King Cotton and His Retainers

King Cotton
and His
Retainers:

*Financing and Marketing the
Cotton Crop of the South,
1800–1925*

by Harold D. Woodman

University of South Carolina Press

Published in Columbia, South Carolina, by the
University of South Carolina Press

Manufactured in the United States of America

Library of Congress Cataloging-in-Publication Data

Woodman, Harold D.
    [King cotton & his retainers]
    King cotton and his retainers : financing & marketing the cotton
crop of the South, 1800–1925 / Harold D. Woodman.
        p.   cm.
    Reprint. Originally published: King cotton & his retainers.
Lexington : University of Kentucky Press, 1968.
    Includes bibliographical references and index.
    ISBN 0–87249–727–5
    ISBN 0–87249–728-3 (pbk.)/
    1. Cotton trade—Southern States—History.   2. Cotton trade—
United States—History.   I. Title.
HD9077.A13W66   1990
338.1′7351′0975—dc20   90–35755

for Leonora

General Editor's Preface

The Southern Classics Series returns to general circulation books of importance dealing with the history and culture of the American South. Under the sponsorship of the Institute for Southern Studies of the University of South Carolina, the series is advised by a board of distinguished scholars, whose members suggest titles and editors of individual volumes to the general editor and help to establish priorities in publication.

Chronological age alone does not determine a title's designation as a Southern Classic. The criteria include, as well, significance in contributing to a broad understanding of the region, timeliness in relation to events and moments of peculiar interest to the American South, usefulness in the classroom, and suitability for inclusion in personal and institutional collections on the region.

Despite its relatively recent date of original publication, Harold D. Woodman's *King Cotton and His Retainers* has most assuredly earned its designation as a Southern Classic. As the first systematic examination of the factors and middlemen who financed and marketed the region's all-important cotton crop, the book has become the standard work on the subject and Woodman's interpretation has been absorbed into the general history of the South. Written in refreshing prose, it is economic history at its best, with appeal both to scholars and to general readers. Its enduring value is now enhanced by the author's new introduction.

John G. Sproat
General Editor, Southern Classics Series

Introduction to Southern Classics Series Edition

King Cotton and His Retainers had its origin in a problem I attempted to investigate early in my graduate student days at the University of Chicago, a problem that I thought would be easily solved. Cotton was the antebellum South's chief commercial crop. The wealth of the planter class depended upon the production and sale of cotton; most of the section's slaves worked in the cotton fields; and even small farmers owning few or no slaves, produced cotton as a cash crop. Almost all of the South's cotton left the section. Some, about 25 percent, went north to supply the rapidly expanding New England textile industry, thereby helping to fuel the nation's early industrialization; the remainder went abroad, mainly to Great Britain but also to the continent, the value of the cotton exports amounting to 50 to 60 percent of the total of U.S. exports during the decades before the Civil War. My initial problem was simply to learn more about the movement of the cotton from the plantations and farms in the South to the consuming mills in the North and abroad. I assumed that my ignorance concerning the institutions and practices of the cotton trade came from my ignorance of the relevant literature on the subject.

I was both surprised and puzzled, therefore, to discover that the antebellum cotton trade, so important to the South, to the nation as a whole, and to consumers abroad, had received little scholarly attention. I found no book-length study of cotton marketing and only a few scattered articles on the subject. When I turned to printed primary sources, I found no published merchants' papers, but planters' papers often contained letters, business accounts, diary entries, and other references to the planters' dealings with merchants—called cotton factors or commission merchants—who sold their cotton and performed other services for them. But comments by the papers' editors, like those of the authors of books and articles about individual planters, provided little analysis of the marketing system and little help in finding analyses written by others. Almost universally, any general comments about marketing mentioned the "cotton factorage system" and referred to a single brief 1915 article by Alfred Holt Stone: "The Cotton Factorage System of the Southern States."[1]

Stone's article was undocumented, but as a Southerner, an economic historian, and, at the time he wrote, a Mississippi cotton farmer, Stone was, it seemed, an eminently qualified expert. Nevertheless, I decided to persist in my research if for no other reason than that Stone's very brief and undocumented study lacked details about the factors themselves and contained no information about the relationship between factors and other middlemen involved in the cotton trade—bankers, buyers, supply merchants, and transporters. I was also suspicious of Stone's insistence that the factors often overcharged for their services, that they would not provide services unless planters agreed to send all their cotton to them, and that they forced planters to guarantee that they would send a stipulated amount of cotton to them or pay a penalty for any shortfall. Stone's conclusion that the factors were the power behind King Cotton's throne seemed at odds with what I knew about the planter class. It seemed unlikely that the politically and economically powerful planters would allow themselves to be dominated by a relatively small group of urban merchants, or, at least, that they would silently acquiesce in that domination. I saw no strident denunciations of factor monopolies in planters' correspondence or in contemporary papers and journals, although at the time, planters and Southern publicists and politicians regularly and vehemently attacked tariffs, abolitionists, reformers, and any other perceived danger to their interests. It was possible, of course, that my limited research had not yet uncovered the relevant evidence; nevertheless I could not help but wonder why historians other than Stone had failed to notice the power of the merchants.

[1] *American Historical Review*, 20 (April 1915), 557–65.

Perhaps, I thought, Stone agreed with the vituperative attacks on postbellum merchants by the Alliances and the Populists and had found them equally relevant to antebellum merchants.[2]

At this stage in my research, however, the evidence I had to support my suspicions was largely negative. The printed sources seldom included evidence of a contract requiring that a planter send all his cotton to one factor and in no case did they refer to penalties; indeed, some sources provided examples of planters changing factors and dealing with more than one factor during a single season. Planter-factor conflict that appeared in the printed sources and in several secondary articles involved disagreements over when and where the factor had sold a planter's cotton and the prices received. But if my evidence consisted primarily of the *absence* of the kinds of merchant-farmer conflict that Stone had described, it did suggest that he might have been mistaken. In any event, he had provided only the briefest discussion of an important historical problem. I decided that additional research might allow me to present a fuller picture of the antebellum cotton marketing system and to assess the place of the cotton merchants in antebellum Southern society.

The most obvious source would have been the papers of the factors themselves, but I was disappointed to learn that only a few had survived. Planters' papers, however, proved to be rich and enlightening. They contained letters and circulars from factors and occasionally copies of letters sent to factors along with numerous accounts from factors. On the debit side of these accounts, factors listed all the money they paid for plantation supplies and personal items ordered by the planter, all the bills of exchange and other notes they paid on the planter's orders, and all marketing expenses, such as costs of transportation, storage, insurance, and drayage. On the credit side, they listed returns on each bale of the planter's cotton. Included among the charges against the planter were commissions for buying ordered goods and for selling the cotton—invariably 2½ percent—

---

[2] I have since learned more about Stone. He was no mere cotton farmer, but the owner-operator of a large Delta plantation. He was critical of merchants but not for the reasons that aroused the ire of the Alliances. Rather, he charged that the merchants, and many landowners as well, failed to give the direction and supervision of cotton farmers that Stone deemed necessary for successful cotton farming. He used tenants, croppers, and hired hands on his plantation, Dunleith, in Washington County, Mississippi, exercised close supervision of their work, provided all advances from his plantation commissary, sold all of his workers' cotton, and was in no way subordinate to merchants.

and interest on funds advanced before the cotton was sold—invariably charged only for the number of days between the time the money was advanced and the time when funds from sales became available.

Written agreements were rare. Factors advanced considerable sums based simply on the expectation that the planters would repay such advances by sending them cotton to sell. When sales did not suffice to pay accumulated debts, factors generally carried over a planter's debt to the following year simply by making a notation to that effect on the final account. Some planters regularly dealt with more than one factor at a time, and did so openly, commonly drawing bills on one factor to pay a debt to another. Factors competed for the planters' business. They advertised in newspapers and sent circulars and letters to planters soliciting all or a part of their trade. Letters that passed between planters and factors revealed a close and friendly relationship between social equals, for the letters often referred to visits to each other's homes and other social connections. Indeed, factors themselves were very often slaveholding planters.

Such close relationships and mutual trust did not preclude disagreements. Planters sometimes complained that the factors did not buy or sell at the most propitious moment, and they would express their unhappiness when a factor announced that a financial pinch temporarily prevented his making further advances. Ordinarily, disagreements resulted in little more than complaining or angry letters, sometimes, but not always, followed by a severing of business relations. On occasion, however, disagreements led to litigation which allowed the courts to define more clearly the planter-factor relationship.[3] The courts ruled that in the absence of a specific written agreement between planter and factor—the usual arrangement—the factor had wide authority to act in the name of the planter. The factor was expected to protect the planter's interests but could not be sued for errors in judgment. The planter, of course, was obligated to pay money owed the factor; indeed, the courts ruled, the factor had a lien on a planter's crop to repay advances. But that lien was sharply limited. It covered only expenses directly related to producing the crop; it did not come into force until the factor received the crop; and

---

[3] Court proceedings turned out to be a rich and valuable source in my research, not merely because decisions set out and clarified the law, but also because the proceedings themselves often described the planter-factor relationship in detail.

it did not obligate the planter to send the crop to the factor making the advances.

Nevertheless, factors regularly provided goods other than plantation supplies long before receiving any crop to sell, and they seldom demanded a written agreement that the planter's crop would be sent to them. Obviously, they simply relied on the planter's good will when making advances. Furthermore, because the factor, except on the rare occasions when he received specific written instructions, was free to buy and sell at times and at prices he deemed most advantageous to the planter, the planter relied on the honesty and good judgment of his factor. Factors expected to receive enough of a planter's crop to reimburse them for the advances they had made, and planters expected that their factors would use their knowledge of market trends to decide on the best time to make purchases and sales. Mutual trust between gentlemen rather than the law and written contracts dominated the relationship.

My research had uncovered more details about the operation of the factorage system and also about others involved in the cotton trade—storekeepers,[4] peddlers, and a variety of itinerants who visited farms and plantations—and had led me to dismiss the contentions of those, mainly following the interpretive lead of Alfred Holt Stone, who wrote that the factors were the power behind King Cotton's throne, overcharging for their services, forcing the reliance on one crop agriculture, stifling the development of interior towns, and, in general, causing many of the antebellum South's economic ills.

Many of the criticisms of the antebellum cotton factors that I had concluded were unfounded had been leveled against the postbellum furnishing merchants. Although Thomas D. Clark found the storekeepers to be as much victims as victimizers in a backward agricultural system,[5] most historians agreed with the angry contemporary criticisms of the furnishing merchants leveled by the Southern Alliances and Populists. If not the sole cause, the merchants were active participants in an economic arrangement that brought increasing tenancy and persisting poverty to the South. Supported by

[4] Lewis E. Atherton's splendid study of *The Southern Country Store, 1800–1860* (Baton Rouge: Louisiana State University Press, 1949) detailed the role of the storekeepers.

[5] Thomas D. Clark, *Pills, Petticoats and Plows* (Indianapolis: Bobbs-Merrill, 1944.)

crop lien laws, merchants charged excessive prices for goods advanced to farmers, assessed exorbitant interest rates, and forced farmers to overproduce cotton to repay loans. They increasingly became the South's leading landlords as their high charges, combined with outright fraud, drove farmers into debts they could not pay. Falling cotton prices and perpetual debt meant that few emancipated slaves could accumulate the money to buy land, and a rapidly growing number and proportion of white landowners, unable to pay their debts, lost their lands and became tenants and sharecroppers on land that was once theirs but now belonged to the merchants.

I decided to extend my study into the war years and beyond in order to assess this view. I hoped to discover what happened to the antebellum factorage system and if—or how—it evolved into the furnishing merchant system. The last three parts of the book were the results of that effort.

I discovered that some factors and merchants by a variety of means were able to hold or to accumulate resources during the war, and that after the war some quickly reestablished their economic connections with Northern merchants, manufacturers, and bankers. These antebellum merchants, along with a number of newcomers, used their funds and their connections to rebuild the factorage system. But times had changed. Planters without slaves who leased their lands to tenants no longer controlled the entire crop; transportation improvements opened hitherto isolated areas populated by small farmers to commercial production of cotton. Tenants and small farmers, like the antebellum planters, required credit in order to grow a crop, but they had little security to offer lenders. Local merchants, familiar with local conditions and knowing the people in the neighborhood, began to supply the credit needed by the growing number of small producers, taking as security a lien on the crop to be grown. At first, these local merchants got credit to pass on to local producers and marketed the cotton they received at the end of the season through the resurrected factorage system, but they soon found they could sell their cotton locally to a growing number of buyers in the interior, and they could deal directly with banks and manufacturers rather than going through a factor. The rebuilt factorage system quickly disintegrated in the face of these changes.

*   *   *

King Cotton and His Retainers has stood the test of time rather well, less because I said the last word on the subjects than because others have not attempted to revise my findings using new sources of information or new methods. In my "Bibliographical Note" I wrote that historians had neglected the economic history of the South in general and especially the commercial history of the region. There were, however, some promising signs of change in 1968. New works on the economics of slavery had begun to appear, spawning new research based upon new methods and raising new questions that went far beyond the matter of profit and loss. Although less evident at the time, there was also renewed interest in the economic and social history of the post-emancipation decades and in the transition from slavery to freedom and its effects on former slaves, former owners, and the small farmers. The past two decades have witnessed an exciting new interest in Southern economic and social history.[6]

But despite the growing interest in the economic history of the South, the commercial history of the section has continued to receive little scholarly attention. My description and analysis of the antebellum cotton factorage system and its disintegration in the postbellum years has not been reinvestigated and challenged by other historians. Some have provided more details in the course of their studies of other matters, and others have studied cotton marketing in places I neglected. Particularly important has been work on Texas. I gave almost no attention to the competition between Galveston and Houston as merchants in these towns sought to establish commercial relations with the increasing numbers of Texas planters in an effort to make their towns key new commercial centers and to divert the Texas business from its traditional market in New Orleans.[7]

The major British and American firms that helped to finance the cotton trade remain largely unstudied. When I wrote in 1968, only the Barings had their scholarly historian.[8] Since then Edwin J. Per-

---

[6] For a full discussion of this new work see the relevant chapters in John B. Boles and Evelyn Thomas Nolen, eds., *Interpreting Southern History: Historiographical Essays in Honor of Sanford W. Higginbotham* (Baton Rouge: Louisiana State University Press, 1987).

[7] See the splendid articles in the *Southwestern Historical Quarterly*, 63 (April 1970): Abigail Curlee Holbrook, "Cotton Marketing in Antebellum Texas," 431–55; Ronnie C. Tyler, "Cotton on the Border, 1861–1865," pp. 456–77; L. Tuffly Ellis, "The Revolutionizing of the Texas Cotton Trade, 1865–1885," 478–508.

[8] Ralph W. Hidy, *The House of Baring in American Trade and Finance* (Cambridge, Mass.: Harvard University Press, 1949).

kins has written a full-length history of the Browns.[9] John R. Killick's studies of the Bolton Ogden & Co. and of the Browns' cotton business provide important insights into the evolution of Anglo-American financing and trading institutions over the nineteenth century.[10] But other international banking firms await their historians.

Similarly, most of the important American firms in the cotton trade have received little or no attention from historians. For example, Lehman Brothers, the firm that began as a country store in Montgomery, Alabama, in the 1850s, participated in the founding of the New York Cotton Exchange in 1870, and eventually became one of the nation's largest investment bankers (known today as Shearson, Lehman, Hutton), has no written history other than a popular, in-house centennial volume published in 1950. Despite their importance, the large cotton merchants who helped to transform the trade in the late nineteenth and early twentieth centuries have not been studied in detail. John R. Killick's essay on Alexander Sprunt shows the importance such studies would have in tracing changes in cotton marketing and financing. Initially very successful in meeting new post Civil War needs, the Sprunt company was unable to adjust to changing conditions and fell before competition from a new group of merchants.[11] But no one has undertaken a scholarly treatment of these newer more successful merchants, such as Anderson, Clayton & Co., George H. McFadden and Brother, S. M. Weld, Weil Brothers, and similar firms that came to dominate the trade in the United States and abroad beginning in the late nineteenth century, often marketing not only American cotton but also that grown and consumed all over the world.[12]

[9] Edwin J. Perkins, *Financing Anglo-American Trade: The House of Brown, 1800–1880* (Cambridge, Mass.: Harvard University Press, 1975).

[10] John R. Killick, "Bolton Ogden & Co.: A Case Study in Anglo-American Trade, 1790–1850," *Business History Review*, 48 (Winter 1974), 501–19; Killick, "Risk, Specialization and Profit in the Mercantile Sector of the Nineteenth Century Cotton Trade: Alexander Brown & Sons 1820–80," *Business History*, 16 (January 1974), 1–16; Killick, "The Cotton Operations of Alexander Brown and Sons in the Deep South, 1820–1880," *Journal of Southern History*, 43 (May 1977), 169–94.

[11] See J. R. Killick, "The Transformation of Cotton Marketing in the Late Nineteenth Century: Alexander Sprunt and Son of Wilmington, N.C., 1884–1956," *Business History Review*, 55 (Summer 1981), 143–69.

[12] Lamar Fleming, Jr., "Growth of the Business of Anderson, Clayton & Co.," edited by James A. Tinsley, *Texas Gulf Coast Historical Association Publication Series*, 10 (September 1966) provides a brief history of that important company. Fleming, a

The changes in cotton marketing procedures that required adjustments by older firms and that brought new firms into the business also produced important institutional changes that began during the Civil War years and continued in the decades that followed. Efforts to establish uniform trading procedures and to provide self-policing mechanisms led to the organization of cotton exchanges in many Southern markets, in New York, in Liverpool, and elsewhere. Exchange members established common grading systems and trading rules in their markets and organized and regulated the new cotton futures system, solving some problems only to raise a rash of new ones. If the exchanges could impose uniformity among their members, they were often less successful in regulating the activities of nonmembers. Even more troublesome was the lack of uniformity among markets in widely scattered areas. Merchants, traders, bankers, and speculators, finding that varying local rules generated uncertainties and controversies, attempted to establish common national and international standards and rules. The effort proved to be long and difficult, eliciting intense rivalry and disagreements as each exchange sought to get the others to adopt its rules. Although there were some voluntary accommodations among the various exchanges, eventually government intervention proved necessary.

Surprisingly, few historians have attempted to describe these developments in any detail. Robert Bouilly has written the only full-length study of the early history of the various cotton exchanges, but unfortunately his 1975 dissertation remains unpublished and his analysis does not extend beyond World War I.[13] The history of the futures system in cotton remains largely unstudied. Southern cotton farmers and many merchants along with their supporters in Congress vehemently attacked the futures system as blatant speculation by parasitic, nonproducers who pocketed enormous profits by rigging cotton prices at the expense of hardworking growers; others, however, supported the system as an effective means for growers, merchants, and spinners to hedge risks. Kenneth J. Lipartito's recent essay on the

company executive, wrote the sketch for the company's internal use. Tinsley published it, adding a few explanatory footnotes and extending the story from where Fleming ended it in 1941 to 1965. The essay remains only a brief, essentially in-house outline of the company's history.

13 Robert Bouilly, "The Development of American Cotton Exchanges, 1870–1916," (Ph.D. diss., University of Missouri, 1975).

development of the futures market in New York provides a brief insight into the history of this important institution, but the subject deserves considerably more attention from historians.[14]

Banking, especially in the antebellum period, has always attracted more historians, but the emphasis of most studies has been on banking organization and regulatory legislation and their effects on the success or failure of banks.[15] The role of antebellum banks in financing the production and sale of cotton by attracting and moving local, national, and international funds has received far less attention. A conspicuous and important exception is George D. Green's study of Louisiana banking, which attempts to relate banking in that state to economic growth and development.[16] Green challenges my contention that the banks were dependent subordinates to Northern banking interests, but no one has written similar studies of other states. If politics and internal operations have dominated antebellum banking histories, historians have almost completely ignored postbellum banking in the South. The rebuilding of banks after the Civil War and their place in the changing cotton trade remains largely unstudied.[17]

Much could be learned from a closer investigation of the interrelationships among international firms, Northern banks, Southern banks, and Southern merchants. Amassing more details about the relationships would be important and relatively easy; more difficult, but much more important, would be to attempt to quantify, if only very roughly, the movement of funds and credit at different times in order to assess the relative importance of various financial intermediaries and their influence on the cotton trade. Studies by Perkins and Killick on the international firms[18] indicate that the data are available, and they provide a start on the task. A similar study of the factorage houses in the South would be more difficult. These firms

[14] Kenneth J. Lipartito, "The New York Cotton Exchange and the Development of the Cotton Futures Market," *Business History Review*, 57 (Spring 1983), 50–72.

[15] The most recent work is Larry Schweikart's richly documented, encyclopedic, and somewhat polemical *Banking in the American South from the Age of Jackson to Reconstruction* (Baton Rouge: Louisiana State University Press, 1987).

[16] George D. Green, *Finance and Economic Development in the Old South: Louisiana Banking, 1804–1861* (Stanford: Stanford University Press, 1972.)

[17] The brief discussion by Roger L. Ransom and Richard Sutch in their *One Kind of Freedom: The Economic Consequences of Emancipation* (Cambridge, Eng.: Cambridge University Press, 1977), 106–25 emphasizes the subordination of banks to the furnishing merchant.

[18] See notes 9, 10, and 11, above.

changed partners (and names) regularly and often did not last over long periods of time, and their records, it seems, have disappeared. But the commercial newspapers in the ports reported the arrival of boats, the amount of cotton each carried, and the factors to whom the cotton was consigned. By combining this information with the letters and accounts in planter's papers, a rough estimate could be derived of the relative importance of various firms and their relationships with other firms.

My argument that the cotton factor was not the power behind King Cotton's throne but rather was the King's chief retainer has not been challenged by other historians. Less acceptable, at least to some, has been my similar contention regarding the postbellum furnishing merchant. As I noted in the book, and as anyone who reads the writings of the Alliances and Populists and of other reformers in the South immediately realizes, Southern farmers and their spokesmen never tired of attacking the furnishing merchants and the crop lien laws that supported them. The litany of the merchants' wrongdoings is familiar. They overcharged for goods from their stores, exacted excessive interest on advances, falsified their books in order to increase the amounts their customers owed and to decrease the returns on the customer's cotton, and forced farmers to concentrate on cotton growing, all of which led to overproduction, low prices, worn-out lands, perpetual farmer indebtedness, increasing tenancy, and persisting poverty. Even a cursory examination of contemporary sources—newspapers, popular journals, Congressional investigations, and political pamphlets—provides ample primary evidence of the menace of the furnishing merchants along with endlessly repeated advice to farmers to avoid dealing with the blood-sucking merchants who were doing such great harm to the cotton farmers and thereby hindering Southern economic progress and general well-being.

Roger L. Ransom and Richard Sutch's recent study of the postbellum Southern economy supports most of the contemporary criticism by providing a new explanation for the merchant's power. They argue that merchants enjoyed "monopoly power" which gave them the ability to make exploitative profits from their farmer customers and to hold them in "debt peonage." Although there were many merchants in the South, the authors explain, they did not compete with one another; rather, individual merchants usually enjoyed a "territorial monopoly," that is, they were located far enough away from potential competitors to prevent farmers from having a choice of merchants with whom to deal.[19]

Ransom and Sutch's evidence does not convince me to revise my view of the furnishing merchants. Contrary to Ransom and Sutch, I have found that all but the smallest villages had more than one merchant, and usually a tenant or small farmer could easily reach more than one town in his search for an accommodating merchant. Like others of their critics,[20] I have found that furnishing merchants operated high-risk enterprises which, if they made a few rich, brought a marginal existence and bankruptcy to many more. Tenants without land or much other property regularly deserted their farms when they realized that returns would not pay out their advances. Merchants could, and regularly did, foreclose if borrowers owned land and other property, but often this property failed to cover debts.

But my own research in recent years convinces me that the issue of the role of the merchant cannot be adequately addressed in simple market terms—monopoly profits versus compensation for the high risks entailed in dealing with small, often propertyless farmers. The furnishing merchants were themselves borrowers. As operators of small, risky businesses where bankruptcies and turnover were common, they paid high interest rates for borrowed money and for goods they purchased on time, and they passed their high costs on to their customers. But the merchants faced other problems as well, problems that I did not fully understand when I first wrote about them in 1968. The postbellum social and economic changes confined most merchants to a limited and marginal existence. Although a few got rich and became large scale landowners with significant political influence, most remained small businessmen, primarily because the law and the organization of production in many areas excluded them from the most profitable business opportunities.

The crop lien laws in every state gave the landlord the primary lien on the crop grown by his tenant. Only after the landlord received his rent and payment for any advances he might have made to his tenant would the merchant's lien take effect. The merchant had no recourse if the landlord's claims left the tenant with insufficient

---

[19] Ransom and Sutch, *One Kind of Freedom,* 126–48 and *passim.*

[20] See the essays in *Explorations in Economic History,* 16 (January 1979). Ransom and Sutch responded to their critics in an article in the same issue of the journal and in another in the April issue of the same volume.

funds to pay his merchant. Furthermore, the largest and most prosperous landowners avoided trading with the merchants, and they discouraged or, in most cases, actually prohibited their tenants and croppers from dealing with merchants, preferring instead to supply advances themselves from their plantation commissaries. These landowners increasingly used croppers rather than tenants on their lands because they could exercise far more control over croppers. The law defined the cropper as a wage laborer rather than a tenant, and, although the croppers' wages were a share of the crop they grew, they did not have legal control over their share until they were paid. Payment was in net returns, the landlord first deducting his share (usually half) and the value of any advances he had made during the year. Merchants were legally free to sell goods on credit to such croppers, but lacking knowledge of how much the cropper owed his landlord (or any other lenders), they had no way to insure that they would be repaid.[21]

Limiting the merchants' power even further were changes in plantation organization. By the end of the nineteenth century, large-scale, centrally administered plantations dominated in the best cotton lands. Using croppers and some wage laborers, plantation owners or their managers directed all work on their land, providing tools, seed, fertilizer, pesticides, and work animals; they often had their own gins and compresses, and they provided any necessary store goods to the croppers from plantation commissaries. Croppers usually received their pay not in a share of the cotton grown, but in the cash value of their share, less the costs of tools, seed, the use of work animals, goods purchased from the commissaries, ginning, and compressing. Merchants had little opportunity to get such croppers' patronage until they were paid off at the end of the season, and even then they faced competition from a flood of itinerants who came to plantation areas at pay-off time and from the landowners themselves who, after final settlement, put in a special stock of items in their plantation commissaries in an effort to get the cash business of the croppers they had just paid.

21 Despite their importance, there is no history of the crop lien laws. For the past several years I have been investigating these laws and the laws concerning sharecropping as part of a larger study of post-emancipation agriculture in the South. Some of my initial findings may be found in "Post-Civil War Southern Agriculture and the Law," *Agricultural History*, 53 (January 1979), 319–37.

The plantation owners, by this procedure, controlled large stocks of the best cotton, grown on the best lands under the best conditions, while most merchants, their business largely confined to small owners and tenants on inferior land, controlled less cotton, much of it of an inferior quality. Small farmers, if they were to improve the quality of their cotton, had to use more fertilizer and better tools and work animals, which would increase their obligations to their merchants, obligations that merchants were reluctant to assume because of the added risk involved.

Because they controlled a large and growing proportion of the South's best cotton, the large plantation owners had access to sources of funding that were less expensive and longer term. As owners of large tracts of the best land and the best available machinery and work animals, they were good risks, and they could, therefore, turn to large banks, insurance companies, and other financial intermediaries for loans at reasonable rates. They produced the best cotton in large quantities which they stored in their own warehouses, and they had the resources to be able to hold the cotton for the best price, a luxury that most small farmers with short-term debts coming due did not enjoy. They organized their cotton into even-running bales (i.e., in groups with similar characteristics), which matched the varying demands of consumers, and as a result, their cotton earned a premium when sold.[22]

Unfortunately, historians have not studied these large, centrally organized plantations in any detail, and therefore we cannot appreciate their significance in the evolution of the Southern economy in general and in marketing and financing procedures in particular. If I were writing *King Cotton* today, I would take into consideration the role of these large plantations and the consequent lesser role of the furnishing merchants in the plantation areas. This would involve more than the sorting out of details. If the merchants played a lesser role than I first thought, they were not unimportant. Their customers

[22] This discussion of the large plantations is based upon my current research. I published some of the results of this research in "The Reconstruction of the Cotton Plantation in the New South," in *Essays on the Postbellum Southern Economy*, ed. Thavolia Glymph and John J. Kushma (College Station: Texas A & M University Press, 1985), 95–119, and in "Postbellum Social Change and Its Effects on Marketing the South's Cotton Crop," *Agricultural History*, 56 (January 1982), 215–30. A brief, but important study of one of the largest of these plantations, the Delta and Pine Lands, is Lawrence J. Nelson, "Welfare Capitalism on a Mississippi Plantation in the Great Depression," *Journal of Southern History*, 50 (May 1984), 225–50.

were mainly the small farmers and tenants, both black and white, but overwhelmingly white. The plantation owners, however, almost exclusively employed black croppers and wage laborers. This meant that the economic and political interests of the various groups involved were more complicated than I realized two decades ago. A fuller understanding of postbellum conditions requires an analysis of the complex interrelationships among class, race, and economic interests.

*   *   *

In the years since I published *King Cotton* the debates concerning the political economy of slavery and the economic and social consequences of the Civil War and emancipation have changed considerably. When I wrote, revisionists had overturned U. B. Phillips's picture of slavery as a benign "school" and the hitherto prevailing picture of Reconstruction as a time of unrelieved corruption and dishonest government. Debates concerning the economics of slavery still turned largely on the narrow grounds of profit and loss, but historians were beginning to ask new questions and use new methods that promised to go far beyond merely revising prevailing views. Eugene Genovese's early work had appeared, and a growing number of economic historians were employing modern economic theory and statistical inference in an effort to provide more precise information about the South. C. Vann Woodward's argument that the Civil War was a significant turning point in Southern history tended to be accepted, but had not been investigated in detail; the hot debates over the economic consequences of the war and emancipation had not yet begun.

I had hoped that my work would make a modest contribution to the new ways in which historians were looking at Southern history, although at the time I had only a vague notion about where the new scholarship was leading. Were I writing the book today, I would, of course, incorporate more recent scholarship, including my own research, and I would attempt to investigate some of the areas which, as I have indicated above, have been neglected by historians. The result would be a richer and more detailed discussion of King Cotton's retainers. At the same time, I would try to sharpen my interpretive analysis in several areas. I would give greater emphasis to the significance of the close relationship between antebellum planters and their factors and relate this to the nature and operation of the slave system as a pre-bourgeois or non-bourgeois economic and political system grounded in master-slave relations.[23] I would also give greater stress to the significance of the Civil War and emancipation. My more recent research has convinced me that although there were elements of continuity that bridged the war, emancipation brought a revolutionary change to the South.

Adding some of the details and sharpening the interpretation would be relatively easy because of the work others have done since *King Cotton* first appeared; other changes, however, would require much new research. My own work and the work of others convinces me that such research would be productive. If in the opinion of the editors of the Southern Classics Reprint Series *King Cotton and His Retainers* qualifies as a "classic," neither they nor I would suggest that it qualifies as the last word on the subject.

Many years ago while still a graduate student, I had the opportunity to introduce a distinguished speaker. In my introduction I said that he had written a "definitive" work in his field. Later the speaker told me that although he was flattered by my words and although such language was often used in introductions and on dust jackets of books, I should be aware that no one ever writes a definitive study on any subject of importance. At that point in my career I was only dimly aware of the philosophical basis for his point, but I nevertheless assured him that I understood. I now know a bit more about the philosophy—and a lot more about financing and marketing the South's cotton crop—which enables me to understand and accept his general point—and to see its relevance to my "classic" book. I am pleased that some still find it useful, but would be even more pleased if it helped to stimulate new research.

Harold D. Woodman

[23] Obviously my thinking in this area has been much influenced by the work of Eugene D. Genovese.

Preface

Who could doubt that cotton was king? Production statistics were unnecessary. Travelers had only to look about them to see the king's domination of Southern life.

A visitor to Charleston in 1827 wrote that he saw the wharves "piled up with mountains of Cotton, and all your stores, ships, steam and canal boats, crammed with and groaning under, the weight of Cotton." Returning to his hotel he found "four daily papers, as well as the conversation of the boarders, teeming with Cotton! Cotton!! Cotton!!!" Nor could he escape the monarch's influence when he left Charleston. In Augusta, Hamburg, Milledgeville, Macon, Montgomery, Mobile, and New Orleans the story was the same. Mobile, he wrote, was a "receptacle monstrous" for cotton. "Look which way you will you see it; and see it moving; keel boats, steam boats, ships, brigs, schooners, wharves, stores, and press-houses, all appeared to be full." And the people seemed to talk of little else: "I believe that in the three days that I was there . . . I must have heard the word cotton pronounced more than 3000 times."

Even so sophisticated an observer as pioneer agriculturist Solon Robinson was astounded by the sight of the New Orleans levee in December 1848:

> It must be seen to be believed; and even then, it will require an active mind to comprehend acres of cotton bales standing upon the levee, while miles of drays are constantly taking it off to the cotton presses, where the power of steam and screws are

constantly being applied to compress the bales into a lesser bulk, at an almost inconceivable rate per day, while all around [bales] are piled up in miniature mountains, which other miles of drays are taking on shipboard, and yet seem unable to reduce in size or quantity, either here or upon the levee; for boats are constantly arriving, so piled up with cotton, that the lower tier of bales on deck are in the water; and as the boat is approaching, it looks like a huge raft of cotton bales, with the chimneys and steam pipe of an engine sticking up out of the centre.

The Civil War taught Southern politicians that their king, however powerful he seemed at home, could not command the world. Even during the war, however, cotton was not toppled from his throne, although at times he had to share it with others. With the war's end, he quickly disposed of his rivals and resumed his former position of power in the South.

Historians have written extensively on cotton production during the nineteenth century and they have commented at length on the influence—or presumed influence—of King Cotton. But few have concerned themselves with the king's retainers: The middlemen involved in financing and marketing the crop have received scant attention.

One possible reason for this neglect is that the merchant has seemed a prosaic figure compared to the planter, the slave, and the "po' white." Marketing and banking might have appeared less exciting than slavery and the sharecropping system. Another reason, perhaps, is that the middleman has never been a popular figure in America. For the most part, he has been considered a necessary evil. Somehow, the man who plows the soil, plants the seed, cares for and harvests the crop is regarded as a more valuable member of the economic society than the one who supplies the money and finds a market for the products of the soil. The agrarian ideology, rhetorically powerful, however ignored as a guide to action, makes the farmer, the initial producer, the most valuable link in the chain from soil to consumer.

Whatever its cause, this neglect of the middlemen in the cotton trade leaves a void in our understanding of the Southern economy and the economic relations between the South and the North. The aim of the following pages is not to disturb the agrarian ideology nor is it to explain away any abuses associated with the middlemen. My purpose, rather, is to provide more information on a neglected facet of the Southern economy: To show how cotton was marketed in the ante bellum period and how this method changed in the post bellum period; to show the effects that the various marketing systems had on Southern economic life; to show the political and social changes the marketing systems illustrated and engendered.

Acknowledgments

This book could not have been written without the help of many people. To Professor Daniel J. Boorstin of the University of Chicago I am particularly grateful. He encouraged my work in its earliest stages and directed a different version of this study as a doctoral dissertation. Most important, he has taught me by precept and example what a historian must do and for this I shall always be in his debt. I have also benefited from discussions with Professor Richard C. Wade and Dr. Roger Shugg of the University of Chicago and with Professor Bernard Weisberger of the University of Rochester. Professor Meyer Weinberg of Wright Junior College in Chicago first introduced me to the excitement of American economic history and my education has been enhanced by my association with him ever since. I owe a special debt to my colleague, Lewis Atherton, whose books revealed to me the significance of middlemen in American economic history and who has given freely of his time and advice over the past several years.

Librarians and archivists have with intelligence and celerity made pertinent manuscript collections available to me. I am happy to acknowledge the aid given by the staffs of the following institutions: Mississippi Department of Archives and History (Jackson); Southern Historical Collection, University of North Carolina Library (Chapel Hill); Manuscript Division, Tennessee State Library and Archives (Nashville); Emory University Library (Atlanta); Arkansas History Commission, Department of Archives and History (Little Rock); Department of Archives and Manuscripts, Louisiana State

University (Baton Rouge); Georgia Historical Society (Savannah); South Carolina Historical Society (Charleston); Joint Collection, Western Historical Manuscripts Collection, State Historical Society of Missouri Manuscripts (Columbia); Burrow Library, Southwestern at Memphis (Memphis).

I have profited from the comments and suggestions of several of my students and in particular want to acknowledge my indebtedness to Mr. Alan S. Weiner. Generous grants from the University of Missouri Research Council provided me with a needed summer's leave and paid for the typing of the manuscript and preparation of the maps. Mrs. Earl E. Orye of Columbia, Missouri, not only typed the manuscript but saved me from many embarrassing errors. To Professor James H. Shideler, editor of *Agricultural History* and Professor Henry R. Winkler, managing editor of the *American Historical Review* I am grateful for permission to reprint articles which originally appeared in their journals.

Acknowledgment is also due to the University of North Carolina Press for permission to use the information on railroad routes contained in John F. Stover's *The Railroads of the South, 1865-1900* (copyright 1955) in preparation of the endpaper maps.

My greatest debt is to my wife Leonora who took precious time from her own research to read and reread what I had written from first draft to page proof. Where my language has grace and my exposition has clarity, she may take the credit. When these qualities are lacking, it means simply that I lacked the wit to take her advice.

Columbia, Missouri   H. D. W.
August, 1967

Contents

ANTE
BELLUM

PART ONE

The Cotton
Factorage System

Every planter dealt with a firm of "Factors." These businessmen of a high type . . . were indeed the people who "did" things for the planter, as their designation imports.

> —D. E. Huger Smith, A *Charlestonian's Recollections, 1846-1913* (Charleston, 1950), 47.

The Factor was the factotum of our business life, our commission merchant, our banker, our bookkeeper, our adviser, our collector and disburser, who honored our checks and paid our bills. Many of the planters did not really always know what money they possessed. One year's accounts would overlap another's and sometimes years would pass before the accounts were balanced and settlement made.

> —I. Jenkins Mikell, *Rumbling of the Chariot Wheels*, p. 200, as quoted in David Duncan Wallace, *The History of South Carolina* (New York, 1934), III, 70.

Early in February 1812, a rice and cotton planter wrote to Hayne and Waring, a firm of Charleston merchants whom the planter called "Factors":

> I have not had the pleasure of hearing from you since I saw you. I conclude that you have recieved [sic] and sold my rice, and recieved, if not sold at least some of the cotton. I have not heard from the manager of my plantation since I left there about a month ago, so that I am totally ignorant how much cotton he has made ready for market. I request you to write me as soon as you recieve this letter and inform me on these things. I request you also to send me some money if it be in your power. . . . Send a bill of fi[f]ty Dollars if you can. . . .[1]

While Hayne and Waring's answer is not extant, the firm probably answered promptly giving the planter the information he desired and enclosing the $50 he requested. In addition the reply most likely contained information about the state of the market in Charleston, the latest advices from New York and Liverpool, and an invitation to the planter to call upon the firm for any further services he might require. In so doing the Charleston merchants were merely carrying out their duties as cotton and rice factors.

Undoubtedly Hayne and Waring considered the planter's request as minimal. The services they were prepared to perform were far more extensive, for they not only received and sold the crops but they purchased supplies for the plantation, secured credit when needed, and provided numerous other services for their planter customers. Located in various towns throughout the world, but concentrated primarily in the Southern ports, the cotton—and sugar, rice, and tobacco—factors were the most important of the middlemen involved in financing and marketing the Southern staple crops in the ante bellum period.

Despite his conspicuous position in the Southern economy, the factor was not peculiar to the ante bellum South. His historic antecedent had emerged with the quickening of trade during the Middle Ages. Merchants whose business had expanded beyond their local markets often found it expedient to remain at home, contracting with agents abroad to handle their transactions for them. By the late fifteenth century this procedure had apparently become so common and specific that the word "factor" had entered the English language to designate individuals so engaged.[2]

The factor, then, was simply the agent of individuals or firms empowered to transact business for them. He was engaged to buy, sell, receive, or forward goods and received a commission—called factorage—for his service. By the nineteenth century the foreign trade of a great part of the world was carried on in this manner.[3]

Although there were numerous agents active in foreign trade, the factor became an agent of a special kind. Unlike a direct representative or a broker who was authorized to act only in the name of his employer, the factor dealt in his own name. Although merchandise consigned to the factor remained the property of the consignor, the factor, unless given definite instructions to the contrary, was free to deal with the consignment at his own discretion and under conditions which he deemed most satisfactory and advantageous. If the owner suffered any loss or if he were in any way dissatisfied with the results of his factor's actions, he had no redress unless he could show that the disputed transaction was

[1] L. D. Parks to Hayne & Waring, White Bluff [Ga.], Feb. 8 [1812], Waring & Hayne Papers, South Carolina Historical Society, Charleston, S.C.

[2] The *Oxford English Dictionary* records the first use of the word in its commercial sense in 1491. The word came into English via the French and Latin words meaning "doer" or "maker."

[3] J. R. McCulloch, *A Dictionary, Practical, Theoretical, and Historical, of Commerce and Commercial Navigation* (American ed., by Henry Vethake; Philadelphia, 1854), I, 669; William Anderson, *The London Commercial Dictionary and Sea-Port Gazateer* (London, 1826), 274.

fraudulent or that the factor was guilty of gross negligence. Moreover, since the factor often incurred expenses (payment of duties, transportation, storage, insurance, and the like) and frequently gave partial payment on goods consigned to him prior to their sale, he acquired a lien on his principal's property, which gave him the right to deal with it in a manner that would protect his acquired interest.[4]

[4] McCulloch, *Dictionary of Commerce*, I, 669, 671; Anderson, *London Commercial Dictionary*, 273-74; L. de Colange, *The American Encyclopaedia of Commerce, Manufactures, Commercial Law, and Finance* (Boston, 1881), I, 354; J. Smith Homans and J. Smith Homans, Jr. (eds.), *A Cyclopedia of Commerce and Commercial Navigation* (New York, 1859), 646-47. Since the advent of modern agencies of trade and exchange, factoring as here described has all but disappeared. As will be shown below, it continues to exist on a very small scale in the Southern cotton trade; but with this exception, modern factoring is merely a short-term credit operation where the factorage house takes over the credit held by another company. For example, company "A" ships a quantity of goods to "B" and "B" is billed payable in 30, 60, or 90 days. "A" then turns over the unpaid bill to the factorage house which pays it immediately and then collects from "B" when the bill falls due. The factorage house charges a commission for this service. It is used by "A" because it enables him to extend some credit but does not require him to have large amounts of his capital tied up in unpaid bills. For a detailed discussion of this modern factorage business see Clyde William Phelps, *The Role of Factoring in Modern Business Finance* (Baltimore, 1956); Owen T. Jones, "Factoring," *Harvard Business Review*, XIV (Winter 1936), 186-99.

CHAPTER ONE

The Rise of Cotton Factorage

During the seventeenth and eighteenth centuries the factorage system was the principal means for marketing the Southern tobacco and the West Indian sugar crops. Planters consigned their tobacco to British merchants who sold the crop, purchased and shipped manufactured goods, and advanced credit when required. In truth, this arrangement was a slight departure from the usual factorage relations, for it was a case of a merchant's dealing with a planter rather than of a merchant-to-merchant relationship. This variation, however, was more apparent than real, for the Tidewater tobacco planter, especially in the early years of the colonial period, was in a very basic sense a merchant as well as a farmer. Planters with landholdings on the banks of the deep Southern rivers often provided imported manufactured goods to their inland or upcountry neighbors on credit. After the tobacco was harvested in the fall, they would take payment in the staple or sometimes buy it outright. It was this tobacco, along with their own, that they consigned to their merchants in London.[1]

As population grew and moved further inland and as production increased, the proportion of Southern planters who dealt directly with English merchants decreased. Instead, many planters and farmers began to trade with representatives of English firms who established themselves at various coastal and inland points in the colonies. Although some of these representatives were merely employees of British firms, many colonials moved into this business, often combining tobacco planting with their mercantile activities. The proportion of Americans among these resident merchants—

or "factors," as they were called—increased, especially during the Revolutionary War years when ties with England were cut. By the time trade with England reopened, there had developed in America a group of resident merchants with ties to the planting class in the South and with capital resources adequate to help finance the tobacco trade.[2]

Such was the pattern of trade when the industrial revolution, the invention of the cotton gin, and the availability of fertile lands combined to stimulate the growth of the cotton kingdom. The resultant Southern demand for foodstuffs and manufactured goods had an exhilarating influence on the West and the Northeast. To transport Western, Eastern, and foreign goods to the South and to bring Southern products to market required a vast expansion of the internal and foreign commerce of the country.[3] The factorage system rapidly adapted itself to the needs of the cotton growers, linking them to their markets and sources of supply in the North and abroad. Merchants of every description began to congregate in the older settlements, particularly in the seaports, and farmers and planters, often a long way from these areas, began to rely upon agents there to handle their business for them.

The cotton factorage system did not, of course, spring into

[1] The planter also provided manufactured goods in the form of clothing and tools to his slaves. In the strictest sense, of course, the planter when so doing was not acting as a merchant. He was, however, serving as a distributor of goods and in this broader sense was indeed carrying on the functions of a merchant.

[2] John Spencer Bassett, "The Relation Between the Virginia Planter and the London Merchant," in American Historical Association, Annual Report, 1901 (Washington, D.C., 1902), I, 551-75; Alfred Holt Stone, "The Cotton Factorage System of the Southern States," American Historical Review, XX (April 1915), 557-58; David Ramsay, The History of South Carolina (Charleston, 1809), II, 222, 428; Wesley Frank Craven, The Southern Colonies in the Seventeenth Century, 1607-1689 (Baton Rouge, 1949), 236-38, 339; Daniel J. Boorstin, The Americans: The Colonial Experience (New York, 1958), 105-10; Curtis P. Nettels, The Roots of American Civilization (New York, 1938), 252-58; Lewis Cecil Gray, History of Agriculture in the Southern United States to 1860 (Washington, D.C., 1933), I, 409-33; Curtis P. Nettels, The Emergence of a National Economy, 1775-1815 (New York, 1962), 13-22, 46-51, 230-32.

[3] For a description and an assessment of the immense significance of these changes for the economic development of the United States see Guy Stevens Callender, Selections from the Economic History of the United States, 1765-1860 (Boston, 1909), 271-75; G. S. Callender, "The Early Transportation and Banking Enterprises of the United States in Relation to the Growth of Corporations," Quarterly Journal of Economics, XVII (Nov. 1902), 111-62; Lewis Bernard Schmidt, "Internal Commerce and the Development of National Economy Before 1860," Journal of Political Economy, XLVII (Dec. 1939), 798-822; Douglass C. North, The Economic Growth of the United States, 1790-1860 (Englewood Cliffs, N. J., 1961), passim; Nettels, The Emergence of a National Economy, 183-84, 201-204.

being full blown. It evolved gradually, not, it appears, from a conscious desire to emulate the system of tobacco marketing in colonial times but rather as a practical effort to meet certain immediate needs. For example, in the early decades of the nineteenth century many planters and farmers hauled their cotton into Charleston themselves and either sold it directly to local buyers or traded it for manufactured goods or other items they desired. Merchants who received cotton in this way then resold it on the wharves either to representatives of shippers or to speculators. Such a system, however, proved cumbersome, especially for the larger planters, since it required their personal chaperonage each time a wagonload of cotton was ready for market. It was also expensive. The planter had to sell or barter his cotton immediately without the option of storing and holding it to await the best price during the marketing season. As a result, more and more of the planters began to use the services of agents in town—the factors.[4]

Cotton factors had been in business in Charleston at least since the turn of the century and the advantages they offered the planter became increasingly obvious. For example, early in February 1800 a factor wrote to a planter that his cotton had been received but not sold. The shipment was being held, he said, because the market was uncertain but he predicted a price rise later. Unless given orders to the contrary, he would continue to await improved conditions before selling.[5] Thus, the planter had not been forced to sell in an unfavorable market, nor had he been required to be on the scene awaiting the propitious moment to dispose of his crop. The factor had handled all this for him.

A similar evolution in the cotton trade occurred in Savannah. The business of Robert Goff, a general merchant in that city during the second decade of the nineteenth century, illustrates a transitional stage. His books show that his customers either sold their crops for cash or bartered them for merchandise. At the same time, however, some of his regular customers periodically

[4] Charles Fraser, *Reminiscences of Charleston* (Charleston, 1854), 15-16; J. N. Cardozo, *Reminiscences of Charleston* (Charleston, 1866), 12.

[5] Joseph Winthrop to Frederick Fraser, Charleston, Feb. 5, 1800, Fraser Papers, South Carolina Historical Society, Charleston, S.C. For correspondence and accounts of other Charleston factors in the early years of the nineteenth century, see the Waring & Hayne Papers and the Bacot-Huger Collection, both in the South Carolina Historical Society, Charleston, S.C.

received advances in the form of supplies and cash and then paid their accounts with the products of their farms, often cotton. Goff sold some of the products locally and consigned other items for sale elsewhere.[6] Goff, then, often supplied credit to farmers and planters, but he appears to have functioned only as a partial factor since he did not serve as the selling agent for the crops. At the same time (and probably earlier) true factorage firms were being organized in Savannah and planters and farmers began to use their services because of the extra advantages they offered.[7]

During the same period an analogous development occurred in the Mississippi Valley trade. Farmers there hauled their crops to the local village—in the newly settled areas this might be no more than a small store near a river—where they bartered them for needed store goods. Having accumulated the products of the neighborhood, the local merchant then loaded them aboard a flatboat and accompanied them to New Orleans. There he either sold the produce and bought a stock of goods to be laboriously poled upstream, or else he transported the goods by coasting vessel to New York, bought his store merchandise there and hauled it home overland by wagon.[8]

Often the trip all the way to New Orleans proved unnecessary. An enterprising Southern merchant with a store near the Mississippi, anxious to stock his shelves, would hail passing riverboats laden with the products of the Northern country—flour, cornmeal, bacon, and the like. If a cargo suited his purposes and if a satisfactory price could be agreed upon, he bought both cargo and boat. Then he advertised his new purchase and advised local planters to bring their cotton to the river to exchange for the supplies they needed. When his stock was exhausted, he loaded the cotton on the flatboat and took it downstream to New Orleans to be sold.[9]

[6] "Account Book" and "Day Book," Robert S. Goff Papers, Georgia Historical Society, Savannah, Ga. Goff began business (according to a statement in the front of the "Day Book") in partnership with Moses Pettingill in Nov. 1818.

[7] See letters and accounts in R. & J. Habersham Papers, Georgia Historical Society, Savannah, Ga. The Habershams sold both rice and cotton.

[8] For a delightful description of this procedure see the accounts by Mrs. Elizabeth L. Topp of her father's business in Clarksville, Tenn.: "Reminiscences of Elizabeth L. Topp" and "Mrs. E. L. Topp's Book of Reminiscences," MSS in Robertson Topp Papers, Burrow Library, Southwestern at Memphis, Memphis, Tenn.

[9] Henry E. Chambers, "Early Commercial Prestige of New Orleans," *Louisiana Historical Quarterly*, V (Oct. 1922), 456-57.

This method, however, was extremely time consuming. Merchants could and did spend as much as six months a year taking their goods to market and returning home with supplies for their stores.[10] A more expeditious (as well as less strenuous) method of disposing of goods taken in trade was to send them to a resident agent in New Orleans to handle the sale. This procedure was noted by a visitor to Nashville in 1802: "There are very few cultivators who take upon themselves to export the produce of their labour, consisting chiefly of cotton; the major part of them sell it to the tradespeople at Nasheville [sic], who send it by the river to New Orleans, where it is expedited to New York and Philadelphia, or exported direct to Europe. These tradesmen, like those of Lexinton [sic] do not pay always in cash for the cotton they purchase, but make the cultivators take goods in exchange, which adds considerably to their profit."[11] The agents in New Orleans either sold the merchandise and (after deducting a commission for their services) remitted the proceeds to the merchant or they purchased goods in the New Orleans market and shipped them to the merchant.[12]

Local merchants were often bypassed as planters found it increasingly advantageous to sell their crop in New Orleans rather than to barter it for supplies from the local merchant. Instead of taking the cotton themselves to New Orleans, they too would deal with a merchant-agent in the Crescent City. During a visit to New Orleans in 1806, Thomas Ashe found that the most important men in commerce there were the "commission merchants to whom the settlers of the upper and adjacent countries consign their produce." These merchants, he wrote, charged a commission for their service in addition to their assessments for storage, wharfage, and labor.[13]

From these varied beginnings, the cotton factorage system gradually developed. In its broadest outlines, the system incorpo-

[10] "Mrs. E. L. Topp's Book of Reminiscences," Robertson Topp Papers.

[11] François Andre Michaux, *Travels to the West of the Alleghany Mountains*, in *Early Western Travels, 1748-1846*, ed. Reuben Gold Thwaites (Cleveland, 1904), III, 252.

[12] John McDonogh, the eccentric Louisiana land speculator, served as such a merchant in New Orleans in the years 1802 to 1804. Lewis E. Atherton, "John McDonogh and the Mississippi River Trade," *Louisiana Historical Quarterly*, XXVI (Jan. 1943), 37-43; Arthur G. Nuhrah, "John McDonogh: Man of Many Facets," *Louisiana Historical Quarterly*, XXXIII (Jan. 1950), 16-40.

[13] *Travels in America* (London, 1808), III, 259.

rated both the old methods used in the colonial trade and the newer methods practiced by commission merchants in other branches of the internal trade of the country.[14] When Southern merchants, like their counterparts in other sections of the country, began to specialize,[15] and as some concentrated their attention on the cotton trade and sought to build up a cotton-planter clientele, Southern cotton factorage began to develop certain special characteristics.[16]

Within the first two decades of the nineteenth century the cotton factorage system had settled into a pattern which would vary little throughout the ante bellum period—and even beyond. New firms might arise and old ones disappear, a general merchant might evolve into a cotton factor, a sleepy crossroads village with one or two general stores might become an important inland market with a number of large factorage houses—but despite minor local variations cotton factorage showed a remarkable uniformity.

[14] For a brief general description of the part played by factors and brokers in the domestic trade of the United States in the first half of the nineteenth century, see Fred Mitchell Jones, *Middlemen in the Domestic Trade of the United States, 1800-1860* (Urbana, 1937), 19-32.

[15] See George Rogers Taylor, *The Transportation Revolution, 1815-1860* (New York, 1951), 10-14.

[16] The terms "factor" and "commission merchant" were often used interchangeably in contemporary writings, and even in court cases. Cf. Ralph W. Haskins, "Planter and Cotton Factor in the Old South: Some Areas of Friction," *Agricultural History*, XXIX (Jan. 1955), 1, n. 3. In his discussion of the agencies in Anglo-American trade, one student maintained that "there is no practical difference" between the two terms. Norman Sydney Buck, *The Development of the Organization of Anglo-American Trade, 1800-1850* (New Haven, 1925), 6. Indeed, the factor was a commission merchant—i.e., he served as an agent for another party and received a commission for his services—but not all commission merchants were factors. Listings in city directories would often distinguish between cotton factors and commission merchants and factors would often list themselves in newspapers and advertisements as factors *and* commission merchants. For example, three New Orleans directories listed commission merchants, cotton factors, rice factors, sugar factors, and tobacco factors separately. Most, but not all, of the factors were listed also as commission merchants, but the number of commission merchants exceeded the combined number of factors of every description. H. & A. Cohen, *Cohen's New Orleans Directory for 1855* (New Orleans, 1855), 252-53, 263, 265; Wallace A. Brice, *New Orleans Merchants' Diary and Guide for 1857 and 1858* (New Orleans, 1857), 16-23, 25-27, 60-61, 63-64; A. Mygatt & Co., *New Orleans Business Directory* (New Orleans, 1858), 89-102, 106-10, 206, 215, 227-28.

Anyone buying and selling for a commission, regardless of who employed him and the article handled, was considered a commission merchant. The term "factor," however, was reserved for those commission merchants who were the agents of the planters growing the Southern staple crops. The distinction was not a legal one, nor did it reveal an especially subtle differentiation. Rather, it arose out of custom and usage.

The factor became the cotton planter's commercial alter ego, his personal representative in the marketplace. Although his primary concern was with the sale of the crop and the needs of the plantation, he also performed many other personal services for the planter. However far from the city the planter lived and however seldom he visited, he had the city's facilities available to him through his factor.

CHAPTER TWO

Selling the Crop

A planter with cotton to sell found buyers as near at hand as the gates of his plantation or as far away as the wharves of Liverpool. To secure the highest net return he had to select the proper buyer in the right market at the most propitious time. This was no easy task and planters with a substantial crop to sell ordinarily entrusted the responsibility to an expert—the cotton factor. Every town had factors or their representatives eager to serve the planters.

Closest at hand for most plantations were the larger interior towns. Situated at river, road, and railroad junctions, these towns became important cotton markets as production spread and increased in volume. By 1860 the most important interior cotton markets were Fayetteville, Columbia, Augusta, Milledgeville, Macon, Atlanta, Montgomery, Nashville, Memphis, and Shreveport.[1]

Sales close to home obviously kept marketing expenses low. Yet, despite the extra costs (higher transportation and insurance bills, extra handling, and the like) most planters found it advantageous to have their crop sold in the coastal cities where buyers in greater numbers produced a more active demand. Charleston, Savannah, Mobile, and New Orleans became the largest cotton markets in the South.[2]

A few shipped their cotton directly to factors in Liverpool. Fanny Kemble, in her account of her stay at her husband's cotton plantation on the sea islands of Georgia, recorded that a "gentlemen in Liverpool . . . has been factor for this estate for thirty years."[3] Similarly, the Mississippi planter, Charles Whitmore, consigned his crop directly to the Liverpool firm of Thomas B. Barclay and Company, bypassing middlemen in both New Orleans and Natchez.[4] Planters consigning their products directly to European factors were, of course, following the pattern of the colonial tobacco trade. But notwithstanding the pull of tradition, most planters during the ante bellum period preferred to deal with a factor in the South. A London merchant told a committee of Parliament in 1833 that three-fourths of the staple sent to Liverpool was on consignment from merchants, not from planters. In later years the proportion of direct consignments from planters to Europe probably decreased even further.[5]

Preference for Southern factors arose not from sectional patriotism but from concrete economic advantage. If he shipped directly to Liverpool the planter limited himself to a sale in that market; peculiar indeed would be price conditions in the Northern markets which could support the expense of two trips across the Atlantic. If, however, he chose a Southern factor to sell his crop, the planter was not confined to that market in which his factor resided. A system of partnerships and other business relationships existed among factors in various towns and cities in the South, the North, and abroad, which facilitated the movement of cotton from place to place as conditions—or whim—dictated.

Factors in the interior markets enhanced their commercial position by having business connections with firms in the port cities to whom they could send cotton for sale. Philo Goodwyn, for example, established himself as a commission merchant in

[1] Lewis Cecil Gray, *History of Agriculture in the Southern United States to 1860* (Washington, D.C., 1933), II, 711, 714; Ulrich B. Phillips, *Life and Labor in the Old South* (Boston, 1929), 141-42. If he chose, a planter might sell his crop to a storekeeper in the local village or to speculators who came to the plantation. These buyers are dealt with in detail in chap. vii and viii below.

[2] Gray, *History of Agriculture*, II, 711.

[3] Frances Anne Kemble, *Journal of a Residence on a Georgia Plantation in 1838-1839*, ed. John A. Scott (New York, 1961), 202.

[4] Mack Swearingen, "Thirty Years of a Mississippi Plantation: Charles Whitmore of 'Montpelier,' " *Journal of Southern History*, I (May, 1935), 208.

[5] Gray, *History of Agriculture*, II, 711; James H. Lanman, "The American Cotton Trade," *Hunt's Merchants' Magazine*, IV (March 1841), 221; [Joseph Holt Ingraham], *The Southwest. By a Yankee* (New York, 1835), II, 93; Charles S. Davis, *The Cotton Kingdom in Alabama* (Montgomery, 1939), 141; Edward Baines, Jr., *History of the Cotton Manufacture in Great Britain* (London, [1835]), 317, citing evidence of Mr. Gabriel Shaw of Thomas Wilson & Co., London, before Select Committee of the House of Commons on Trade, Manufactures, and Shipping, 1833; Norman Sydney Buck, *The Development of the Organization of Anglo-American Trade, 1800-1850* (New Haven, 1925), 91-93.

Memphis in 1845 and announced that he would sell cotton consigned to him there. If his customers preferred, however, he would send the staple on to the New Orleans firm of Franklin and Henderson for whom he served as an agent.[6] Similarly, a Montgomery factor and warehouseman, John T. Murphy, advertised that in addition to selling in the Montgomery market he would also ship cotton for sale through "his friends" in either New Orleans or Mobile.[7]

Partnerships commonly linked coastal factorage houses with firms in the interior or in other coastal cities. For example, Leigh Maddux and Company of New Orleans announced in August 1836 that Branham Merrill of Tuscumbia, Alabama, had been taken in as a partner and would conduct business in the Alabama town under the firm name of Merrill, Maddux and Company.[8] In 1850 William Knox of Montgomery became a partner in the large New Orleans factorage firm of Hill, McLean and Company. Knox declared he would either sell cotton in Montgomery or would forward it to his partners in New Orleans.[9] The Augusta factors, Adams, Hopkins and Company, formed an association with a Savannah firm and announced that they could "therefore (if desired) give our planting friends the advantage of both markets."[10] A group of New Orleans firms advertising in 1860 indicated that they had partners in such tiny interior areas as Indianola, Texas; Attalaville, Brandon, and Yazoo City, Mississippi; in the larger interior markets such as Montgomery, Louisville, St. Louis, Shreveport, Vicksburg, and Wetumpka; and in the port city of Mobile.[11]

Not only were a number of Southern markets available to the planter through his factor; Northern and European markets were equally accessible. Partnerships sometimes united Northern and European firms with Southern factorage houses. Such was the relationship which joined Washington Jackson and Company (New Orleans), Jackson, Todd and Company (Philadelphia), and Todd, Jackson and Company (Liverpool). "We either sell here or

---

[6] *Semi-Weekly Appeal* (Memphis), Jan. 24, 1845 in typescript MSS dated April 1962 in envelope marked "Biography: Goodwyn, William Adolphus," Goodwyn Institute Library, Memphis, Tenn.

[7] *Tri-Weekly Flag & Advertiser* (Montgomery), Feb. 23, 1847, Nov. 4, 1848.

[8] *New Orleans Price Current*, Aug. 13, 1836.

[9] *Daily Alabama Journal* (Montgomery), Feb. 27, 1851.

[10] *Daily Chronicle & Sentinel* (Augusta), Jan. 2, 1850.

[11] *New Orleans Price Current*, Sept. 1, 1860.

ship to our house at Liverpool, as our friends may desire," wrote
the New Orleans branch of the firm to a Mississippi planter,
". . . as it is mostly the same thing to our Mr. Jackson—whether
we sell here or in Liverpool."[12] A family relationship joined
factorage firms in Savannah and New York: Robert Habersham
and Son would sell in Savannah and I. Rae Habersham headed
the New York firm.[13] One need only glance at the announcements
and advertisements appearing in the newspapers of the day to
recognize that such partnerships were common.[14]

Actually, Southern factors did not need a partner in Europe
or the North before they could send a planter's cotton there.
Numerous New York and European firms took cotton on consignment from Southern factors. For instance, the great English firm
Baring Brothers and Company during the three decades before
the Civil War arranged to receive cotton from factors in the great
coastal cities of Charleston, Mobile, Savannah, and New Orleans
as well as from those in interior markets such as Macon and
Columbus. Besides these dealings with Southern factors, the
Barings also had their own agents in the port cities of the South
and in major Northern markets who bought cotton outright
or who took it on consignment for later sale in Liverpool.[15] The
various companies organized by the Brown family (Brown Brothers
and Company, New York; Brown, Shipley and Company, Liverpool
and London; and other allied firms in Boston and Baltimore) also
had Southern factors with whom they dealt as well as their own
agents in major Southern cities.[16]

[12] Jackson, Todd & Co. to Leverich, Philadelphia, April 16, 1840, Charles P.
Leverich Papers, Mississippi Department of Archives and History, Jackson, Miss.;
Washington Jackson & Co. to Johnson, New Orleans, Jan. 23, 1844, William John-
son Papers, also in Mississippi Department of Archives and History.

[13] I. Rae Habersham to Jones, New York, Oct. 19, Nov. 10, 1854, Feb. 16, 1856,
Wm. Neyle Habersham to Jones, New York, March 31, 1856, George Noble Jones
Papers, Georgia Historical Society, Savannah, Ga.

[14] The *New Orleans Price Current*, for example, would regularly carry notices
announcing the formation of "co-partnerships" with partners in New Orleans and
New York. The same paper would carry advertisements of New Orleans firms
offering to forward cotton to their "friends" in New York or Liverpool, or Havre,
or London. Firm names of the various companies would often be similar. For
example, on Dec. 10, 1859 Hewitt, Norton & Co. (New Orleans) advertised that
it would send cotton to be sold in Liverpool by James Hewitt & Co. or to New
York, consigned to Hewitt & Co.

[15] Ralph W. Hidy, *The House of Baring in American Trade and Finance*
(Cambridge, Mass., 1949), 174-75, 185-86, 359, 363.

[16] *William and James Brown and Company v. Thomas McGran*, 14 Peters (U.S.)

Thus, through a system of partnerships or other agreements, the factorage system made virtually every cotton market in the world available to the cotton grower. If the planter were dissatisfied with prices in one market he needed only to instruct his factor to send his cotton elsewhere.[17] Factors themselves might take the initiative in shipping to another market,[18] or they might discourage such a course.[19] Their decisions rested simply on a personal judgment as to which of the many markets available would offer the most advantageous sale at any given moment. For example, in a single crop year, the Augusta factors, Heard and Simpson, sold cotton not only in Augusta but in Charleston, New York, Baltimore, and Liverpool as well.[20]

The best market of course was one that netted the planter the highest return and it was the factor's responsibility to find it. With prices fluctuating as much as 5 cents per pound—and more—

479 (1840); *Brown Shipley & Co.* v. *P. A. Clayton*, 12 Cobb (Ga.), 564 (1853); John Crosby Brown, *A Hundred Years of Merchant Banking* (New York, 1909), 255, and circular announcing the opening of the New York firm reprinted on 190-91.

17 In 1804 Andrew Jackson and his partner John Hutchings were dissatisfied with the price their New Orleans factors, Boggs, Davidson & Co., were able to get for cotton in the Crescent City and they instructed the Southern firm to send the cotton to Liverpool for sale. The New Orleans firm quickly complied. N. Davidson to Jackson, New Orleans, July 14, 1804, Jackson and Hutchings to Boggs, Davidson & Co., Hunters Hill, Tenn., July 31, 1804, in John Spencer Bassett (ed.), *Correspondence of Andrew Jackson* (Washington, D.C., 1926), I, 96-98, 99-101.

18 In June and July of 1841 many factors in New Orleans were still holding cotton from the previous summer's crop, reluctant to take the prices the local buyers were offering. Rather than reduce their prices, the city's commercial journal reported, the factors "have commenced shipping their stocks to Liverpool and Havre." *New Orleans Price Current*, June 19, June 26, July 10, 1841.

19 "We are ourselves opposed to shipping any produce out of this market," wrote a New Orleans merchant to a planter, "having found it, by experience and an insight into the transactions of others, in nine times out of ten the best spot for the planter." The factor warned that great losses had been sustained by those who did ship to the North or to Europe but hastened to add that if so directed he would send cotton to New York for sale. John Hagan & Co. to Hamilton, New Orleans, May 7, 1829, W. S. Hamilton Papers, Southern Historical Collection, University of North Carolina Library, Chapel Hill, N.C.

20 See letters during the first seven months of 1859 to Heard & Simpson from A. Gardelle in Charleston, J. E. Clemm in Baltimore, and Isaac Low & Co. in Liverpool. Gardelle mentioned shipments to New York but there is no indication as to which firm received the cotton there. Stephen D. Heard Papers, Southern Historical Collection, University of North Carolina Library, Chapel, N.C. In a single year a planter might sell his crop in more than one market. For example, Coffin & Pringle, cotton factors of Charleston, sold part of John Fripp's 1856 crop in Charleston and part the firm shipped on to Liverpool for sale. A/c current, Fripp with Coffin & Pringle, Charleston, June 10, 1857, John Edwin Fripp Papers, Southern Historical Collection, University of North Carolina Library, Chapel Hill, N.C.

throughout the season in every market,[21] he was expected to be wise enough to make a sale when prices reached their peak. This meant that a successful factor had to be an expert salesman, aware of the needs of the local buyers, and alert to the trends in supply and demand in his own and in other markets of the world.

Once he consigned his crop to a factor, the planter did not lose sight of it. He could and did keep informed. Newspapers published in the market cities brought him estimates of the quantity of cotton produced and the prices being paid in the Southern, Northern, and European markets. Factors, too, regularly sent him reprints of this information,[22] as well as letters and circulars which offered estimates of the probable size of the crop, the prospects for prices, and appraisals of the demand based on their assessment of political and economic conditions in Europe and at home and guesses as to the amount of raw cotton in the hands of the manufacturers.[23]

Advice on the best time to sell often accompanied such information. For example, in the late summer of 1827 a New Orleans factor urged one of his customers to take advantage of an early

---

[21] For figures showing high and low prices paid in various markets for various grades of cotton during the ante bellum period see E. J. Donnell, *History of Cotton* (New York, 1872), *passim.* Cf. figures given in James E. Boyle, *Cotton and the New Orleans Cotton Exchange* (Garden City, N. Y., 1934), 155, 176-80. Each issue of the commercial journals carried information on prices and sales since the last issue and each year at the start of the marketing season (Sept. 1) an "Annual Statement" would summarize the trends for the previous year.

[22] The *Price Currents* published in the port cities printed abridged editions of their paper, reduced in size and available in bulk orders. They also printed letter sheets, a folded page on one side of which was reprinted information from the latest edition, the other side left blank for the merchant's letter. Almost every collection of planter's papers contains such reprinted or letter sheets.

[23] For example of such letters and circulars see Reynolds, Byrne & Co. to Walker, New Orleans, Sept. 20, 1830, Oct. 16, 1830, Sept. 25, 1831, Zachariah Walker Papers, Mississippi Department of Archives and History, Jackson, Miss.; Gribble & Montgomery's "Annual Circular," dated New Orleans, Aug. 16, 1848 in Eli J. Capell and Family Papers, Meritt M. Shilg Memorial Collection, Department of Archives and Manuscripts, Louisiana State University, Baton Rouge, La. Almost every collection of planters' papers contain such letters.

Factors provided information to the planters; they usually did not solicit it. On one occasion, however, the planter did have better information than his factor. Maunsel White wrote to Andrew Jackson (Jan. 29, 1831) that the trend in cotton prices would depend on whether there would be war in Europe. "On this subject however, you Must be better advised than any one else in these states, and if it were not asking too much, or what might be improper for me to ask, I would ask yr opinion on that subject." Bassett, *Correspondence of Andrew Jackson*, IV, 228.

demand. Stocks of cotton in the hands of Northern manufacturers were very low, he wrote, "from which we infer that they will be forced into this market with their orders at the opening of the Season, and this with the aid of speculators, will probably enable us to obtain better prices than at a later period when the trade falls into its regular channels."[24] Several years later Reynolds, Byrne and Company gave similar advice for different reasons. The prospects for a large crop were very great, they wrote, and therefore "we advise our friends very particularly to ship as early as possible and accept the then market prices in preference to holding on for still higher rates," for prices would soon decline in the face of a heavy crop.[25]

Armed with such information, planters sometimes insisted that they, rather than their factors, make the decision when to sell. A Georgia planter was adamant on this point:

> It has been my custom to sell my cotton when I have been in Augusta & I expect ever to do the same—I have Heard [sic] that you did not want cotton sent you, unless you had to selling of it. Now when I want my cotton sold & I am not in Augusta, then I shall expect my Factor to sell—not otherwise. This being the case, if you would rather not have me send my cotton to you, say so & I will try & Make some other arrangements—otherwise, I shall be pleased to send my cotton to you. . . . If you conclude to take it, under the circumstances, then I want the cotton Insured . . . & Held for further instructions—as I would rather have it all sold together & besides, I will risque getting more for it.[26]

Perhaps it was the thrill of gambling along with the expectation of greater gains which induced a planter to retain control over the sale of his own crop. Mississippi planter James W. Monette, following the New Orleans market from his plantation, in early December 1846 wrote his New Orleans factors, Buckner and

24 John Hagan & Co. to Hamilton, New Orleans, Aug. 24, 1827, W. S. Hamilton Papers.

25 To Johnson, New Orleans, Aug. 19, 1833, William Johnson Papers. As will be shown, factors did not always advise an immediate sale once the cotton was in their hands. Preseason advice that an early sale would be best was common, probably because the factors wanted the planters to hurry the cotton to them.

26 B. W. Heard to Heard & Simpson, Redmont, Ga., Jan. 14, 1859, Stephen D. Heard Papers.

Stanton, that he wanted his cotton held "for better prices" which he hoped would soon be available. Two weeks later he indicated that "if the next steamer from Liverpool brings favorable news, we think the Orleans market must have an upward tendency." His expectations were realized when the market began to advance after the first of the year but Monette wrote that he would hold for at least 12 cents per pound on his best cotton "unless an unexpected decline should overtake the European market." By the end of January prices had improved still further, but the planter had upped his demands to no less than 12.5 cents per pound. Mid-March found him still predicting a further rise, but by the first week of April conditions had changed so radically that he indicated he would settle for a sale at 11 cents.[27]

Planters like Monette who bound their factors so closely were at a distinct disadvantage. News about market conditions was often stale by the time it arrived in the mails. Information about a rise in prices might not reach the planter before a contrary tendency governed the market and the advantage lost. If the cotton was being held until the planter came to town to sell his own crop, peak prices might have come and gone before the planter arrived.

Usually, therefore, planters allowed their factors wide discretion. Typical were the instructions of a South Carolina planter: consider the crop "as committed to your better judgement."[28] "Still you must bear in mind that I leave all to your own judgment which in such matters, is no doubt better than mine," a Mississippian wrote the New York factors who had his cotton.[29]

A factor was expected to have the skill, experience, and sources of information that would make his judgment superior to that of the planter. Superior judgment was expected to lead to profitable

[27] Letters dated Washington, Miss., Dec. 3, Dec. 16, 1846, Jan. 8, Jan. 25, March 18, March 31, April 7, 1847, James W. Monette Papers, Mississippi Department of Archives and History, Jackson, Miss.

[28] John B. Bull to Stoval & Simmons, Willington, S. C., Jan. 22, 1838, Bull-Morrow Papers, Georgia Historical Society, Savannah, Ga.

[29] W. Newton Mercer to Leverich, Laurel Hill [near Natchez, Miss.], June 20 [1840], Charles P. Leverich Papers. Even James Monette, who kept his factors under such close instructions in 1846-1847, gave his factors more leeway in 1848— perhaps because of his own lack of success earlier. He instructed them in mid-September "to make the best disposition" they could. "If you think speedy sales best—select your own time." To Buckner & Stanton, Washington, Miss., Sept. 16, 1848, James W. Monette Papers. See also *ibid.*, Oct. 17, 1848.

results, as Richard J. Dunett's advice—and warning—to his Augusta factor made clear:

> I hope, gentlemen, that you will look well to my interest & sell at the proper time, (even at once if you think it safest). I have been strongly solicited to patronise another house, but my invariable reply has been that I never give up an old friend for a new one, without a good reason. I have thought that whilst a market is regularly going up, it may be safe to hold, but I hope you will not allow it to go down with the cotton on hand; but you are in the market with more lights before you than we have so far off, & of course have more facilities to form correct conclusions, & I doubt not, but that you will do what your judgement dictates to be best in the premises.[30]

Few customers were so minatory. The factor was aware of his duties and needed no reminders of it. When the cotton consigned to his care arrived, he would dispatch a letter to the planter acknowledging receipt. Soon the planter would be advised of the quality of his cotton and the prospects for prices. Unless under specific instructions, the factor would sell when he deemed best without waiting for the planter's approval and the planter would usually hear about the sale only after it had already been made.[31]

Often a factor bound by a planter's specific orders would urge him to change his instructions when market conditions seemed to warrant it. Maunsel White wrote a customer that he would hold for better prices as instructed but urged a prompter sale: "The demand is now good, & brisk sales making at 9 to 10 cts. & if very fine a little [hig]her & I doubt much if they will be better in a month hence."[32]

[30] To Simpson & Heard, Montevideo, Dec. 6, 1858, Stephen D. Heard Papers.

[31] Most collections of planters' papers contain such letters. A convenient source illustrating the general procedure are letters from factors who sold cotton from Mrs. James K. Polk's plantation published in John Spencer Bassett, *The Southern Plantation Overseer as Revealed in His Letters* (Northampton, Mass., 1925). See esp. Pickett, Perkins & Co. to Mrs. Polk, New Orleans, Jan. 3, 1850 (p. 229), Jan. 5, 1852 (pp. 231-32), Pickett, Macmurdo & Co. to Mrs. Polk, New Orleans, March 1, 1854 (pp. 237-38), W. S. Pickett to Mrs. Polk, New Orleans, June 23, 1854 (p. 239).

Price was not the only item determining when a sale would be made. If the planter needed ready cash to pay a debt or to make a purchase, or if the factor was unable to continue carrying a previously incurred debt, it was necessary to make a sale at an early date to meet these needs. These problems of credit and forced sale, and the rights of the factor in such situations, are treated below.

[32] To Walker, New Orleans, April 9, 1829, Zachariah Walker Papers.

Sometimes explicit instructions were ignored. For example, in May 1823 a New Orleans merchant informed his planter customer that his 50 bales of cotton had been sold at one-half cent below the planter's minimum instructed limit. "This may be improper," the factor admitted, "and you have a right to claim the half cent." But, after close examination of the cotton "we were convinced that more than the 12¢ offered could not be obtained. . . . We hope you will be satisfied that we consulted your interest, if we disobeyed your instructions."[33]

One New Orleans factorage firm made it very clear to its customers that it would use its own discretion if it would be to the advantage of the planter: "As factors, we shall endeavor to act with reference to the *interest* of our Correspondents, even if for the moment, it should be at variance with their wishes, unless we are laid under positive instructions."[34]

A profitable sale involved more than mere timing. The factor also had to decide the best way of selling. A planter's crop often contained several grades, which could be sold separately at varying prices or together at an average price for the lot. Furthermore, the factor usually had the bales of many planters in his possession at one time and could, if he thought it advantageous, sell the crop of several planters in a single transaction. For example, the New Orleans factor Maunsel White informed one of his customers that he had just made a sale of some eleven hundred bales at "the highest offer I could get or expected to get" and that "I have included yours in the number." Proceeds of this sale would vary according to the quality of each planter's cotton and therefore, he explained, "it will take some time to go thro' the entire, so that I cannot send you the a/c [account] Sales for a few days."[35]

A planter might dictate the way his cotton should be sold,[36] but usually this decision was left to the factor. Buyers often required

[33] Dicks, Booker & Co. to Hamilton, New Orleans, May 16, 1823, W. S. Hamilton Papers. See also *Ward et al.* v. *Warfield et al.*, 3 Robinson (La.) 468 (1848).

[34] Gribble & Montgomery's "Annual Circular," New Orleans, Aug. 16, 1848, Eli J. Capell and Family Papers.

[35] To Walker, New Orleans, Jan. 29, 1828, Zachariah Walker Papers.

[36] James Monette, directing his factor's actions in 1847 very closely, insisted that his better cotton be sold separately from the inferior grades and dictated the minimum price he would accept for each lot. To Buckner & Stanton, Washington, Miss., Jan. 8, 1847, James W. Monette Papers. Another Mississippi planter, while giving his New York factor free rein to make the best sale nevertheless urged the merchant to sell his cotton in small lots to insure high prices. W. Newton Mercer to Leverich, Laurel Hill, Feb. 7, 1840, Charles P. Leverich Papers.

a special grade, variety, and quantity of cotton and these needs had to be recognized in the interests of a good sale. A New Orleans factor described how a buyer entered his office in early February 1851 expecting to purchase about four hundred bales for shipment to Spain, "whereupon, I took down the samples of a number of small crops of Prairie cottons, suitable for the Spanish market, placed them on the table for sale, made a list of them and sold them."[37]

Obviously, a factor could not discharge his responsibility to seek out the best sale without being able to classify, grade, and sample cotton in his possession. Since the value of the staple varied considerably according to quality and grade, an error in classification could be costly. There is some evidence, however, that this danger was lessened through the skilled aid of another group of merchants, the cotton brokers.

The exact role these cotton brokers played is unclear. Directories and newspapers carried advertisements of numerous firms calling themselves cotton brokers. When in 1836 New Orleans brokers organized themselves and appointed a committee "to give a correct report of sales, and to revise the prices each week," the leading commercial newspaper of that city announced that its list of cotton sales would thenceforth be "taken from their register" and its price quotations would be "in conformity to their views."[38] The brokers also seem to have been given certain regulatory powers over the cotton trade. A meeting of "cotton buyers and cotton brokers" was held in October 1859 "for the purpose of devising means to redress certain abuses and grievances existing in connection with the cotton trade of New Orleans." After agreeing on a set of rules, the group set up a committee of fifteen cotton brokers to enforce these regulations and empowered the committee "to adopt such other rules amongst themselves to secure a more uniform and satisfactory method of receiving cotton."[39]

That brokers were in the best position to have a "correct report" of weekly sales and prices and to enforce trading rules indicates that they were participants in cotton sales. Often their participation is noted in the records. A New Orleans factor, describing a sale, wrote that the buyer came to his office "accompanied by A.

---

[37] C. Toledano, *Appeal to the Public* ([New Orleans, 1851]), 1.
[38] *New Orleans Price Current*, Dec. 10, 1836.
[39] *Hunt's Merchants' Magazine*, XLII (1860), 105-106.

Desmare, Broker."[40] Many—but not all—accounts of sales rendered by factors to planters listed the name of a broker along with the name of the individual or firm making the purchase.[41]

It is clear that the cotton broker, in addition to other duties, was often an intermediary between buyer and seller, probably helping the two parties to agree on the grade and quality of the cotton under consideration. "We had the cotton valued by one of our best brokers," a New Orleans factor testified during litigation arising over a dispute concerning the price received for a planter's cotton.[42] In another case, testimony showed both buyer and seller hiring brokers "to inspect" the list of cotton offered for sale to determine quality.[43]

Even with the help of brokers, factors had to be experts, alert to price movements, buyers' needs, crop size and quality, and the like. The need for expert knowledge inevitably led to specialization. Although some factors sold more than one commodity,[44] by and large it appears that factors in the larger markets specialized in the selling of one or another of the South's staples. Advertisements in journals, directories, and newspapers usually indicated that the merchant was a factor exclusively for cotton or rice or sugar or tobacco. Rarely was more than one commodity handled by a single house.[45]

[40] Toledano, *Appeal to the Public*, 1.

[41] For examples of such accounts see Washington, Jackson & Co. to Capell, New Orleans, Dec. 16, 1841, Jankins & Bonner to Capell, New Orleans, Dec. 31, 1841, Sales by Gribble & Montgomery for Capell, Eli J. Capell and Family Papers.

[42] *Ward et al.* v. *Warfield et al.*, 3 Robinson (La.), 468 (1848).

[43] Buckner, Stanton & Newman v. Delany, Rice & Co., as reported in *Hunt's Merchants' Magazine*, XLIII (1860), 322.

[44] A Charleston factor, for example, sold both cotton and rice for the South Carolina planter James Gregorie in 1858. John Colcock to Gregorie, Charleston, May 21, 1858, Gregorie-Elliott Papers, Southern Historical Collection, University of North Carolina Library, Chapel Hill, N. C. Another Charleston factor sold "ground nuts" for one of his customers. See a/c sales on a/c of Mrs. A. Lovell by A. W. Campbell, Charleston, May 1, 1834, Langdon Cheves Collection, South Carolina Historical Society, Charleston, S. C. This sale of 133½ bushels of nuts (along with the sale of 55 bales of cotton) was probably an accommodation rather than a regular practice. Other accounts with Campbell in this collection, at least, show no other sales than cotton.

[45] For material dealing with sugar factorage see J. Carlyle Sitterson, "Financing and Marketing the Sugar Crop of the Old South," *Journal of Southern History*, X (May 1944), 188-99; Wendell Holmes Stephenson, *Alexander Porter, Whig Politician of Old Louisiana* (Baton Rouge, 1934), *passim*. Information on rice factorage may be found in J. H. Easterby, *The South Carolina Rice Plantation* (Chicago, 1945), 357-439 and in the same author's "The South Carolina Rice Factor as Revealed in

Every cotton market had many different kinds of buyers with whom the factor dealt. Some were mainly speculators. "The purchases yesterday were principally on Speculation," wrote a Charleston factor, "Cotton to be restored and resold later."[46] The extent of such speculative activity varied from day to day and from year to year, depending on estimates of crop size, anticipated demand, political conditions, and the vitality of the hundreds of rumors circulating in the market. With the characteristic exaggeration of a foreign visitor, Edward Sullivan described cotton speculation in the New Orleans market:

> During the whole winter the city is thronged with cotton speculators. . . . I had no idea mercantile affairs were so entirely a matter of speculation. People make bets about the probable rise and fall in the price of cotton, and book them in the same way as a man does his bets on the "Derby." It appears that the real amount of the yield of cotton is never exactly known, and all the great speculators have touts, who are despatched into the different cotton districts to send information to their employers. As their accounts differ considerably, so does the spirit of gambling increase, each man considering his information better than his neighbor's, and backing it accordingly. Fortunes are made and lost as quickly as on the Stock Exchange, and numbers of bankruptcies occur every winter.[47]

Such frenzy was not a regular feature of the market. Sometimes a rash of speculation would take hold of the market as it did briefly in 1843 when "many parcels of Cotton changed hands repeatedly."[48] In other seasons it could be reported that "speculation has been comparatively unknown."[49]

Most sales were made to buyers who expected to ship the cotton to another market. Some of these buyers also were primarily

the Papers of Robert F. W. Allston," *Journal of Southern History*, VII (May 1941), 160-72.

[46] Gardelle to Heard & Simpson, Charleston, March 25, 1859, Stephen D. Heard Papers.

[47] *Rambles and Scrambles in North and South America* (London, 1852), 217-18.

[48] *New Orleans Price Current*, Sept. 2, 1844.

[49] *Ibid.*, Sept. 1, 1848. The extent of speculation at any given time can be accurately gauged by reading the reports on the state of the cotton market published in each edition of the commercial newspapers in each port city. In their "Annual Statements" the amount of speculation during the year under review as well as when it was most prevalent were carefully reported.

speculators, hoping to resell and still realize a profit after transportation costs had been paid. Thus, for example, a buyer would purchase cotton from a Memphis factor and then order it shipped down the Mississippi to a New Orleans factor with instructions to seek out another buyer in the Southern port.[50]

Such buyer-speculators usually operated between Southern markets and those in the North or Europe. William C. Murray of Charleston, for instance, purchased cotton from factors in the South Carolina port and shipped it to merchants abroad to be resold, hoping that the proceeds less transportation, insurance, selling commissions, and other costs, would leave a profit.[51]

A buyer-speculator could utilize the possibilities of several of the world's cotton markets. He might make purchases in one of the Southern ports and then order the cotton sent to New York. If satisfied with prices offered there, he would order a sale. If not, he would have the cotton sent to one of the European markets. Since most of the cotton shipped to New York in this manner was later exported to Europe,[52] speculators in this trade developed a simpler method of shipment. The cotton was sent directly from the Southern ports to Europe, but samples taken from each bale went to New York. This method—called selling "in transit"—gave the speculator the option of selling out in New York (by sample) or of holding for a European sale, and it saved the extra expense of sending the cotton first to New York and then to Europe. First begun in the early 1850's, "in transit" sales by 1858 came to some two hundred thousand bales per year in New York. Buyers in New Orleans and Mobile were the largest users of this method, but merchants in Charleston, Savannah, and other ports also took advantage of it.[53]

[50] *The Farmers and Merchants Bank of Memphis* v. *Franklin et al.*, 1 Robinson (La.), 393 (1846).

[51] L. Trapmann to Murray, Charleston, Jan. 21, 1839, April 22, 1839, May 28, 1839, June 1, 1839, Bacot-Huger Collection. Murray sold cotton in Liverpool, Antwerp, and Havre. In some of these transactions—many of them very large, involving hundreds of bales—Murray had partners, once including the captain of the ship on which the cotton was sent.

[52] Even as late as the 1850's only about one bale in five grown in the United States was consumed in this country. James L. Watkins, *King Cotton* (New York, 1908), 30.

[53] New York Chamber of Commerce, *Annual Report, 1858* (New York, 1859), pp. 13-14; Henry Hentz, "Reminiscences of the Cotton Trade of Old," *New York Times*, Dec. 29, 1890, as reprinted in *Cotton and Finance* (New York), I (Nov. 30, 1912), 396.

Many buyers were not themselves speculators but were buying on orders from others. Northern and European merchants and manufacturers would order a quantity of cotton purchased for them, often stipulating a maximum price and a certain grade. Buyers, working on a commission for their services, would bargain with factors in an attempt to fill the order at the limits set. Available evidence seems to indicate that these buyers sometimes speculated as well; that is, they bought and shipped cotton on their own as well as on other's account. The Savannah firm of Cohen and Fosdick, for example, bought cotton on order for a Boston company, Coffin and Weld. The Northern concern resold the staple in Boston. Sometimes Cohen and Fosdick would merely fill the order as directed; at other times they shared the risk (and, hopefully, the profit) by investing some of their own funds in a shipment sent to the Boston merchants.[54] Godfrey Barnsley carried on a similar business as a buyer for English merchants and cotton spinners. He bought large lots of cotton from local factors, sorted the bales according to the quality ordered, and then shipped the staple to the various British firms as instructed. He also bought cotton on his own account; he never resold it in Savannah but consigned it for sale in England.[55] Advertisements and "Business Cards" in newspapers and directories indicate that large numbers of firms in the South were engaged in this "buying on foreign account."

Through his factor, then, the cotton planter could deal with buyers of every description in an intricate worldwide marketing system. His factor supplied him with information and advice concerning the sale of his crop, or, as was so often the case, took the whole responsibility for selling his cotton. But this was only a part of the factor's responsibilities. The planter usually turned to his factor for aid long before he had any cotton to sell.

[54] The course of business between these two firms can be followed in the letters from Cohen & Fosdick to Coffin & Weld during 1844, 1848, 1849, 1850, and 1851, Cohen & Fosdick Papers, Georgia Historical Society, Savannah, Ga.

[55] "Barnsley v. MacLellan, Copy Correspondence," Godfrey Barnsley Papers, Emory University Library, Atlanta, Ga. Cotton could replace cash as a means to remit funds abroad. Thus the New York hardware merchants Phelps Dodge & Co. instructed Southern merchants who had been selling their goods to use the proceeds to buy cotton. This cotton was shipped to the Liverpool firm of Phelps James & Co. and sold. The proceeds were then invested in metal products for export to the parent firm. Richard Lowitt, *A Merchant Prince of the Nineteenth Century: William E. Dodge* (New York, 1954), 40-54.

CHAPTER THREE

Providing Plantation Supplies and Credit

As the planter's representative in the marketplace, the factor served as a buyer as well as a seller. Throughout the year as food, rope, bagging, clothing, and other items were needed, the planter—or his overseer—would simply order them from the factor. It was his responsibility to fill the order promptly at the lowest possible cost.

Some planters made annual purchases,[1] but most sent orders as the need arose. In either case, the procedure was the same: a letter from the planter brought a promise from the factor to send the merchandise ordered and soon afterward the planter received the goods along with an invoice showing the prices paid.[2]

Factors might have goods on hand to meet the requests of their customers. In the 1830's and 1840's, for example, several Savannah factors sold woolen cloth for a Rhode Island merchant.[3] Presumably, they filled any orders for woolens from their own stock. Others had a more complete stock. When Philo Goodwyn, a Memphis cotton merchant and agent for a New Orleans factor, opened his business, he advertised that he intended "to keep on hand a constant supply of groceries, western produce, bagging and rope, etc." for his customers.[4]

For the most part, however, it appears that factors (especially those in the larger markets) bought the merchandise after it was ordered. In doing so, of course, they were expected to respect their client's purse. A small Georgia planter, whose difficulties with the language did not obscure his intent, made this point clear when he placed an order with his Augusta factors: "... as I presume that you inten to do me justice wich I wish you not to cheat me out one cent I wish you to Send me the following articles to Lexinton depot and pay the freight to that point and wrte me when you start them their so that I may send my waggon after them. . . ."[5]

Thus the factor in addition to his other duties had to keep a watchful eye on the market for plantation supplies and decide when and from whom to buy. If the supplies ordered were not immediately needed, he might delay: "I have *not* yet purchased the Cotton Goods," wrote a New York factor to his Southern customer, "ascertaining they can be had at *any* time next month."[6]

[1] The overseer on the James K. Polk plantation was in the habit of ordering his supplies for the entire year. After estimating his needs for the coming season, he would send an order to Mrs. Polk who would then forward it to her factor in New Orleans. W. S. Pickett & Co. to Mrs. Polk, New Orleans, Jan.. 21, 1857, Feb. 5, 1857, Perkins & Co. to Mrs. Polk, New Orleans, Dec. 4, 1857, printed in John Spencer Bassett, *The Southern Plantation Overseer as Revealed in His Letters* (Northampton, Mass., 1925), 249-50, 255-56.

[2] For typical examples from various Southern markets see Welman & Phillips to Walker, New Orleans, March 31, 1815, Maunsel White to Walker, New Orleans, Nov. 10, 1827, May 24, 1828, Reynolds Byrne & Co. to Walker, New Orleans, Oct. 28, 1830, Zachariah Walker Papers, Mississippi Department of Archives and History, Jackson, Miss.; a/c current of Mrs. Eliza Bull with John S. Holt, Augusta, Nov. 14, 1823, Holt & Ware to E. & J. Bull, Augusta, Feb. 26, 1827, a/c current of John B. Bull with Baird & Rowland, Augusta, May 3, 1839, Baird & Rowland to John B. Bull, Augusta, Nov. 14, 1839, Bull-Morrow Papers, Georgia Historical Society, Savannah, Ga.; a/c current of Fripp with Coffin & Pringle, Charleston, June 10, 1857, a/c current of Fripp with Coffin & Pringle, Charleston, March 23, 1859, John Edwin Fripp Papers, Southern Historical Collection, University of North Carolina Library, Chapel Hill, N. C.; a/c of Pickens with Franklin Robinson, Mobile, July 1, 1832, as printed from Samuel Pickens Papers by Charles S. Davis, *The Cotton Kingdom in Alabama* (Montgomery, 1939), 147.

Planters who consigned to New York factors received the same service. See Charles P. Leverich to Stephen Duncan, New York, Aug. 30, 1839, invoice for shoes sent by Leverich to Duncan, New York, Jan. 1, 1860, invoice for supplies sent by Leverich to Duncan, New York, Jan. 15, 1860, Stephen and Stephen, Jr., Duncan Papers, Louisiana Department of Archives, Louisiana State University, Baton Rouge, La.

[3] See letters to Hazard from R. & W. King, Savannah, 1831 and 1832 and from R. Habersham, Elias Reid, Way & King, Savannah, 1841-1849, in Isaac Peace Hazard Papers, Georgia Historical Society, Savannah, Ga. The Savannah factors would also sell cotton to the Rhode Island merchant.

[4] *Semi-Weekly Appeal* (Memphis), Jan. 24, 1845 in "Biography: Goodwyn, William Adolphus" (typescript; April 1962), Goodwyn Institute Library, Memphis, Tenn.

[5] John G. Higginbotham to Heard & Simpson, Elbert County, Ga., Sept. 4, 1858, Stephen D. Heard Papers, Southern Historical Collection, University of North Carolina Library, Chapel Hill, N. C.

[6] Charles P. Leverich to Stephen Duncan, New York, Aug. 30, 1859, Stephen and Stephen, Jr., Duncan Papers.

High prices might induce a factor to send part of a planter's order and delay purchase of the remainder if he expected a decline later. Thus, in early August 1827 Maunsel White of New Orleans wrote a Mississippi planter that he was sending only part of a requested order. The factor explained that he was sure the planter did not want the full order at the high prices which then prevailed.[7]

Listings in directories and newspapers indicate that the factor had a wide market from which to choose when he made a purchase for the planter. "Our dealers are well supplied with all descriptions of foreign and domestic merchandise direct from Europe, and from the markets and manufactories of the North, and are prepared to supply their customers on the most liberal terms" ran a typical statement in a New Orleans newspaper at the height of the cotton season.[8]

The factor, however, did not make all the planter's purchases. It was not uncommon for planters to buy goods from nearby merchants or even to order merchandise from city merchants who did not handle their cotton. Stephen Duncan, one of the wealthiest ante bellum planters, purchased goods not only from his New Orleans and New York factors but also placed orders with a merchant in St. Louis.[9] Small planters did the same thing. John W. Brown, for example, sold his cotton through factors in New Orleans but made regular purchases from merchants in Camden, Princeton, and Tulip, towns near his Arkansas plantation.[10]

Even under these circumstances the factor was usually involved in the transaction, as he often paid the bill. John W. Brown paid local merchants with checks drawn on his New Orleans factors.[11] When the Alabama planter Hugh Davis purchased goods from a merchant other than his factor he either gave the merchant his

[7] To Walker, New Orleans, Aug. 4, 1827, Zachariah Walker Papers. The way in which prices would act in the future was of course at best a guess and all factors did not agree. Less than three weeks after White had written that he expected a later decline, another New Orleans factor wrote a Louisiana planter that he had filled his order in full as he did not expect price reductions. John Hagan & Co. to Hamilton, New Orleans, Aug. 24, 1827, W. S. Hamilton Papers, Southern Historical Collection, University of North Carolina Library, Chapel Hill, N. C.

[8] *New Orleans Price Current*, Nov. 10, 1838.

[9] Duncan Journal, 1851-1861, *passim;* invoice of sundries ordered of Stephen G. Miller, St. Louis, Nov. 1960, Stephen and Stephen, Jr., Duncan Papers.

[10] Entries for Jan. 15, 17, and 18, 1854, John W. Brown Diary, Arkansas History Commission, Department of Archives and History, Little Rock, Ark.

[11] *Ibid.*

personal note (which the merchant would present to Davis' factor for payment) or requested the merchant to bill the factor directly. In either case, the factor paid the charges, just as if he had made the purchase, and added the bill to Davis' account.[12]

Planters sometimes came to the city to fill their needs personally, but again the factor was usually involved. John W. Brown, after arriving in New Orleans in April 1853 for his regular annual visit, went first to his factor to check his accounts and then roamed the city "to ascertain where I should deal, learn prices, see what changes had taken place" since his last visit. After his factor introduced him "to some wholesale houses, in view of purchasing," he set about "to make my purchases for family use." He bought groceries and meat "from or through Henderson," his factor, and placed orders for supplies with two other firms. His factor paid all the bills. His work and pleasure finished, Brown boarded a steamboat for home, having spent about four days in the city.[13]

This system of buying "from or through" the factor was not confined to plantation supplies. Personal luxury items were also ordered in the same manner. Eli Capell's factors filled his requests for not only the obviously utilitarian plantation supplies (bagging, rope, lime, firebrick, cultivators, twine, nails, seed, hammers, plaster), for clothing and bedding, but also for the civilized amenities of planter life such as sherry, books, a tuning fork, and other items to be used by the Capell family.[14] Similarly, when George Noble Jones ordered quail from a New York merchant

[12] Weymouth T. Jordan, *Hugh Davis and His Alabama Plantation* (University, Ala., 1948), 120. Many of the supplies for the estate of Isaac Franklin were purchased and paid for in this manner. For example, in April and July of 1846 the New Orleans grocers, Peters & Millard, filled an order and the estate's factors, Hill, McLean & Co. of New Orleans, were asked "please pay the above account and charge the same to the account of Estate of Isaac Franklin." Invoice in Franklin plantation records, printed in Wendell Holmes Stephenson, *Isaac Franklin, Slave Trader and Planter of the Old South* (University, La., 1938), 243. Similar invoices illustrating this procedure from the Franklin estate are printed *ibid.*, 233, 245-48.

[13] Entries for April 22, 23, 25, and 26, 1853, John W. Brown Diary. Brown recorded his visit to New Orleans the following year also. Part of this diary is printed in Horace Adams (ed.), "Arkansas Traveler, 1852-1853: Diary of John W. Brown," *Journal of Southern History*, IV (Aug. 1938), 377-83. The experiences recorded here may be found on 382-83.

[14] See invoices of purchases by Gribble & Montgomery for Capell, dated variously, New Orleans, 1848-1849, Eli J. Capell and Family Papers, Meritt M. Shilg Memorial Collection, Department of Archives and Manuscripts, Louisiana State University, Baton Rouge, La.

and fine ale from a merchant in Philadelphia, he was indulging tastes far removed from the practical necessities of plantation life, but tastes which the factor was expected to gratify.[15]

Furnishing supplies was only one small part of the credit provided by the factor. The security of cotton—grown, growing, and to be grown—served as the basis of an immense credit system in the ante bellum South. Although the planter's property provided the security, it was the factor who organized and operated the credit system which enabled the planter to provide for his needs and to sell his cotton.

The simplest form of credit, common to factoring throughout the world in all commodities, was the system of "advances." A firm to which goods were consigned for sale would pay the consignor a part of the expected sale price in advance of the sale. In this way, the consignor—be he manufacturer, grower, or merchant —did not have to wait until his goods were sold before he received any funds; partial payment was made immediately. After a sale was finally made, the seller deducted his expenses and commissions and then remitted any additional proceeds over and above the amount advanced.[16]

Anyone with cotton on hand could easily get an advance from the merchant to whom he chose to consign it, be that merchant in the interior, in the large port cities, in the North, or in Europe. Moreover, he could get his advance—in cash—immediately, even if he planned to consign his cotton to a merchant a long way off. In the interior, agents and partners of coastal factors gave advances on the spot for cotton to be shipped to the coast. "We are prepared to make Advances upon Cotton shipped to our house in New Orleans," ran a typical advertisement in a Montgomery news-

---

[15] J. A. Sanderson to Jones, New York, Aug. 25, 1851, Robert Smith to Jones, Philadelphia, April 29, 1852, George Noble Jones Papers, Georgia Historical Society, Savannah, Ga. A Charlestonian recalled the factor's role as a purchaser: "If he [the planter] lived all the year, as many did, in the country, they bought his household groceries and his wines and liquors, shoes and stockings for his family, silks and linens for his wife and daughters." D. E. Huger Smith, *A Charlestonian's Recollections, 1846-1913* (Charleston, 1950), 47. This is without doubt overstated. Trips to the city were much more common than implied here, and, although it is possible that a planter would trust his merchant to select his wines, it is difficult to imagine a planter's wife and daughters allowing a busy merchant to choose their dresses and linens.

[16] See J. R. McCulloch, *A Dictionary, Practical, Theoretical, and Historical, of Commerce and Commercial Navigation* (American ed. by Henry Vethake; Philadelphia, 1854), I, 669.

paper.[17] Should a Northern or European sale be preferred, there was still no need to wait for an advance. "Liberal advances in cash will be made by us on property shipped to our address, from the interior, either for sale here, or to be forwarded to our friends in New York or Boston," announced the New Orleans firm, Fellowes, Johnson and Company. Gorrissen Brothers of the same city offered advances on cotton shipped to "their friends" in New York, Liverpool, Havre, Rotterdam, Antwerp, Hamburg, and Bremen.[18] Similar advertisements appeared in every issue of the commercial papers in the Southern markets and examples could be endlessly expanded. It is doubtful if any firm in the United States—North or South—or abroad refused a requested advance.[19]

Another form of credit extended by the factor arose from his responsibility for the sale of the planter's crop. Service costs began the moment the cotton left the plantation. The journey to market meant charges for transportation and insurance against fire and water damage. Upon arrival the cotton had to be hauled to a warehouse or other storage place, weighed, sampled, and exposed for sale. Any damage the bales had suffered in transit had to be repaired. If the cotton were to be shipped on to another market, more transportation costs and insurance premiums were involved. In the event of an ocean voyage the bales had to be recompressed to a higher density so that they would occupy less space on the ship. Moreover, a European shipment meant import duties and further charges for transportation, insurance, handling, and storage.[20]

[17] *Daily Alabama Journal* (Montgomery), Feb. 27, 1851.

[18] *New Orleans Price Current*, Sept. 2, 1844.

[19] Firms would differ, however, on the size of advance they would give—i.e., how large a part of the expected sale price they would risk in advance—depending upon their estimate of the price trend in the market.

Merchants would give advances to other merchants as well as to planters directly. Thus, if an interior merchant decided to ship to the coast for sale, he could receive an advance from the coastal factor and then, if necessary, pass it on to his planter customer. Similarly, factors in the coastal markets could get advances from Northern or foreign houses for consignments. The economic significance of the resulting capital flow is treated elsewhere in this study.

[20] A planter, writing in 1852, listed the service charges which were made on his cotton shipped to Europe: Services in the United States included baggage, mending, wharfage, cartage, storage, fire insurance, and maritime insurance; in Europe the planter was charged for dock dues, cartage, porterage, weighage, mending, warehouse rent, freight, and duties. In addition he had to pay for the cost of materials such as twine and canvas needed to repair damaged bales. *DeBow's Review*, XIII (1852), 301-302.

Although the planter eventually paid these marketing expenses, it was the factor who paid them as they arose and the planter was not billed until his cotton was sold.[21] Actually the procedure was much like the advance noted earlier, the only difference being that in this case the advance was in the form of services rather than cash.[22]

However important the advance on cotton already consigned, it provided only a limited measure of credit. Such funds after all became available only at the end of the growing season. But the planter often needed money long before he had any cotton to sell. Again, the cotton factor solved the problem. He provided advances in both merchandise and cash on the security of a crop still growing in the fields or even on cotton not yet planted. Such expenditures he carried on his books until he sold the planter's next crop. Here indeed was a peculiar form of credit. The security was something that did not yet exist; an advance was made on cotton not yet grown.

It is impossible to determine to what extent planters borrowed on the growing crop. Clearly, some planters did not find it necessary to do so. Mrs. James K. Polk, for example, waited until her factor had her cotton before making her yearly order. Thus, in 1857, the $553.52 worth of supplies furnished by Mrs. Polk's factor stood as a debt for only nine days, or until he sold the 120 bales he already had on hand for $6,227.93. Moreover, it was her practice to leave funds with her factor to cover other bills she might incur during the year.[23] Similarly, the Charleston factor, A. W. Campbell, held the proceeds of cotton sales from the plantation of Mrs. Ann Lovell, sending her funds during the year as she requested them.[24]

On the other hand, there is ample evidence that the practice of borrowing on anticipated crops was common. Indeed, it was wide-

[21] When accounts of sales were rendered by factors to the planters they showed the various services performed and the costs. For a typical account see a/c sales of cotton by Reynolds Byrne & Co. for Johnson, New Orleans, June 10, 1834, William Johnson Papers, Mississippi Department of Archives and History, Jackson, Miss.

[22] The bookkeeping convention was strictly adhered to, however; factors carefully distinguished between service costs and advances in their accounts.

[23] W. S. Pickett & Co. to Mrs. Polk, New Orleans, Feb. 5, 14, March 9, 1857, printed in Bassett, *Southern Plantation Overseer*, 250-51.

[24] Campbell to Mrs. Lovell, Charleston, July 15, 1834, a/c current of Mrs. Lovell with Campbell, Charleston, Oct. 17, 1834, Langdon Cheves Collection, South Carolina Historical Society, Charleston, S. C.

spread enough to draw the attention of contemporary travelers and commentators. "The system of credit in this country is peculiar," wrote a Northerner visiting Mississippi in 1834. "The planters have their commission merchants in New-Orleans and Natchez, who receive and ship their cotton for them, and make advances, if required, upon succeeding crops."[25] The prevalence of this practice was common knowledge, declared a Northern financial journal: "Everybody knows that the cotton planters of the southwestern states, procure large supplies of clothing for their slaves, and of every article required for their own consumption, upon credit from the neighbouring merchants, in anticipation of the next year's crop. . . ."[26] It "is well known," echoed the author of an article describing "The American Cotton Trade" that "the harvest of one year is, as it were, mortgaged for the expenses of the next" for the majority of the cotton planters.[27] A Louisianian who had lived for a time in the North told Frederick Law Olmsted that most planters in his state would borrow to buy slaves and land in anticipation of a good crop which would cover their debts.[28] New Orleans railroad promoter and banker, James Robb, noted that the capital of the Southern merchants "is absorbed in high rents, high interest, and by advances to planters."[29] Mississippian Benjamin Wailes recorded in his diary in 1857 that Southern planters had participated in the speculation which precipitated the hard times of that year by borrowing from their factors on the "growing cotton crop" to purchase land and slaves at inflated prices.[30] The planter borrows funds from his factor "long before his 'fields are white unto harvest,'" wrote the author of a popular history of banking in New York.[31]

Planters' and factors' records indicate clearly that borrowing on future crops was commonplace. Usually the advance was in the form of supplies or cash needed by the planter during the summer

[25] [Joseph Holt Ingraham], *The Southwest. By a Yankee* (New York, 1835), II, 93.

[26] *Financial Register*, I (Aug. 16, 1837), 63.

[27] *Hunt's Merchants' Magazine*, IV (1841), 226.

[28] Olmsted, *The Cotton Kingdom*, ed. Arthur M. Schlesinger (New York, 1953), 330-31.

[29] *DeBow's Review*, XI (1851), 77.

[30] Entry of Oct. 17, 1857, as quoted in Charles Sackett Sydnor, *Slavery in Mississippi* (New York, 1933), p. 198, n. 60.

[31] J. S. Gibbons, *The Banks of New-York, Their Dealers, The Clearing House, and The Panic of 1857* (New York, 1858), 214.

before his crop was ready to harvest. The cost of supplies purchased for the planter as well as charges for transportation from town to plantation were carried on the factor's books until the planter's cotton was sold. South Carolina planter John B. Bull's accounts with his factor in 1839-1840 are typical. In May 1839 and then again in November of the same year Bull ordered and received supplies from his Augusta factor, Baird and Rowland, but it was not until April, eleven months after the first order, that the bills were paid.[32]

Even if a planter bought merchandise from merchants other than his factor, his factor often paid the bill and then carried the debt until cotton was received and sold. The Augusta factors Heard and Simpson were asked to pay a note for $600 that a planter had given for the purchase of a pair of horses. "I will if possible forward you cotton enough to pay the note, but if it should so happen that I can not get the cotton there in time please advance the amount, and I will send the cotton as early as possible. . . ."[33]

If the planter needed cash, the factor often supplied that too. When John W. Brown visited his New Orleans factor in April 1853, he was supplied with merchandise and also authorized to borrow "on the faith of the next crop," a crop which would probably not be ready for sale for at least six months. Brown promptly used this authority; just before starting for home, he drew $75 in cash from his factor and recorded that he was "well pleased" with his visit and was leaving his "business matters in as favorable a fix as I could have hoped for."[34]

Again, the factor provided aid for plantation expansion or improvements or unforeseen expenses of one kind or another before a planter's crop was ready for sale. In January 1859 a planter wrote Heard and Simpson requesting $2,000 to make some improvements on his plantation. He would repay this money, he wrote, "with my next crop of cotton—say in December next."[35]

[32] John B. Bull in a/c with Baird & Rowland, Augusta, May 3, 1839, Baird & Rowland to Bull, Augusta, Nov. 14, 1839, Bull-Morrow Papers. Both bills are marked paid, April 4, 1840. Examples from the accounts of planters with their factors showing this procedure could be multiplied endlessly.

[33] M. W. Gray to Simpson & Heard, Elbert County, Ga., Sept. 6, 1858, Stephen D. Heard Papers.

[34] Entries of April 25 and 26, 1853, John W. Brown Diary.

[35] A. S. Brown to Heard & Simpson, Sparta, Jan. 22, 1859, Stephen D. Heard Papers.

Less specific was the request a few months later from a plantation near Sparta, Georgia, for a loan of $1,500 for *"an especial purpose."* The planter promised to repay the loan the following November "by which time I will have cotton in your hands."[36]

In granting a loan the factor sometimes simply sent cash to his customer. Usually, however, he granted a loan in much the same way a bank today gives a deposit loan. He informed the planter that he was extending a line of credit on which the planter could draw to pay bills, receive cash, or otherwise use as he saw fit. "We have to inform you of our willingness to accommodate you with the sum you require," wrote a New Orleans factorage house to a planter customer. The letter went on to indicate that the firm would pay drafts from the planter under this credit.[37] The amount of credit the factor gave depended, of course, both on his own financial status and the amount of cotton he could expect to receive from the planter. John W. Brown's "letter of credit" was for $800,[38] whereas the more substantial planter, Charles Clark of Bolivar County, Mississippi, was authorized to draw on his factors "to the extent of fifteen thousand Dollars" in drafts "to suit your convenience."[39]

Business connections provided a great deal of flexibility in the credit system. Through their "friends" in the North or in Europe, Southern factors provided letters of credit for their customers traveling far from home. For example, while in Paris in June 1856, wealthy planter George Noble Jones received notice that his Savannah factor, R. Habersham and Son, had arranged for the credit he had requested to cover the expenses of his European trip: "Messrs R. Habersham & Son having authorized a credit in your favor for £3000—by their instructions we request Messr Haywood & Co to send you enclosed their Circular Letter for the amount in force to 9 June 1857 for which you will please send us your acknowledgement."[40]

When a factor indicated his willingness to grant a line of credit he could at the same time shift part of the credit burden to others.

---

[36] A. I. Lane to Heard & Simpson, Granite Hill, May 5, 1859, *ibid.*

[37] John Hagan & Co. to Hamilton, New Orleans, March 12, 1828, W. S. Hamilton Papers.

[38] Entry of April 25, 1853, John W. Brown Diary.

[39] Fellowes & Co. to Clark, New Orleans, March 13, 1860, Charles Clark and Family Papers, Mississippi Department of Archives and History, Jackson, Miss.

[40] Brown Shipley & Co. to Jones, Liverpool, June 9, 1856, George Noble Jones Papers.

When John Hagan authorized William Hamilton to draw on him, he asked that Hamilton do so "at as long date as possible, not under 30 days." Similarly, Charles Clark's factor asked that Clark value on him at from 60 days to 12 months.[41] Under such an arrangement the person receiving the note (say, a produce merchant or a slave trader) could not collect for 30 days or more. He could present it to the factor who would "accept" it. But this meant simply that the factor agreed to pay the note when it fell due. Thus, a merchant who took payment from a planter in such time notes shared the credit burden with the factor. The longer the note (i.e., the longer the length of time it had to run before it could be cashed) the greater the amount of credit being given by the merchant rather than the factor. For example, on January 1, 1848 one of the executors of the estate of Isaac Franklin purchased slaves for one of the estate's plantations from Thomas Williams, a Washington, D. C., trader, and paid the $8,000 cost with a 40-day note drawn on Hill, McLean and Company, the estate's New Orleans factors. In this instance the factor did not have to make payment until mid-February; in the 40-day interval, the slave trader provided the credit.[42] Another instance, though on a much smaller scale, involved a purchase by John W. Brown. The Arkansas planter noted in his diary in March 1852 that he bought a horse for $65, paying for it with a 2-month bill on Cherry, Henderson and Company, his New Orleans factors.[43]

Frequently, the factor would be asked to lend only his name and credit standing instead of cash. By "endorsing" a planter's note, the factor guaranteed that it would be paid when due. The planter would receive credit, but the factor would not be called upon to make any cash outlay unless the planter defaulted. Such was the arrangement worked out between Robert Habersham, Savannah, and planter John A. Cobb. Habersham agreed to accept, i.e., endorse, certain drafts drawn by Cobb and payable to various parties in the future. To secure Habersham, Cobb gave him a mortgage on forty slaves. If the notes were not paid when

41 John Hagan & Co. to Hamilton, New Orleans, March 12, 1828, W. S. Hamilton Papers; Fellowes & Co. to Clark, New Orleans, March 13, 1860, Charles Clark and Family Papers.
42 Draft on Hill, McLean & Co. in favor of Thomas Williams, New Orleans, Jan. 1, 1848, printed in Stephenson, *Isaac Franklin,* 222.
43 Entry of March 28, 1852, John W. Brown Diary.

due, Habersham could take possession of the Negroes and sell them to pay the debt (which he, as the endorser would be required to pay) and, after deducting expenses and damages, remit any surplus to Cobb.[44] Usually such guarantees by the factor were based on the growing crop rather than on slave property. For example, in May 1832 William Hamilton's factor suggested that the planter ask one of his creditors to await payment of a debt until his first batch of cotton was harvested and sold. "We will guarantee this to them if this is required," the factor added.[45]

Through his endorsements and acceptances the factor was able to open credit resources all over the world to the planter. His endorsement usually meant that the local banks would discount the planter's note, and the bank's added endorsement would mean it, in turn, could get funds from banks in the North and abroad. Thus, the world's money markets, like the world's commodity markets, became available to the cotton planter through his factor.[46]

The entire credit structure was built on the presumption that cotton, when it finally came to market and was sold, would cancel all debts. But this was not always the case. Often sales failed to net the sum needed to pay off loans granted during the year. When that happened, one year's accounts would run into another, with factors advancing additional funds before prior loans were retired. For example, early in 1822, after his cotton had been sold, William Hamilton received notice that a balance was due his factor. When Hamilton replied that he did not have the funds, his merchant was apologetic: "I did not think when I addressed you yesterday on the subject of accts that yr situation was so embarassing [sic] and that the dificulty [sic] of paying was so great with you, or I assure you, notwithstanding my own wants, I should not have mentioned the subject." The merchant went on to promise Hamilton that he would not be pressed for payment and that the debt would be carried over "for the next crop."[47]

[44] Indenture between Habersham and Cobb, Savannah, May 24, 1834, Robert Habersham Papers, Georgia Historical Society, Savannah, Ga.

[45] John Hagan & Co. to Hamilton, New Orleans, May 5, 1832, W. S. Hamilton Papers.

[46] The part played by banks in the financing and marketing of cotton is treated below.

[47] Robert M. Chinn [of Chinn & Johnson] to Hamilton, St. Francisville, Feb. 28, 1822, W. S. Hamilton Papers.

Knowing that Hamilton was a chronic debtor—he regularly finished the season owing a balance—his factor usually did not even bother to ask him for immediate payment. Instead, Hamilton was simply asked to sign notes to fall due "at such periods as your new Crop can meet and cancel."[48] Nor was Hamilton's experience unique. A student of the plantation records of Lavinia Erwin found that despite proceeds from crops during 1831 to 1836 totaling almost a quarter of a million dollars, Mrs. Erwin would end each year owing money to her New Orleans factors. The balance due would always be carried over to the next crop.[49] Thus, the credit available to the cotton planter ranged from a short-term advance of funds while his cotton was being sold to long-term credit running through many years.

[48] John Hagan & Co. to Hamilton, New Orleans, June 6, June 27, 1828, *ibid.* See also Hagan to Hamilton, May 28, 1832, *ibid.*

[49] Alice Pemble White, "The Plantation Experience of Joseph and Lavinia Erwin, 1807-1835," *Louisiana Historical Quarterly*, XXVII (April 1944), 390-91.

CHAPTER FOUR

Banker, Bookkeeper, and Friend

Often in the course of attending to the planter's affairs the factor functioned as a personal banker. He held the planter's funds or made funds available through credit and he disbursed them as ordered. Instructions, verbal or written or in the form of a draft drawn on the factor, allowed the planter to pay bills from merchants, slave traders, and physicians, overseers' wages, taxes, and other expenses and to procure cash. Thus the factor provided services similar to those provided by a checking account today. In addition, the factor kept a set of books for the planter showing income, expenditures, debts, and surpluses. These "Accounts Current" and year-end rendering of accounts were for many planters the only records they kept. In the absence of a centralized banking system and a common currency, these banking services were not unimportant. Living, as he often did, far from the commercial centers, the planter was enabled to buy and sell, contract and pay his debts, and in general have his affairs cared for without being required to travel to town or to concern himself with problems of exchange, transfer of funds, discounts, and the like.[1]

The business acumen of some factors was so well respected that sometimes wealthy planters would ask their factors to handle business transactions other than those connected with planting. Stephen Duncan, for example, used his factor's services in his money-lending operations. Duncan, who made it a practice to lend large sums of money to his planter neighbors and friends, would send the borrowers' notes to his factor, who would collect the money owed as the notes became due. In December 1857

Washington Jackson and Company held notes for money due Duncan during the following January and February to a total of $154,691.98.[2] George Noble Jones' factors, Robert Habersham & Son, sold stock, slaves, and town lots for him in addition to handling his plantation business.[3]

Sometimes a factor managed plantation affairs when the planter was away. Writing from Philadelphia in July 1823, Alex Telfair requested that his Savannah factor investigate to see if "my man

---

[1] Almost any collection of planter's papers containing correspondence with factors can be used to illustrate the banking function of the factor. Among the fullest records are those kept by R. Habersham & Son (Savannah factors) for various members of the Telfair family. The Savannah firm handled both the business affairs of the plantations owned by members of the family as well as the personal affairs of these people. The factor kept a complete set of books for each plantation showing expenditures and income and drawing a yearly balance. See "Account Book 1832-1844—Retreat Plantation in Acct with R. Habersham & Son," "Account Book 1842-1856—Retreat Plantation in Acct with R. Habersham & Son," "Account Book, 1845-1860—Mills Plantation in Account with Robert Habersham and Son," "Sabine Fields Plantation Account Book, 1845-1858 In account with R. Habersham & Son," Telfair Family Papers, Georgia Historical Society, Savannah, Ga. Habersham also served as the personal banker for several members of the Telfair family, paying their personal bills, advancing them money when they needed it, and keeping their personal records. These personal accounts were kept separately from the plantation accounts but like the business accounts show income, expenditures, and draw a yearly balance. See "Accounts of Miss Mary Telfair 1832-1847 with R. Habersham," "Accounts of Mrs. Sarah G. Haig and Misses Mary and Margaret Telfair with R. Habersham," "Account of Mr. and Mrs. W. B. Hodgson and Miss Mary Telfair with R. Habersham & Son, 1854-1864," "Mr. and Mrs. W. B. Hodgson in Account with R. Habersham & Son, 1845-1856," *ibid.* Two full collections in print illustrating the banking functions of factors are Wendell Holmes Stephenson, *Isaac Franklin, Slave Trader and Planter of the Old South* (University, La., 1938), 222-39 and Alice Pemble White, "Plantation Experience of Joseph and Lavinia Erwin, 1807-1835," *Louisiana Historical Quarterly,* XXVII (April 1944), 430-65.

[2] Memorandum of notes held in collection by Washington Jackson & Co. for a/c of Duncan, New Orleans, Dec. 14, 1857, Stephen and Stephen, Jr., Duncan Papers, Louisiana Department of Archives, Louisiana State University, Baton Rouge, La.

[3] Robert Habersham & Son to Jones, Savannah, Jan. 29, April 1, 1856, George Noble Jones Papers, Georgia Historical Society, Savannah, Ga. Factors themselves probably did not make slave sales but arranged such sales through a slave trader or auctioneer. See A. Ledoux to Hamilton, New Orleans, Sept. 2, 1848, W. S. Hamilton Papers, Southern Historical Collection, University of North Carolina Library, Chapel Hill, N. C. Factors would sometimes advertise plantations for sale (often with slaves, if desired). See, for example, advertisements by Fellowes & Co., M. B. Brady & Co., and Foley, Avery & Co. in *The Daily Picayune* (New Orleans), Jan. 21, March 6, 11, 1860. It is not clear whether in these instances the factor was selling for a planter. Factors could come into possession of land through a defaulted debt, in which case they might attempt to sell it. Maunsel White tried to sell some 7,000 acres which he "was compelled to purchase some time ago to secure the payment of a large debt." White to P. E. H. Lovelace, Deer Range, Aug. 30, 1847, Maunsel White Papers, Southern Historical Collection, University of North Carolina Library, Chapel Hill, N. C.

Isaac" (apparently his overseer) was following the instructions Telfair gave him before he left.[4]

All sorts of favors, both of a personal and a business nature, were asked of a factor by a planter unable to travel to the city. In the absence of through bills of lading from distant markets to the plantation, the factor's help was often needed to receive goods and to arrange (and pay for) suitable transportation to the plantation. In October 1828, for example, John Hagan and Company received three boxes of "Tomb Stones" which had been ordered by William Hamilton from New York. Hagan sent them on to Hamilton and among his charges were freight (from New Orleans to the Louisianian's plantation) and draying.[5] Similarly, an Appling, Georgia, planter ordered a horse from New York with instructions to ship it to his factors in Augusta. The factors in turn were asked to receive the horse, pay any expenses involved, and to notify the planter when the animal arrived.[6]

Personal favors, too, were customary. "We are just compleating [sic] a school House at this place and I am chairman of the building committee," wrote a planter from Bath, Georgia, to his factor. He asked that the merchant send him 5,000 bricks and 2 barrels of lime to finish the job.[7] A few days later another customer wrote the same firm requesting that it investigate the whereabouts of some wool which the planter had sent to another merchant to sell.[8] Still another planter asked the factor to inquire about the city to find out if any carriage maker would take the son of "a clever Widow Lady of Sparta" as an apprentice.[9] Factors indeed expected to be asked to perform such favors and even urged the planters to solicit their aid. W. S. Pickett wrote to Mrs. James K. Polk that "it will afford me pleasure to attend to any order of yours *outside of our regular business.*"[10]

[4] To Robert Habersham, Philadelphia, July 10, 1823, R. & J. Habersham Papers, Georgia Historical Society, Savannah, Ga.

[5] John Hagan & Co. to Hamilton and a/c—Hamilton with John Hagan & Co., both dated New Orleans, Oct. 25, 1828, W. S. Hamilton Papers.

[6] Thomas J. Jones to Heard & Simpson, Appling, Sept. 8, 1858, Stephen D. Heard Papers, Southern Historical Collection, University of North Carolina Library, Chapel Hill, N. C.

[7] Gideon Dowse to Heard & Simpson, Sept. 5, 1858, *ibid.*

[8] W. H. Harris to Simpson, Oakland, Sept. 8, 1858, *ibid.* The letter also included news of the planter's crop, which would soon be sent to the factor for sale.

[9] A. I. Lane to Heard & Simpson, Granite Hill, Jan. 11, 1860, *ibid.*

[10] Letter dated New Orleans, June 23, 1854, printed in John S. Bassett, *The Southern Plantation Overseer as Revealed in His Letters* (Northampton, Mass., 1925), 229.

Unsolicited favors of a personal nature were also routine. A Charleston factor, concerned about the health of his customer, offered medical aid: "This dreadful Cholera seems to be approaching us very near, and I feel much apprehension, that it may prevail in all parts of our State. I have therefore sent a Box containing medicine with instructions how to use it—one Box for yourself & one for Colo. Richardson.—I hope sincerely we may escape this dreadful scourge, but I think it prudent to be prepared."[11] Often the factor sent gifts for the planter and his family. Along with a shipment of sugar the planter had ordered, the New Orleans factor Charles Clark, in October 1819, sent several presents for the planter's children.[12] "The merchants in New Orleans . . . usually send . . . a barrel of oysters or oranges, as a New Year's or Christmas present," recorded a Southern school teacher upon receiving a "beautiful orange" from one of his students.[13] Nor was the frivolous forgotten. A New Orleans factor rushed a planter news of "the greatest event of the day," information of an American record set by a racehorse.[14]

Special favors and gifts might be merely good business. Often they meant more than that, for close personal relations between factors and planters were not uncommon. In January 1832 Mrs. Ann Lovell received a formal letter from her Charleston factors, Cheesborough and Campbell, informing her of the state of her accounts. Below, on the same sheet, was an informal note from J. W. Cheesborough: "Mrs Cheesb'o will write to you . . . & in all probability soon after pay you a visit with 2 or 3 of the children —She is at present sorely afflicted with influenza & I recover from my late indisposition very slowly."[15] Andrew Jackson's factor,

11 A. W. Campbell to Mrs. Ann Lovell, Charleston, Sept. 3, 1834, Langdon Cheves Collection, South Carolina Historical Society, Charleston, S. C.

12 To Hamilton, New Orleans, Oct. 22, 1819, W. S. Hamilton Papers.

13 A. de Puy Van Buren, *Jottings of a Year's Sojourn in the South* (Battle Creek, Mich., 1859), 199.

14 M. Gillis to St. John R. Liddell, New Orleans, April 3, 1855, as quoted in Wendell H. Stephenson, "Ante Bellum New Orleans as an Agricultural Focus," *Agricultural History*, XV (Oct. 1941), 170. Looking back long after the event, a Louisianian remembered that the factor had social as well as economic duties: "His province was to receive and sell their [the planters'] crops, to forward such supplies as were needed, to keep them abreast of the market reports, to secure boxes at the opera and invitations to all the balls, so they were entertained royally [when they visited the city]." Louise Butler, "The Louisiana Planter and His Home," *Louisiana Historical Quarterly*, X (July 1927), 362.

15 Letter dated Charleston, Jan. 20, 1832, Langdon Cheves Collection.

Maunsel White, was an ardent Jacksonian and a personal friend of the general. When Jackson in February 1842 ordered supplies from White, he added a personal note: "It would afford me great pleasure to see you this summer at the Hermitage where, my dear friend, you would receive a hearty welcome."[16] By 1848 the Wilmot Proviso had soured White on the Northern democrats and he wrote that he preferred a Southern man for the presidency, General Taylor, "the friend of my youth & my old age."[17]

Friendships between factor and planter sometimes even resulted in a family union. Christopher Fitzsimons was Wade Hampton's Charleston factor and also his close personal friend. In June 1811, Fitzsimons invited Hampton "to bring Mrs. Hampton and the little ones to spend a few days with us."[18] Whether Hampton accepted that particular invitation or not is not recorded. But the families did meet socially and one of the "little ones," Wade Hampton II, married Fitzsimons' daughter, Ann, in 1833.[19]

Personal letters[20] obviously indicate friendships beyond any business connection. They show clearly that some factors at least were accepted as social equals by the planter class. Rosser Howard Taylor's conclusion that in South Carolina "factorage was the one branch of trade which was not regarded as derogatory to social standing"[21] is equally valid in other Southern states.

It would be a mistake, however, to assume that all factors were considered the social equals of the wealthy planters, that by merely taking the title "factor" a merchant could reach the top rung of the social ladder. He needed other credentials as well. The wealthier factors, those with the largest businesses and incomes, were frequently planters and slaveowners as well as merchants. Indeed, the line separating factors from planters was

16 Letter dated Hermitage, Feb. 28, 1842, Maunsel White Papers.

17 To H. M. Hyams, Deer Range, Sept. 4, 1848, *ibid.* See also White to Geo. F. Allen, Deer Range, Oct. 11, 1849, *ibid.*

18 Letter dated Charleston, June 11, 1811, printed in Charles E. Cauthen (ed.), *Family Letters of the Three Wade Hamptons, 1782-1901* (Columbia, S. C., 1953), 17. For other letters showing both the personal and business relationship between Hampton and Fitzsimons, see *ibid.*, 6-10, 13.

19 *Ibid.*, introduction by editor, p. xiv.

20 For other examples see Charles S. Davis, *The Cotton Kingdom in Alabama* (Montgomery, 1939), 157; Stephenson, "Ante Bellum New Orleans as an Agricultural Focus," 170.

21 "The Gentry of Ante-Bellum South Carolina," *North Carolina Historical Review*, XVII (April 1940), 117; also the same author's *Ante-Bellum South Carolina: A Social and Cultural History* (Chapel Hill, 1942), 44.

often blurred. Christopher Fitzsimons, whose daughter married Wade Hampton II, owned a plantation about fifty miles southeast of Augusta.[22] Maunsel White owned and operated a plantation, Deer Range, in Louisiana on which he grew large crops of cotton and sugar cane.[23] Harry R. W. Hill, one of the largest of the New Orleans cotton factors, owned some seven sugar and cotton plantations and more than a thousand slaves.[24] Steamboat owner and banker Gazaway Bugg Lamar was also for a time a Savannah commission merchant. Part of his business came from his several cotton plantations in south Georgia.[25] Savannah cotton buyer Godfrey Barnsley was also a cotton planter, having purchased Woodlands, a Georgia plantation, in about 1840.[26] Edmund Richardson, a partner in the large New Orleans factorage firm, Thornhill and Company, operated a cotton plantation in Mississippi.[27] Such merchants easily moved in the highest social circles and suffered no social ostracism because of their commercial calling.

If factors and storekeepers who operated on a smaller scale did not move in these circles, the same may be said of the small planter or farmer. The accumulation of wealth could easily move a man up the social scale in the ante bellum South. Factors Hill and Richardson had origins as humble as those of many of their planter customers but their wealth opened the highest social circles to them. Not all factors became wealthy and entered the ranks of high society, but not all farmers did either.[28]

---

[22] The young Hampton subsequently inherited the plantation and its 75 slaves. Cauthen, *Hampton Family Letters*, p. xiv.

[23] The Maunsel White Papers contain numerous letters from White in which he refers to his plantation and also an extensive correspondence with his overseers. White did not sell through his own firm but through Robert Patterson & Co. of Philadelphia, Dunlop Moncure & Co. of New Orleans, and others.

[24] Freeman Hunt, *Lives of American Merchants* (New York, 1858), II, 502.

[25] Thomas Robson Hay, "Gazaway Bugg Lamar, Confederate Banker and Business Man," *Georgia Historical Quarterly*, XXXVII (June 1953), 95.

[26] See numerous references to the plantation in Barnsley Collection, Archives Division, Tennessee State Library and Archives, Nashville, Tenn.

[27] "Edmund Richardson," in Latham, Alexander & Co., *Cotton Movement and Fluctuations, 1876 to 1883* (New York, 1883), 42-43. Richardson at the same time owned stores in Jackson, Brandon, Canton, Morton, and Newton, Miss.

[28] See Lewis E. Atherton, *The Southern Country Store, 1800-1860* (Baton Rouge, 1949), 205-206.

CHAPTER FIVE

Commissions, Service Charges, and Interest

For most of the factor's services, of course, there was a charge. When a planter received his year-end account, he would find among his expenses commissions exacted for buying and selling and interest charges for advances and loans he had received during the year. These, along with the cost of transportation, insurance, storage, drayage, and the like, were deducted from the gross proceeds from the sale of the crop.

The usual commission for selling cotton was 2.5 percent of the gross price. This had been the standard commission paid London factors to whom tobacco was consigned in the seventeenth and eighteenth centuries,[1] and from the earliest years it seems to have been accepted as the charge for selling cotton. Accounts of sales in Charleston during the first years of the nineteenth century uniformly show the 2.5 percent charge.[2] Thomas Ashe, on a visit in 1806, was told that New Orleans merchants "to whom the settlers of the upper and adjacent countries consign their produce" charged 4.5 percent;[3] but three years later, planters were paying factors only 2.5 percent to sell cotton in the Crescent City.[4]

Sales records among planters' and factors' papers, schedules of charges published in newspapers and journals,[5] letters and announcements from factors to their customers (or prospective customers)[6]—all indicate that, with few exceptions, planters throughout the ante bellum period paid 2.5 percent commission to their factors regardless of the market in which they chose to sell. This charge for "selling the crops," declared the Louisiana Supreme

Court, was "well established by the custom of merchants, and recognized by law."[7]

Any deviation from this general practice seems to have been in the direction of a lesser, rather than higher, charge[8] and

[1] Curtis P. Nettels, *The Roots of American Civilization* (New York, 1938), 254; Lewis Cecil Gray, *History of Agriculture in the Southern United States to 1860* (Washington, D. C., 1933), I, 424.

[2] See accounts of sales of cotton sold by Joseph Winthrop in Charleston for Frederick Fraser for various dates beginning in 1800, Fraser Papers, South Carolina Historical Society, Charleston, S.C. In the second decade of the nineteenth century Daniel Huger sold rice and cotton in Charleston and paid a 2.5 percent commission to both his cotton factor and his rice factor. Daniel Huger in a/c with Dart & Spears, Charleston, Nov. 24, 1817, sales [of rice] by F. Mottle, Sept. 30, Dec. 10, 1811, June 10, 1812, May 7, 20, 1814, and a/c current with Mottle, Charleston, June, 1814, Bacot-Huger Collection, South Carolina Historical Society, Charleston, S. C.

[3] *Travels in America* (London, 1808), III, 259.

[4] Sales of cotton on a/c of John M. Pintard by Flower & Faulkner, New Orleans, May 25, 1809, John M. Pintard Papers, Department of Archives and Manuscripts, Louisiana State University, Baton Rouge, La.; sales of cotton on a/c of Mr. Jno Bisland by Mitchell & McCullagh, New Orleans, Dec. 9, 1809, document reproduced in Beatrice Marion Stokes, "John Bisland, Mississippi Planter, 1776-1821" (unpublished M.A. thesis, Louisiana State University, 1941), ff. 86.

[5] The New Orleans, Charleston, Memphis, and Baltimore chambers of commerce published schedules of charges which would be made for various services rendered in their markets. All listed as the commission for selling cotton (as well as other produce) 2.5 percent. For copies of these schedules see *DeBow's Review*, I (1846), 172-73, III (1847), 84-85; *Hunt's Merchants' Magazine*, III (1840); 541-42, V (1841), 81, XI (1844), 185, XV (1846), 613, XVII (1847), 96.

[6] A circular announcing the opening of the New York firm of Brown Bros., Oct. 31, 1825, informed planters (and merchants) that cotton consigned for sale to the New York house would be sold for a commission of 2.5 percent. If customers preferred to sell in Liverpool, they could direct the New York house to ship the cotton to the Liverpool house of the firm where it would be sold at the same rate. In the case of cotton ordered reshipped to Liverpool from New York, the New York house would make no charge for its services. Circular reproduced in John Crosby Brown, *A Hundred Years of Merchant Banking* (New York, 1909), 190-91.

Washington Jackson & Co., in a letter soliciting business from a Mississippi planter, informed him that they would sell in New Orleans or through a branch house in Liverpool as the planter desired. If the New Orleans house were ordered to ship to Liverpool, it would make no charge for its service. Washington Jackson & Co. to Johnson, New Orleans, Jan. 23, 1844, William Johnson Papers, Mississippi Department of Archives and History, Jackson, Miss.

[7] *Byrne, Vance & Co.* v. *D. Y. Grayson*, 15 Ogden (La.), 457 (1860). The leading historian of pre-Civil War Southern agriculture wrote that 2.5 percent was the "customary commission" for selling cotton. Gray, *History of Agriculture*, II, 711. A student of the cotton kingdom in Alabama concluded that the 2.5 percent commission was standard in that state from the time of early statehood until the turn of the twentieth century. Charles S. Davis, *The Cotton Kingdom in Alabama* (Montgomery, 1939), 146, n. 22.

[8] Alfred Holt Stone wrote that a 2.5 percent commission was the "customary charge for selling the crop" but, he added, "sometimes this was as high as four." "The Cotton Factorage System of the Southern States," *American Historical Review*,

appears, moreover, to have been both rare and temporary. In June 1857, a Milledgeville, Georgia, newspaper announced that beginning on the first day of August, factors in that market would begin to charge 2.5 percent commission instead of the town's prevailing rate of 50 cents a bale.[9] An identical increase took place in two Virginia markets, Norfolk and Petersburg, in the late 1850's. An Enfield, North Carolina, cotton planter sold his cotton through factors in Norfolk in 1852 and in Petersburg during the years 1856 to 1859 and paid only 50 cents a bale commission. In the 1859-1860 season, however, his merchants in both these markets raised the commission to 2.5 percent of sales.[10]

An effort was made in 1858 to force a decrease in commission charges. A Cotton Planters' Convention in Macon that year appointed one Isaac C. West as an "agent for receiving, selling, and shipping cotton for planters." Planters using either the Savannah or Charleston markets were urged to patronize West, who was forbidden "in any case" to charge more than 50 cents a bale for cotton consigned to him.[11] Later the same year, a committee of the convention reported that the action had been highly successful. Because of the competition offered by West, factors in Savannah were said to be selling cotton for a commission of 50 cents a bale.[12] The committee report undoubtedly contained more wishful thinking than fact. It was presented on September 14, long before the bulk of the cotton had come to market and

XX (April 1915), 561. This writer finds no evidence to support Stone's higher figure except the statement by Thomas Ashe concerning New Orleans in 1806.

[9] *Federal Union*, June 16, 1857, as quoted in Norman Sydney Buck, *The Development of the Organization of Anglo-American Trade, 1800-1850* (New Haven, 1925), 78. The paper added that some of the factors had not agreed to the change and would continue to charge the old rate.

[10] A/c sales of cotton sold for F. H. Whitaker by A. & H. Harris, Norfolk, various dates, 1852, a/c sales of cotton sold for Whitaker by McIlwains Son & Co., Petersburg, various dates in 1856-1857, 1857-1858, and 1858-1859 seasons, a/c sales of cotton sold for Whitaker by McIlwains Son & Co., Petersburg, various dates in 1859-1860 seasons, a/c sales of cotton sold for Whitaker by Kader Biggs & Co., Norfolk, various dates in 1860, Ferdinand Hannon Whitaker Papers, Southern Historical Collection, University of North Carolina Library, Chapel Hill, N. C.

The higher commission probably reflected increased specialization in a growing market. A storekeeper who sold cotton as part of a general merchandising business could afford to provide his services at lower prices and make up the difference in profits from sales in his store. Once he began to specialize in selling cotton on commission, however, he would have to charge the higher rate. As will be shown, this specialization was a recurring feature of the ante bellum economy.

[11] *DeBow's Review*, XXV (1858), 217.

[12] *Ibid.*, 713.

before the committee could be sure of the rates charged. Furthermore, accounts of sales in Savannah, Augusta, and Charleston for the last years of the 1850's do not show the decrease.

When factors purchased goods for their planter customers, the standard commission was also 2.5 percent. The same charge was made both in cases where the factor used the planter's funds and where money was advanced to make the purchase.[13]

Interest was charged on money loaned or advanced, either as cash or supplies. Rates varied, but in general they were high by modern standards; 8 percent and more was frequently assessed. Thus, although Stephen Duncan in 1859 was charged only 5 percent interest by his New York factor on an order for more than $2,000 worth of supplies,[14] most planters paid considerably more than that. In 1839 a Louisiana planter recorded in his diary that he had "changed Merchants" in New Orleans. Obviously satisfied, he wrote he could "obtain money from them at 10 pr ct & they are considered the best salesman [sic] in the city."[15]

In Louisiana the maximum rate of "conventional" interest[16] was 10 percent until 1844, when it was lowered to 8 percent.[17] Planters probably expected to pay at least the maximum allowed, and usually even more. William Hamilton, in need of funds in early 1824, was informed by his factors that money was available in New Orleans only "at Shaving interest, say, one and a half pr cent a month."[18] In November 1860 a New Orleans factor wrote that "money is worth 5 % pr month here."[19]

[13] Published schedules give 2.5 percent for buying as the standard commission; see n. 5, above. Invoices of purchases and accounts current in planters' and factors' papers invariably show this same charge.

[14] Invoice for supplies purchased by Chas. P. Leverich for Duncan, New York, Nov. 15, 1859, Stephen and Stephen, Jr., Duncan Papers, Louisiana Department of Archives, Louisiana State University, Baton Rouge, La.

[15] Entry of Oct. 5, 1839, "Plantation Diary of Bennet H. Barrow," printed in Edwin Adams Davis (ed.), *Plantation Life in the Florida Parishes of Louisiana 1836-1846 as Reflected in the Diary of Bennet H. Barrow* (New York, 1943), 165.

[16] For conventional interest to be charged there had to be written evidence of an agreement between both parties that that rate would be paid. In the absence of such an agreement a lower rate prevailed. *Maunsel White v. Charles Jones,* 14 Ogden (La.), 693 (1859).

[17] *Civil Code of the State of Louisiana: With the Statutory Amendments, From 1825 to 1853 inclusive,* ed. Thomas Gibbs Morgan (New Orleans, 1861), 377.

[18] Dicks, Booker & Co. to Hamilton, New Orleans, Feb. 10, 1824, W. S. Hamilton Papers, Southern Historical Collection, University of North Carolina Library, Chapel Hill, N. C.

[19] Watt & Noble to J. R. Simpson, New Orleans, Nov. 26, 1860, Stephen D. Heard Papers, Southern Historical Collection, University of North Carolina Library, Chapel Hill, N. C.

Similarly, in Mobile, Harriet Martineau noted the legal interest was 8 percent "but double is easily to be had."[20] Nor were New York rates necessarily lower than those in the South. George Noble Jones had to pay at the rate of between 11 and 12 percent for a loan in that city in 1856.[21]

Interest was frequently only part of the cost of loans and advances. Factors often charged commissions for making advances or for endorsing the notes of planters. The New Orleans Chamber of Commerce, for example, decided that merchants would charge 2.5 percent commission "for drawing, accepting, negotiating or endorsing notes or drafts without funds, produce, or bills of lading in hand." If cash were advanced, the same commission would be charged "in all cases."[22] These commissions—really service charges —were often the subject of litigation, as many claimed they served merely as a means to evade usury laws.

In 1832 the Louisiana Supreme Court declared that a charge of 2.5 percent commission for accepting a draft was illegal. Neither law, custom, nor the "value of the service" rendered warranted such a charge, the court ruled.[23] The court's interpretation of the law may have been correct, but its understanding of commercial usage was limited. Such commissions were customary and they continued to be charged. Less than a decade later the Louisiana court recognized this and modified its position. The case involved a factor who had charged a planter, in addition to interest, 2.5 percent commission for accepting his draft and the same for advancing funds to pay the draft when it came due. In its decision, establishing a precedent followed until the Civil War, the court allowed the commission for accepting the planter's note but declared illegal the charge for advancing funds to pay the note.[24]

Despite this ruling, some factors continued to charge the commission for advancing. In 1842 the Louisiana court reviewed a case involving a planter who had paid his factor 2.5 percent

20 *Society in America* (London, 1837), II, 258.

21 I. Rae Habersham to Jones, New York, Feb. 16, 1856, George Noble Jones Papers, Georgia Historical Society, Savannah, Ga.

22 "Tariff of Charges, etc. Agreed Upon and Adopted by the New Orleans Chamber of Commerce, at a Special Meeting Held on the 2d of November, 1846," *Hunt's Merchants' Magazine*, XV (1846), 613. Similar charges were agreed upon by members of the Charleston and Memphis chambers of commerce. See *ibid.*, XI (1844), 185, XVII (1847), 96.

23 *Millaudon v. Arnaud*, 4 Miller (La.), 542 (1832).

24 *Taylor, Gardiner & Co. v. Wooten*, 19 Curry (La.), 518 (1841).

commission for accepting his notes, the same commission for paying the notes, and 10 percent interest on both the funds advanced and the commissions. When cotton sales proceeds did not cover the advances and commissions, the factor carried the balance but charged (in addition to interest) a 2.5 percent commission on the balance. The court was outraged. The records, it declared, showed "a series of charges and extortions, which we hope, for the mercantile character of New Orleans, is without a parallel, although one witness testifies that such charges are customary among commission merchants." Reiterating its decision of the year before, the court allowed the commission for accepting the drafts but denied the other commissions.[25]

The Louisiana court insisted on the distinction between charges for accepting and endorsing notes and charges for advancing cash. In the former case the factor was paid for "loaning his credit and incurring the risk of inconvenience at the maturity of the bill," and the charge was considered both reasonable and "consonant to usage."[26] A commission charge on cash advances, however, "must be regarded as interest." Therefore, if the maximum interest rate were charged, an additional commission would bring the interest rate over the maximum and the resulting contract would be illegal.[27] In short, if the factor merely loaned his name (by accepting or endorsing a draft) but did not actually lend money (and hence charged no interest) he could legally charge a commission for this service. If, on the other hand, he loaned money or paid a bill with cash (and then charged the maximum legal interest on the money advanced) he was legally barred from levying a commission.

Subsequent litigation made it amply clear that both charges continued to be assessed in Louisiana. In 1856 the court admitted that commissions added to maximum interest on cash advances were "in accordance with a commercial usage very prevalent in the State" but insisted, and continued to insist, that the practice "is contrary to law."[28]

[25] *Henry S. Buckner et al.* v. *John L. Chapman,* 2 Robinson (La.), 360 (1842).
[26] *Joseph Lalande* v. *Breaux & Matherne,* 5 King (La.), 505 (1850).
[27] *Barrett* v. *Chaler, Syndic.,* 2 Robinson (La.) 874 (1847).
[28] *Haven & Co.* v. *B. Hudson,* 12 Ogden (La.), 660 (1856). That the same matter repeatedly came to court is in itself evidence of its persistence. See *Robert Patterson & Co.* v. *Leake & Tucker,* 5 King (La.), 547 (1850); *H. Gilly* v. *George Berlin,* 12 Ogden (La.), 723 (1857); *Byrne, Vance & Co.* v. *D. Y. Grayson,* 15 Ogden (La.), 457 (1860).

The Louisiana story was repeated in South Carolina. An 1833 court decision ruled that a commission added to interest was illegal. Such commissions were commonly charged, the court admitted, but if allowed would be merely an additional interest levy making possible the evasion of the usury statute.[29] As in Louisiana, the practice continued. In 1855 the South Carolina Court of Appeals again heard testimony that commissions in addition to interest for cash advances were generally paid in Charleston, but the court persisted in declaring such commissions illegal.[30]

A somewhat different conclusion was reached by the Alabama Supreme Court. It was the custom, declared the court in 1850, for Mobile factors to charge commissions both for accepting the planters' notes and for advancing cash, with these charges being added to interest. The legality of the charges would depend upon their purpose. If commissions were merely a "device to avoid the statute of usury," they would be illegal; if, on the other hand, they served as payment for the merchants' "trouble, risk, inconvenience, &c. incurred in accepting and paying the bill," such commissions would be legal. The determination was for a jury, not the court, to make.[31]

In Texas, commissions for cash advances and for acceptances of time drafts were declared legal by the Supreme Court in 1859. The former charge served as payment to the factor for his trouble in keeping the books, securing the money, and making it available to the planter; the latter charge served as payment for the factor's loan of credit and the risk he took for possible nonpayment when the note fell due.[32]

A commission charge for the acceptance and endorsement of the planter's drafts therefore seems to have been generally authorized by law in the ante bellum period.[33] A commission for cash

---

[29] *Cheesborough and Campbell v. James Hunter, Survivors*, 1 Hill (S. C. Ct. App.), 400 (1833).

[30] *Walters & Walker v. McGirt, Meekins & Son*, 8 Richardson (S. C. Ct. App.), 287 (1855).

[31] *Brown v. Harrison & Robinson*, 17 Alabama 744 (1850).

[32] *Robert Mills v. Alexander S. Johnston and Another*, 23 Texas 309 (1859).

[33] Planters' and factors' records usually (but not always) show this charge being assessed. William Johnson, for example, paid a bill to Cline & Williams, local merchants, with a draft on his New Orleans factor, James Armour. Armour charged 2.5 percent of the bill for "accepting." Johnson in a/c current with Armour, New Orleans, Jan. 14, 1842, William Johnson Papers. The Savannah factorage firm Young, Wyatt & Co. recorded in their books that they charged 2.5 percent "for

advances was legal in Texas and could be allowed by a jury in Alabama; although declared illegal in both South Carolina and Louisiana, continual litigation on this matter evidenced the persistence of the practice.

It should be noted that even if the letter of the law were followed, the planter in Louisiana might legally be charged two commissions. If the planter gave a note for a debt and the creditor required a factor's endorsement (as he usually did), the factor could then charge a commission (for endorsing) and the lender would be allowed to charge maximum interest.[34] Thus, maximum interest rates—high as they were—often reflected only a part of the cost the planter was forced to pay to obtain funds.[35]

The length of the loan or advance varied according to the needs of the planter. An advance on a consigned crop might run for as little as a week or two; if the cotton was held for a rise, it could run to several months. An advance given during the growing season could mean a loan for six months or more. Finally, if the proceeds of the crop did not cover the credit advanced, the factor might carry the balance as an advance on the next crop and the resultant loan would be for a duration of a year or more. Although computed on an annual basis, interest was charged only for the time the loan was actually outstanding.[36] Ordinarily, interest

---

accepting . . . Dft. when not covered by Produce." Daybook (Oct. 29, 1855-Dec. 17, 1856), Young, Wyatt & Co. Papers, Georgia Historical Society, Savannah, Ga.

[34] S. S. Hall, *Laws of Louisiana, Relative to Cotton Factors and Commission Merchants* (New Orleans, 1861), 72. This work offers a convenient summary of the statute law and the court decisions of Louisiana on the subject.

[35] Young, Wyatt & Co., for example, in addition to the commission for advancing, charged 2.5 percent more when the bill was paid. One typical entry in their "Daybook" shows a commission charge for accepting a draft on Feb. 27, 1856 and another commission charged for paying the same draft on April 22. Thus the planter paid 5 percent over and above any interest he was charged for this loan, which was in force for a period of less than two months.

[36] Stone ("Cotton Factorage System," 561) wrote that often interest was charged for an entire year regardless of the time used. This writer has found no evidence of this practice. Any commission charges, however, were not dependent upon the length of time a loan was outstanding, and, if the money was borrowed for a short time, the resulting rate would be very high indeed, if figured on an annual basis; see n. 35. Sometimes an advance would be given for a set time and a renewal of the advance would mean new commission charges even though interest would be assessed only on the time the loan was outstanding. Thus, for example, the Charleston factor, A. Gardelle, advanced for 30 days, charging 2.5 percent commission. When a customer wanted to renew the advance the factor requested an additional commission. Gardelle to Heard & Simpson, Charleston, Jan. 21, 1859, and other letters throughout the year, Stephen D. Heard Papers.

charges were calculated to the day, running from the time the advance was given to the day on which cotton was sold, proceeds realized, and an account current rendered. The debit side of the account current listed the advance given, the date on which it was made, the number of days the debt was outstanding, and the resultant interest charge.[37]

In some instances, the credit side of the account current showed interest paid to the planter. Usually, the factor allowed the planter interest credit from the time of the sale to the date the account current was rendered. Seldom, however, was the amount significant because the account current was customarily rendered within a few days after the cotton was sold. If, however, a planter's entire crop were not sold together, interest credit might amount to a considerable sum. Thus, for example, Mrs. M. A. Hickman's account current for 1857-1858 showed sales of cotton over the period from March 12, 1857, to May 25, 1858. The account, rendered on July 15, 1858, credited Mrs. Hickman with $148.76 in interest.[38]

Such payments were merely credits which simplified bookkeeping. Instead of applying proceeds as they came in to debts already incurred (and thereby stopping interest on these debts), the factor simply continued charging interest on debts but credited interest at the same rate on the proceeds of the cotton as it was sold. This obviated the need to render separate accounts each time a parcel of cotton was sold.

On rare occasions the planter was a lender rather than a borrower and received interest on money held by his factor. After final settlement, the planter might draw interest on the balance due him, provided he left the funds with his factor and provided also that he requested such interest.[39] Eli Capell, for example, on

---

On occasion, interest would be charged for less than the time funds were advanced. In May 1828, for example, Maunsel White purchased and shipped supplies to one of his customers. He indicated that interest would not be charged on the bill until the following September. White to Walker, New Orleans, May 24, 1828, Zachariah Walker Papers, Mississippi Department of Archives and History, Jackson, Miss.

[37] For a typical example, see a/c current, Fripp with Coffin & Pringle, Charleston, March 23, 1859, John Edwin Fripp Papers, Southern Historical Collection, University of North Carolina Library, Chapel Hill, N. C.

[38] Mrs. Hickman in a/c current with Rhorer Higginbothom & Co., New Orleans, July 15, 1858, Hickman-Bryan Papers, Joint Collection, Western Historical Manuscripts Collection, State Historical Society of Missouri Manuscripts, Columbia, Mo.

[39] A South Carolina court ruled that until the planter requested the balance due

at least two occasions was credited with 8 percent interest on funds left with his factor.[40] Such interest payments to planters were rare, however. Some factors actually discouraged the practice. Robinson and Caldwell of Charleston informed a customer that they allowed no interest on money left with them "inasmuch as the money is of no use to us, as it is subject to *call* at any moment." For them to allow interest on such funds, they concluded, "would be doing business on a false capital."[41] By and large, the planters were borrowers, not lenders. Records usually show any balance after final sales to have been remitted to the planter. Moreover, when funds were left with the factor, they were ordinarily used up during the year. Wealthier planters with excess funds readily found investment opportunities in stocks and bonds.

Chambers of Commerce in their published schedules listed numerous other charges levied by merchants for services rendered.[42] Goods received from other markets and forwarded were subject to a commission charge for the service. Thus, when William Hamilton ordered tombstones in New York, his New Orleans factor charged him a commission of 75 cents for receiving the shipment in New Orleans and for forwarding it to Hamilton's home.[43] Most planters, however, seldom paid such commissions because they purchased most goods in their factor's markets.

Price schedules also indicated that if a planter consigned cotton to a factor and subsequently ordered it reshipped, the planter could be charged a full commission of 2.5 percent just as if the original factor had made the sale. This charge was probably seldom assessed. When Simpson and Heard ordered their Charleston factor to reship cotton consigned to him to New York, the

---

him, the factor was merely holding the planter's money in safekeeping and could not be considered to have borrowed it. *Cheesborough & Campbell* v. *James Hunter, Survivor*, 1 Hill (S. C. Ct. App.), 400 (1833).

[40] In general a/c with Gribble & Montgomery, New Orleans, Oct. 17, 1848, in general a/c with Gribble & Montgomery, New Orleans, Aug. 30, 1850, Eli J. Capell and Family Papers, Meritt M. Shilg Memorial Collection, Department of Archives and Manuscripts, Louisiana State University, Baton Rouge, La.

[41] Robinson & Caldwell to James M. Nelson, Charleston, Jan. 15, 1851, James M. Nelson Papers, Southern Historical Collection, University of North Carolina Library, Chapel Hill, N. C.

[42] *Hunt's Merchants' Magazine*, III (1840), 541-42, XI (1844), 185, XV (1846), 613, XVII (1847), 96, XXVIII (1853), 370-71; *DeBow's Review*, I (1846), 172-73, III (1847), 84-85.

[43] John Hagan & Co. to Hamilton and a/c—Hamilton with John Hagan & Co., both dated New Orleans, Oct. 25, 1828, W. S. Hamilton Papers.

Charleston firm merely asked that the advance it had given be returned.[44] Inasmuch as so many firms volunteered to sell in any market the planter chose without additional commissions, it is unlikely that any one firm could regularly make the extra charge and keep its business.

[44] A. Gardelle to Heard & Simpson, Charleston, June 6, 7, July 6, 1859, Stephen D. Heard Papers.

CHAPTER SIX

Planter-Factor Relations: The Law, Tradition, and Expediency

Once his cotton had been grown, harvested, and ginned, the planter's livelihood was entrusted to his factor. With so much at stake, it is not surprising that disagreements arose which led to bickering and litigation.[1] The federal and state courts were thereby given the opportunity to scrutinize custom and to define and describe the rights and duties of planter and factor. Given, however, the importance of the factor-planter relationship, it is surprising how little litigation did take place, how general were the laws and court decisions, and how much of the relationship was governed by custom and tradition rather than by formal law.

The basic law was clear, wrote Justice Joseph Story for the majority of the United States Supreme Court in 1840; it arose from the "ordinary relation of principal and agent." The consignor had the privilege of setting conditions controlling the sale of his goods "according to his own pleasure," and the factor was bound to obey any instructions given him. When specific instructions were not given, however, the factor was to sell the goods "according to his own judgment," using "sound discretion" and taking into consideration "the usages of trade at the place of sale."[2]

Southern courts agreed. Barring specific instructions, the factor was merely obligated "to do the best he can" to protect the interests of the planter, explained a Louisiana court. He would be responsible for any damages which might arise from his "fault or neglect," but, so long as he "acts in good faith," he could not be held responsible for "errors of judgment."[3]

Definite orders, however, had to be followed and any losses

which occurred because instructions were deliberately disobeyed had to be sustained by the factor.[4] Testimony in a case before the Georgia Supreme Court in 1852 showed that a factor had ignored a planter's order to sell his cotton in Savannah and instead had shipped it to New York. The factor, obviously banking on a higher price in New York, had advanced the planter the current Savannah price. Expectations were not realized; prices in New York were so low that the sale there did not net enough even to cover the advances given the planter. When the factor demanded that the planter reimburse him for the difference between the advance and the actual sale proceeds, the planter refused, declaring that the factor would not have suffered a loss had he followed instructions. The court upheld the planter.[5]

Under certain circumstances planters' instructions could be disregarded with impunity. A factor might ignore an order setting a minimum sale price and sell at a lower figure if he felt the higher price would not be attained. If his judgment proved correct and prices did not go up, the planter had no redress. If, on the other hand, the factor's judgment proved erroneous, he would have to sustain any losses because he had deliberately ignored instructions.[6]

[1] A brief summary of some of these disagreements may be found in Ralph W. Haskins, "Planter and Cotton Factor in the Old South: Some Areas of Friction," *Agricultural History*, XXIX (Jan. 1955), 1-14.

[2] *William & James Brown & Co. v. Thomas McGran*, 14 Peters (U.S.), 479 (1840). This important decision was given in full summary in *Hunt's Merchants' Magazine*, II (1840), 328-34.

[3] S. S. Hall, *Laws of Louisiana, Relative to Cotton Factors and Commission Merchants* (New Orleans, 1861), 77.

[4] When specific instructions were given, the factor had to do all in his power to obey them. He could only be held responsible for losses sustained from his deliberate disobedience, not from his lack of skill or poor judgment. Thus in Louisiana a factor was instructed to sell at a certain price. When the cotton arrived, cotton was freely selling at prices over the planter's minimum but the factor was unable to find a buyer on the levee and he put the cotton in storage where it later burned. In the suit which followed, the Louisiana court held the factor blameless. He "had not been guilty of any fault or neglect" but had done the best he could and was therefore not responsible. *Ibid.*, 76.

[5] *Hardeman & Hamilton v. Gary G. Ford*, 12 Cobb (Ga.), 205 (1852). A similar ruling was made by the Supreme Court of Louisiana four years later. With cotton selling at 12½ cents a pound, the planter ordered his factor to sell. The factor, hoping for further increases, delayed. Instead of rising, cotton prices dropped sharply and the factor was forced to sell at 7 cents. The court ruled that the factor's actions would have been justified had no instructions been given. However, since a specific order to sell had been disregarded by the factor, he was responsible for the loss and consequently had to pay the planter the additional 5½ cents a pound. *B. Maggoffin v. Cowan, Dykers & Spalding*, 11 Randolph (La.), 554 (1856).

[6] Hall, *Laws of Louisiana*, 80. Time limit was from time of sale to start of suit.

The factor was also able to depart from orders if he gave the planter notice of his intentions and received no objections from him. In 1844, a New Orleans factor, instead of selling a consignment in New Orleans, shipped it to Liverpool for sale. The factor informed the planters by mail of what he had done, indicating that he believed the best interests of the planters had been served but offering them the current New Orleans price for their cotton if they refused to take the risk of a Liverpool shipment. The planters delayed answering, but later, after news of a decline in Liverpool reached the United States, they wrote that they would take the New Orleans price as offered. The factor now refused to pay, contending that the planters had forfeited their right to the option by raising no immediate objection to the Liverpool shipment. The Louisiana Supreme Court agreed. When a factor, "acting in good faith," informed the planter that he had disobeyed instructions, the planter had to voice his objections "within a reasonable time"; failure to do so meant that the planter accepted the decision and assumed the risk.[7]

When factors made advances on consignments, they could, the courts decided, under certain circumstances, dispose of the goods in order to protect their investments even if this meant disregarding specific instructions. This matter was dealt with by Justice Story in his 1840 decision. The consignor's right to control the sale was unlimited only when "no advances have been made or liabilities incurred" on the consignment. Where such liabilities had been incurred the factor "has a right to sell so much of the consignment as may be necessary to reimburse such advances or meet such liabilities." The factor had this right despite any instructions given him, unless a specific agreement to the contrary had been made or unless the consignor indicated his willingness "to reimburse and discharge such advances and liabilities." In short, by virtue of his advances, the factor acquired special rights—or a lien— on the property consigned to him and was free to act in any manner he deemed necessary to protect these rights, even if it meant going counter to the explicit instructions of the planter.[8] Two years later, a case from the Alabama courts provided the

---

[7] Ward, et. al. v. Warfield, et. al., 3 Robinson (La.), 468 (1848). The court reaffirmed this principle in another case three years later. William Flower v. S. W. Downs, 6 King (La.), 538 (1851).

[8] William & James Brown & Co. v. Thomas McGran, 14 Peters (U.S.), 479 (1840).

Supreme Court with the opportunity to reconsider this decision, and Justice John McLean reaffirmed the earlier ruling.[9]

Decisions in the state courts narrowly defined the nature of the lien, thereby severely circumscribing the factor's powers. For a factor to have a lien on the crop he must not only have made advances on it but the crop must also have been consigned to him. He had no lien on goods not yet consigned to him or on goods consigned to another factor, even if he had made a loan on these goods.[10]

Another limitation on the factor's rights was based on the nature of his advances. The Louisiana civil code declared that when one furnished "necessary supplies" to any farm or plantation, one established a prior lien on the products of that farm. But the courts interpreted this very narrowly, insisting that the lien was established only when the factor furnished the supplies directly. If a planter purchased his supplies from another merchant and his factor paid the bill no lien existed under the law. Nor did advances of money or credit establish a lien, according to Louisiana court decisions.[11] South Carolina courts came to a similar decision. The Court of Appeals in 1847 ruled that the factor had a lien on cotton consigned to him to the extent of that portion of his advances which were earmarked for plantation supplies, but he had no special rights because of advances used for family supplies and personal expenses.[12]

Since advances and loans were often given to planters long before the cotton was picked, and since the courts had ruled that factors had special privileges over the crop only after it had been consigned to them, the factor was faced with the problem of securing guarantees that a crop upon which he had advanced money would finally be given him to sell. Either he had to trust

9 *Brander & McKenna v. Phillips & Co.*, 16 Peters (U.S.), 121 (1842).

10 *Shaw & Zuntz v. Andrew Knox*, 12 Ogden (La.), 41 (1857); *George J. Kallock, et al. v. John Jackson*, 5 Kelly (Ga.), 153 (1848); *Brown, Shipley & Co. v. P. A. Clayton*, 12 Cobb (Ga.), 564 (1853). See Arts. 3184 and 3214, *Civil Code of the State of Louisiana: With the Statutory Amendments, from 1825 to 1853 inclusive*, ed. Thomas Gibbs Morgan (New Orleans, 1861), 411, 416, for the law upon which the Louisiana decision was based. The Louisiana case concerned a sugar planter but the language of the decision makes it clear that the ruling refers to all factors.

11 Art. 3184, *Civil Code of Louisiana*, 411; *Shaw & Zuntz v. Andrew Knox*, 12 Ogden (La.), 41 (1857); *Shaw & Co. v. A. Grant, Sr., & A. Grant, Jr.*, 13 Ogden (La.), 52 (1858); Hall, *Laws of Louisiana*, 87.

12 *Sylvanus Hunton v. Ingraham & Webb*, 1 Strobhart (S. C. Ct. App.), 271 (1847).

the planter to send his cotton or else he had to get a written guarantee from the planter. In the absence of a written agreement, the court ruled, the planter was not legally bound to send cotton to a particular factor for sale despite any advances that may have been made and despite any custom which may have prevailed to the contrary.[13] Where an agreement was made, however, it stood as a contract and the planter was obligated to fulfill the terms of the agreement. If the planter failed to do so, the factor could legally charge him the commission on the crop which he would have received had the agreement been honored.[14]

It might be expected that factors would uniformly have required their planter customers to sign such agreements. Some undoubtedly did,[15] but available evidence indicates that most probably did not.[16] Custom, tradition, and perhaps the word (spoken or implied) of a gentleman provided adequate security.

Planters often dealt with two or more factors simultaneously. This practice was more prevalent among the larger planters, but it was also found among those operating on a smaller scale. Some sold part of their crop through a local merchant and sent part to a factor in the larger markets. William Johnson, for example, sent most of his cotton to James Armour in New Orleans, but in 1842 he also had Cline and Williams, merchants of Fort Adams, Mississippi, sell for him.[17] Planters sometimes had more than one factor in the same market, as did William Hamilton who in 1823

[13] *Harrod v. Constant*, 5 Martin (La.), 575 (1818); *Taylor, Gardiner & Co. v. Wooten*, 19 Curry (La.), 518 (1841); *Henry A. Lyons v. J. Lallande*, 9 Randolph (La.), 601 (1854).

[14] *Thompson v. Packwood*, 2 Robinson (La.), 624 (1847).

[15] For a copy of such an agreement see "Mortgage on the Cotton Crop of 1836 to James Hamilton & Son," printed in Kathryn Abbey (ed.), "Documents Relating to El Destino and Chemonie Plantations, Middle Florida, 1826-1868," *Florida Historical Society Quarterly*, VII (April 1929), 210. The planter William B. Nuttal pledged to send his entire crop for the year to Hamilton & Son, New York factors.

[16] But see Alfred Holt Stone, "The Cotton Factorage System of the Southern States," *American Historical Review*, XX (April 1915), 562-63. Stone wrote that most factors required formal agreements. These contracts, he maintained, stipulated that the planter ship a certain amount of cotton to the factor; if the planter fell short of the agreed-upon number of bales, he was required to pay a penalty commission based on the shortage. In addition, most agreements stipulated that all of a planter's crop, including any part that exceeded the minimum pledge, be sent to the same factor for sale. Available evidence indicates that planters were not as completely obligated as Stone argues. His article, unfortunately, is undocumented.

[17] Cline & Williams to Johnson, Fort Adams, Jan. 6, 1842, Johnson in a/c current with Armour, New Orleans, Jan. 14, 1842, William Johnson Papers, Mississippi Department of Archives and History, Jackson, Miss.

dealt with two New Orleans factors, Dicks, Booker and Company and Samuel Elkins.[18]

Usually no effort was made to hide these dealings. A Georgia planter, placing an order for supplies with an Augusta factor, informed the factor that he was planning to send half his crop to Augusta and half to Savannah.[19] Hugh Davis, the Alabama planter, began dealing with the Mobile factorage firm, W. M. Pleasant, in 1851. The following year, while still sending cotton to Pleasant and receiving advances from him, Davis sold a part of his crop in the local market near his plantation. He continued dealing in two markets despite his factor's entreaties to send all his cotton to Mobile. Apparently the factor employed no pressure other than requests and made no effort to enforce an agreement—there in all probability was none—for he continued to advance Davis money and Davis continued to sell a portion of his crop in the local market.[20]

Planters encountered few problems in changing factors. The freedom with which planters could deal with more than one factor at once as well as shed them at will can be well illustrated from the records kept by the Mississippi planter, Eli Capell. In the two decades prior to the Civil War, Capell dealt with no fewer than ten different factors in New Orleans. Only in a few of the years did he employ a single merchant; usually he had at least two factors in the Crescent City. In the 1852-1853 season, he sold cotton through four New Orleans firms and in addition made several sales through local merchants at Clinton, Mississippi.[21]

Differences between a planter and his factor might induce the planter to change merchants in midseason. In 1854 John Brown's regular New Orleans factor refused to accept some of his drafts and the Arkansas planter turned to another firm which accepted the drafts and later received 20 bales of Brown's cotton. Brown did not

[18] See accounts of sales from these firms in Feb. and May, 1823, W. S. Hamilton Papers, Southern Historical Collection, University of North Carolina Library, Chapel Hill, N. C.

[19] James Thomas to Heard & Simpson, Elberton [?], Sept. 19, 1858, Stephen D. Heard Papers, Southern Historical Collection, University of North Carolina Library, Chapel Hill, N.C.

[20] Weymouth T. Jordan, *Hugh Davis and His Alabama Plantation* (University, Ala., 1948), 141-47.

[21] This paragraph is based on an examination of accounts of sales and accounts current, 1841-1861, in the Eli J. Capell Papers and Eli J. Capell Plantation Diaries and Record Books, Louisiana Department of Archives and Manuscripts, Louisiana State University, Baton Rouge, La.

terminate his business relations with the first firm; a month after sending the 20 bales to a competitor, Brown was in New Orleans buying supplies through his original firm.[22]

Switching factors in the middle of the season was a relatively simple matter, but sometimes rancor and bitterness accompanied the move, as the experience of James W. Monette, a Louisiana cotton planter, demonstrates. Monette had apparently paid a debt with a time draft on his New Orleans factors, Buckner and Stanton. The person to whom he had given the note transferred it, in turn, to Fellowes, Johnson, also New Orleans factors. When Fellowes, Johnson presented the note to Buckner and Stanton for collection, the latter replied that they could not pay until they had sold Monette's cotton. This angered the planter who wrote to Fellowes, Johnson informing them of his dissatisfaction with his factors and offering to give them his future business if Fellowes, Johnson would pay the note it now held. Fellowes, Johnson accepted the offer, paid the note, and received the remainder of Monette's crop. Buckner and Stanton wrote to Monette protesting the loss of business and complaining that the planter was obligated to send them his cotton. They made no mention, however, of any written agreement to that effect. Monette answered in language clearly indicating that he was bound by no formal agreement. "You have never lost a cent by me; in no advance or acceptance for me have you incurred more risk than I have in confiding my crop to your care. Hence I conceive that no obligation has been created on my part which is to control the future disposition of my crop." He went on to explain that he changed factors in the middle of the season because his new factor had helped him where his old firm had refused. Then, taking the offensive in the dispute, the planter argued that Buckner and Stanton had been consistently overcharging him. The debate continued, but Monette was not moved and in the following season sent all his cotton to the new firm.[23]

[22] Entries of March 13, April 20, 1854, John W. Brown Diary, Arkansas History Commission, Department of Archives and History, Little Rock, Ark. Later when his regular factor again refused to honor one of his drafts, Brown recorded his determination to change factors. Entry of July 5, 1854, *ibid.*

[23] Monette to Fellowes, Johnson & Co., Islington Plantation, Madison Parish, La., Oct. 10, 1849, Jan. 2, 23, 1850, March 25, 1850, Monette to Buckner & Stanton, April 2, 28, 1850, and numerous letters to Fellowes throughout the 1850-1851 season, James W. Monette Papers, Mississippi Department of Archives and History, Jackson, Miss.

Bitterness was avoided by John Hagan and Company of New Orleans, who made no effort to hold on to a customer who wanted to change. The firm even suggested that dissatisfied planters seek a new factor. When, in the spring of 1829, a dispute arose with William Hamilton, Hagan made his position clear in a polite but firm letter: "It is our way of thinking that those doing business with us find their interest in it, and when otherwise that some one else will be selected—We ask no more from any of our correspondents desirous to change than payment of their accounts, and so little blame do we attach to them for trying other houses, that we have frequently received them back, after an absence of a Season, with as much good will as if we had never parted."[24] It is noteworthy that there is no mention of any agreement nor is there a word about the law of the matter.

It was expected, of course, that when a factor gave an advance he would receive some cotton to sell. But, it seems, this was largely an unwritten agreement, one which would have no standing in the courts. Not until 1861 did the factors in the South's largest market, New Orleans, take steps to insure their receiving cotton from a planter to whom they had given advances. Even then, it was not the law to which they turned, but rather to cooperation among themselves. They agreed "to establish a black book" in which they would record the names of all planters who had received "advances, supplies, endorsements, or acceptances" and afterward "disregarded such obligations by sending their Cotton to other houses, or selling it at home."[25] Ironically, this decision by the Crescent City factors was being made at the same time that planters were being urged to hold their cotton on the plantation until the federal blockade was lifted.[26]

A legal agreement was probably not expedient. It would not be binding for more than one season; the planter would then be free to change factors. Even if he remained in debt to the old factor, his new merchant, eager for his business, would be willing to advance

[24] John Hagan & Co. to Hamilton, New Orleans, April 13, 1829, W. S. Hamilton Papers. Hamilton stayed on with Hagan who, true to his word, continued to advance the planter large sums in later years. He required no legal agreement. John Hagan & Co. to Hamilton, New Orleans, June 6, 29, Dec. 3, 12, 1829, May 28, 1832, *ibid.*
[25] *New Orleans Price Current*, July 27, 1861. The editors, in reporting the decision, called it "a good move" which "should have been done years ago."
[26] *Ibid.*

the necessary funds to pay the debt. The agreement in any case would be hard to enforce because it was difficult for a factor to determine whether a planter's entire crop had been sent to him. In 1858, for example, the *New Orleans Crescent* complained that "many small planters" were informing their factors (who had given them advances) that their crops were not as large as expected and were asking that their debt be continued for the following year. The planters, the paper charged, were sending only a part of the crop to their regular factors "and the balance takes another course."[27] Presumably, the balance of the crop went to a different merchant, who could then be asked for an additional advance. The factor who was, in effect, being cheated, even if he had an agreement, had to prove that he was not receiving the entire crop. This required a careful surveillance of numerous plantations in the interior, for the competing factor could not be expected to divulge the necessary information and thereby deprive himself of new sources of profit. The factor probably could do no more under the circumstances than to urge that the cotton be sent to him as did Reynolds, Byrne and Company in a letter to one of their customers: "We are aware that contracts for crops are now making freely in the country and as we consider this not only hazardous to the Planter but may prove to be a serious loss to him, we recommend our friends to decline all such operations, which it is not probable would be proposed to them, if they were not likely to result advantageously to the purchaser."[28]

The preponderance of evidence, therefore, points to the fact that the planters were not, for the most part, tightly bound to their factors by legal contracts. Expediency, hardened into tradition, dictated otherwise.

It was expected that there would be no conflict of interest between the planter and his factor. The higher the price the factor was able to get for a planter's cotton, the higher his commission and the greater his reputation as a good salesman. Still, opportunities arose for the factor to profit at the possible expense of his planter customer. Should he be hired to buy cotton or should he decide to speculate in the staple, the factor's interests might not coincide with those of the planter.

27 No date given, as reprinted in *The Daily Confederation* (Montgomery), Oct. 13, 1858.
28 To Johnson, New Orleans, Aug. 19, 1833, William Johnson Papers.

No law prohibited a factor from buying cotton for others or from buying it on his own account for speculation. The courts simply ruled that in a single transaction the factor could not serve as a commission merchant for both buyer and seller. As a merchant selling cotton consigned to him, he was obligated to seek the highest possible price; as a merchant buying on commission, he was expected to get the cotton at the lowest possible price. "It is impossible that a commission merchant who has bound himself under such incompatible obligations, can do justice to either of the persons by whom he is employed."[29] This, of course, did not mean that the factor was barred from both buying and selling or from buying on his own account; he was merely prohibited from buying cotton he was hired to sell.

This was a fine legal distinction which critics of the factors did not always make. For these critics, all buying and speculating on the part of the factor was suspect. When a cotton planters' convention appointed its own agent to undersell factors in Savannah and Charleston, it specifically forbade this agent to deal in cotton on his own or to act as an agent for a buyer. A factor representing both buyers and sellers, no matter how honest he might be, declared a convention report, would, "perhaps, unperceived by himself" tend to act in the interests of one or another of the parties.[30]

Planters were advised against placing complete reliance on their factors. When a Mississippi planter proposed that cotton prices could be kept up through an association of factors to counteract the organized brokers and manufacturers in Liverpool and Manchester,[31] he was told that factors could not be trusted with that power. Many commission merchants bought as well as sold, declared M. W. Phillips, and, as long as this was the case, their reports would be designed primarily to advance their own interests.[32] Similar advice, warning the planter to be wary of factor's reports, appeared in an agricultural journal in 1858: "As it is strongly suspected that many cotton Factors are also cotton Speculators, having interests directly opposed to the interests of the planters and interior shippers, it behooves the latter to scan with

[29] *Beal v. M'Kiernan*, 6 Curry (La.), 407 (1834). See also *Thomas Symington v. Thomas McLin*, 18 North Carolina 292 (1835) for a similar decision.
[30] *DeBow's Review*, XXV (1858), 713-14.
[31] *Ibid.*, VII (1849), 74-75.
[32] *Ibid.*, pp. 410-12.

a suspicious eye, the singular and improbable statements and estimates of the supply of cotton, put forth by the former."[33] Misleading a planter could be profitable. An Alabama paper in 1825 charged that factors, being in a good position to judge a prospective rise in price, often bought cotton consigned to them before the rise and sold it afterward, pocketing the difference.[34]

Planters could hardly be expected to approve of such speculation by their factors. Obviously responding to planter concern, some factors sought to reassure prospective consignors by advertising that they engaged in no such speculation.[35] Pope, Aikin and Company of Mobile, for example, pledged to "confine ourselves to a business of a strictly legitimate character."[36] Similarly, a Savannah firm announced: *We are mutually bound not to speculate in Cotton or any other article of Merchandize.*"[37]

While there is ample evidence that some ante bellum factors were buyers as well as sellers,[38] probably most were not—even though such actions might have been legally permissible. When Ward, Jones and Company of New Orleans shipped a crop to Liverpool without prior instructions, they wrote to the planter and offered to pay the New Orleans price if he did not want to risk the European shipment. But, the merchants added, "we do not wish . . . to do so, as we have bought no cotton and are averse to doing so."[39]

That more cases did not come to court, or that evidence of a more widespread and vehement attack against such practices is lacking, or that many factors advertised that they would not or wrote that they preferred not to buy cotton—cannot be considered conclusive evidence that the practice was not common. The planter,

---

[33] *Farmer and Planter*, IX (1858), 150, as quoted in Lewis Cecil Gray, *History of Agriculture in the Southern United States to 1860* (Washington, D. C., 1933), II, 711.

[34] Charles S. Davis, *The Cotton Kingdom in Alabama* (Montgomery, 1939), 145, citing *The Tuscumbian*, June 27, 1825.

[35] *DeBow's Review*, XXV (1858), 714.

[36] *Tri-Weekly Flag & Advertiser* (Montgomery), Jan. 11, 1849.

[37] *Daily Chronicle & Sentinel* (Augusta), Jan. 2, 1850. Emphasis in original.

[38] For other examples see Disposition of Samuel D. Corbitt in Barnsley v. Mac-Lellan, Copy Correspondence, Godfrey Barnsley Papers, Emory University Library, Atlanta, Ga.; "Daybook" (Oct. 29, 1855–Dec. 17, 1856), Young, Wyatt & Co. Papers, Georgia Historical Society, Savannah, Ga.; James Brown to Henry Clay, Paris, Nov. 12, 1825, Jan. 30, 1826, printed in "Letters of James Brown to Henry Clay, 1804-1835," James A. Padget, ed., *Louisiana Historical Quarterly*, XXIV (Oct. 1941), 975, 987-88.

[39] *Ward, et al.* v. *Warfield, et al.*, 3 Robinson (La.), 468 (1848).

far from the marketplace, could have been totally ignorant of the details of his factor's business.

On the other hand, there were also great pressures tending to keep the buying and selling functions separate. First of all, the force of tradition dictated this distinction. A description of commerce in Savannah clearly differentiated among the various businessmen in the cotton trade. Factors handled the business of the planters; other commission merchants "buy and sell for foreign parties." Both were "usually pledged not to speculate in produce; and the *speculators* form a distinct class of business men."[40]

Moreover, the planter was in a position to check up on his factor. The commercial journals noted the arrival of every steamship or other conveyance into the market and therefore the planter knew exactly when his cotton arrived. By noting price fluctuations on the days following the arrival of his cotton, he could get a fairly accurate idea of the price his cotton should fetch. Although he might not have legal redress in case the prices he received seemed too low, he could easily change firms if he thought he was not being adequately represented.

Finally, if there was a danger that the planter as a seller would suffer because of the divided interest of his factor, so too was there the same danger for the buyer. English and Northern firms would in all probability hesitate to engage as their buying agents those who were dealing on such intimate terms with the planters as were the cotton factors.

As seller of the planter's crop, supplier of the plantation, banker, and general business representative of the planter, the factor played a significant part in the marketing of the cotton crop. Although disagreements sometimes led to litigation, what is more important is that, for the most part, the relationship between factor and planter was one of cordial trust. Lacking the means of communication that would allow him to have precise and timely knowledge of market conditions, the planter came to trust the judgment of his factors in most of his business dealings. Differences and complaints about the system were not absent, but they were relatively rare. Generally, the planter was free to choose a factor he liked and trusted and the relationship which developed rested on mutual consent and for mutual advantage.

[40] *Hunt's Merchants' Magazine*, XXIX (1853), 60.

PART TWO

Storekeepers, Itinerants, and Bankers: Attendants to the Factor

Wherever the middling classes are a considerable proportion of the population, there the country stores are numerous.

—J. W. Dorr in the *New Orleans Crescent*, 1860.

The principal operations of the banks are in exchange, seeing that the large exports of cotton, with the small comparative amount of imports, involves a large excess of bills in the market.

—*Hunt's Merchants' Magazine,* XL (1859), 184.

The factor was King Cotton's chief retainer, but he was not the only one. Many planters and farmers did not deal with a factor at all, while others sent him only a part of their crops. If they wished, cotton growers could easily dispose of their crops in the immediate vicinity of their plantations and farms.

One convenient outlet was the country store in the nearby town where the farmer could either sell his cotton outright or barter it for store goods. Often, however, there was no need to travel even the few miles to the village: buyers would appear right at the plantation gates. They might be itinerant peddlers willing to take cotton in lieu of cash for their goods, or they might be speculators, offering hard cash for a crop they later hoped to resell at a profit.

The dominant position of the factor, then, did not prevent hundreds of small operators from entering the marketing business. Lethargic villages, far from the great markets, became animated at harvest time, as storekeepers, speculators, peddlers, and factors' representatives vied for a share of the local crop.

CHAPTER SEVEN

The Country Storekeeper

Early in the 1850's Henry Strong ran a store in Montroy, Arkansas, a tiny village on the Ouachita River in Dallas County. The land in the area was suitable for cotton growing and the Ouachita provided a convenient connection with the New Orleans market. Like other storekeepers in cotton country, Strong combined a cotton business with his other trade. Most of his customers during his first decade of business were small farmers growing from 5 to 20 bales each season, but he also numbered among his patrons farmers producing as little as 150 pounds annually as well as planters with a yearly crop of well over a hundred bales.

Strong offered his customers a variety of services. For those who preferred the New Orleans market, he acted as a receiving and forwarding agent. Farmers sent their cotton to the store and Strong shipped it by boat to the designated factor in the Crescent City. If a customer ordered merchandise in New Orleans, Strong received the shipment, paid the freight charges, and then delivered it.

Cotton growers whose crop was too small to merit a shipment on consignment to a factor and those who desired an immediate sale were easily accommodated in Montroy. Strong took cotton in trade for goods and he bought some outright. Other buyers were also available in Montroy. Strong regularly received cotton from growers and then shipped it in the name of a third party, indicating that he served as an intermediary for buyers in the neighborhood.

From Montroy the cotton traveled down the Ouachita toward New Orleans. Some went to merchants on the way, such as McCollum and Fellows in nearby Camden—probably to pay a bill; however, most was consigned to one of a dozen factors in New Orleans and went directly to that city. In part, this reflected the specific instructions of planters using the Montroy storekeeper as a forwarding agent, but Strong also divided his own cotton among several factors in New Orleans.

Not all of Strong's customers elected to make purchases in New Orleans. Some bought food and other supplies directly from his store. Frequently such sales were on credit, payment being deferred until the end of the season when cotton was available to meet the bill.

Strong followed no consistent policy regarding charges for the many services he provided. To the price of credit sales from his store, he would sometimes add what he called a commission, usually 2.5 percent, but at times, 3 percent. Goods from New Orleans which he received for his customers also, on occasion, carried an extra charge, designated variously as a "commission" or a cost of "advancing." But not all Strong's customers paid these extra costs, for often his records show no charges for these services.[1]

Next to the factors, country storekeepers such as Henry Strong were the most important Southern middlemen in the cotton trade.[2] Located in the smallest crossroads villages as well as in the larger market towns, grocers, dry goods merchants, and general storekeepers regularly handled cotton in addition to their other business. As Strong's business procedures illustrate, storekeepers provided the same important services in the marketing of cotton as did the factors. Like the factor, the storekeeper assisted in the sale of the crop, provided long-term credit, and facilitated the movement of supplies to the cotton grower. But these country

[1] The description of Strong's business operations is based on an analysis of Account Book of Henry Strong, Montroy, Manchester Township, Dallas County, Ark., 1852-1897, microfilm copy of MSS in Arkansas History Commission, Department of Archives and History, Little Rock, Ark.

[2] The outstanding, full-scale discussion of the ante bellum country store is Lewis E. Atherton, *The Southern Country Store, 1800-1860* (Baton Rouge, 1949). I have profited greatly from this pioneering work and have drawn from it freely. Atherton deals with all aspects of the store; the institution is considered here only in its role in the financing and marketing of the cotton crop.

stores were not substitute marketing agencies existing parallel to the factorage system. Rather, they were appendages to the system, relying ultimately upon the services of the factor.

The country storekeeper who combined cotton transactions with his business of selling merchandise for the most part serviced the farmers and small planters. Owning few or perhaps no slaves and producing a relatively small crop, this group required on a lesser scale many of the same services the large planter did. However small the amount, cotton produced on the farms had to find its way to market, and farmers as well as planters often required supplies on credit. The factorage system could not always meet the needs of the farmer and small planter. The crop was not large enough and the security was usually inadequate to induce factors to take the trouble and risk involved in dealing with hundreds of tiny cotton growers. The country storekeeper stepped into the breach. He offered equipment, food, and dry goods to the farmer as needed and allowed bills, rendered at the end of the season, to be paid in cotton. By providing this service to as many as three or four hundred farmers within shopping distance of his store, the storekeeper accumulated enough cotton to enable him to deal with a factor. The storekeeper thus became an important customer of the factor, and he could, if necessary, receive advances and credit on cotton shipped or to be shipped (just as a planter could), thus enabling him to pass this credit on to his farmer customers.[3]

The smallest producer could market his crop through the storekeeper. Henry Strong's practice of accepting cotton in quantities of less than a single bale was not unique. Evidently no amount was too small for the storekeeper to handle. For example, J. M. Bradford of Wetumpka, Alabama, owned a general store and warehouse and took an average of 2 or 3 bales per farmer to be shipped to Mobile for sale.[4] In White Plains, Alabama, A. A. Causby bought local farmers' cotton in lots as small as 20 pounds,[5] while in Claysville, Alabama, a merchant accepted cotton in the seed in quantities valued as little as $10.[6]

[3] Ibid., passim, but esp. pp. 12-15, 106, 109; Fred Mitchell Jones, Middlemen in the Domestic Trade of the United States, 1800-1860 (Urbana, Ill., 1937), 45-46.
[4] Charles Davis, The Cotton Kingdom in Alabama (Montgomery, 1939), 154.
[5] Ibid.
[6] Atherton, Southern Country Store, 105.

Likewise, goods from the markets of the world were available to the small farmer through his storekeeper. Patrons of A. and J. M. Gordon and Company of Lewisburg, Conway County, Arkansas, for example, could find "a splendid assortment" of clothing, dry goods, shoes, hardware, drugs, and other merchandise "just received from Philadelphia and New-York."[7] A number of Mississippi storekeepers dealt with R. G. Hazard, a Peacedale, Rhode Island, merchant, who purchased and shipped goods ordered from various Northern markets.[8]

Unlike the factor, the storekeeper rarely specialized: his cotton business was but one part of his varied mercantile activities. He would buy and sell, not only cotton but all other merchandise of the community.[9] In this manner he replenished his stock of store goods, filled orders for buyers, and accumulated goods for sale elsewhere. How complex the business activities of a country store could become can be seen in the records of H. R. Johnson and Company of Americus, Georgia. The Americus merchants had extensive dealings with Thomas Wood and Company of New York City, who supplied them with a variety of merchandise which they sold on commission, remitting the proceeds in both cash and cotton. In addition to buying cotton and taking it in trade in order to send it to New York to pay Wood, the Americus firm also purchased cotton on their own account and sent it on consignment to Wood. Nor did the Georgians confine themselves to trade with New York. They also made purchases of groceries in Savannah, Macon, and other markets for resale in the vicinity of Americus; and they bought cotton on order from, and in partnership with, Savannah merchants. Finally, H. R. Johnson played still another role; he was the Americus agent of the Merchant's and Planter's Bank of Savannah.[10]

[7] [John P. Campbell (ed.)], *The Southern Business Directory and General Commercial Advertiser* (Charleston, 1854), I, 118.

[8] P. H. Skipwith to Hazard, Commerce, Miss., Aug. 5, Oct. 16, 1841, B. Stanton, Jr. to Hazard, Belmont, Miss., Dec. 13, 1841, R. G. Hazard Papers, Mississippi Department of Archives and History, Jackson, Miss. Hazard not only sold goods to Southern merchants but also sent items on consignment. See E. B. Baker to Hazard, Natchez, June 6, 1843, Jan. 15, 1846, Apr. 10, 1851, *ibid.*

[9] Mills & Heeth of Marietta, Ga., urged local residents to send them "any, and every thing, which may be desired to be sold at Auction, or privately, on Commission." [Campbell], *Southern Business Directory*, I, 237.

[10] The Harrold Brothers Papers, Emory University Library, Atlanta, Ga., amply

A varied business, of course, made for diverse sources of income for the storekeeper. Charges made, however, were neither as uniform nor as consistently assessed by the storekeeper as they were by the factor. As has been shown, Henry Strong sometimes added a separate charge for his services and at other times did not. But the absence of a specific service charge or commission did not necessarily mean that the service was made as a complimentary accommodation. There is ample evidence that storekeepers had a two-price system, charging more for supplies advanced on credit.[11] Charges undoubtedly varied depending upon the nature of the storekeeper's business and the relationship he had with a particular customer. Thus, cotton was sometimes forwarded free of charge in hopes that the good will created would be repaid in trade at the store. In other instances the factor charged the planter a single commission and then returned a part of this commission to the storekeeper for his services.[12]

Although the small farmer was the main support for the country store, it does not follow that these stores were found only in newly or sparsely settled areas outside the plantation belt. Throughout the ante bellum period fertile lands and an increasing demand for cotton drew settlers west. If the larger plantations came to dominate the richer black belt areas, small farmers were never completely absent from these lands.[13] New country brought wealthy

illustrate their business. See especially the following: Behn & Foster to Johnson, Savannah, Nov. 1, 1858, Cohens & Hertz to Johnson, Savannah, May 6, 1859, a/c sales of cotton for sale on 3/3rd a/c for L. A. Smith, Johnson and Cohens & Hertz, Savannah, Jan. 13, Feb. 8, March 30, May 5, 1859, J. M. Selkin & Co. to Johnson & Harrold, Savannah, May 3, 1861, Charles C. Walden & Co. to Johnson & Harrold, Savannah, April 6, 1861, Fears & Pritchett to Johnson & Harrold, Macon, July 7, 1861, Thomas Wood & Co. to U. B. Harrold, New York, March 30, 1861, Thomas Wood & Co. to Johnson & Harrold, New York, Feb. 5, 6, 7, 13, 1861, and numerous others from the New York firm.

11 In 1848 Maunsel White wrote to a merchant for some supplies for his plantation asking that they be of the best quality at cash prices: "nor must you charge *your country Credit* prices. (It was the reason I quit the Laytons.) you know you can have the cash the moment you call for it & therefore I want things at cash price." White to W. B. McCutchon & Co., Deer Range, Oct. 2, 1848, Maunsel White Papers, Southern Historical Collection, University of North Carolina Library, Chapel Hill, N. C. White, a planter and factor of long experience, was well aware of current mercantile practices.

12 See *Davis* v. *Larguier et al.*, 2 Robinson (La.), 327 (1847).

13 Scholars, led by Owsley, have given great emphasis to the small farmer. See Frank Lawrence Owsley, *Plain Folk of the Old South* (Baton Rouge, 1949); Frank L. and Harriet C. Owsley, "The Economic Basis of Society in the Late Ante-Bellum South," *Journal of Southern History*, VI (Feb. 1940), 24-45; Harry L. Coles, "Some

planters from the East; it also provided new opportunities for wealth. A small farmer today might become a planter tomorrow and a lord of thousands of acres and hundreds of slaves the day after. As a result of the dynamics of the expanding cotton kingdom, planter and farmer frequently lived side by side and local storekeepers had both planters and farmers for customers. There never was a clear demarcation between a farmer and a planter and no precise point at which the cotton grower suddenly merited the attention of a factor. Moreover, even when a planter had a regular factor, he often gave part of his business to a local merchant.

Wherever cotton was grown there were merchants on hand to market it. In the largest markets, the port cities, the factors dominated the cotton trade, but the level of business in the interior seldom supported such highly specialized firms. In the important interior markets, such as Montgomery and Augusta, increasing cotton receipts might justify specialization, but even here the general merchant shared the cotton business with more specialized firms. In Montgomery, during the last decade before the Civil War, cotton marketing occupied the energies of a varied group of merchants. H. Lehman and Brothers advertised themselves as "Wholesale and Retail Dealers in Dry Goods, Clothing, Groceries, Hardware, Boots, Shoes, Hats, Caps, Bonnetts, Cutlery, Flowers, Combs, etc., etc., etc.," making them probably as "general" as merchants could be.[14] Cotton marketing became a significant aspect of the brothers' business. They regularly sold their multifarious merchandise on long-term credit to neighboring planters and farmers, and, more often than not, year-end accounts were settled with cotton rather than cash. To the stock they accumu-

Notes on Slave Ownership and Land Ownership in Louisiana, 1850-1860," *ibid.*, IX (Aug. 1943), 381-93; Blanche Henry Clark, *The Tennessee Yeoman, 1840-1860* (Nashville, 1942); Herbert Weaver, *Mississippi Farmers, 1850-1860* (Nashville, 1945). For an able critique of these studies which denies the emphasis given to the plain folk but does not deny their existence, see Fabian Linden, "Economic Democracy in the Old South," *Journal of Negro History*, XXXI (April 1946), 140-89. On the importance of cotton for the growth of the West see the perceptive studies by Douglass C. North: "International Capital Flows and the Development of the American West," *Journal of Economic History*, XVI (Dec. 1956), 493-505 and *The Economic Growth of the United States, 1790-1860* (Englewood Cliffs, N. J., 1961), 122-34.

14 [Campbell], *Southern Business Directory*, I, 10.

lated in this way, the brothers occasionally added even more through outright cash purchases.[15]

While the Lehman Brothers and other general merchants in Montgomery were taking cotton in trade for merchandise or buying it for cash,[16] the level of trade allowed other firms to specialize. Grant and Nickels, "Dealers in Choice Groceries, at Wholesale & Retail,"[17] also ran a commission business, announcing their willingness to "make liberal CASH ADVANCES ON COTTON to be shipped to Mobile, New Orleans or New York, where they have arrangements with the best houses to receive and sell their consignments."[18] Even more specialized was Thomas B. Maddox who in September 1848 advertised that he had leased a warehouse in Montgomery and "offers his most devoted personal services to his friends and the public, in receiving and forwarding Cotton and Merchandize [sic], for the sale of Cotton and as General Commission Merchants."[19]

If towns grew larger and cotton receipts increased, further specialization would follow. By the mid-1850's, Augusta had such firms as Scranton, Seymour and Company, which sold groceries and plantation supplies and, in addition, took produce on consignment.[20] A firm might divide its consignment business from its other concerns if volume warranted the move. Beall and Stovall, for example, announced that they would "continue the Grocery Business in all its branches, at their old stand, opposite the Planter's Hotel," but they moved their cotton business to a warehouse elsewhere, promising that "one of the firm may at all times be found" there to sell cotton on commission.[21] This might

---

[15] Lehman Brothers, A *Centennial: Lehman Brothers, 1850-1950* (New York, 1950), 4. This is the same firm prominent today as investment bankers in New York. The business began in 1845 when the first of three brothers opened a store in Montgomery. Subsequently, two other brothers arrived from Europe and joined the business. In 1850 the firm name became Lehman Bros. *Ibid.*, 2.

[16] P. Abraham & Bros., for example, dealt in dry goods and groceries but also advertised that they would purchase cotton. [Campbell], *Southern Business Directory*, I, 10.

[17] *Ibid.*, I, 11.

[18] *Tri-Weekly Alabama Journal* (Montgomery), Oct. 10, 1853.

[19] *Tri-Weekly Flag & Advertiser* (Montgomery), Sept. 7, 1848.

[20] [Campbell], *Southern Business Directory*, I, 294. See advertisements of Davis, Kolb & Fanning ("Wholesale Grocers and Commission Merchants") and Antoine Poullain ("Cotton Factor and Dealer in Groceries") for similar firms. *Ibid.*, 293-94.

[21] *Ibid.*, I, 293.

be the first step toward further specialization should the cotton transactions justify the full attention of both members of the firm.[22] Indeed, at this very time a few Augusta merchants gave all their attention to selling cotton, running typical factorage houses.[23]

Few Southern towns could support the specialization which arose in Montgomery and Augusta. In most, general storekeepers were the only resident merchants in the area.[24] For the nearby planter, the store was another market in which he could buy and sell, and the storekeeper became a helpful intermediary between him and his factor. But for the small farmer, the store might be his only market. Indeed, the storekeeper was in fact—if not in name—the farmer's factor, providing the same necessary services for the small grower that the factor furnished the planter.[25]

[22] The business might be permanently divided between partners or among members of a family. Thus while John W. L. was the Stovall in the firm Beall & Stovall, M. P. Stovall advertised himself as a warehouseman and commission merchant and Thomas and Joseph Stovall united as Thos. P. Stovall & Co., general commission merchants. *Ibid.*, I, 294.

[23] See the Stephen D. Heard Papers, Southern Historical Collection, University of North Carolina Library, Chapel Hill, N. C., for an example of an Augusta factorage house.

[24] This is apparent from the listings in [Campbell], *Southern Business Directory*, I, *passim*. See also Atherton, *Southern Country Store*, 164-70.

[25] Like the factor, the storekeeper might be asked to perform a personal favor for one of his customers. A Griffin, Ga., planter notified an Americus storekeeper that he had sent a slave to be hired out and asked the merchant to try to get $20 per month. "I consider him low at the price above named," the farmer added, "But *confidentially*, rather than he should come back home, I will authorise you to hire him, for a little less. But I shall depend upon you in confidence, to make the concession only in case they [the firm to whom the slave is to be hired] positively [*sic*] refuse to give the price named. Do the best you can for me. . . ." J. S. Jones to H. R. Johnson, Griffin, Dec. 31, 1861, Harrold Brothers Papers.

CHAPTER EIGHT

Itinerant Merchants

Storekeepers were not the only local buyers available to the cotton grower.[1] He could turn to hundreds of others who, lured by the scent of profit, entered the cotton-buying business. Some were peddlers, taking cotton in payment for their merchandise; most were simply itinerant buyers intent on a speculative purchase.

The dominant position of the factor and storekeeper in cotton marketing has tended to obscure the role of these itinerant merchants in bringing the South's principal crop to market. To be sure, they were not independent of the factors; like the storekeepers, the traveling merchants sold their cotton by consigning it to factors. For the cotton grower, however, they provided another market for his crop.

The significance of the itinerant merchants transcends their role in moving the cotton crop. Indeed, an analysis of their business activities helps to describe a changing Southern economy. The earliest of these itinerant buyers, the peddlers, were the product of a scattered and exceedingly shallow market, served by the most rudimentary transportation facilities. Improvements in transportation almost eliminated the peddler, but at the same time stimulated the rise of a new group of itinerant merchants. Better transportation combined with this new group of buyers signaled important changes in the Southern economy; both tended to alter the nature of cotton marketing, to change the character of the cotton factorage system, and, indeed, to portend its ultimate collapse. The Civil War simply delayed changes already evident in the 1850's.

The peddler, the earliest of the itinerant merchants, played an interesting, though minor, part in marketing cotton. Of ancient, if somewhat tarnished, lineage, the peddler was a well-known figure among backcountry folk, North and South. Often he was one of the few visitors these people saw and his news and gossip were usually as welcome as his goods.[2] The lack of currency which often plagued the largely subsistence farmers with whom he dealt did not prevent sales. The peddler frequently bartered his merchandise for farm commodities and furs which he would later sell in town.[3]

Cotton was one such commodity taken in trade. In exchange the peddler offered a variety of wares often difficult for the isolated country folk to obtain. Under some conditions, he might have a great range of goods to offer. Robert Sutcliff, on a visit to the United States in 1805, was told of floating stores on the Ohio River, riverboats "fitted up with counters, shelves, and drawers, in the same manner as are shops on land, and well stored with all kinds of goods." At each stop the local people would gather about the boat to make their purchases. Payment would be in "the produce of their plantations; such as grain, flour, cotton, tobacco, dried venison, the skins of wild animals, &c. &c."[4]

Not all peddlers, of course, could be so well stocked. Since most conducted their business overland on horseback, cotton, low in value relative to its weight, could not be taken in barter for goods. This problem was solved by some who established business

[1] This discussion of itinerant merchants appeared in a slightly different form in *Agricultural History*, XL (April 1966), 79-90.

[2] For an entertaining and informative discussion of the peddlers and other pre-Civil War itinerants see Richardson Wright, *Hawkers & Walkers in Early America* (Philadelphia, 1927). More scholarly and specialized is Lewis E. Atherton's study of peddlers in the South: "Itinerant Merchandising in the Ante-Bellum South," *Bulletin of The Business Historical Society*, XIX (April 1945), 35-59. See also R. Malcolm Keir, "The Tin Peddler," *Journal of Political Economy*, XXI (March 1913), 255-58; Fred Mitchell Jones, *Middlemen in the Domestic Trade of the United States, 1800-1860* (Urbana, Ill., 1937), 12, 61-63, 66-67.

[3] Wright, *Hawkers & Walkers*, 37-38, 65, 74, 246-47.

[4] Robert Sutcliff, *Travels in Some Parts of North America, In the Years 1804, 1805, & 1806* (York, 1815), 90-91. See also Atherton, "Itinerant Merchandising," 46-48; Henry E. Chambers, "Early Commercial Prestige of New Orleans," *Louisiana Historical Quarterly*, V (Oct. 1922), 456-57.

connections with country stores. Peddlers received their mail and fresh supplies of merchandise at these stores;[5] they also used them as depots for the cotton and other produce taken in exchange for their goods.

When such facilities were available, peddlers in the South conducted their business in much the same way as the country storekeepers. They often distributed their goods on credit and then took payment in cotton at harvest time. Such were the business arrangements among Rensselaer Upson, a Connecticut clockmaker; George Bartholomew, a peddler; and Philip Barnes, a storekeeper in Athens, Alabama.[6]

"I shall want you to forward me some goods in the spring early . . . and you must get credit for a year," wrote the peddler to Upson in the winter of 1825. "I shall get no money through the summer." Ten months later the peddler reported that business was dull and collections slow, but, he added, there was no chance to do any business at all except "on a credit." During the previous spring he had visited his customers and had collected some fourteen hundred dollars in cash and three hundred dollars in fur which he promised to sell in order that a payment might be made to Upson.[7]

In the meantime the storekeeper, Philip Barnes, had been collecting cotton in payment for merchandise. "There is no money and cotton is the only chance to collect debts," he reported in November 1826. Early the next year he was still trying to make collections, announcing that although "business in this country is dull in the extreme both in selling and collecting" he had managed to accumulate about five thousand dollars in cotton.[8]

After the first decades of the nineteenth century the general merchandise peddler who took cotton and other produce in return for his wares became a rarer figure, although he never completely disappeared.[9] The proliferation of interior stores meant disastrous

---

[5] Keir, "The Tin Peddler," 256.

[6] A description of this business arrangement may be found in Priscilla Carrington Kline, "New Light on the Yankee Peddler," *New England Quarterly*, XII (March 1939), 80-98.

[7] Bartholomew to Upson, Athens, Ala., Dec. 27, 1825, Oct. 22, 1826, April 16, 1826, as printed *ibid.*, 81, 83-84, 86.

[8] Barnes to Upson, Athens, Ala., Nov. 8, 1826, Jan. 21, 1827, as printed *ibid.*, 83.

[9] Jones, *Middlemen*, 62. Frederick Law Olmstead reported meeting a German

competition. Writing from Mississippi in early 1827, George Bartholomew complained that business was getting steadily worse and that he was suffering greatly from the competition of local merchants.[10] Not only were there more stores available to the rural population, but the storekeepers themselves often dispatched wagonloads of goods on peddling expeditions, selling suplies or bartering merchandise for agricultural produce.[11] A general antagonism, legal restrictions, and taxation added to the burdens of the peddler and hastened his decline.[12]

Far more significant than the peddlers in the marketing of cotton was another group of itinerant merchants—the speculators. Sometimes these men worked from their own stores, but often a particular town served only as a base of operations—and a temporary one at that. Although they might buy on order for others, they frequently made purchases for their own accounts, purchases often financed by factors who either provided them with cash or guaranteed their notes in local banks. Whatever their methods, their aim was usually profit through speculation.

The activities of several of these merchants can be followed in detail through their correspondence in the late 1850's with Heard and Simpson, cotton factors of Augusta, Georgia, with whom they dealt.[13] They did their cotton buying in western Georgia, centering

---

peddler in Mississippi in the 1850's. His customers, he told Olmstead, were "all poor folks" who exchanged eggs, chickens, and other farm goods for the peddler's trinkets, calico, and handkerchiefs. The people had no money and were unaware of town prices for the goods they bartered. Olmstead, *The Cotton Kingdom*, ed. Arthur M. Schlesinger (New York, 1953), 421-22.

[10] To Upson, Columbus, Miss., Jan. 16, 1827, Mount Zion, Miss., Feb. 18, 1827, as printed in Kline, "New Light on the Yankee Peddler," 82.

[11] Atherton, *Southern Country Store*, 96-97.

[12] Atherton, "Itinerant Merchandising," 53-59.

[13] Unless otherwise indicated, the letters cited and quoted in the following discussion are from the Stephen D. Heard Papers, Southern Historical Collection, University of North Carolina Library, Chapel Hill, N. C. Brief descriptions of similar speculators working in other markets through other factors may be found in the decisions and testimony in the following court cases: *Hamilton, Donaldson & Co. v. Cunningham*, reported in John W. Brockenbrough (ed.), *Reports of Cases Decided by the Honourable John Marshall . . . in the Circuit Court of the United States for the District of Virginia and North Carolina From 1802 to 1833 Inclusive* (Philadelphia, 1837), II, 352; *Solomon v. Solomon*, 2 Kelly (Ga.), 18 (1847); *D. A. Johnson & Co. v. Mechanics & Savings Bank*, 25 Martin (Ga.), 643 (1858). It is clear from these cases as well as from references in the letters discussed below that Heard & Simpson were not the only factors supporting these itinerant merchants. It is unfortunate that full factors' records are no longer extant so that similar operations elsewhere cannot be fully described.

in the towns of West Point, La Grange, and Newnan, and in northern Alabama, working out of the towns of Athens and Huntsville. These towns were in the center of what had become wealthy cotton producing areas.

By the 1850's planters in these districts could elect to sell their crops in a number of markets which had become accessible because of multifold improvements in transportation facilities. The ante bellum South's investment in internal improvements had been designed to supplement natural communication links between major markets and the backcountry which could support cotton and other staple production. A glance at maps showing navigable rivers, canals, and railroads indicates clearly how transportation resources opened numerous markets to cotton growers in western Georgia and northern Alabama.[14] Newnan, La Grange, and West Point were all on the Atlanta and West Point Railroad. Crops from these towns could move north on this railroad to Atlanta and then across the state via the Georgia Railroad to Augusta and thence very easily either to Savannah or Charleston. But other routes were equally convenient. Macon could siphon off cotton moving eastward, for the Macon and Western Railroad connected with the West Point and Atlanta at the town of East Point, just below Atlanta. The Chattahoochee and Apalachicola rivers opened a southern route from West Point to the Gulf. Alabama markets were also available. Crops might move eastward on the Montgomery and West Point Railroad. From Montgomery the Alabama River led to Mobile and the Alabama and Florida Railroad led to the Gulf at Pensacola. Nor did these routes exhaust the possibilities. The Western and Atlantic Railroad ran northward from Atlanta, where it met the Memphis and Charleston (and related lines), which provided a route to Memphis to the west and to Richmond, Petersburg, and Norfolk, Virginia, to the east.

Obviously, then, planters in western Georgia and northern Alabama could choose factors in every major cotton market in the

[14] Good railroad and canal maps may be found in Ulrich Bonnell Phillips, A History of Transportation in the Eastern Cotton Belt to 1860 (New York, 1908); George Rogers Taylor and Irene D. Neu, The American Railroad Network, 1861-1890 (Cambridge, Mass., 1956). Phillips' book also gives information concerning the navigable river system. It may be supplemented admirably with a map in Robert William Fogel, Railroads and Economic Growth: Essays in Econometric History (Baltimore, 1964), 250.

South and many of the minor ones as well. Not surprisingly, these factors, keenly alert to competitive dangers and anxious to channel cotton to their houses, employed whatever means they could to achieve this end. Nor should it be surprising that large stocks of valuable cotton brought to the area a number of men anxious to speculate in the commodity.

In the fall of 1858, W. H. Sims of La Grange wrote Stephen Heard in Augusta that he and another man had "formed a partnership in the Grocery & Cotton business." His description of intent plainly indicates that Sims was more interested in cotton than in groceries. He did not plan simply to trade store goods for cotton; he expected to buy and speculate in the article. "We intend to buy right & when it looks right to take hold liberally, & when it does not have presence enough to keep out." Sims' purchases in the La Grange area would be resold in a number of markets, including Augusta, and Heard and Simpson, he averred, might have the opportunity to profit by the transactions if they were willing to offer aid. Sims informed the Augusta factor that he was "anxious to make arrangements to make shipments to Heard & Simpson for all or most of my Augusta shipments." The "arrangements" he required involved financial backing. Heard and Simpson were to authorize the local bank "to take bills drawn by Sims Gorham & Co." so that "we will then have no difficulty in getting money when we want." The money, of course, would be used to buy the cotton.[15]

Sims wanted to borrow money in La Grange for his cotton purchases. Apparently the local bank had indicated that it would discount Sims' note provided an established Augusta house guaranteed payment. The arrangement requested was promptly concluded, for less than a week later Sims wrote that he had sent 26 bales to Augusta to be sold. He indicated that he had drawn an advance from Heard and Simpson based on the expected proceeds from the cotton sent (the money, presumably, to be used to pay his note at the bank, or, if that was not yet due, to make more purchases).[16] The La Grange merchant's advice paralleled the

[15] Letter dated La Grange, Sept. 11, 1858.

[16] *Ibid.*, Sept. 17, 1858. See a description of similar arrangements made in Tennessee in Thomas B. Abernathy, "The Early Development of Commerce and Banking in Tennessee," *Mississippi Valley Historical Review*, XIV (Dec. 1927), 317.

usual planter-to-factor instructions at the time of crop consignment: "Sell to best advantage at such time as you think best, this will be our general instructions."[17]

Initial sales were hardly to Sims's "best advantage." When the Augusta factors sold his cotton, prices in Augusta were depressed and Sims was faced with a considerable loss. He complained that his cotton should not have been sold until prices had improved. But Sims was not to be deterred by a temporary setback. Falling prices in Augusta seemed to offer the opportunity to recoup through further speculation, this time in Augusta: "We hope you will when you think Cotton is lowest buy us about the same number of bales . . . or more & hold as long as possible hoping to make up our loss," he advised.[18]

Lack of success in this venture did not discourage the intrepid Sims. He maintained relations with Heard and Simpson and continued his speculative buying in the La Grange area, shipping to Augusta and, at times, ordering a purchase to be made in Augusta.[19]

Sims was only one of several La Grange buyers dealing with Heard and Simpson in 1858-1859. Less than three weeks after Sims had written asking for financial backing, W. P. Delph wrote Heard and Simpson from the same town announcing that he had just arrived but had not yet begun making purchases as he had no money. He noted that although the prices seemed to him to be too high, others were already buying in La Grange "mostly for the Augusta market."[20] Apparently financial arrangements had already been made with Delph; he seemed to be waiting for the arrival of funds. Indeed, a week later he reported that he had made some purchases, but, because of "the recklessness of the buyers of this place," prices had been driven up beyond what he felt would return a profit and he had discontinued purchases even though he still had $7,500 belonging to Heard and Simpson on hand.[21]

While Sims, Delph, and others were buying in the La Grange area, another buyer-speculator, A. M. Benson, was active in West Point. Apparently Benson was not a storekeeper; he was much too

---

[17] Sims to Heard, La Grange, Sept. 17, 1858.

[18] Sims Gorham & Co. to Heard & Simpson, La Grange, Nov. 6, 1858.

[19] See their many letters exchanged during the 1858-1859 season.

[20] Letter dated La Grange, Sept. 28, 1858.

[21] *Ibid.*, Nov. 6, 1858. Also in La Grange was W. C. Darden.

peripatetic, visiting many markets in search of cotton. Like Sims, Benson was financed by Heard and Simpson, who arranged a credit in local banks upon which Benson could draw. The Augusta factors guaranteed credits from $5,000 to $10,000 at a time as requested.[22] Should the local banks be unable to supply the cash, Heard and Simpson would be asked to send it from Augusta. "We wrote you yesterday for a package of $5000—as the Auga. Bank. and R R Bank have neither a dollar in their agencies, nor do they know when they will get any—."[23]

Benson faced strenuous competition from many buyers representing other markets. If prices were higher in these markets than they were in Augusta, buyers for Augusta would have a difficult time getting cotton at prices which would leave them a profit after resale in Augusta. Benson therefore had to be alert to price trends in a number of markets. Heard and Simpson were expected to provide the latest information from Augusta to help Benson determine the bid he would make on available cotton. On September 28, 1858, for example, he wrote his Augusta factor that he was buying cotton at 11.5 cents a pound "and will continue at these prices unless otherwise instructed by you."[24]

Price fluctuations and differentials created the risk. On November 9 Benson complained of troublesome competition. "Several opperators [sic] are buying and shipping to Montgomery," he wrote, adding, however, that he was continuing his purchases "and getting our share."[25] Two days later he reported that resales in Montgomery had been very profitable, and that consequently buyers for that market had pushed prices up in West Point. Wetumpka prices were also up, he complained. As a result, "the planters bordering on the Talapoosa, are going to that market, which is cutting off a large and profitable Custom from that section, legitimately belonging to our market."[26]

Augusta prices were not advancing as fast as those in the Alabama markets and Benson was faced with a loss. "We fear we

[22] Benson & Rosamond to Heard & Simpson, West Point, Sept. 30, Nov. 8, 1858. Rosamond, Benson's partner, might have been a storekeeper in West Point, although there is no direct evidence to this effect. When Benson left West Point in search of cotton elsewhere, he signed his letters with just his name. Correspondence from West Point carries the name of both partners. All letters are in the same hand.

[23] *Ibid.*, Nov. 11, 1858.

[24] *Ibid.*, Sept. 28, 1858.

[25] *Ibid.*, Nov. 9, 1858.

[26] *Ibid.*, Nov. 11, 1858.

have done our do for the season, and have made a bad do of it, unless things change to our advantage, which we cannot now forsee [*sic*]," was his pessimistic prognosis in mid-November.[27] He was now in a quandary. Buyers for Montgomery were taking up the available crop at prices that meant a loss in Augusta and Benson could not decide whether to chance purchases on the supposition that Augusta prices would advance. He appealed to Heard and Simpson for advice.[28]

Benson's difficulties seemed endless. News from Augusta was wretched. As of November 22 his speculations had netted a loss of almost two thousand dollars. His competitors, he darkly grumbled, were undermining his reputation among the planters; he had heard "remarks . . . made about us" which were "not polite to our ears." He noted that he "will trust to providence, and your judgement to extricate us" from the unprofitable venture. His advice to Heard and Simpson would seem to indicate that complaints about him in West Point were not completely unjustified. "We will have to ask your assistance, and indulgence . . . to help us out of the difficulty as well as you can," he wrote suggesting that the Augusta factors help him at the expense of their other customers. Benson wanted his remaining cotton sold along with better grades belonging to others; the average price for the lot therefore would be higher than what he would receive if his cotton were sold alone—and lower than what the better cotton would fetch alone.[29]

Within the week, Benson seemed more confident. He was sure that prices in Augusta would improve and he began buying again in West Point in anticipation of rising prices.[30] Competition was still fierce, keeping the West Point market active. Even a planter tried his hand at speculation, much to Benson's disgust: "Ben Johnson (a rich planter from Harris Co) is in Competition with us, and you know when planters take a notion to buy they are such fools, and being no judges of Cotton, that we cant [*sic*] compete with them."[31]

27 *Ibid.*, Nov. 16, 1858.
28 *Ibid.*, Nov. 18, 1858.
29 *Ibid.*, Nov. 22, 1858. Benson repeated this advice a few days later (*Ibid.*, Nov. 27, 1858), but there is no evidence that Heard & Simpson did what he asked.
30 *Ibid.*, Nov. 26, 27, 1858.
31 *Ibid.*, Nov. 26, 1858. Speculation by planters was not commonplace, but

Prospects for more profitable purchases soon took Benson out of the West Point area. Perhaps it was Heard and Simpson who suggested that he try his luck in northern Alabama. The Augusta factors had written to one E. P. Beirne in Huntsville and on January 20 Beirne provided them with market information. The crop in the area was very large, exceeding the previous year "by ¼ or ⅓," he wrote. "A considerable portion" had already been marketed via Memphis and New Orleans, but very little had gone east as "we have had very few buyers here from Carolina & Georgia."[32]

Five days later Benson wrote Athens, Alabama. The crop in the immediate area was almost all sold, he reported, but he planned to go further north, up the Elk River into Tennessee, "to see what the prospects are."[33] His trip convinced Benson that more purchases could be made in that area, but all the cotton was not yet ready for market. Writing from Huntsville, he described his decision to engage in a highly speculative venture—buying cotton in the field: "I can buy some cotton there [in Tennessee] at 10¢ all round [i.e., as an average price regardless of grade], and let them have their own time to deliver it, and it is the only possible terms on which we can get it, and inasmuch as Cotton is getting quite scarce, I am determined on going back in that section, and buy all I can, which I hope may be 4 or 500 bales, but at the same time I have no idea, but some of the Cotton will be three months in delivering. . . ."[34] For the next few days Benson scoured the

---

Benson's reaction to it was one of scorn, not surprise, indicating that he was not unfamiliar with it. Benson ran into planter competition again in 1860. Writing from Athens, Ala., on Jan. 28, Benson recorded that a local planter had purchased some eight hundred bales of cotton in the area on speculation. On a much larger scale was the speculation by a planter in Mobile in 1855. One Captain Rice purchased some eighteen hundred bales in a venture that soured so badly that he reportedly lost $25,000! [William A. Witherspoon] to Reynolds, Mobile, July 10, 1855, Henry Lee Reynolds Papers, Southern Historical Collection, University of North Carolina Library, Chapel Hill, N. C. Planters would sometimes buy cotton in the seed from their farmer neighbors who did not have a gin and who did not want to be bothered with marketing the crop themselves. See Diary of John W. Brown, Arkansas History Commission, Department of Archives and History, Little Rock, Ark., *passim*.

32 To Heard & Simpson, Huntsville, Jan. 20, 1859.
33 To Heard & Simpson, Athens, Ala., Jan. 25, 1859.
34 *Ibid.*, Huntsville, Jan. 27, 1859. This method is obviously very speculative for Benson had to take a chance on the market conditions three months in the future. It also has a very modern flavor, for Benson is, in a manner, buying "futures." Farmers

countryside looking for cotton. Apparently there was more available than he first thought, for he raised his anticipated purchase from 500 to 1,000 bales.[35] No opportunity to secure cotton was overlooked. So that he might not miss any available purchases while he was away, he employed John T. Tanner, a storekeeper in Athens, to buy up "the little small lots coming into town, during my absence."[36]

In the following crop year Benson continued his itinerant cotton buying with the support of Heard and Simpson in Augusta. From West Point he moved northward in Georgia to the area around Rome, and thence once more into northern Alabama. Again he faced competition from buyers from other markets. On January 24, 1860 he reported that he could not make profitable purchases there unless the Augusta market improved.[37] Three days later he was in Athens, Alabama, making the same complaint. He noted, however, that he had been advised of some virgin territory for his speculations. He planned to go to Triana and Whitesburg, two little towns on the Tennessee River in Madison County a few miles south of Huntsville. "These places have no buyers—and . . . we might do some good there."[38]

Benson was probably much too sanguine in his expectations of a buyerless market. The smallest towns had storekeepers who would buy cotton or trade it for merchandise from their stores; a business directory for 1854 listed two merchants in Whitesburg and four in Triana.[39] Moreover, nearby Huntsville had a sizable merchant community and, as Benson's experience has already shown, numerous itinerant cotton merchants were roaming the general area in search of cotton.

Among Benson's many competitors were a number who resold in Augusta, some of whom dealt with Heard and Simpson. Such

---

selling to Benson for 10 cents are "hedging" against a drop in the market price in the future when their crops would be ready for market.

[35] *Ibid.*, Athens, Jan. 29, Feb. 1, 1859.

[36] *Ibid.*, Jan. 29, 1859. A directory lists Tanner & Co. as general merchants in Athens. [John P. Campbell (ed.)], *The Southern Business Directory and General Commercial Advertiser* (Charleston, 1854), I, 20. Tanner wrote that he performed this service of buying on order for anyone, charging 50 cents a bale for his trouble. Tanner to Benson, Athens, April 11, 1859.

[37] Benson & Co. to Heard & Simpson, Rome.

[38] *Ibid.*, Athens, Jan. 27, 1860.

[39] [Campbell], *Southern Business Directory*, I, 22.

was N. L. Atkinson, who made purchases in the West Point area and shipped to Augusta and Charleston.[40] Also in West Point was a part-time cotton buyer, Kindseel Tayler. In September 1858 Tayler wrote that he had been employed as a cotton weigher for a local firm and had good opportunities to buy cotton. All he lacked was money and he asked Heard and Simpson to finance his buying, promising to send all he purchased to Augusta for sale. Tayler was clearly no neophyte in the cotton business, nor was he unknown to the Augusta factors. He had apparently been financed by them in earlier speculations, for his letters acknowledge an outstanding debt and contain a pledge of early payment.[41]

Sims, Benson, and others, although financed by Heard and Simpson, bought on their own account and at their own risk. They hoped for a speculator's profit; the Augusta factors financed their operations so as to benefit from the commissions they charged for selling the speculators' cotton. At times, however, the Augusta firm itself sought to profit from speculation, as can be seen in its dealings with Thomas A. Grace, who worked out of Newnan. Grace would buy on order and consequently at the risk of the Augusta factors.[42]

The evidence describing the activities of these itinerant speculator-buyers is limited; it is ample enough, however, to warrant an assessment of the part they played in the marketing of cotton in the ante bellum period. By gathering up scattered crops and directing them to one or another market, they helped to extend the factorage system far into the interior—even to the farm itself. In so doing they not only facilitated the marketing of small crops but also provided the large grower with the opportunity for an immediate sale; planters who did not want to pay the cost or take the risk of a shipment to a more distant market could easily sell at home for cash on the line.

The itinerant merchants were therefore an adjunct to the cotton factorage system. They were clearly dependent upon the cotton factors, who financed them and sold their purchases. Ironically,

40 Atkinson Clark & Co. to Heard & Simpson, West Point, Nov. 16, 1858. Atkinson also made purchases in Augusta through Heard & Simpson for resale in Charleston. Atkinson to Heard & Simpson, West Point, May 7, 1859.

41 Taylor to Heard, West Point, Sept. 13, 22, 1858.

42 Grace to Heard, Newnan, Sept. 28, 1858, Jan. 20, 1859, to Heard & Simpson, Nov. 6, 1858.

however, the factors, by extending this aid, helped to destroy their own hegemony over the cotton trade in the South. The pattern is clear enough.

Ordinarily, the cotton factor dealt with a planter. One of his key duties was to sell cotton. In his business with the itinerant buyers, however, the factor was dealing with fellow merchants, not planters, and when he financed these buyers, he was moving in the direction of becoming a buyer himself, an activity frowned upon by custom and law.[43]

This procedure itself was not entirely new. Throughout the ante bellum period factors numbered storekeepers among their customers and these storekeepers were often buyers of cotton. The new feature was simply that the itinerant speculators were one more type of interior buyer.

Their significance, however, goes beyond the fact that they were a new agency in the cotton trade. More importantly, they represented the beginnings of a procedure and an institution which was to become established after the Civil War. In the ante bellum South, the itinerant merchant had the cotton he bought resold by a factor. After the war, however, the factor dropped out of the picture. Itinerant merchants sold directly to the spinner or, perhaps, represented a consumer. Improved transportation facilities made possible direct shipments from the interior to the consuming markets on a through bill of lading; improved communications provided instantaneous information everywhere about prices in all markets from La Grange, Georgia, to Liverpool, England. The intervening services of the cotton factor became superfluous.[44]

Thus, it was no accident that itinerant buyers were so active in those areas that were well supplied with transportation facilities. Competitive rivalry had led market towns to sponsor transportation to the interior, but this had only heightened competition. Cotton in some areas could now move in any number of directions, and the result was that factors in one market found themselves competing with merchants in markets hundreds of miles away, markets that had never before offered competition, in the days of limited transportation. Here was obvious opportunity for a speculator to buy and then choose the best of many markets in which to resell.

[43] See Chap. VI, above.
[44] See below, Chap. XXIII.

Moreover, he could expect the aid of factors, who, feeling the pinch of competition, financed him in return for his business.

Technological change, then, was bringing about significant economic change in the South before the Civil War. The war served to alter the pace of this change. Blockade and devastation would slow it, but the end of slavery, the rise of the tenant system, the rebuilding and expansion of the rail network, and the extension of the telegraph and telephone into the South would accelerate it again. The seeds of change, however, had germinated in the black belt before the war. The itinerant cotton buyers in western Georgia and northern Alabama were a few of these hardy new plants.

CHAPTER NINE

Bankers and Planters

In the South, as elsewhere in the nation, banks were organized to meet the financial needs of a growing new economy. Secretary of the Treasury William H. Crawford noted the trend—and the dangers inherent in it—early in 1820: "banks have been incorporated, not because there was capital seeking investment; not because the places where they were established had commerce and manufactures which required their fostering aid; but because men without active capital wanted the means of obtaining loans, which their standing in the community would not command from banks or individuals having real capital and established credit."[1] Southerners, eagerly turning the wilderness into plantations, winked at the dangers and expected their states to charter banks designed to meet their financial needs. By 1838 the cotton states of South Carolina, Georgia, Alabama, Louisiana, Mississippi, Arkansas, and Tennessee had sixty-five chartered banks with eighty-one branches.[2]

The purpose of all of these banks, as Guy S. Callender has written, "consisted in providing the capital for producing and marketing the cotton and sugar of this region."[3] Producing and marketing the South's staple crops required capital improvement loans, that is, long-term mortgage loans for land, slaves, equipment, and buildings. Commercial agriculture also necessitated ample provisions for exchange and, to a lesser extent, for a circulating medium. These were formidable tasks for banks in a new country with little accumulated capital, but Southerners expected their banks to provide the services they required.

To do so, it was often necessary to call upon the states to aid in the creation of banks; until the depression following the crisis of 1837, many of the important Southern banks relied upon extensive state support. One group of banks, the so-called property or plantation banks, were authorized to raise their capital through the sale of mortgage bonds tendered by resident planters. The first of this type of bank, the Consolidated Association of Planters, chartered by the Louisiana legislature in 1827, found it impossible to sell the mortgage bonds, whereupon the state came to the rescue by issuing its own bonds, taking the mortgages as security. The state bonds sold readily to foreign and domestic investors, and subsequent property banks were chartered with the provision that state bonds, backed by real estate mortgages, be sold to supply the banks' capital. Thus did the states lend their credit to bring into existence such banks as the Union Bank and the Citizens' Bank of Louisiana, the Real Estate Bank of Arkansas, and the Union Bank of Mississippi.

State banks of various kinds often received more direct aid from the states. Some, such as the Central Bank of Georgia and the Bank of the State of Alabama, were state owned, with operating capital made up of state monies and the proceeds of the sale of state securities. Others were mixed enterprises; thus the state of Louisiana sold bonds to raise the funds to subscribe for half the stock in the Bank of Louisiana, and the state of Mississippi sold bonds to provide two-thirds of the capital of the Planters' Bank. Even when states did not invest directly in banks their aid was apparent. Until the advent of free banking in the 1840's virtually every Southern bank owed its existence to a special act of the legislature; chartering provisions, by stipulating some state regulation and control, provided a measure of public confidence and thereby helped to draw investment.

[1] Letter dated Feb. 12, 1920, reprinted in U. S. Congress, House, *Report of the Secretary of the Treasury* . . . , 23rd Cong., 1st Sess., House Exec. Doc. 51 (Jan. 14, 1834), 2. Cf. Amasa Walker's dictum that "banks never originate with those who have money to lend, but with those who wish to borrow." *The Nature and Uses of Money and Mixed Currency, with a History of the Wickaboag Bank* (Boston, 1857), 53, as quoted in George Rogers Taylor, *The Transportation Revolution, 1815-1860* (New York, 1951), 311.

[2] U. S. Congress, House, *Condition of State Banks*, 25th Cong., 3rd Sess., House Exec. Doc. 227 (Feb. 27, 1839), 672-79.

[3] "The Early Transportation and Banking Enterprises of the States in Relation to the Growth of Corporations," *Quarterly Journal of Economics*, XVII (Nov. 1902), 162.

The state and property banks regularly offered long-term loans to planters. The property banks especially were organized precisely for this purpose; planters who had given mortgages to secure the state bonds were allowed to borrow from the bank up to 50 percent of the value of their mortgages. State banks also usually made provisions for long-term capital-improvement loans to planters. Combined with their mortgage activities, Southern banks also carried on extensive commercial banking operations. As commercial banks they were expected to facilitate trade through the discounting of notes, bills of exchange, and bills of lading, and as banks of issue they were expected to provide a circulating medium in the absence of adequate supplies of specie.[4]

Although banking theory was rather primitive in the first decades of the nineteenth century, Southerners were not unaware of possible dangers in combining commercial with mortgage banking. If notes, the principal indication of loan liability in the days before deposit loans became important, were to be convertible on demand to specie—a requirement for a sound circulating medium—then banks had to be in a position to convert loans to cash quickly so as to meet sudden demands by holders of notes. Long-term mortgage loans to farmers did not meet this requirement. At best, warned William H. Crawford, in the midst of hard times following the crisis of 1819, only half a bank's capital might safely be loaned to agriculturalists. Nor were short-term loans to farmers the answer. "The returns of capital invested in agriculture are too slow and distant to justify engagements with banks, except upon long credits." The economic difficulties many farmers were facing, Crawford argued, stemmed from their being called upon to repay

---

[4] There is no full-scale study of ante bellum Southern banking. A convenient summary of the charter provisions of some of the leading Southern banks may be found in Earl Sylvester Sparks, *History and Theory of Agricultural Credit in the United States* (New York, 1932), 84-111. See also Davis R. Dewey, *State Banking Before the Civil War* (Washington, D. C., 1910), *passim*, but esp. 19, 33-36, 48, 158, 160-61; Fritz Redlich, *The Molding of American Banking: Men and Ideas* (New York, 1947), I, 205-208; J. Van Fenstermaker, *The Development of American Commercial Banking: 1782-1837* (Kent, Ohio, 1965), *passim*. For state studies see Milton S. Heath, *Constructive Liberalism: The Role of the State in Economic Development in Georgia to 1860* (Cambridge, Mass., 1954), 159-230; Stephen A. Caldwell, *A Banking History of Louisiana* (Baton Rouge, 1935), 30-89; W. A. Clark, *The History of the Banking Institutions Organized in South Carolina Prior to 1860* (Columbia, S. C., 1922); William H. Brantley, *Banking in Alabama: 1816-1860*, Vol. I (Birmingham, Ala., 1961); Charles Hillman Brough, "The History of Banking in Mississippi," *Publications of the Mississippi Historical Society*, III (1900), 317-40.

short-term loans before returns from their agricultural operations were available.[5]

Despite such warnings, Southern states regularly chartered institutions that combined commercial with mortgage banking. Charters usually set down stringent rules to regulate mortgage loans, ordinarily placing a maximum on the size of loan any single individual could receive and limiting long-term agricultural loans to a proportion—usually half—of the capital stock of the bank. Had such regulations been universally observed, most Southern banks might have remained both solvent and liquid while granting long-term loans to planters. But the exhilaration of flush times, "that golden era, when shin-plasters were the sole currency; when bank-bills were 'as thick as Autumn leaves in Vallambrosa,' and credit was a franchise,"[6] often made charter restraints meaningless. Not only were long-term loans made on dubious security but often on the basis of capital not yet paid in, or paid in in the form of a personal note, or even with funds first borrowed from the bank itself.[7]

Such dubious banking practices might go unnoticed during flush times, but they could not be sustained in times of economic contraction. The crisis of 1837 and the depression that followed devastated Southern banking. Unable to meet their obligations, the banks were forced to suspend specie payments. Many proved to be insolvent and closed their doors forever; others managed to resume specie payments and eventually to reopen. Everywhere suspension and failure brought renewed attention to banks and banking policies. In some states a revulsion against banking virtually ended the chartering of banks after the depression. Mississippi in 1850 reported only one bank "with a very limited capital" in the state and seven years later, when the country again faced financial panic, the governor took pride in the fact that the state had only two small banks, "Mississippi having almost wholly rid herself of the banking system for more than fifteen years past."[8]

[5] Letter dated Feb. 12, 1820, reprinted in U. S. Congress, House, *Report of the Secretary of the Treasury* [1834], 12.

[6] Joseph G. Baldwin, *The Flush Times of Alabama and Mississippi* (New York, 1853), 1.

[7] See Reginald Charles McGrane, *The Panic of 1837* (Chicago, 1965), 24-27. (First published in 1924.)

[8] Samuel Stumps (Mississippi secretary of state) to W. M. Meredith (U. S. secretary of the treasury), Jan. 22, 1850, Jackson, Miss., in U. S. Congress, House,

A similar revulsion against all banking gripped Arkansas and Florida, and when Texas entered the union in 1845, its constitution forbade the chartering of banks by the state.[9]

Other states, recognizing the continued need for banking facilities, sought to correct abuses and to institute stringent regulation. The dangers of combining commercial banking with mortgage banking once again were raised. A joint committee of the Kentucky legislature insisted that the only safe banking was commercial banking; long-term mortgage banking could not be combined with commercial banking without doing injury to both the agricultural and business community.[10] This contention was disputed in 1843 by F. H. Elmore, the president of the Bank of the State of South Carolina. Admitting the hazards inherent in allowing commercial banks of issue to grant long-term loans, he would not, however, agree that the hazards justified prohibiting long-term loans. He argued that a bank could "safely and profitably loan a part of its funds on bonds and mortgages and long notes, and yet perform the functions of a bank of circulation—promptly redeeming its notes with specie." It was the duty of responsible bank officials to determine the proper proportion of short- and long-term loans so as to promote safety while providing for the legitimate needs of the people.[11] Edmond J. Forstall, New Orleans merchant,

Condition of the Banks in the United States, 31st Cong., 1st Sess., House Exec. Doc. 68 (May 16, 1850), 299; Gov. McRae to Mississippi Legislature, Nov. 2, 1857, in U. S. Congress, House, Condition of the Banks Throughout the United States, 35th Cong., 1st Sess., House Exec. Doc. 107 (April 27, 1858), 214.

[9] Paul B. Trescott, Financing American Enterprise: The Story of Commercial Banking (New York, 1963), 33; Bray Hammond, Banks and Politics in America from the Revolution to the Civil War (Princeton, N. J., 1957), 614-17. Hammond mistakenly writes that Arkansas entered the Union in 1846 with a constitutional prohibition against chartering of banks. Arkansas, of course, entered the Union in 1836. The first act of the first general assembly was to set up the Real Estate Bank. As a result of what the legislature considered abuses by the bank during the panic, a constitutional amendment declaring that "no bank or banking institution shall be hereafter incorporated or established in this State" was ratified during the 1846-1847 session of the legislature. "Report of a joint committee of the legislature . . . January, 1857," in U. S. Congress, House, Condition of the Banks, Doc. 107, 216, 229.

[10] U. S. Congress, House, Condition of State Banks, 25th Cong., 2nd Sess., House Exec. Doc. 79 (Jan. 8, 1838), 760-62.

[11] Report of F. H. Elmore . . . , Nov. 23, 1843, in U. S. Congress, House, Bank Returns, 29th Cong., 1st Sess., House Exec. Doc. 226 (Aug. 10, 1846), 630-31. Elmore added that he was speaking from his experience in 1839: "Of the seven banks in Charleston, six were purely commercial—rejecting bonds and such securities in their operations; and of these, five suspended specie payments, while this bank

banker, and sugar planter, concurred in this opinion. It is necessary to separate long-term accommodation paper from short-term business paper, he warned the stockholders of the Citizens' Bank of Louisiana in January 1839. "Any bank, be its capital what it may, trusting the repayment of its loans on accommodation to meet its circulation, places itself in the power of the public, and loses its efficiency," he explained.[12]

The experiences of bank failure led bankers and legislators to take such advice seriously. While banks disappeared altogether in Mississippi and Arkansas, they became much more conservative in the other cotton states. The Alabama legislature, which had created the state-owned Bank of the State of Alabama in 1823, severed completely its relationship with banking institutions. Deprived of the state's credit, sobered by the experiences of the depression, and aware of the constant scrutiny of the legislature, Alabama banking was sharply curtailed in the period after 1840. Total banking capital in the state declined from almost twelve million in 1838 to a little over three million in 1858; total loans and discounts dropped from almost twenty-six million to about five and a half million during the same period, while specie holdings remained about the same.[13]

Banking facilities remained more abundant in Georgia and South Carolina, although banks in these states also limited loans. In both states, legislative enactments in 1840 required chartered banks to resume specie payments and imposed penalties including loss of charter and foreclosure of any bank suspending in the future.[14] Bankers were understandably cautious. In Georgia it was not until 1857 that banking facilities reached 1838 levels. South Carolina was more liberal; by the end of 1857 bank capital had risen about 66 percent and loans and discounts about 45 percent over 1838 levels.[15] Neither state enacted legislation dealing

---

met and redeemed in specie all its notes as presented, and at the same time paid off more than a million of dollars of other liabilities."

[12] Forstall to the Stockholders of the Citizens' Bank of Louisiana, New Orleans, Jan. 23, 1839, in U. S. Congress, House, *Condition of the State Banks*, 26th Cong., 2nd Sess., House Exec. Doc. 111 (March 3, 1841), 792.

[13] U. S. Congress, House, *Condition of State Banks*, Doc. 227, p. 675; U. S. Congress, House, *Condition of the Banks*, Doc. 107, pp. 192, 193-96.

[14] Heath, *Constructive Liberalism*, 209; Clark, *History of Banking Institutions in South Carolina*, 149-52; Alfred Glaze Smith, Jr., *Economic Readjustment of an Old Cotton State: South Carolina, 1820-1860* (Columbia, S. C., 1958), 196-216.

[15] See reports from the banks of these two states in U. S. Congress, House,

with the vexing problem of the proper relationship between long-
and short-term loans; proper discretion was left to responsible bank
officials.

Only in Louisiana did legislation clearly delimit the extent of
long-term loans which could be given by the banks. Authored by
Edmond J. Forstall, the Louisiana banking law of 1842 was
rigorously conservative. Under its provisions, long-term credit
could be extended only to the extent of the bank's capital; deposits
could be loaned only on a short-term basis (90 days maximum),
and banks were required to keep at least one-third of their public
liabilities—notes and deposits—on hand in specie. The law gave
the state a sound currency backed by ample specie reserves and
short-term commercial paper; at the same time it severely restricted
the long-term loans available to the agricultural community.[16]

Thus in every cotton state before 1839, long-term mortgage loans
were available to planters. The depression following the crisis of
1837 diminished but did not completely dry up these loans in the
1840's and 1850's. A combination of restrictive legislation and
caution born of experience led to stringent limitations on long-term
mortgage or capital-improvement loans. Adding to the clamor in
the early 1840's for restrictions on banks were the complaints of
those who had suffered from the unfortunate participation of many
Southern banks in cotton speculation which had followed the crisis
of 1837.

Ordinarily Southern banks, like those elsewhere in the country,
did not participate directly in marketing but confined their
business to financing production and trade.[17] Early charters usually
prohibited banks from buying and selling real estate[18] (except that
needed for the carrying on of business) and commodities, but

Condition of State Banks, Doc. 227, pp. 672, 673; U. S. Congress, House, *Condition
of the Banks,* Doc. 107, p. 328.

[16] Caldwell, *Banking History of Louisiana,* 71-89; Bray Hammond, "Long and
Short Term Credit in Early American Banking," *Quarterly Journal of Economics,*
XLIX (Nov. 1934), 97-100; Redlich, *Molding of American Banking,* II, 32-40;
Leonard C. Halderman, *National and State Banks* (Boston, 1931), 91-97; Hammond,
Banks and Politics, 680-85. When Georgia banks suspended in the crisis of 1857-
1858, many urged that the state enact laws similar to those in Louisiana, pointing
out that Louisiana banks did not suspend during the crisis. See Heath, *Constructive
Liberalism,* 225.

[17] Dewey, *State Banking Before the Civil War,* 43-48.

[18] See Clark, *History of Banking Institutions in South Carolina,* 53, 61 for examples of charter restrictions.

custom rather than law seems to have kept Southern banks out of the cotton business before 1837. Two Alabama banks, the Planter's and Merchant's Bank of Huntsville and the Tombeckbe Bank in St. Stephens, were exceptions. Although neither bank purchased cotton outright, both were actively engaged in marketing the crop during 1819 and 1820. In October 1819, Israel Pickens, the president of the Tombeckbe Bank, announced that the board of directors of the bank had appointed an agent "to take charge of all cotton which may be delivered for shipment." The bank was to pay all marketing costs, which were then to be repaid out of the proceeds of the crop. Pickens' announcement gave no further details, but his action did prompt a local paper to charge that the bank had become a commission merchant.[19] The following year LeRoy Pope, the president of the Planter's and Merchant's Bank, proposed a similar plan to planters in the Huntsville area. His proposal was much more specific. He proposed "to receive on consignment, from one to six thousand bales of cotton, which he will ship on account and risk of the owner to any port in the United States that the owner may direct; and will advance on the delivery of the cotton in Huntsville, or any safe place on the Tennessee River, TEN CENTS per pound; and will play the balance of the net proceeds at the Huntsville Bank as soon as the cotton is sold and the money received.[20] The bank itself did not make the sale; this was left to the factors to whom the bank shipped the cotton. The bank did provide an advance (for which interest was charged) and did pay the expenses of the sale.[21] By this procedure it assumed the risks inherent in advancing on unsold cotton, risks ordinarily taken by the factor.[22] The evidence indicates that this practice was extremely rare and, with one important exception, the banks usually remained only indirect participants in the marketing of the cotton crop.

The one exception occurred in the few years following the crisis

[19] Brantley, *Banking in Alabama*, I, 43-44.

[20] "To the Cotton Planters of Madison County and the Tennessee Valley," *Alabama Republican*, Oct. 13, 1820, as reprinted *ibid.*, 26.

[21] *Betts* v. *The Planter's & Merchant's Bank of Huntsville*, 3 Stewart (Ala.), 18 (1830).

[22] As will be shown, banks often shared the risks with the factor by discounting factors' notes, bills of lading, and planters' notes carrying a factor's endorsement. In these instances the primary risk was borne by the merchant. The procedure of the Alabama banks described here reversed the process and thereby increased the risk taken by the bank.

of 1837 and ended in disaster for bankers and planters alike. The failure of many of the leading cotton factors and the disruption of regular channels of trade and credit drew first the United States Bank of Philadelphia and then many Southern banks into cotton speculation. Nicholas Biddle provided the initial leadership; in a public letter to John Quincy Adams, he explained that the move was a temporary expedient made necessary because "the derangement of the currency placed the staples of the south entirely at the mercy of the foreign purchaser, who could have dictated the terms to the prostrated planter. It was thought proper to avert that evil by employing a large portion of the capital of the bank in making advances on southern produce. . . . These . . . were measures of emergency, adopted in the midst of a public calamity, and to be discontinued with the necessity which caused them."[23]

Obviously aware that he was departing from ordinary banking procedures, Biddle felt himself justified by the extraordinary state of the market.[24] He and other officers of the United States Bank advanced money on cotton which they then sent to their own agent, Humphreys and Biddle, in Liverpool with instructions to hold for a rise in prices. The transaction was financed through the sale of United States Bank securities in Europe. The plan was simple enough: by advancing funds on cotton Biddle allowed planters to meet their current obligations without forcing a sale at low prices; it was hoped that by withholding substantial amounts of cotton from the market prices would be forced up.[25]

[23] Letter dated Philadelphia, Dec. 10, 1838, printed in *Financial Register* (Philadelphia), II (Dec. 19, 1838), 393.

[24] Banker-historian Bray Hammond, a warm admirer of Biddle, wrote that his action was "irregular." "Banks," he explained, "like women, are not supposed to take the initiative. They consider proposals and say yes or no. This spreads the risk inherent in enterprise; it subjects the judgment of enterprisers to independent scrutiny, and though the banks, if they acquiesce, take some risk, they retain recourse upon the enterprisers and their property if the projects fail." *Banks and Politics*, 469. Nevertheless, Hammond argued, the times called for irregular action. The inaction of the Democratic administration "clutching its inheritance of Jacksonian clichés" forced Biddle to take the initiative in an attempt to save the economy. Hammond compared Biddle's action to the "humming, untrammeled energy with which the administration of Franklin D. Roosevelt moved against a similar crisis ninety-six years later." *Ibid.*, 528-29. Arthur M. Schlesinger, Jr., who also finds New Deal parallels in the Jacksonian period, does not find them in Biddle; he comes to quite contrary evaluations of Biddle's cotton transactions. *The Age of Jackson* (New York, 1945), 264-65.

[25] For details concerning Biddle's activities see Thomas Payne Govan, *Nicholas Biddle* (Chicago, 1959), 320-25, 336, 339-41, 344-46, 349-51, 357-59, 370-71, 381-82, 385-87; Hammond, *Banks and Politics*, 467-77, 502-504, 519-22; 528-31;

While Biddle was advancing on cotton, a number of Southern banks were drawn into similar activities. A convention of Georgia bankers meeting in Milledgeville in September 1837 resolved "to increase their loans for the purchase of the ensuing crop of cotton."[26] The Mobile branch of the Bank of the State of Alabama, after noting the distress in the market, decided on May 15, 1837 "to purchase bills predicated on the shipments of cotton, on the express condition that the cotton should be sent to a known agent in Liverpool, to be sold to meet bills drawn on such shipments."[27] The first year of such operations seemed successful; indeed, Biddle and others pocketed a substantial profit and cotton prices rallied. "But for the United States Bank, and the other banks of our country that came into the market," a Liverpool correspondent wrote to the *New York Herald* in July 1838, ". . . the value of our present cotton crop would have been $10,000,000 less than it will fetch."[28]

Initial success, however, was followed by disaster. After first indicating that he would stay out of the market, Biddle changed his mind and began buying and making advances on the crop of 1838-1839. Similarly, numerous Southern banks continued their operations in cotton during the new crop year. This time British money was not readily available. A crop failure in England forced British money into the purchase of grain imports. The resulting stringency of funds along with a falling demand forced cotton onto the market, leading to a serious decline in prices. Sale proceeds seldom covered the large advances given to planters and the result was often financial ruin.

The disastrous results which followed the banks' direct participation in moving the cotton crop apparently ended this practice. Indeed, objections to the practice and warnings of its probable effects had been raised even before the final calamity. The *New York Journal of Commerce*, while granting that the banks had

---

L. H. Jenks, *The Migration of British Capital to 1875* (New York, 1938), 88-98; Ralph W. Hidy, *The House of Baring in American Trade and Finance* (Cambridge, Mass., 1949), 240-42; Halderman, *National and State Banks*, 69-76, 85-86; Rose Irene Mautz, "Anglo-American Trade Relations in Cotton, 1830-1840" (unpublished M.A. thesis, University of Chicago, 1937), 67-90.

[26] U. S. Congress, House, *Condition of State Banks*, Doc. 79, p. 504.

[27] *Ibid.*, 510-12.

[28] Letter from Liverpool dated July 10, 1838, reprinted from *New York Herald* in *Financial Register* (Philadelphia), II (Aug. 29, 1838), 140. See also *Niles' Register*, LIV (Aug. 11, 1838), 384.

acted correctly in aiding the movement of the crops in 1837—"for there seemed no other means of moving the produce of the country"—objected to the banks' continued "interference." The business of marketing the crop should return to the merchants and the banks should resume their normal sphere of operations, the paper argued in the fall of 1838. Conditions no longer warranted continued direct participation in cotton marketing by the banks and such action "ought to meet the most determined resistance." Both the merchant and the banking community will suffer, the paper warned. Since only the banks had the power to issue bills, they could exert undue influence by depriving the merchants of these bills in order to take the business for themselves. Moreover, a bank engaging in trade "hazards its solvency, and consequently the soundness of the currency. Institutions charged especially with issuing money, it will never be safe to trust in the hazards of speculation and general trade."[29]

There was already ample evidence in the South that this concern was not without foundation. In Mississippi, for example, the banks bought and accepted on consignment large quantities of cotton, giving good prices and advances in the form of their own notes. Relief, however, was illusory; Mississippi bank currency soon depreciated sharply. "The planters find the depreciated currency will not pay for their supplies, unless at exorbitant prices, and that the high rates they received for their cotton was a mere delusion of the bank system," warned a financial journal. The merchants, too, suffered. Having bought their goods from the North on credit and sold them for Mississippi currency, they found that their money was greatly discounted when sent to New York to pay their bills.[30] In August 1838 the Mississippi bank commissioners reported that the currency issued by the bank for the advances given on cotton was inflated and that the planters could buy no more for their money than if they had been given only legitimate advances.[31] Hardship was common in the state; many planters lost their plantations when unable to make up the difference between the advance they had received and the proceeds on their crops. There was even a reported danger of violence and bloodshed.[32]

29 Reprinted in *Financial Register* (Philadelphia), II (Oct. 10, 1838), 234-35.
30 *Ibid.* (July 11, 1838), 29.
31 *Ibid.* (Oct. 24, 1838), 268.
32 *Ibid.* (July 18, 1838), 43.

Nevertheless, Southern banks continued to give advances for the 1838-1839 season. At the end of August 1838, the board of directors of the Bank of the State of Alabama at Tuscaloosa offered advances to planters who consigned cotton to be sold by the bank's agents in New Orleans, New York, Liverpool, or Mobile. The bank guaranteed that the cotton so shipped would be held a minimum of four months so that the best price could be obtained. In addition, the bank indicated it would give advances on the growing crop provided planters promised to send a sufficient amount of their crop to the bank to cover the advances.[33] Mississippi bankers also continued their cotton transactions. The Mississippi Union Bank at Natchez, for example, offered advances of $60 per bale "to planters who desire to postpone their sales" until prices went up.[34] At the same time, Mississippi banks attempted to maintain the value of the currency they were issuing. They purchased provisions and other plantation supplies which they resold to planters for Mississippi bank notes at New Orleans prices.[35]

As it became increasingly evident that these extraordinary activities by the banks were not producing the desired results, indeed that they were compounding the difficulty by undermining the currency, opposition grew stronger. Bank commissioners in Alabama, in a report dated December 3, 1839, charged that the cotton transactions of the State Bank were illegal and unwise. After investigating the bank's charter the commissioners concluded that the bank managers "had no legal authority" to create agencies to give advances on cotton. Moreover, they noted, the bank had advanced over a million dollars through these illegal agencies, a sum they estimated as at least $300,000 more than the cotton was worth. The tragedy was being compounded by the fact that "the bank is still engaged in making advances on cotton."[36]

In Mississippi the governor in January 1839 charged that the banks of his state were "all . . . more or less, engaged in speculation." Furthermore, they issued notes far beyond their capacity to redeem them and thereby saddled the state with a depreciated currency.

[33] Statement dated Aug. 29, 1838, reprinted from the *New York Journal of Commerce, ibid.* (Oct. 10, 1838), 235-36.

[34] *Ibid.* (Dec. 12, 1838), 380.

[35] U. S. Congress, House, *Condition of the State Banks,* 26th Cong., 1st Sess., House Exec. Doc. 172 (April 9, 1840), 522-42.

[36] *Ibid.,* 451-52.

"Excess of circulation has increased the cost of producing cotton at least three fold, but has not enhanced the price of the article a single farthing. Its direct tendency is to impoverish the planting and ruin the mercantile interest." The governor accused the banking interest of a "monstrous assumption of power," inasmuch as it sought "to monopolize the cotton crop of the State" and become "a factor and shipper of our great staple."[37]

By 1840 it had become very clear that direct participation by the banks in moving the crops was unwise and unprofitable and business resumed its accustomed channels. The brief foray of the bankers into cotton marketing had left many banks insolvent and had caused hardship and ruin to many planters, an experience which helped to reinforce the prevailing antibank sentiments in many Southern states and which gave added ammunition to those who would prohibit or severely restrain the banks. Nicholas Biddle had argued that his cotton operations had been undertaken simply to revive trade; Southern bankers could—and did—point out that without their help cotton would not be sold, debts could not be paid, and the planting and mercantile interest of the South would meet with ruin.[38] Biddle's biographer, Thomas P. Govan, agrees: "Once Biddle's agents commenced buying cotton, others joined in, and the bills of exchange thus provided were used to pay interregional and international debts."[39] Thus the actions of the banks were serving to expand the currency in a period of disastrous contraction. Govan concludes that it was not Biddle who was in error, but rather the Van Buren administration and its followers with their delusions of hard money and a return to specie payments combined with their refusal to countenance government aid in heading off a depression. With proper cooperation between government and the banks, "many of the subsequent economic troubles of the nation would have been avoided."[40]

[37] *Ibid.*, 474-78.

[38] "So soon as the embarrassments of the commercial world began to develop themselves, exchange was declined; still, much cotton was on hand and unsold; the planters could not pay debts due, nor purchase supplies; all demands for curtailments of accounts were answered by an entire failure to pay; exchange based on cotton began to return, and the suspended debt rapidly increased." Thus did the Mobile branch of the Bank of the State of Alabama describe the distress which induced its cotton operations. U. S. Congress, House, *Condition of State Banks*, Doc. 79, p. 510.

[39] *Nicholas Biddle*, 371.

[40] *Ibid.* Bray Hammond agrees with this evaluation, describing Biddle's actions

It is beyond the scope of this study to evaluate Biddle's activities on a national level. Suffice it to note, however, that the cooperation was absent—understandably, given the conflict between New York and Philadelphia and the general antagonism toward Biddle engendered by the long bank fight. Initial success in ending commercial stagnation in 1837 could not be sustained, perhaps as Douglass C. North has suggested, because by 1839 "monetary and external influences . . . were combined with the real effects of a decade of uninhibited expansion of productive capacity, which necessarily entailed a long period of adjustment."[41] In any case, economic difficulties in Europe and the raising of the interest rate on bills of exchange by the Bank of England marked a renewed downturn in 1839. Nor did the continued cotton operations by the United States Bank in 1839 aid matters. English manufacturers, fearing the bank was attempting a monopoly, cut back production and lowered demand for cotton as Biddle was accumulating large stores of the article.[42]

If Biddle and the Southern bankers could argue that their aid was required in 1837, there seemed to have been less justification for continued investment in cotton after prices rallied. Matters other than the desire to promote the nation's trade were involved. Biddle's agents were anxious to continue making purchases so as to continue their profitable ventures of the previous year.[43] Moreover, a group of Southerners, heartened by Biddle's success in 1837, had organized a Cotton Planters' Convention through which they hoped to centralize the cotton trade through Southern ports, bypassing Northern and European middlemen. The dream of direct trade from Southern ports to European manufacturers, controlled by a Southern association backed by Southern banks, led them to urge the banks to continue cotton operations.[44] In a word, the very success of the 1837 operations led those who had profited to continue.

---

as "a major resort to monetary measures for the alleviation of economic disorder, inertia, and distress." *Banks and Politics*, 529.

[41] *The Economic Growth of the United States, 1790-1860* (Englewood Cliffs, N. J., 1961), 202. For a similar contemporary evaluation, see *DeBow's Review*, IV (1847), 85-86.

[42] See the discussion of these matters in McGrane, *The Panic of 1837*, 177-208.

[43] Govan, *Nicholas Biddle*, 357-58.

[44] *Ibid.*, 321, 358-59; Thomas Payne Govan, "An Ante-Bellum Attempt to Regulate the Price and Supply of Cotton," *North Carolina Historical Review*, XVII (Oct. 1940), 302-12.

In the South, interstate rivalry was also a factor inducing continued cotton operations by the banks. Many Mississippians, for example, saw the banks' cotton loans as a means to free planters from local, but especially New Orleans, middlemen. In January 1839, a joint committee of the Mississippi legislature reported that the cotton operations of the Union Bank were beneficial to the planter:

> When your committee remembered the extravagant and unlimited extent to which, on former periods, the banks of the State permitted the mercantile houses of our own State and New Orleans to absorb their means, thus constituting them the only channels through which the planter could obtain any banking facilities, they have been gratified to find that the Union Bank have pursued a more correct course, and one better calculated to advance the planting interest, and put it on a footing with other pursuits, by furnishing the planter directly from the bank, without his incurring additional expense in the way of commissions, acceptances, &c.[45]

Henry S. Foote, a member of the joint committee, disagreed with this positive assessment of the Union Bank's cotton business and issued a minority report. He did not disagree with the aim of bypassing the New Orleans factors; his objection was that the bank's cotton operations would not have the salutary effect described in the majority report. The purpose of the bank, he argued, was to end the situation where "the substantial citizens of the State" were unable to get funds "except upon the presentation of the *acceptance* of one of those thrice glorious potentates, the commission merchants of New Orleans." Yet the cotton policy of the bank, if continued, would have the reverse effect. Indeed, he pointed out, the cotton business was already falling into the hands of a favored few. One member of the bank's cotton agency —that is, the firm selling the cotton consigned to the bank—was also a member of the board of managers of the bank; moreover, two of the commission merchants who had received the greatest number of acceptances from the bank were also members of the board of managers. Although he did not question the honesty of these men, Foote did raise the specter of monopoly.[46]

---

[45] U. S. Congress, House, *Condition of the State Banks*, Doc. 172, p. 557.
[46] *Ibid.*, 583-87.

Thus there was no coordinated plan in the cotton operations carried out by Biddle and his associates and the Southern banks. If Biddle saw his activities as a temporary expedient to meet a short-term problem, others had very different ideas. The banks did not have the resources to sustain the market in 1839 and the inevitable revulsion set in. In early 1840, just a year after the majority of the Mississippi committee investigating the Union Bank had found the cotton operations beneficial, another committee came to precisely opposite conclusions. The whole of the cotton transactions was probably illegal, the committee concluded; but even if legal, the transactions were unwise as far too much was advanced on the cotton. Again, the question of special privileges was raised: "Another great evil of the cotton business was its tending to create a monopoly of bank facilities in the hands of a few large planters and cotton speculators to the prejudice of other meritorious classes of the community, and contrary to any principle of discounts prescribed by the charter of the bank."[47]

The committee suggested that the banks be prohibited from carrying on such operations in the future,[48] and the Mississippi legislature complied with appropriate legislation on February 21, 1840.[49] A similar law was passed in Georgia in the same year.[50] Although the role of the banks in marketing cotton had apparently not been illegal,[51] it had obviously proved unsound. In the future, popular pressure and explicit law, both born of the disasters of 1837-1840, would keep Southern banks primarily in the area of exchange, with only a limited portion of their resources being made available for long-term capital-improvement loans.

[47] *Ibid.*, 682.
[48] *Ibid.*
[49] *Ibid.*, 687.
[50] Dewey, *State Banking Before the Civil War*, 48.
[51] In Alabama, a planter who had suffered heavy losses through his participation in the cotton activities of the Bank of the State of Alabama initiated litigation against the bank. The Alabama Supreme Court in 1841 decided that the bank's actions were not illegal. William Garrett, *Reminiscences of Public Men in Alabama* (Atlanta, 1872), 267-77.

CHAPTER TEN

Bankers and Factors

Emphasis on short-term commercial loans usually forced planters to deal with the banks indirectly through their factors. This was very obvious, but puzzling, to an English visitor to Charleston late in the 1850's: "It must strike every one as a singular feature in the banking system of Charleston, that a broker [factor], who may be a mere man of straw, can get his bills cashed at the banks, whereas, those of a really substantial planter, owning large and most valuable properties would not be looked at; yet, such is the practice of these banks. I presume that there must be some good and sufficient reason for this, but I certainly failed in discovering it."[1] There was reason enough, of course. Loans to factors were short-term commercial loans, usually running from 30 to 90 days and secured by bills of exchange, merchandise in storage or transit, and the good name and reputation as well as the tangible assets of the factors. Experience had taught Southern bankers that such loans protected the liquidity and hence the safety of their banks.

Planters in need of funds, then, turned most often to their factors rather than to the banks. Yet it might be the bank and not the factor that ultimately supplied the credit required. Thus, a planter in need of an advance from his factor might be asked to sign a note which the factor, if necessary, could discount at the bank. Typical was the procedure of John Hagan and Company, factors of New Orleans, who in March 1828 wrote the Louisiana planter William S. Hamilton that they were willing to advance him money on the security of his next crop. Hamilton was authorized to draw on the factors for whatever funds he might need. The merchants added that "as we may not find it very convenient to lay out . . . this money during the summer months, we enclose a note for your signature for which if necessary we can obtain the funds through [the] Bank."[2] The planter's note, then, was more than an indication of his indebtedness; it also served, with the factor's endorsement, as a means for receiving money from the bank.

Should problems arise in sending cotton to market, a factor who had advanced large sums of money to a planter might arrange to be reimbursed via a bank before the cotton was sold. For example, in April 1855, Peter T. Hickman was unable to ship his cotton to his New Orleans factor, R. W. Estlin and Company, because of low water in the Red River. "If Red River does not rise soon we will send you up some paper to sign to reimburse us for advances," the factor wrote on April 26. Four days later the factor calculated the planter's debt at about $27,000 and sent five notes of $5,000 each, "which please sign and return to us & we will try to have them negotiated on the best possible terms to reimburse us." Two of the notes were subsequently discounted "in the Citizens Bank at 100 and 120 days date at 8%."[3]

Although it was the planter's note which was being discounted, making him the actual borrower, he required the intervening services of the factor.[4] The planter's notes were discounted only after the factor had added his endorsement. This, of course, changed the whole nature of the loan: banks were lending not on the security of a plantation, slaves, or cotton but on the liquid assets of a city merchant. In a word, by adding his endorsement

[1] Leonard Wray, "The Culture and Preparation of Cotton in the United States of America, &c.," *Journal of the Society of Arts*, VII (Dec. 1958), 82.

[2] Letter dated New Orleans, March 12, 1828, W. S. Hamilton Papers, Southern Historical Collection, University of North Carolina Library, Chapel Hill, N. C.

[3] Letters dated New Orleans, April 26, 30, May 23, 1855, Hickman-Bryan Papers, Joint Collection, Western Historical Manuscripts Collection, State Historical Society of Missouri Manuscripts, Columbia, Mo.

[4] See Thomas P. Govan, "Banking and the Credit System in Georgia, 1810-1860," *Journal of Southern History*, IV (May 1938), 178-79; Charles S. Davis, *The Cotton Kingdom in Alabama* (Montgomery, Ala., 1939), 155-56. Factors dealing in the other staple crops could discount planters' notes at banks in much the same way. See J. Carlyle Sitterson, "Financing and Marketing the Sugar Crop of the Old South," *Journal of Southern History*, X (May 1944), 191.

to the planter's note, the factor was guaranteeing the payment of the note at maturity. Even when a planter dealt directly with a bank, the factor's endorsement was usually necessary. Thus, for example, a Savannah factor informed the agent of a bank in Americus, Georgia, that one William M. James "is authorized to draw on us." James' notes "will be at 40 days" and the factor promised to "accept and pay his dfts at Maturity."[5]

Some endorsements were better than others; that is, they would be more likely to be readily discounted by the banks. A well-known house in a major market with a large business would be a better risk than a smaller firm. This is amply illustrated in a letter to an Augusta factor from his agent in Montgomery. The agent had been asked to collect a debt owed the Augusta factor by one K. L. Cunningham:

> According to agreement Mr Cunningham came down today to effect a settlement of your claim. I was very much in hopes he would have given me a Mobile acceptance as he had written to a house to get their acceptance but had received no answer but rather than delay or defer the settlement longer I agreed to take his bill of Exchange payable here at five Months with Gilmer & Co acceptance and have made a settlement with him in that way believing that after the bill has run 80 or 90 days it can be discounted with Interest off which would make the settlement equal to a 90 day paper a little longer than you suggested in your note to me. It may be that the note can be discounted even before that time as it is as good as need be and will be met promptly.[6]

Mobile was a larger market than Montgomery and the Augusta factor hoped for a ninety-day note endorsed by a Mobile merchant. He knew that such a note would be readily discounted. By taking a longer note out of Montgomery, the Augusta factor had to wait for his money although his agent assured him that Gilmer and Company, the Montgomery acceptor, was a good risk.

In essence, when banks discounted planters' notes with their factors' endorsements, they were lending on promissory notes

[5] Behn & Foster to H. R. Johnson, Savannah, Nov. 1, 1858, Harrold Brothers Papers, Emory University Library, Atlanta, Ga.

[6] E. M. Burton to J. R. Simpson, Montgomery, Sept. 10, 1858, Stephen D. Heard Papers, Southern Historical Collection, University of North Carolina Library, Chapel Hill, N. C.

rather than on the exchange of real property. Such notes were fraught with danger because they were limited not by specific transactions but rather by the judgment of the banker concerning the solvency of the planter and his factor. Often termed "accommodation paper," these promissory notes could be—and sometimes were—transformed into long-term agricultural loans by means of periodic renewals or through the acceptance of a second note to pay the first.[7] This was a typical means whereby a factor carried his planter customer over a year without tying up large sums of his own money. Thus in late May 1832, John Hagan and Company informed William S. Hamilton that his account showed a balance owed the factor. The factor asked Hamilton to draw on him and then discount the note at the bank. The proceeds were then to be forwarded to the factor.[8]

The discounting of accommodation paper was an important element in the flush times of the 1830's, although few seemed to have understood its implications. An exception was Edmond J. Forstall, who argued that accommodation paper was long-term paper as distinct from business paper and should be treated as such. This distinction was included in the Louisiana Bank Law of 1842, which he wrote.[9]

Accommodation paper continued to be important in the 1840's and 1850's in part because its real nature was imperfectly understood, in part because it was the accustomed method of doing business, and in part because it was not always possible to distinguish accommodation from business paper.

Often other forms of paper in the market took on the appearance of accommodation paper. It was common practice, for example, for a planter or storekeeper to draw upon his factor after shipping cotton to him. The bill, accepted by the factor who had the cotton on hand, would seem to be the best of business paper. Sale of the cotton would put the factor in funds and he could then easily pay the bill which had been drawn on him when it was presented by the bank. The bill was short-term and secured

[7] See Fritz Redlich, *The Molding of American Banking: Men and Ideas* (New York, 1947), I, 10-12, 43-48.

[8] Letter dated New Orleans, May 28, 1832, W. S. Hamilton Papers.

[9] See Edmond J. Forstall to the Stockholders of the Citizens' Bank of Louisiana, New Orleans, Jan. 23, 1839, printed in U. S. Congress, House, *Condition of the State Banks*, 26th Cong., 2nd Sess., House Exec. Doc. 111 (March 3, 1841), 790-94. See also Redlich, *Molding of American Banking*, II, 34, 38-39.

by a real transaction in actual produce. The bank would merely be lending its resources for the period between the time the cotton was shipped and when it was sold. The planter (or store-keeper) by having funds available immediately would be able to pay his bills and his creditors would then be able to pay theirs. Thus, the bank's credit, issued in the form of its bills, would eventually return to the bank for redemption. The result was obvious: a bank's issue was limited and secured by real values while at the same time ample funds were available for smooth commercial transactions.[10]

Yet, this entire procedure rested on the assumption that the original advance did not exceed the value of the crop when sold. Should prices fall before a sale were made, the proceeds might not cover the advance and the result would be that a part of the original note (the difference between the advance and the actual proceeds) was an accommodation loan based merely on the credit of the factor and not on merchandise on hand.

It was the bankers' responsibility, therefore, to be discreet when discounting paper. Forstall, who argued that accommo-dation and business paper had to be kept separate, stated that loans on business paper were short term, "payable in full at maturity." Therefore, he suggested, renewals of such business paper should be prohibited "unless forced by extraordinary circum-stances," in which case the loan should be considered as an accommodation and real estate security should be required.[11] In the Louisiana Bank Law of 1842, business paper had to be payable in full at maturity and those who applied for an extension or renewal were to have their accounts closed and their failure to meet their obligations publicized.[12] This, of course, provided no automatic safeguard; the responsibility for wise loans still lay with the banker.

After the panic of the late 1830's bankers were understandably

---

[10] "The bill business is limited by the actual operations of commerce; the accom-modation business is as limitless as the want of money, the rage of speculation, or the spirit of gambling. In discounting a note, the bank exchanges its own credit for that of an individual, and receives six per cent. per annum for the difference. In purchasing a real bill, the bank buys a certificate of real substantial value." U. S. Congress, House, *Condition of State Banks*, 25th Cong., 2nd Sess., House Exec. Doc. 79 (Jan. 8, 1838), 762.

[11] E. J. Forstall to the Directors of the Citizens' Bank of Louisiana, Parish St. James, Aug. 31, 1838, printed in U. S. Congress, House, *Condition of the State Banks*, Doc. 111, p. 787.

[12] Stephen A. Caldwell, *A Banking History of Louisiana* (Baton Rouge, 1935), 79.

more cautious, but the separation of business from accommodation paper still remained a problem. In January 1847, for example, the president of the Farmers' and Merchants' Bank of Memphis noted that his bank had discounted a large quantity of bills of exchange based on cotton and therefore presumably good business paper. Closer examination, however, led the bank's board of directors to conclude that "the drawers and acceptors . . . [were] generally weak and uncertain." Cotton prices were high at the moment because of "speculative operations" but there was evidence of an impending drop in cotton prices which would lessen the ability of planters and merchants to meet their obligations, thereby undermining the safety of the bank. The directors decided to tighten up the discount policy by accepting no paper "without the most undoubted endorsements . . . on it" and also by refusing to give more than fifty percent of the face value of the bill discounted.[13]

The exercise of caution was not a simple matter. Planters' notes, endorsed by their factors, were only one of many kinds of commercial paper in the market seeking discount at the Southern banks. When, for example, a sale was made abroad, foreign bills would enter the market. This may be typically illustrated from the correspondence of William Johnson, a Mississippi planter, with his factor, Washington Jackson and Company of New Orleans. In the 1844-1845 season, Johnson had the New Orleans firm sell part of his cotton in Liverpool through Todd, Jackson and Company, the Liverpool branch of the firm. After shipping his cotton to New Orleans, Johnson drew on Washington Jackson and Company, thereby creating a domestic bill for discount. The New Orleans firm reimbursed itself for this advance by drawing on the Liverpool house after shipping the cotton there, thus creating a second bill for discount. When a sale was made in Liverpool, Todd, Jackson and Company sent a sterling bill for the proceeds over and above the advance drawn upon them. The New Orleans firm sold the sterling bill to a bank for local currency and then authorized Johnson to draw another bill to cover his returns over the advance he had drawn originally.[14]

[13] Report of J. Fowlkes to the General Assembly of Tennessee, Oct. 25, 1847, printed in U. S. Congress, House, *Bank Returns*, 30th Cong., 1st Sess., House Exec. Doc. 77 (Aug. 10, 1848), 534-35.

[14] Washington Jackson & Co. to Johnson, New Orleans, Nov. 19, 1844, Dec. 24,

Thus a relatively simple sale of Mississippi cotton in Liverpool brought no less than four different bills of exchange—all good paper, based on cotton—into the market. A more complex sale involving interior merchants as well as coastal merchants could bring even more paper into the market.

Cotton buyers brought still more paper into the market. As representatives of firms in the North or in Europe, buyers were given the right by the firm they represented to draw on them for funds in order to buy cotton. This would bring in bills drawn on New York, Boston, Philadelphia, Liverpool, London, and many other places which had to be sold for local currency that was then used to buy cotton. Resident cotton buyers carrying on business on their own accounts would draw a bill on themselves, sell it to the bank, and with the proceeds buy cotton. After shipping the newly purchased cotton to a merchant in the North or in Europe, the buyer would then draw on the Northern or foreign merchant and use this bill to meet his original obligation.[15]

Here too caution by the banker was required. A sudden decline in cotton prices, a drop in the demand for a particular class of cotton purchased by a buyer, the failure of a foreign merchant— these and a number of other possibilities would lessen the real value of the bills and leave the bank in possession of bills which could not be fully repaid at maturity. In 1844 a South Carolina bank president reported that his bank had regularly discounted buyers' bills in the early 1830's, but in 1834 the failure of a number of buyers led the bank to discontinue the business. Yet, he noted, there was a great demand on the bank to discount these buyers' bills and in 1840 the bank again entered this business. To protect itself, the bank required "ample security" and reduced the time of the bills to 30 days or less. As a result "a healthy action and safe business grew up, of real transactions, . . . which has banished

---

1844; Johnson in a/c current with Todd, Jackson & Co., Liverpool, Nov. 30, 1844, a/c sales by Todd, Jackson & Co., for a/c of Johnson, Liverpool, Nov. 30, 1844; Todd, Jackson & Co. to Johnson, Liverpool, Dec. 3, 1844, Jan. 10, 1845; Johnson in a/c current with Washington Jackson & Co., New Orleans, Dec. 23, 1844; all in William Johnson Papers, Mississippi Department of Archives and History, Jackson, Miss.

[15] For a typical example of a buyer who bought for others as well as for his own account see the Account Books of William Scarborough in the Barnsley Collection, Archives Division, Tennessee State Library and Archives, Nashville, Tenn. Scarborough kept a detailed record of bills drawn, showing the date, on whom drawn, the time of the bill, the amount, to whom discounted, and the rate paid.

the reckless and speculative spirit out of which had arisen so much distress to individuals, and losses to the bank."[16]

In addition to notes based on cotton, Southern banks, of course, also handled bills on the South's other staples as well as the bills of merchants dealing in Western, Northern, and foreign merchandise. In every case, the banks were called upon to furnish local funds for the purchase and sale of commodities. Thus, they provided a measure of short-term credit since when they bought or discounted notes based on commodities bought or sold they made cash immediately available before the notes came due. At the same time these transactions facilitated the movement of funds from one area to another. As banks of issue, the Southern banks were able to exchange their currency for notes based on currency from markets outside the state, region, or nation, a crucial service in a day when there was no common currency and when central banking was either of a very rudimentary nature or (after the destruction of the Second Bank of the United States) completely nonexistent.[17] Had such exchange provisions been unavailable, payment for goods imported into and exported from the South would have had to be in specie, and the transfer of cash would have been an additional expense in cotton marketing. Merchants would be required to tie up a large proportion of their funds by having deposits in many banks in the neighborhood of their customers so that checks could be drawn on these banks to transfer funds.[18] More important, since the supply of specie was more or less fixed and certainly could not be expanded (as bank notes could) to meet the increased demand when cotton was being marketed, complete reliance on specie would have clogged the channels of trade and depressed prices.[19]

[16] R. H. Goodwyn, president Branch Bank at Columbia of the Bank of the State of South Carolina, to the President and Directors of the Bank of the State of South Carolina, Columbia, Oct. 1, 1844, printed in the U. S. Congress, House, *Bank Returns*, 29th Cong., 1st Sess., House Exec. Doc. 226 (Aug. 10, 1846), 637-38.

[17] Alexander Trotter noted that the Second Bank of the United States always purchased bills and paid them in its own currency redeemable at every branch. This, he argued, made exchange operations easier and cheaper. *Observations on the Financial Position and Credit of Such of the States of the North American Union as Have Contracted Public Debts* (London, 1839) 33-34.

[18] Sometimes factors did have deposits in interior banks and remitted funds to their planter customers by sending a check drawn on a local bank. For an example see Maunsel White to Walker, New Orleans, Nov. 10, 1827, Zachariah Walker Papers, Mississippi Department of Archives and History, Jackson, Miss. This method, which required funds to be held in idleness, was not commonly used.

[19] This is exactly what happened when financial panic interrupted the purchase

Southern banks had no monopoly of the exchange business. Throughout the ante bellum period private bankers (that is, unchartered firms), brokers, and factors bought and sold exchange in both the coastal cities and in the interior. In Montgomery, Alabama, in 1858, for example, S. Cullom and Company advertised themselves as bankers and listed their services:

> Purchase Time Bills on Mobile and New Orleans, &c., at the usual rates.
> Sight Exchange on all the Principal cities bought and sold.
> Long and short time LOCAL PAPER, negotiated on favorable terms.[20]

Firms such as Cullom and Company had been buying and selling promissory notes in Charleston and elsewhere as early as the 1790's.[21] As the Southern staple trade expanded in the nineteenth century, so too did the activities of note brokers and private bankers. A Southern business directory in the mid-1850's carried advertisements of private bankers in Montgomery, Mobile, New Orleans, Charleston, and Nashville.[22] Often these advertisements described the firm's business as did that of J. C. Martin of Charleston, which announced that the firm would buy and sell "all kinds of uncurrent funds and specie."[23] Virtually every issue of commercial newspapers such as the *New Orleans Price-Current* carried business cards of private exchange dealers. On the eve of the Civil War, a listing by *Bankers' Magazine* showed 101 private bankers in the states of Arkansas, Alabama, Georgia, Louisiana, Mississippi, South Carolina, and Tennessee.[24]

As their advertisements indicated, these firms would buy and sell "uncurrent funds" or "time bills," that is, notes drawn on a merchant and payable at some future time. Once he had purchased the note, the private banker might rediscount it at a local bank, his endorsement added to that of the person from whom he had

---

and sale of paper by the banks of the country.

[20] *Daily Confederation* (Montgomery), Oct. 12, 1858.

[21] Albert O. Greef, *The Commercial Paper House in the United States* (Cambridge, Mass., 1938), 7-8; Bray Hammond, *Banks and Politics in America from the Revolution to the Civil War* (Princeton, N. J., 1957), 193.

[22] [John P. Campbell (ed.)], *Southern Business Directory and General Commercial Advertiser* (Charleston, 1854), I, 13, 41, 81, 161, 363.

[23] *Ibid.*, I, 363.

[24] *Bankers' Magazine*, XV (1860), 49-64.

bought it increasing the safety of the note, thereby making the bank more likely to accept it at a lower rate. Alternatively, the banker might hold the note to maturity.[25]

Like the incorporated banks, the private bankers, by discounting notes, would make local funds immediately available in the market. They also aided in the transfer of funds. Thus, Fisher and Armor of New Orleans advertised that they would collect notes and bills "on all the principal cities of the Union" and indicated in their advertisement that they had business connections with firms in Boston, Philadelphia, Louisville, Nashville, New York, St. Louis, Mobile, and Washington, D. C.[26] In the collection of such bills, the firm would be acting as a broker rather than a banker. A factor in receipt of a New York bill for the purchase of cotton, could, by paying a brokerage fee, have Fisher and Armor collect the bill for him in New York. In this case the banker was simply acting as an intermediary between the New Orleans factor and the New York merchant.[27] If, on the other hand, Fisher and Armor bought the bill (as their advertisement indicated they would), then the firm was acting in the capacity of a banker, making its funds immediately available and taking the risk that the note would actually be collected in New York.

It would not always be necessary to send a purchased bill to the place where it was drawn in order to collect it. Like the chartered banks, the private bankers sold as well as bought bills. Thus, a New Orleans factor with a debt to pay in New York might buy a New York bill in New Orleans and then mail it to his creditor.[28]

Should their resources warrant it, private bankers might be able to give long-term loans which the chartered banks were unable or unwilling to give. Peter T. Hickman arranged such a loan through his New Orleans factors in 1853 and 1854. In March

[25] See Greef, *Commercial Paper House*, 14.

[26] [Campbell], *Southern Business Directory*, I, 161.

[27] Bray Hammond argues that brokerage was the main function of the private bankers. "Banking in the Early West: Monopoly, Prohibition, and Laissez Faire," *Journal of Economic History*, VIII (May 1948), 16. See also Greef, *Commercial Paper House*, 31. Planters' records and advertisements indicate, however, that numerous firms, especially after 1840, purchased bills and risked their own funds.

[28] In Sept. 1855 Peter T. Hickman's New Orleans factor bought drafts on a Philadelphia firm and a Memphis firm, sent the two drafts to Hickman, and charged the planter's account. The drafts were probably for Hickman's use in a trip he was about to take. When he arrived in Memphis and Philadelphia he could present the drafts for payment and receive local funds. R. W. Estlin & Co. to Hickman, New Orleans, Sept. 26, 1855, Hickman-Bryan Papers.

1853, Hickman's factor, H. R. W. Hill, informed him that he owed some $15,000. "I can now have your paper discounted at 9% the same rate which the Bank charges," Hill wrote. He urged Hickman to send his notes for discount so as to allow the factor to carry the planter's "indebtedness into another season." Hickman sent the requested notes. Fourteen months later the note was still not paid, but the banker was willing to continue the loan. Hickman's new factor, Estlin, Lee and Company, had worked out a new agreement: "We have arranged with the holder of your note to discount a note of $7000. in part payment, at 10% which is 2% lower than the best paper in the city can be done at."[29]

When private bankers were merely brokers, their capital resources did not have to be extensive. Purchase of time bills and long-term loans, however, required a larger store of funds. Many private bankers augmented their personal funds by accepting deposits, offering interest payments on such deposits to attract them.[30]

Exchange operations were also carried on by factors and other merchants. Factorage firms with branches or partners in several cities could send bills to one another for collection. More important in these activities were the larger general merchants with Northern and European connections. Brown Brothers and Company and allied firms, Baring Brothers and Company, and Hope and Company were among the firms which combined exchange with their other business.[31]

The exchange and loan services offered by private bankers, brokers, and merchant-bankers became especially important during the last two decades before the Civil War. The bitter experiences of 1837 and 1839 virtually ended chartered banking in some states and seriously limited it in others. The chartered banking facilities were never adequate to meet the growing needs of com-

[29] H. R. W. Hill to Hickman, New Orleans, March 22, 31, 1853, Estlin, Lee & Co. to Hickman, New Orleans, May 2, 1854, *ibid.*

[30] Cochran & Co. of New Orleans advertised: "Deposits received and interest allowed." [Campbell], *Southern Business Directory*, I, 41. See also Redlich, *Molding of American Banking*, II, 65, 72.

[31] Ralph W. Hidy, "The Organization and Functions of Anglo-American Merchant Bankers, 1815-1860," *Journal of Economic History*, I (Dec. 1941), 56; Brown Bros. & Co., *Experiences of a Century, 1818-1918* (Philadelphia, [1919]), 40; John Crosby Brown, *A Hundred Years of Merchant Banking* (New York, 1909), 255, 279; Frank R. Kent, *The Story of Alexander Brown & Sons* (Baltimore, 1925), 128-29; Redlich, *Molding of American Banking*, II, 66-69.

mercial agriculture, and a growing proportion of the exchange business was carried on by private bankers and brokers.[32]

It is obvious that Southern banks played an important role in the financing and marketing of the cotton crop. For the most part, however, the credit services available from the banks, both chartered and private, came through the agency of the cotton factorage system. Loans based directly on the cotton crop had proved speculative and unsafe; long-term mortgage loans were limited by law or by the caution of bankers who feared freezing their assets in such loans. The discounting and exchange of business paper, secured by cotton and the endorsement of a recognized and responsible cotton merchant, proved to be the safest form of business for the Southern banks. The planter in need of a loan or an advance on his crop could seldom turn directly to the banks; instead, he turned to his factor, for only through him could he tap the bank's resources. For some Southerners this procedure seemed wasteful and unnecessary. The South has a system of banking, wrote H. C. Cabell of Richmond, Virginia, on the eve of the Civil War, "which has no parallel except in a pawn-broker's shop." The planter was unable, he explained, to borrow from a bank "upon a pledge of his land and negroes, or on good personal security, or even upon a promise to turn over to the bank the proceeds of his crop when sold. He can, however, borrow by drawing on his factor, who sells his cotton."[33]

But Southern bankers could argue that their banking system had evolved to its present state through long and often bitter experience. If the Southern banking system was inadequate—and many agreed with Cabell that it was—it was not because Southern bankers lacked imagination or courage. The problems went deeper than that. Indeed, many argued that the entire cotton marketing system was exacting an unnecessary and burdensome toll from the Southern economy.

[32] Redlich, *Molding of American Banking*, II, 69-70; Davis R. Dewey, *State Banking Before the Civil War* (Washington, D. C., 1910), 180-81; Hammond, *Banks and Politics*, 625-26; Trescott, *Financing American Enterprise*, 33; Charles Hillman Brough, "The History of Banking in Mississippi," *Publications of the Mississippi Historical Society*, III (1900), 340.

[33] "Banking at the South, With Reference to New York City," *Hunt's Merchants' Magazine*, XLII (1860), 321.

PART THREE

Cotton Marketing and the Southern Economy

By mere supineness, the people of the South have permitted the Yankees to monopolize the carrying trade, with its immense profits. We have yielded to them the manufacturing business. . . . We have acquiesced in the claims of the North to do all the importing, and most of the exporting business, for the whole Union. . . . Meantime, the South remains passive— in a state of torpidity—making cotton bales for the North to manufacture, and constantly exerting ourselves to increase the production as much as possible.

> —Vicksburg *Daily Whig*, Jan. 18, 1860, as reprinted in Dwight Lowell Dumond (ed.), *Southern Editorials on Secession* (New York, 1931), 13-14.

The wealth of the cotton growing states . . . is . . . greatly augmented by the borrowing of foreign capital, and the condemnation of so advantageous a policy, comes with a bad grace from a cotton planter.

> —*Financial Register* (Philadelphia), I (Aug. 16, 1837), 63.

The factorage system was as much a part of the Southern economy as slavery and the plantation system. Yet, although historians and economists have studied the effects of slavery and the plantation system on the Southern economy and have produced an extensive and sophisticated literature on the subject, they have paid scant attention to the economic influence of the factorage system. The general neglect of the subject is especially ironic because those few scholars who have considered the factorage system have attributed to it far-reaching effects on the Southern economy.

Most of these writers have condemned the system.[1] The process, it has been argued, was exceedingly costly and helped keep the planter in debt.[2] Nor was there any escape for the planter. The factor, through his control of credit vital to production, in effect controlled production. As a result, he encouraged and indeed perpetuated a single-crop economy in order to maintain his economic pre-eminence.[3] Furthermore, so the argument goes, the factorage system impeded the growth of interior towns and the development of commerce because planters transacted most of their business with factors who were concentrated, in the main, on the coast.[4] Profits from planting and farming were siphoned out of the countryside and concentrated in the hands of a few factors in the coastal ports.[5] In short then, the factors, through

their control of the planters, dominated the Southern economy.[6]
"If cotton was king, the cotton factor was the power behind the
throne," wrote the leading student of the system in 1915.[7]

The factorage system has thus been blamed for some of the
most important economic problems that plagued the ante bellum
South—chronic debt, lack of diversification, and rural backward-
ness. All stemmed from the concentration of Southern capital in
the hands of a merchant elite that was able to maintain economic
dominance over farmers and planters. Such evaluations imply
an economic independence on the part of the factors which ignores
the realities of the Southern economic scene in the pre-Civil War
period. Moreover, they postulate the existence of a merchant
class in the South, steadily growing richer but never turning to
other, varied forms of economic enterprise as did their counterparts
in the North and West. In reality, the power behind King
Cotton's rickety throne was located in New York and Liverpool
rather than in New Orleans, Mobile, Savannah, and Charleston.
If the metaphor may be extended further, the factors were little
more than royal retainers with no more power than the throne
they served. Moreover, to attribute to factorage such major

[1] A conspicuous exception is Clement Eaton. See *The Growth of Southern
Civilization, 1790-1860* (New York, 1961), 200-204; *A History of the Old
South* (2nd ed.; New York, 1966), 229, 357-58. In the latter book, Eaton states
that many planters were "in semivassalage to their factors" and that planters "frequently paid a high price" for their factors' services, but concludes that the view of
the factor as "an outrageous exploiter" is "one-sided."

[2] James L. Watkins, *King Cotton* (New York, 1908), 40; Alfred Holt Stone, "The
Negro and Agricultural Development," *The Annals of the American Academy of
Political and Social Science*, XXXV (Jan. 1910), 12-13.

[3] David L. Cohn, *The Life and Times of King Cotton* (New York, 1956), 114;
Alfred Holt Stone, "The Cotton Factorage System of the Southern States," *American
Historical Review*, XX (April 1915), 562.

[4] Charles S. Davis, *The Cotton Kingdom in Alabama* (Montgomery, Ala., 1939),
160-61; Lewis E. Atherton, *The Southern Country Store, 1800-1860* (Baton Rouge,
1949), 34-35; Norman Walker, "Commercial and Mercantile Interests," *Standard
History of New Orleans, Louisiana*, ed. Henry Rightor (Chicago, 1900), 568.

[5] Stone, "Cotton Factorage System," 563. See also Alfred Holt Stone, "The Influence of the Factorage System," in James Curtis Ballagh (ed.), *Economic History,
1865-1909*, Vol. VI of *The South in the Building of the Nation* (Richmond, 1909),
351.

[6] "The whole agricultural country along the Lower Mississippi and its bayous and
streams became, in a manner, the commercial slaves of the New Orleans factors. . . ."
William F. Switzler, *Report on the Internal Commerce of the United States*, 50th
Cong., 1st Sess., House Exec. Doc. 6, Pt. 2 (1888), 205.

[7] Stone, "Cotton Factorage System," 562. Most writers in dealing with the
factorage system have relied extensively on this article by Stone.

authority over the Southern economy is to ignore its real effects on Southern economic and social life. The factorage system reveals much about the Southern economic scene; but blaming the factors for the South's economic woes obscures rather than illuminates the picture.

CHAPTER ELEVEN

The Need for Credit

At the end of the planting season of 1829, planter William Hamilton was faced with an unavoidable delay in the ginning of his cotton. Respectfully, but with an obvious sense of urgency, his New Orleans factors wrote him on December 3 to express regret about the delay. The factors noted that they had advanced Hamilton cash "to some amount" and hoped that his cotton would soon be ready as they needed the money. The ginning problem solved, Hamilton sent his cotton to New Orleans and in a few days it was sold.[1]

Such pressure to supply cotton to repay debts often led to criticism. Usually, however, contemporary observers directed their complaints not against the factorage system as such, but rather at the procedure of advances associated with it. When notes fell due, cotton had to be sold even if prices on the market were depressed. The solution to this problem seemed simple enough to a planter writing in 1849: "*Keep out of debt*, and *control your cotton*." He drew on his own experience to support his point. Because he had been in debt he had been forced to sell his cotton for 5 cents a pound, whereas a friend, free of debt, had been able to refuse 7 cents in anticipation of an even better price at a later date.[2]

J. A. Turner appended like advice to his *Cotton Planter's Manual*: "Create no liens on this crop, or necessity for selling. Never spend the money which it is to produce until it is sold. You are then free to choose your own market, and time of selling; and as cotton is a controlling article, it will greatly regulate the value of all property to be purchased, except the redemption of an out-standing promise."[3] This, of course, is a part of the rhetoric of King Cotton, the "controlling article" in the market. If the planter were wise enough to stay out of debt—to become more "self-dependent" as Israel Andrews put it[4]—he would be able to demand a high price from the buyers.

But, if advances were bad because they prevented planters from controlling their crops, the factor who provided the advances and then sold cotton to pay the debts was not at fault. He too was under pressure: he needed money to meet his own debts and to lend to other planters and therefore was "compelled" to sell his customer's cotton. The factor's expert services were required to sell the crop, but if "mutual good faith and good will" were to prevail between factor and planter, "the planter must preserve his independence" by eschewing advances.[5] Such was the opinion of an Alabama planter when he proposed cooperation between planters and factors, "whose interests are identical." Planters and their merchants should agree to refuse to sell unless prices were high. This would be possible, he noted, only if advances were avoided so as to obviate the danger of a sale under pressure.[6] At an 1855 Commercial Convention in New Orleans, a Louisiana planter offered more far-reaching suggestions for cooperation between planters and their factors. One of his proposed resolutions asked that the "Chambers of Commerce and Commission Merchants" in Southern cities agree not to give advances to planters; another of his resolutions proposed that his first suggestion be given the sanction of legislation in each state, "making it a penitentiary offence for the planters to ask or the merchants to make such pecuniary advances."[7]

Despite its constant reiteration, such advice was largely ignored

[1] John Hagan & Co. to Hamilton, New Orleans, Dec. 3, Dec. 12, 1829, W. S. Hamilton Papers, Southern Historical Collection, University of North Carolina Library, Chapel Hill, N. C.

[2] *DeBow's Review*, VII (1849), 411.

[3] *The Cotton Planter's Manual: Being a Compilation of Facts from the Best Authorities on the Culture of Cotton* (New York, 1857).

[4] U. S. Congress, Senate, *Report on the Trade and Commerce of the British North American Colonies and Upon the Trade of the Great Lakes and the Rivers*, 32nd Cong., 1st Sess., Senate Exec. Doc. 112 (1853), 830-31.

[5] *DeBow's Review*, VII (1849), 412.

[6] *Ibid.*, XIII (1852), 640-41.

[7] *Ibid.*, XVIII (1855), 359.

—and with good reason. Planters were well aware that if an advance sometimes forced a sale because a due bill had to be paid, on other occasions an advance allowed cotton to be held for a favorable price while at the same time providing funds for the start of a new crop. "When planters hold back a portion of their crops, it is for the most part held . . . under advances generally from factors or warehousemen," wrote the commercial editor of the *Charleston Mercury*,[8] and few planters lacked experiences that would support him.[9] A suggestion to avoid advances was tantamount to a suggestion that they give up this advantage. Planters would most certainly refuse to deal with factors who refused to give such advances. Nor would legal restraints be possible. When the Louisiana planter proposed that state legislatures prohibit advances, the Commercial Convention took no action on his resolutions.[10]

The basic weakness of the suggestion that advances be avoided was that it was impractical and uneconomical. Planters were being asked to conduct a cash business; that is, they were expected to have funds on hand to pay expenses of production and marketing as well as the costs of expansion. If this were the case, production would be restricted to those with a vast accumulation of capital—enough to buy land, slaves, seed, and tools, support a work force through the year, pay transportation and marketing costs, and start a new crop before proceeds from the old were available. At any time an obvious misallocation of resources, this procedure would have been an impossible allocation of resources in the nineteenth century, when Americans, North and South, were attempting to carve farms and plantations from the wilderness.

If all commercial farmers required credit,[11] the Southern producer had certain special and peculiar problems that influenced and aggravated his credit needs. The ownership of slaves and land

8 *Ibid.*, XIII (1852), 69.

9 See discussion of advances in Chap. III.

10 *DeBow's Review*, XVIII (1855), 359-60. Among the resolutions was one recommending that planters deal only with Southern merchants, a necessary stipulation if restraints on advances were to be effective. One speaker denounced the resolutions saying that he was "opposed to any legislation that should undertake to tell them [the planters] who [*sic*] they shall or shall not deal with."

11 See Paul W. Gates, *The Farmer's Age: Agriculture, 1815-1860* (New York, 1960), 403-13.

was both economically and socially important to the planter. It is unnecessary to enter into the controversy over the profitability of slavery to accept the institution's significance. Whether slavery persisted because it was profitable, or despite its profitability,[12] the facts are that it remained, that the planter relied upon it for his economic well-being, that most of the cotton was grown with slave labor, and that the ownership of slaves was an indication of social prestige.

Consequently, the planter persistently sought to expand his holdings of slaves and land, a fact few visitors to the South failed to notice. Wrote a traveler in 1834: "To sell cotton in order to buy negroes—to make more cotton to buy more negroes, 'ad infinitum,' is the aim and direct tendency of all the operations of the thorough going cotton planter; his whole soul is wrapped up in the pursuit. It is, apparently, the principle by which he 'lives, moves, and has his being.' "[13] Slaves and cotton "are the law and the prophets of the men of the South," wrote James Stirling in 1857. Seeking to increase his slave force and to grow more cotton, the planter would spend not only his profits but would also borrow on future profits—or hoped-for profits—by securing advances on a crop not yet grown. "This I believe is the secret of the notorious 'indebtedness' of the Southern planters," Stirling explained. "Not one in fifteen, I am assured, is free of debt."[14]

The difference between planters in Louisiana and farmers in New York "was the impulsive and unreflective habit of the former, in doing business," Frederick Law Olmsted was told by one who had lived in both places. An indication of this habit was the "almost universal passion among the planters for increasing their negro-stock." Ignoring the fact that prices for slaves were "much higher than the prices of cotton and sugar warranted," Olmsted's informant continued, most planters

> would always run in debt to the extent of their credit for
> negroes, whatever was asked for them, without making any

[12] See Harold D. Woodman, "The Profitability of Slavery: A Historical Perennial," *Journal of Southern History*, XXIX (Aug. 1963), 303-25; *Slavery and the Southern Economy* (New York, 1966), *passim*.

[13] [Joseph Holt Ingraham], *The Southwest, By a Yankee* (New York, 1835), II, 91.

[14] *Letters from the Slave States* (London, 1857), 179, 181-82. This letter was written from Macon, Ga., and dated Feb. 4, 1857.

calculation of the reasonable prospects of their being able to pay their debts. When any one made a good crop, he would always expect that his next one would be better, and make purchases in advance upon such expectation. When they were dunned, they would always attribute their inability to pay, to accidental short crops, and always were going ahead risking everything, in confidence that another year of luck would favour them, and a big crop make all right.[15]

Critical visitors were not the only ones who recognized—and lamented—this state of affairs. When the bottom fell out of the cotton market in 1839, New Orleans cotton factor Maunsel White decided to change his manner of business by restricting credit. Writing to his friend Andrew Jackson in June 1840, he explained his new business policy and the reasons for it: "We have . . . given up the old System of accepting D[ra]ft[s] except on cotton immediately shipped to our address, because it was those acceptances and the general custom of giving Credit facilities that brot [sic] on the Ruin of the Country, and induced the planter to purchase more Land and negroes than he wanted, and others who had no Capital, to Buy large Estates on Credit, paying a part down, raised on Drafts on Merchants in this City at 12 mos."[16]

These critics viewed the Southern credit problem from a somewhat different perspective than did those who simply condemned all borrowing. It was not borrowing as such which created problems, they asserted, but rather the inordinate borrowing stimulated by what Robert Y. Hayne of South Carolina condemned as the mistaken view that the "acquisition of more land, and the production of more cotton . . . [were] the only objects worthy of . . . attention."[17] Maunsel White's solution was to curtail his loans by refusing funds to a planter until he sent cotton to him. Presumably this would prevent the planter from borrowing excessively during the year because he would not get loans until his cotton was ready to sell; since the factor would limit the loans to the value of cotton already produced, loans would not exceed expected returns.

15 *The Cotton Kingdom*, ed. Arthur M. Schlesinger (New York, 1953), 330-31.
16 To Andrew Jackson, New Orleans, June 3, 1840, printed in John Spencer Basset (ed.), *Correspondence of Andrew Jackson* (Washington, D. C., 1926), VI, 64.
17 Report delivered to Charleston Commercial Convention (1839), reprinted in *DeBow's Review*, IV (1847), 343.

The logic of White's plan was to eliminate long-term credit. The advance given after cotton was shipped would provide funds for marketing the cotton and allow the planter to buy supplies for the coming year, repair or replace needed equipment, and begin production of a new crop. When the cotton was sold, the advance would be repaid and the planter would be out of debt until the next year after the new crop was harvested and ginned.

George McDuffie had made the same point in 1838 when he attacked the planters' unending emphasis on cotton, slaves, and land, an emphasis, he argued which required long-term credits, to the detriment of Southern interests. "Their [the planters'] habit of laying out their incomes before they get them, and requiring a credit in all their dealing for the year, till the close of it, or until they sell their crops, even if it be longer, is the root of the evil of our whole system of credit." Short-term credits, based on bills of exchange and used merely to balance transactions, should be adequate, he argued.[18]

Although they rejected the simplistic notion that the planters could get along entirely without credit of any kind, White and McDuffie had accepted the equally naive notion that the South's cotton growers could dispense with long-term loans. But the desire for economic gain and social prestige continued to induce planters to expand their holdings and to demand long-term loans. If White would not supply them, others would—and did. In 1847 the New Orleans editor, J. D. B. DeBow, bemoaned the failure of the South to change its ways. The "profound and eleborate reports" of Hayne, McDuffie, and others had come to nothing. "But they shall not be forgotten," he resolved in his introduction reprinting the reports.[19] A year later a New Orleans factor, J. B. Gribble, complained that the planters' debts were forcing them to sell their cotton at inopportune times. He sounded a familiar lament: "Planters, as a body, must cease to be dependent on their credit for the means of raising their crops, and increasing beyond propriety their negro force."[20] But this

[18] Report of George McDuffie of South Carolina to Augusta Commercial Convention (1838), reprinted *ibid.*, 220-21.

[19] *Ibid.*, 209. DeBow reprinted the reports again in 1853 in his *The Industrial Resources, Etc., of the Southern and Western States* (New Orleans, 1853), III, 92-117.

[20] *DeBow's Review*, VI (1848), 127. Gribble was a partner in the firm, Gribble & Montgomery; see his business card in *New Orleans Price Current*, Sept. 1, 1848.

was not statement of policy; it was little more than a plea for caution. How much borrowing was possible before the bounds of "propriety" were exceeded he did not say.

Indeed, the line was often more visible after it was passed, when due bills led to distress selling at inadequate prices. In 1851 a Mobile factor explained to his planter customer that large quantities of cotton would soon be on the market and that this would keep prices low. "I fear the negro mania, pork mania, mule mania & land mania of Nov. & Dec. has drawn too many drafts to allow much to be held."[21]

The criticism of the system of advances was not merely an agrarian debtor complaint against local middlemen, the factors and other merchants in the South. Although local merchants often came under attack, criticism of them, as well as of the planters, was usually coupled with a more far-reaching critique of the entire Southern economy. Southerners, it was argued, had allowed themselves to become dependent upon outsiders for manufactured goods, services, and credit. The South, lacking economic independence, was being robbed of its wealth.

[21] J. R. Goree to Hugh Davis, Mobile, Feb. 26, 1851, as quoted in Weymouth T. Jordan, *Hugh Davis and His Alabama Plantation* (University, Ala., 1948), 139-40.

CHAPTER TWELVE

The Dependent South

The economic collapse of the late 1830's prompted widespread concern over the nature of Southern economic development. In July 1837 a group of Georgians issued a call for a convention of Southerners to consider steps to solve a very pressing problem: "we furnish nearly all the articles of export in the great staples of cotton, rice and tobacco. This is a singular advantage for any people to enjoy. Yet, with all this in our favor by nature, we employ the merchants of the Northern cities as our agents in this business. They export our immense valuable productions, and import our articles of consumption—and from this agency they derive a profit which has enriched them; and as long as it continues, will enrich them at our expense."[1] South Carolinians, who had warned of the economic hardships engendered by the tariff, responded enthusiastically to the convention call. The end of expansion, easy credit, and profits of flush times provided more fertile soil for the complaints of these Southern nationalists. George McDuffie, Robert Y. Hayne, and Franklin H. Elmore, all of whom had been associated with John C. Calhoun in the abortive nullification movement in South Carolina (1830-1832), gave the major reports to the series of conventions held in Augusta and Charleston in 1837, 1838, and 1839.

To these people, the link between the older problems of the tariff and the national bank and the present plight of the South seemed obvious enough. McDuffie made the connection in Augusta in 1838. The costs of the duties, he explained, fell mainly on the exporting agricultural South, yet the North derived all the benefit because the funds collected were concentrated in the North in the United States Bank. This forced the commerce of the South "into artificial, circuitous, and unnatural channels." True, the tariff had been lowered and the bank's power diminished, but the "effects . . . for some time survive their causes" and the South remained dependent. Exchange of the South's agricultural products for needed manufactured goods was a part of American commerce which was "appropriately *our own*," yet it was carried on and controlled by Northern cities. These Northern cities exacted a tribute for their services, a charge "voluntarily paid, to be sure, but utterly incompatible with a just and enlightened view of our own interests."[2]

The charges of Southern economic dependency made sense to many—even to some who might quibble with the politics of the South Carolinian.[3] A convention committee issued a public "Address to the People of the Southern and Southwestern States" describing the drain of Southern wealth to the North:

> The northern merchant has come hither and bought [produce] from the southern planter . . . abating from the price all the expenses, direct and incidental, of transportation. He has insured them in northern offices, and shipped them abroad in his own vessels—exchanged them at a small profit for foreign merchandise—brought it home—paid one-fourth of its value to the government—added that amount and all the expenses of importation, and fifteen to twenty per cent. for his profits, to the price, and exposed it for sale. The southern merchant has now gone to him—lingered the summer through with him at a heavy expense—bought a portion of these goods—reshipped them in northern vessels to southern ports—added twenty-five per cent. more to the price, to cover his expenses and profits—and sold them to the southern planter. All the disbursements made in this process, save such as are made abroad, are made among northern men; all the profits, save the southern merchant's, are made by northern men; and the southern planter, who supplies nearly all the foreign goods of the country, gets his portion of them burdened with every expense that the government, merchant,

---

[1] Circular reprinted in Herbert Wender, *Southern Commercial Conventions, 1837-1859* (Baltimore, 1930), 11.

[2] *DeBow's Review*, IV (1847), 213.

[3] DeBow in reprinting the "valuable paper" carefully disassociated himself from the "political doctrines in it." *Ibid.*

insurer, seaman, wharfinger, drayman, boatman, and wagoner can pile upon them. . . . Every item in the endless catalogue of charges, except the government dues, may be considered a voluntary tribute from the citizens of the South to their brethren of the North: for they would all have gone to our own people, had we done our own exporting and importing.[4]

To the losses sustained by virtue of Northern domination of Southern trade and commerce, others added the costs of buying manufactured goods outside the South. In twenty years, DeBow argued, the South spent more than enough on transportation and purchases of cotton goods to "put into successful operation a sufficient number of cotton mills to manufacture all the cotton that she grows."[5]

For twenty years Southerners decried their economic dependence. "We are paying bounties and premiums which, if enforced by authority, would put every southern man in armor to the teeth," raged a Mississippi planter in 1850.[6] Familiar arguments were endlessly repeated. In reprinting the 1838 "Address to the People of the Southern and Southwestern States," DeBow noted that "the main points of argument are irresistible, and quite as true and applicable in 1852 as they could have been in 1838."[7] *Southern Wealth and Northern Profits* was the title and theme of Thomas Prentice Kettell's discussion of the problem on the eve of Civil War. His book was a solemn reminder to Northerners that their prosperity depended on the Southern trade, a prosperity which would disappear should the Union dissolve.[8]

Virtually every complaint attempted to explain the causes of Southern dependency and contained proposals for change. Indeed, as dangerous and abiding as the problem was, solution seemed deceptively simple: Break the overwhelming emphasis on staple crop agriculture, especially on cotton production. A diversified agriculture would free the planter from dependence upon Western foodstuffs; Southern investment in commerce and manufacturing would free the South from dependence upon Eastern and foreign

[4] *Ibid.*, XIII (1852), 483-84.

[5] DeBow, *The Industrial Resources, Etc., of the Southern and Western States* (New Orleans, 1853), II, 115.

[6] *DeBow's Review*, VIII (1850), 99.

[7] *Ibid.*, XIII (1852), 478.

[8] *Southern Wealth and Northern Profits as Exhibited in Statistical Facts and Official Figures: Showing the Necessity of Union to the Future Prosperity and Welfare of the Republic* (New York, 1860), *passim.*

merchants and manufacturers. Both of these steps would remove resources from cotton production, diminish the size of the crop, and thereby cause prices to rise. Dependence, it seemed, would end at no real cost. Therefore the agricultural community was advised to stay out of debt, diversify crops, invest in commerce and manufacturing, improve transportation, and open up direct trade with Europe.

Many, recognizing the problem, recognized also that concerted, cooperative action was required if change were to come about. Individually, cotton growers could do little; "we are too numerous, and scattered over too large an extent of territory, without the means of communicating with each other," a Mississippi planter argued.[9] From such feelings came the Southern Commercial Conventions and the Planters' Conventions. Both these convention movements had their origins in the crisis of 1837 and both urged direct trade with Europe as a means of bypassing middlemen and thereby decreasing the costs of marketing staple crops and purchasing supplies. Beyond this, however, the emphasis of each movement was quite different; at times the two were somewhat contradictory.[10]

The Southern Commercial Conventions emphasized freeing the Southern economy from its dependence upon the North. Direct trade was seen as the most important means to this end but the

[9] *DeBow's Review*, VII (1849), 74. In calling for a cotton planters' convention to meet in Macon, Ga., in 1851, a group of Florida planters resolved that "nothing is likely to be accomplished . . . without a reasonable amount of concert of action among cotton planters." DeBow, *Industrial Resources*, I, 133.

[10] Full reports of the proceedings of these conventions may be followed over the years in *DeBow's Review*. DeBow reprinted published material from both sets of conventions in his *Industrial Resources*, I, 128-39, III, 92-117. Southern Commercial Conventions are discussed in detail in Wender, *Southern Commercial Conventions*; William Watson Davis, "Ante-Bellum Southern Commercial Conventions," *Transactions of the Alabama Historical Society*, V (1904), 153-202; John G. Van Deusen, *The Ante-Bellum Southern Commercial Conventions* (Durham, N. C., 1926). Historians have given much less attention to the Planters' Conventions, but an excellent survey of the work of these meetings can be found in Weymouth T. Jordan, *Rebels in the Making: Planters' Conventions and Southern Propaganda* (Tuscaloosa, Ala., 1958). An excellent study of an early planters' convention is Thomas Payne Govan, "An Ante-Bellum Attempt to Regulate the Price and Supply of Cotton," *North Carolina Historical Review*, XVII (Oct. 1940), 303-12. A more general discussion of the various attempts by the South to break out of economic dependency, including valuable interpretive insights on the effect of the economic situation on the coming of the Civil War, may be found in Robert Royal Russel, *Economic Aspects of Southern Sectionalism, 1840-1861* (Urbana, Ill., 1924). A similar approach on the state level is John G. Van Deusen, *Economic Bases of Disunion in South Carolina* (New York, 1928).

conventions also urged the establishment of a more rounded economy in the South through the development of manufacturing and the building of railroads. During the last half decade before the Civil War the question of reopening the slave trade also became a major issue in the discussions. The main concern of the Planters' Conventions was to cut marketing costs and raise the price paid for cotton. Little emphasis was given to manufacturing and railroads at these meetings; rather, the stress was on marketing, banking, and credit reform in the South. The Commercial Conventions urged the expansion of Southern commerce and trade, belittled prejudice against Southern merchants and factors, and sought means to bypass both Southern and Northern merchants in their commercial dealings.

The problem had been recognized, yet solutions proved elusive. Convention reports and resolutions proposed fundamental alterations in the Southern economy, and reformers expected "the public spirit and zealous co-operation of their fellow citizens"[11] to bring about change. When change did not come, angry writers condemned Southern planters and merchants. "Habit and indolence" led planters to accept their subordinate position, insisted a Mississippi planter. "The truth is, that the COLONIAL SPIRIT still adheres to the South."[12] The South's economic problems arose from "our own supineness and lack of energy," charged another Southerner. Merchants were timid. They would not import merchandise themselves but were content merely to sell goods imported by Northerners. If successful, they did not seek to enlarge and expand their business but instead retired to a plantation. "Let our merchants be no longer content to be mere *peddlers*, but become *merchants* in *deed* as well as in *name*," he concluded.[13]

What appeared to some as a lack of energy was seen by others as a lack of interest. James S. Buckingham, visiting the South in 1842, noted that some were discussing direct trade with Europe. But he found most people apathetic:

> The planters and merchants of the interior, however, are not so eager on this subject as those of the seaports, because their

---

[11] *DeBow's Review*, XIII (1852), 478. See also *ibid.*, IV (1847), 212.
[12] *Ibid.*, VIII (1850), 99.
[13] *Southern Standard*, reprinted *ibid.*, XII (1852), 299-300.

interests are not so deeply involved. They dispose of their cotton to buyers here [Augusta], or at the ports on the coast, and trouble themselves no further, as they find all the supplies they want in the stores of the towns at which their sales are made; but the ship-owners and merchants of the coast naturally look with jealousy on a state of things which leads to the importation of all their European supplies through the ports of the North.[14]

If some were apathetic, others were opposed to suggested changes. In a very real sense, the outlook of the reformers clashed with the agrarian outlook many Southerners held dear. Thus, for example, Elwood Fisher, in a long article, proclaimed the virtues of the Southern economy, arguing that the failure to develop commerce and manufacturing did not mean the South did not enjoy "general prosperity." On the contrary, he maintained, the South had less poverty, a more equal distribution of wealth, and, in general, higher living standards than the North because of the agrarian base of its economy.[15] Certainly implicit in such an evaluation was resistance to any movement that aped the North and thereby undermined this prosperity.

More explicit was the opposition of those who felt it was the North that was dependent upon the South rather than the reverse. Cotton was king and could command the world; the South controlled the world's supply of cotton and the manufacturing areas, Northern and European, for all their vaunted wealth, were dependent upon the South for their cotton.[16] Less than a month after the first shells had been fired on Fort Sumter, an Alabama politician confidently described the South's strength to a British visitor. In stridently Jeffersonian terms he made explicit what Fisher had only implied:

[14] *The Slave States of America* (London, [1842]), I, 185.

[15] *DeBow's Review*, VII (1849), 134-45, 262-66, 304-16.

[16] "The subject that most interests them [the Southerners] is the fleecy product of the cotton plant. It is cotton in the morning, cotton at noon, and cotton at night. A kind of cotton insanity appears to affect all classes. To their distempered imaginations, cotton is pablum that nourishes and sustains the entire North and 'the rest of mankind;' cotton, the 'open sesame' to wealth, power, honor, and personal and national aggrandizement; cotton, the Atlas which upholds and the lever that moves the entire world. In fact, they consider cotton the *vis vitae*—'the one thing needful.' Upon it is based the boasted power of the South, which, without it, would sink into comparative insignificance, and the inhabitants lose their prestige with foreign nations, and in point of influence *be but little above the 'mudsill'* Yankees at the North*." [Carlton H. Rogers], *Incidents of Travel in the Southern*

We are an agricultural people; we are a primitive but a civilized people. We have no cities—we don't want them. We have no literature—we don't need any yet. We have no press—we are glad of it. We do not require a press, because we go out and discuss all public questions from the stump with our people. We have no commercial marine—no navy— we don't want them. We are better without them. Your ships carry our produce, and you can protect your own vessels. We want no manufactures; we desire no trading, no mechanical or manufacturing classes. As long as we have our rice, our sugar, our tobacco, and our cotton, we can command wealth to purchase all we want from those nations with which we are in amity, and to lay up money besides. But with the Yankees we will never trade—never. Not one pound of cotton shall ever go from the South to their accursed cities; not one ounce of their steel or their manufactures shall ever cross our border.[17]

Another, but related, ideological problem reformers faced, was the fact that their criticism opened the door to antislavery arguments. When Hinton Rowan Helper published his vitriolic book, *The Impending Crisis*, in 1857, he painted a dismal picture of what he called the "unmanly and unnational dependence" of the South on the North, using much the same rhetoric as the reformers but blaming the situation on slavery.[18]

Force of habit, apathy, and outright opposition undoubtedly played a part in preventing change. The problem, however, went deeper. Southerners who argued that federal law in the form of the tariff and the national bank brought about Northern dominance shrank from advocating similar legislative enactments to develop the Southern economy. Planters and merchants were merely urged to make changes and to form voluntary associations

---

States and Cuba (New York, 1862), 234-35. Though published in 1862, the letters in this unsympathetic account are dated 1856.

17 William Howard Russell, *My Diary North and South* (Boston, 1863), 179.

18 "It is a fact well known to every intelligent Southerner that we are compelled to go to the North for almost every article of utility and adornment, from matches, shoepegs and paintings up to cotton-mills, steamships and statuary; that we have no foreign trade, no princely merchants, nor respectable artists; . . . that, owing to the absence of a proper system of business amongst us, the North becomes, in one way or another, the proprietor and dispenser of all our floating wealth, and that we are dependent on Northern capitalists for the means necessary to build our railroads, canals and other public improvements; . . . and that nearly all the profits arising from the exchange of commodities, from insurance and shipping offices, and from the thousand and one industrial pursuits of the country, accrue to the North." *The Impending Crisis of the South: How to Meet It* (New York, 1857), 21-25.

to carry them out. A critic of the 1838 Augusta Commercial Convention scoffed at resolutions "not to buy Northern goods when they can get Southern, unless the Northern are cheapest; not to freight Northern vessels when they can freight Southern, unless the Northern freight is less." Such advice sounded like the sailor's injunction "never kiss the maid, if he could kiss the mistress unless he liked the maid best." But this critic did not propose legislation to force Southerners to deal only with their own merchants. His answer was to provide better facilities in the South which could compete successfully with the North.[19]

This, of course, was the key to any change. Lacking legal coercion, Southerners would alter patterns of trade only when local merchants and manufacturers became economically competitive and thereby able to draw business away from the North. In this way public spirit would be buttressed by private gain. But standing in the way of such goals were serious problems that Southerners were never able to solve.

When it was suggested that the South organize its own cotton mills, A. A. Lawrence, the Massachusetts textile manufacturer, asked an embarrassing question: "Have our Southern friends such resources of money now at their command as to create these immense works, or are they borrowers?" The question was rhetorical. From his own experience Lawrence knew of the South's lack of ready cash: "We sell our fabrics, which are made at the North, to the Southern buyers, on a credit of from six to ten months. Neither do we receive a similar credit in return, for the reason that they are not in a condition to grant it. All the great staples sent from the Southern market are sold for cash, or on a credit of sixty days. It is in this way that the foreign and the home manufacturers supply themselves with cotton."[20]

---

[19] Article from *Southern Literary Messenger*, as quoted by Wender, *Southern Commercial Conventions*, 25-26.

[20] *Hunt's Merchants' Magazine*, XXI (1849), 628. Lawrence added that "though there are many rich men in the large cotton-growing States, the number of moneyed men is very small, and they are not usually the projectors of new enterprises." In January 1839, Fanny Kemble, visiting her husband's Georgia sea island plantation, noted that a canal was being built on the mainland adjacent to one of the islands. The project, she indicated, was being financed primarily by Northern capital, "Yankee enterprise and funds being very essential elements, it appears to me, in all Southern projects and achievements." Francis Anne Kemble, *Journal of a Residence on a Georgia Plantation in 1838-1839*, ed. John A. Scott (New York, 1961), 122. See also *ibid.*, 104, n. 2.

Here was a rock upon which Southern plans foundered. To build cotton factories and fleets of ships required capital investment. So too did an expansion of Southern merchandising. In calling for the avoidance of long-term credits, McDuffie had touched upon this problem in 1838: "If the planters require a long credit, the merchants, wholesale and retail, through whom they were supplied, would at least require an equally long credit, so far as they purchase upon a credit. A large money capital becomes thus necessary for the importing merchants, that a long credit may be extended to the planters. . . ."[21] But Southern planters required long-term credit and lacked the necessary "money capital" or liquid capital. When a planters' convention tried to reform the cotton marketing mechanism, it ran into the same problem.

In October 1851 a group of Florida cotton planters came to a Cotton Planters' Convention in Macon, Georgia, with a plan which they thought would solve the problem of low cotton prices. They proposed the creation of a Cotton Planters' Association "chartered by the States of South Carolina, Georgia, Alabama, Louisiana and Florida, with a capital of at least $20,000,000, to be increased in amount as the wants of the business may require." The association would take over and monopolize the cotton marketing business. It would set up a warehouse and organize "a regular commission business, with a view to the storage and sale of the entire [cotton] crop of the United States." A minimum price for cotton would be set by the association; planters unable to obtain this minimum price on the open market would sell their cotton at the set price to the association which would then hold the staple, refusing to sell except at the minimum price plus storage and commission charges. "Under such a system," declared the Florida planters, "the planter would not crowd the market with cotton, as is now the case, and speculators at the minimum price would purchase freely and hold with confidence."[22] In short, the plan envisioned a kind of price support for cotton.[23]

The proposal was approved by the Macon convention,[24] but it

---

[21] DeBow's Review, IV (1847), 221.

[22] Ibid., XI (1851), 501-502; James L. Watins, King Cotton (New York, 1908), 108.

[23] Present-day government price supports for cotton operate in almost the same manner, except, of course, the undertaking is public, not private.

[24] DeBow's Review, XII (1852), 121.

failed to materialize. A critic of the plan pointed to the major obstacle: "How will the capital of twenty millions of dollars be obtained?" Capital could come only from the sale of cotton and at least one-third of the current crop would have to be sold to raise the funds necessary to support the undertaking. This would mean that one-third of the crop would have to be sold at depressed prices in order to support the prices of the other two-thirds; that is, the owners of the one-third would have to be willing to sacrifice for the benefit of the others. To believe this possible one "must have faith in the existence of folly amounting to infatuation," he declared. An alternative plan for raising the capital had been proposed by the Florida planters: "The planters will deposit their cotton with the company, and take its stock in payment." This was no real alternative, the critic insisted. Even if enough cotton were so withdrawn to raise prices (he thought 40 million would be a more realistic figure), only those who still had their crop on hand would benefit. The others would have no returns except stock in the association, and the association itself would still have cotton which it could not put on the market (without lowering the price) until a future short crop would allow the stored cotton to be sold. "Where will the author of the scheme find such public-spirited and self-sacrificing stockholders?" he asked.[25]

The critic of the Florida scheme, like A. A. Lawrence who scoffed at Southern plans to introduce cotton manufacturing, had pointed to the obvious: The South lacked the liquid capital required for such commercial and industrial enterprises.[26] Re-

[25] Ibid., 124-26. The association, of course, could not dump the cotton it held for that would depress prices. Thus, in its second year, the problem of capital would be raised again. Even when supply was short, if the association then sold its holdings it would raise the supply and thereby counteract the advantages of short supply.

[26] But see George R. Woolfolk, "Cotton Capitalism and Slave Labor in Texas," *The Southwestern Social Science Quarterly,* XXXVII (June 1956), 43-52. Woolfolk, in attacking what he called the "Helper-Phillips" thesis which, he said, maintained that slavery was economically unprofitable because it froze great wealth in slaves, argues that on the contrary slaves could be, and were, used as liquid capital because of the great ease with which they could be sold. This argument merely begs the question. Slavery was restricted to the South; when one planter sold slaves to another, the amount of liquid capital in the South was not increased but merely redistributed. Presumably, a planter desiring to do so could sell his slaves and invest the proceeds in any economic activity he desired. But what is true for any individual could not be true of the South as a whole. Obviously everyone could not sell his slaves for then there would be no buyers. Nor could a sizable number do so without driving prices down disastrously.

formers, of course, were aware of this problem; indeed, a significant aspect of their complaint against Southern dependency was that it drained capital from the section. Solving the problem, however, seemed easy enough. Hayne suggested three ways to raise the "*capital* necessary to carry on the direct trade to the extent desired." He proposed that planters divert some of the capital invested in agriculture to commerce, that Southern merchants follow the example of New York merchants and borrow from abroad on drafts based on cotton and other produce, and, finally, that foreign (particularly English) capitalists be induced to invest in the South. Such measures would be "abundantly sufficient," Hayne concluded, to supply the capital "necessary to the perfect success of our great scheme."[27]

Hayne's advice was applauded and repeated but, for good reason, never followed. It revealed a combination of wishful thinking, Southern nationalism, and muddled economic reasoning which characterized most attempts to end Southern dependence. An evaluation of Hayne's suggestions will serve to reveal the fundamental problems faced by the South and the reasons for its continued economic dependence despite efforts at reform by some of its most articulate and energetic leaders.

In explaining his first proposal, Hayne made it clear that he did not expect planters to "leave the cultivation of their fields to engage in the business of the countinghouse." Only a "portion of their annual surplus" would be invested in commerce; his specific suggestion was the "tenth part of a single crop," the funds being invested in firms with limited liability so as to protect the planters' other holdings. He concluded this aspect of his proposal on a contradictory and revealing note:

> We confidently believe that the profits to be derived from such an investment, would be greater than if the same amount were applied to the usual purpose of making more cotton—indeed, we are persuaded, that the profits of agriculture would not thereby be sensibly diminished, while the profits of commerce would be greatly enlarged. We are well aware, that it is not in the course of human affairs that such a concert of action could be brought about among our planters. But we do hope and believe, that the example already set by so many of

27 *DeBow's Review*, IV (1847), 350-53. Subsequent references to Hayne's position are all from this source.

our public-spirited and patriotic citizens in this respect, will
be followed by others. . . .

That all he could do is "hope" that planters would shift part
of their investments to a more profitable enterprise indicates
either that he expected that planters would have little confidence
in his promise of profits or that they would prefer to devote their
full resources to cotton planting despite promises of better returns
elsewhere. Southerners faced no legal restrictions on their investment activity. They simply invested their money in those
areas which they thought promised the best returns—monetary,
social, or both. That funds found their way into planting with
slave labor and that merchants sought to invest their profits in
planting[28] was simply an indication that Southerners felt this
practice to be more beneficial to them. Constant reference by
reformers to public spirit and patriotic motives indicates that
individual Southerners were being asked to undertake a sacrifice
of some kind for the public good.

Hayne's second and third proposals for securing capital—drawing in foreign investments of various kinds—were no more practical than his first suggestion. In the first place, foreign capital
already played a major role in financing and marketing the crop.
Indeed, many decried British financial domination just as vehemently as Hayne and others complained of Northern domination.[29] Second, his argument that British capitalists could be

---

[28] There is ample evidence that merchants were so impelled and also, it should be
added, that profit was not the sole motivation. Daniel Robinson Hundley, a well-
educated contemporary Southerner with a decided bias in favor of the gentleman
planter, wrote a devastating attack on the oily and knavish merchant. But before
leaving his subject, he noted that there were some who were honest. The honest
storekeeper, "truly a gentleman at heart," did not spend his profits foolishly, Hundley
explained, "and so soon as he finds himself possessor of more cash capital than
his business requires, he invests it in a suburban farm—small at first, but enlarged
and added to from year to year, until after a while it assumes the stately proportions
of a plantation. . . ." This storekeeper's children, Hundley added, will usually be
well educated and enter "the best society." D[aniel] R[obinson] Hundley, *Social
Relations in Our Southern States* (New York, 1860), 106-17. A Mississippian,
looking back from the postwar period, recalled that when he arrived in Rodney,
Miss., in 1836 "the town had an active and profitable mercantile business. . . .
Sometimes a three or five years business would be so profitable to a sober and
prudent merchant as to enable him to retire—to sell out to his clerks and go to
planting, or to New Orleans to engage in larger operations." H[orace] S. Fulkerson,
Random Recollections of Early Days in Mississippi (Vicksburg, Miss., 1885), 8. See
also Lewis E. Atherton, *The Southern Country Store, 1800-1860* (Baton Rouge,
1949), 203-204.

[29] For examples see Commercial Convention (Charleston, 1854), *The Journal*

induced to invest in direct-trade agencies in the South rested on the questionable assumption that the only reason they had not done so was that they lacked adequate information. "Let the proper measures, then, be taken to inform foreign capitalists of the opening now presented at the South for the profitable employment of their capital among us." Hayne was asking his readers to believe that British money went into banks and railroads (North and South) and into Northern commerce and manufacturing but stayed out of Southern shipping simply because the English were ignorant of the opportunities available to them.

It was not ignorance but lack of opportunity which was to blame. A Boston paper scorned what it called the "thoroughly fruitless" efforts to get English investments in Southern commercial agencies: "Capital goes where the owner think he can make it ultimately profitable to *himself*, and not where it has merely the prospect of benefiting *others*." The South lacked a large market and hence goods did not come to it. "If the Charleston merchant wonders why fewer commodities are imported into that market than into Boston, cannot he find a ready answer in the fact that commodities go only where they are wanted. . . . Commodities come to *us* because we want them —and we want them because we consume them. Commodities are not carried to South Carolina because they are not consumed there, and of course not wanted there."[30]

Southerners were aware that markets were important. Hayne had included a proposal for internal improvements which he termed "indispensable to our success." Good transportation, he noted, was necessary if the seaports engaged in direct trade were to find markets for their imports.[31] But Hayne gave the matter relatively little attention, whereas later conventions, beginning in 1845, stressed this point. Visions of lines of transportation connecting Southern ports with Western markets, with the Pacific, and even with the Far East marked speeches and resolutions at

---

of Proceedings (Charleston, 1854), 42-43; *DeBow's Review*, XVIII (1855), 633, 758-59, XXV (1858), 40-45.

[30] *Boston Courier*, as reprinted in *DeBow's Review*, XIII (1852), 96. In a brief paragraph introducing this extract (p. 95), DeBow poked fun at a part of the argument presented, but he made no effort to answer it. There was much about the article with which DeBow undoubtedly agreed since it stressed the importance of the development of manufacturing, a subject close to DeBow's heart.

[31] *Ibid.*, IV (1847), 353-55.

conventions in the late 1840's and early 1850's.[32] Yet, the South lagged behind the North in railroad construction, and those roads that were built tended to open up new cotton lands rather than the hoped-for markets which would support large-scale direct trade.

Here, then, was the crux of the matter. Cotton production (and to a lesser extent the production of other staples) possessed a great comparative advantage in the South.[33] This attracted capital from the North and Europe and, along with the social benefits arising from ownership of plantations and slaves, led to concentration on staple production. At the same time, the South lacked the extensive market necessary to induce widespread investment in commerce and manufacturing. Eugene D. Genovese has blamed the shallow market on slavery;[34] perhaps more important was the fact that a great proportion of the free white population were largely self-sufficient farmers, selling and buying little on the market. Had the planters heeded the fervent pleas to spend less and grow their own food so as to lessen their need for credit, the Southern market would have been even shallower. The reformers, of course, wanted the money saved to be put into manufacturing and commerce. They expected that planters, with complete freedom of choice, would give up known social and economic advantages for the broader—and for many, more dubious —advantages of sectional patriotism.

Thus, throughout the ante bellum period, the South remained an agricultural section concentrating on land, slaves, and a few staple crops, and the North and Europe provided the manu-

---

[32] For an able summary and evaluation of these meetings see Van Deusen, *Ante-Bellum Southern Commercial Conventions*, 21-61, 70-73. *DeBow's Review* carried full reports. Banker-politician James Robb of New Orleans was a strong advocate of transportation improvements, noting that New Orleans lacked an import trade to match her export trade because the city merchants lacked adequate transportation to ship imports into the interior. See Harry Howard Evans, "James Robb, Banker and Pioneer Railroad Builder of Ante-Bellum Louisiana," *Louisiana Historical Quarterly*, XXIII (Jan. 1940), 184.

[33] See Douglass C. North, *The Economic Growth of the United States, 1790-1860* (Englewood Cliffs, N. J., 1961) 123. North's brief discussion of "The Economic Structure of the South" (Chap. X) is a brilliant and provocative contribution to Southern economic history.

[34] *The Political Economy of Slavery* (New York, 1965), 157-79. Genovese does not place the entire blame for the shallow market on slavery; his aim is merely to show the effects of slavery.

factured goods, transportation, and many of the other commercial services necessary to market the crop. It is in this context that the factorage system must be understood. As merchant and banker for the planter, the factor played a pivotal role in a dependent South.

CHAPTER THIRTEEN

Cotton Factors and Storekeepers
in a Dependent South

Although the factor served as the planter's banker, factorage
houses were not banks in the real meaning of the word; that is,
unlike commercial banks, factors did not have the power to
create money either through note issue or deposit loans. They
did, as has been shown, often open a line of credit to a customer,
allowing him to draw on them as funds were required. In doing
so, however, they merely loaned money on hand (their own
funds or those being held for a planter) or they borrowed from
other sources. In the former case they could be compared to
modern savings and loan associations or credit unions; in the latter
case, they acted much as do present-day finance companies. The
factor, then, was the planter's banker only in a very general sense:
he handled his funds, arranged his credit, and paid his bills.

The cotton factor was often wealthy and could use his personal
resources to advance funds to his planter customers. But even such
wealthy factors as Maunsel White of New Orleans, who was said
to be worth a million dollars in 1850,[1] could not support the
credit needs of their customers from their personal assets and had
to rely upon outside funds. It was precisely because the factor
was able to tap capital resources that he was so important in the
credit structure of the South. Through him, capital resources of
the South, the North, and Europe were funneled into financing
and marketing the cotton crop.

The simplest method for drawing on local resources was to
shift the credit burden to another merchant. When he endorsed

a planter's note or allowed a planter to draw a time draft on him, the factor merely loaned his name for the credit it commanded. The merchant who accepted the note or draft actually extended the credit because he would receive payment only when the note or draft later came due. Typical of this procedure was the method used by the executors of the estate of William P. Hickman to pay store bills. Purchases for the Red River, Louisiana, plantation were made at a general store in nearby Alexandria. Bills were rendered annually, usually in January or February, and paid with a 90-day note drawn on the New Orleans factor to whom the estate's cotton was sent.[2]

The Alexandria storekeeper might hold the note to maturity, in which case he would extend the credit; or he might discount the note at a bank; or he might use it to pay his bills in New Orleans, in which case the New Orleans merchant who took it in payment would advance the 90 days of credit. In any event, the factor had three months before he would be called upon to pay the draft, this ordinarily being ample time to receive and sell the Hickman cotton.

Another method by which a factor could secure credit for his customers was to find a merchant who would himself be willing and able to sell goods on credit directly to the planter. For example, in 1824 the Louisiana cotton planter William S. Hamilton wrote his New Orleans factors that he needed a new cotton gin. The factors made inquiries in the city and reported to Hamilton that Lincoln and Green would sell him a gin on a credit of four months, or, if the planter were willing to pay interest, for an even longer credit. "You will please to say the length of credit you wish," wrote the factors.[3] Here again, the

---

[1] Clement Eaton, *The Mind of the Old South* (Baton Rouge, 1964), 55. White did not have this amount in ready cash. Like many other large factors, he was also a planter and part of his estate was in land and slaves.

[2] Hugh Lynch & Co. in a/c with Hickman, Alexandria, La., yearly accounts dated 1840's and 1850's, Hickman-Bryan Papers, Joint Collection, Western Historical Manuscripts Collection, State Historical Society of Missouri Manuscripts, Columbia, Mo. There were sometimes slight variations in the procedure. In 1852, for example, the account with Lynch & Co. came to $1,451.76 and was paid on Feb. 11, 1853 with two notes drawn on H. R. W. Hill, New Orleans factors. One note was dated Jan. 1853 ($483.12) and therefore was a sight draft; the other was dated May 1853 ($968.64).

[3] Dicks, Booker & Co. to Hamilton, New Orleans, July 27, 1824, W. S. Hamilton Papers, Southern Historical Collection, University of North Carolina Library, Chapel Hill, N. C.

factor arranged for the planter to get what he needed on credit, but in this instance it was the gin merchant and not the factor who supplied the credit.

Southern manufacturers and importers of agricultural and manufactured goods often sold their produce on time. In September 1839, a group of New Orleans merchants, "whose business is principally confined to the sale of Produce coming from the sections of country bordering on the Ohio and Upper Mississippi Rivers, and adjacent thereto," announced that they would charge an additional commission for goods sold on credit, explaining that "a very large portion of the vast amount of Western Produce disposed of here is now sold on time."[4] Probably most merchants and manufacturers in extending credit to planters in this way required a factor's acceptance to guarantee the loan or to make discounting possible. "Orders from the country accompanied by the Cash or good city references, promptly attended to," advertised Macon hardware merchant B. A. Wise. Druggist A. Alexander of Atlanta offered his goods "for cash or good paper," while Charleston dry goods dealers, Browning and Leman, called for "cash, or city acceptances."[5] A factor filling an order for food and other supplies from such merchants could delay payment and pass the credit on to his customer without having to use any of his own funds.

But Southern merchants were ill-equipped to extend this credit; it was a rare Southern merchant who had the necessary capital resources. Northern merchants and importers, however, backed by greater capital reserves, were able to supply the need. Often it was their credit which was being extended by Southern merchants to planters, this adding another dimension to the economic dependency of the South.

The procedure was simple enough. Southern storekeepers, wholesalers, and factors were supplied with merchandise on credit by Northern firms. A few examples will serve to illustrate the various relationships. Isaac P. Hazard, a Rhode Island merchant, had an arrangement with several Savannah factors whereby he

[4] Statement signed by 21 firms, dated New Orleans, Sept. 27, 1839, *New Orleans Price-Current*, Oct. 5, 1839.

[5] [John P. Campbell (ed.)], *The Southern Business Directory and General Commercial Advertiser* (Charleston, 1854), I, 225, 255, 357.

bought cotton from them (for cash) and sent woolen cloth to them for sale. The woolens were sent on consignment and could be disposed of in the manner the Savannah firms felt most advantageous. This allowed the factors to sell woolen cloth to planters on a credit that was really being supplied by the Rhode Island merchant.[6] Hazard's brother, R. G. Hazard, dealt with merchants and planters in Mississippi. Orders from storekeepers to stock their shelves and orders from merchants for their planter customers were filled by Hazard on credit; other merchants sold his goods on a commission from their stores, payment being due only after the goods were paid for. Again, it was the Northern firm which supplied the credit that merchants in the South were able to extend.[7]

A business relationship between Johnson and Harrold, country merchants of Americus, Georgia, and Thomas Wood and Company of New York allowed the Americus storekeeers to supply local farmers and planters with a variety of foodstuffs on credit. The New York firm sent fish and groceries to Americus (via Savannah) on consignment, receiving payment when Johnson and Harrold were paid for the goods.[8] Reynolds, Witherspoon and Company of Mobile sold hardware on credit, waiting for payment until after the cotton crop was sold. But the Mobile firm was

[6] See letters from R. & W. King to Hazard from Savannah, dated variously from 1831-1832, and from R. Habersham, Elias Reid, Way & King, also from Savannah during the years 1841-1849, Isaac Peace Hazard Papers, Georgia Historical Society, Savannah, Ga.

[7] P. H. Skipwith to Hazard, Commerce, Miss., Aug. 5, Oct. 16, 1841, B. Stanton, Jr., to Hazard, Belmont, Miss., Dec. 13, 1841, E. B. Baker to Hazard, Natchez, June 6, 1843, Jan. 15, 1846, William St. John Elliot to Hazard, Tilsit Plantation, June 25, 1837, R. G. Hazard Papers, Mississippi Department of Archives and History, Jackson, Miss. Hazard shipped his orders coastwise to New Orleans and sometimes a factor in that city was involved in the transaction. Thus the Natchez merchant E. B. Baker (in letter cited above) ordered shoes from Hazard for a planter, A. W. Dunbar, the order being sent to Ringgold & Ferriday, New Orleans cotton factors, with orders to send them on to Dunbar. The New Orleans firm was probably Baker's factor, since like most storekeepers he probably took cotton in trade for store goods. Elliot was a planter. His order was shipped via Reynolds, Byrne & Co., cotton factors in New Orleans. In his letter to Hazard he promised "to arrange" payment, probably with a draft on Reynolds, Byrne & Co. Planters Moses Liddell and Stephen Duncan also purchased from Hazard.

[8] Thomas Wood & Co. to Johnson & Harrold, New York, Jan. 17, 19, 24, 30, Feb. 5, 6, 7, 13, 1861, Thomas Wood & Co. to U. B. Harrold, New York, Jan. 5, Feb. 25, 1861, J. M. Selkin & Co. to Johnson & Harrold, Savannah, May 3, 1861, Harrold Brothers Papers, Emory University Library, Atlanta, Ga.

simply passing on credit it had received from the half-dozen New York firms who supplied its hardware.[9]

Partnerships linking New York and Southern houses often meant that Northern capital supported Southern firms. Typical was the announcement in 1836 of the formation of Coit and Company in New Orleans: "SAMUEL T. COIT AND JOSEPH NASH are general partners, and PHELPS, DODGE & CO., of the city of New-York, are partners in *commendam* to the amount of Fifty Thousand Dollars, which sum they have contributed to the common stock in cash."[10]

It was to this situation that an angry critic was referring when he charged that Southern merchants were *"mere peddlers"* acting on behalf of real merchants in the North. But such criticism missed the point. It was not a lack of energy which hurt the Southern merchant, but rather the competitive advantages of the North.[11] Southern wholesalers faced disastrous competition from Northern merchants. Price was one factor. In the case of foreign imports, Southern merchants were able to buy directly from Northern importers and jobbers and thereby bypass the costs incurred by Southern wholesalers who had to buy from the same source and then add their own profit markup to the cost. It was this, of course, which induced the movement for direct trade.

Yet, while some Southerners were advocating direct trade with Europe, the South was "importing" an increasing amount of domestic goods from Northern mills and factories, and, at the same time, expressing a decided preference for Northern goods.[12]

[9] Wm. A. Witherspoon to H. L. Reynolds, Mobile, June 15, July 28, Aug. 2, 3, 1855, Henry Lee Reynolds Papers, Southern Historical Collection, University of North Carolina Library, Chapel Hill, N. C.

[10] *New Orleans Price-Current*, Feb. 13, 1836. Similar advertisements appeared regularly in this and other papers and business directories.

[11] In addition to the sources cited directly, this discussion of wholesaling and jobbing in the South is based on Lewis E. Atherton, *Southern Country Store, 1800-1860* (Baton Rouge, 1949), 127-44.

[12] Franklin H. Elmore gave the amount of domestic imports into the South as 33 percent of the total in his report to the Charleston Convention in 1839, noting that Southern consumption of domestic merchandise "has increased greatly and is still increasing." *DeBow's Review*, IV (1847), 496. In 1861 Daniel Lord wrote that Southerners "import from the North ten dollars in domestics for every one imported, directly or indirectly, from Europe." *The Effect of Secession Upon the Commercial Relations Between the North and South, and Upon Each Section* (New York, 1861), 15.

Here again, a price advantage lay in the Northern market. Southern merchants who went North and bought directly from the factory saved the markup added by the Southern jobber or wholesaler. Also, as their advertisements make clear,[13] many Northern manufacturers had retail or wholesale outlets in Southern cities. Finally, Northern manufacturers often sent traveling agents into the Southern cities. These agents offered to sell directly to any customer willing to buy in large quantities; some even visited plantations. They charged wholesale prices and, if necessary, sold on a credit.[14]

Even if price had not been a factor, credit terms gave the Northern firms the advantage. In the summer, complained a Southerner, large numbers of Southern merchants went to the North to buy. They did not make their purchases in the South because "they want *time*, and this grand element in a profitable trade they cannot get here."[15] Northern cities had lured a large part of the wholesale trade from New Orleans, wrote another Southerner. The reason was "not that their markets were better, as convenient, or really cheaper" than the New Orleans market, but that the "wholesale jobbers of the northern cities could afford to extend . . . greater facilities in the way of long credits than could our jobbers and wholesale dealers." Trade which would ordinarily have gone to New Orleans was diverted to Northern cities simply because of "the twelve-months credit system."[16]

Thus, food, clothing, and manufactured goods were available to cotton growers on credit from storekeepers, factors, and other merchants. Although the factor was usually involved—he made purchases, endorsed notes, and paid bills—most of the credit did not come from his own resources. It was usually provided by

---

13 See, for example, the business cards in [Campbell], *Southern Business Directory*, I, *passim*.

14 "Wherever population is at all concentrated in the country, their [northern manufacturers'] commercial agents are to be found. Nay they visit plantations, contract for machinery, hard-ware, cotton and woolen goods, jewelry and other articles, giving time, if necessary, to effect a transaction, and the very sources of business of our great commercial capital are thus undermined." *The Daily Picayune* (New Orleans), Feb. 28, 1860.

15 *Banker's Magazine*, VII (1853), 468.

16 *Commercial Bulletin* (New Orleans), as reprinted in *Hunt's Merchants' Magazine*, XXXIII (1855) 263. See also Harry A. Mitchell, "The Development of New Orleans as a Wholesale Trading Center," *Louisiana Historical Quarterly*, XXVII (Oct. 1944), 956.

other merchants, more often than not, Northerners, or Southerners who had received their goods on credit from Northern firms.

In addition to being able to utilize the credit available from Northern merchants, the cotton factor was also able to draw more directly from Northern or European money markets. Merchants in the North or in Europe allowed factors to draw upon them in anticipation of receiving either the crop to sell or sterling or New York bills which factors might accept for the cotton they sold. This procedure encouraged a general flow of capital from the North and Europe to the South, thereby providing a part of the funds which the factor used to give advances to his planter customers.

The transaction was most easily arranged when a single firm had branches in the South as well as in Europe and the North. A typical case may be taken from the records of William Johnson, a Mississippi planter, who dealt with the allied firms of Washington Jackson and Company (New Orleans), Jackson, Todd and Company (Philadelphia), and Todd, Jackson and Company (Liverpool). The New Orleans branch of the house served as Johnson's factor. He shipped them his cotton, often with instructions to send it on to Liverpool. The New Orleans branch provided Johnson with supplies and cash advances as requested, but it would draw a sterling bill on the Liverpool house which it sold "to reimburse ourselves for cash advances made to you."[17] In this way the New Orleans factor was able to make the advances to the planter. But the funds—and hence, the credit—came from Liverpool.[18]

Factors could also facilitate borrowing by planters directly from

[17] See the numerous letters to Johnson from Washington Jackson & Co. and allied firms, 1844-1850. The quoted words are in Washington Jackson & Co. to Johnson, New Orleans, Nov. 19, 1844, William Johnson Papers, Mississippi Department of Archives and History, Jackson, Miss.

[18] In addition to credit, the procedure facilitated exchange. For example, in 1840, the Natchez planter Stephen Duncan, who also dealt with Washington Jackson & Co. in New Orleans, wanted an advance on his cotton being sent to Liverpool and had the Philadelphia branch of the firm (Jackson, Todd & Co.) draw on Todd, Jackson & Co. of Liverpool. He then instructed the Philadelphia firm to send the sterling bills to Charles P. Leverich & Co. of New York who was to sell the bills for Duncan's account. Jackson, Todd & Co. to Leverich, Philadelphia, April 16, 1840, Charles P. Leverich Papers, Mississippi Department of Archives and History, Jackson, Miss. This allowed Duncan, who had extensive financial dealings in New York, to move funds there. On another occasion, the Philadelphia firm, in possession of a bill on Brown Bros. & Co. of New York—perhaps received by the New Orleans branch in payment for cotton purchased by a Brown Bros. agent of them

a Northern bank. Thus, in February 1856, I. Rae Habersham, a New York partner in the Savannah factorage house of Robert Habersham, wrote Georgia planter George Noble Jones that he had succeeded in getting Jones' note discounted at the Bank of the Republic in New York City.[19] The planter's promissory note probably carried the New York merchant's endorsement; perhaps the Southern house endorsed the note also.

It was not necessary for the Southern firm to be in partnership with a Northern or European firm for it to take advantage of outside credit resources. For example, merchants in the South who planned shipping cotton to William and James Brown and Company of Liverpool were allowed to draw an advance from Brown Brothers and Company of New York. The New York house would reimburse itself by drawing sterling bills on the Liverpool branch. Thus, the Southern merchant's credit in this instance would come from Liverpool via New York.[20] Planters' records indicate clearly that whenever a New York or Liverpool sale was desired, the Southern factor usually used the privilege of drawing an advance on the firm that would receive the cotton.

Not all advances drawn by Southerners on the North or Europe were predicated on the immediate shipment of merchandise; that is, Southern merchants did not always have to send cotton to Northern or foreign merchants before they were allowed to draw on their capital resources. Factors might borrow from Northerners on the security of some of their personal property or upon the promise that cotton which might in the future come into their possession would be consigned to the lending merchant. In June 1842, for example, the New Orleans factor Maunsel White, anticipating a shortage of funds for the coming season, made two proposals to as many New York merchants to supply him with needed cash. To Joshua Clibborn he offered to ship all his firm's cotton in return for the right to draw on the New York merchant when he needed funds.[21] Two days after writing to Clibborn, he

---

there—sent the bill to Leverich & Co. in New York with instructions to get payment from Brown. Jackson, Todd & Co. to Leverich, Philadelphia, June 17, 1840, *ibid.*

[19] Letter dated New York, Feb. 16, 1856, George Noble Jones Papers, Georgia Historical Society, Savannah, Ga.

[20] *William and James Brown and Company v. Thomas M'Gran*, 14 Peters (U. S.), 497 (1840).

[21] Letter dated New Orleans, June 23, 1842, Maunsel White Papers, Southern Historical Collection, University of North Carolina Library, Chapel Hill, N. C.

wrote to Robert Shaw asking for a loan on the security of his sugar plantation.[22]

White was writing in the midst of depression when credit was tight and when bank and business failures in the South had made Northerners justifiably hesitant to lend their own limited funds. Usually Northern and foreign capital was abundantly and easily available and such binding promises were unnecessary. Factors and other merchants found that their notes or planters' notes which they endorsed could be easily discounted or sold. Ultimately, of course, each note would have to be paid by means of the sale of the crop. But each bill or note sold or discounted by a factor was not predicated on a particular shipment of cotton; rather it was based on the expected ability of the factor to sell cotton profitably and pay off bills. The distinction is important. If each loan were based on a particular parcel of cotton, factors could not borrow until the planters had shipped the cotton to them, and hence could not lend beyond the extent of their own savings. But, because factors could borrow on their expected rather than on their immediate ability to repay, they were able to give longer-term loans.

During the 1830's English capital formed the base of an immense credit structure. American importers received credit from British houses and in turn sold on long term to jobbers who passed the credit on. Payment was easily arranged, again with the aid of British funds. Importers, jobbers, wholesalers, storekeepers, factors, and planters easily discounted their notes in the growing number of banks whose resources grew apace as British investors bought bank and state bonds freely. In the South, the cotton factor played a pivotal role in maintaining the credit structure. Factors allowed planters to draw on them or they endorsed planters' notes. This paper was readily discounted in local banks. When notes came due at the bank, they were repaid by factors with bills drawn on New York and European houses which honored factors' drafts because they knew they would be later paid with cotton or foreign bills. In addition, foreign firms such as the Barings gave reputable factors open or uncovered credits ranging up to £20,000, thereby allowing these firms to draw before cotton was actually shipped.[23] While Northern and foreign firms

---

[22] Letter dated New Orleans, June 25, 1842, *ibid.*
[23] Ralph W. Hidy, *The House of Baring in American Trade and Finance* (Cambridge, Mass., 1949), 174, 184.

were allowing Southerners to draw on them for funds, others were
sending agents into the South to buy promissory notes and bills of
exchange.[24] So long as credit came easily and due notes could be
renewed or replaced by new notes, the structure remained intact.
When, however, panic struck in 1837, the structure collapsed. The
National Gazette surveyed the ruins:

> 1. The failure at New Orleans of all but four or five of the
> principal cotton factors, through whose credit and capital the
> planters of Louisiana, Mississippi, Tennessee, and Alabama,
> were enabled to purchase lands and slaves, to improve their
> plantations, and to anticipate the proceeds of their crops, in-
> volving responsibilities estimated at thirty millions of dollars.
>
> 2. The failure at New York and Philadelphia of several large
> houses, who were under acceptance of New Orleans and other
> southern bills of exchange drawn in anticipation of shipments
> of produce, or remittances of sterling bills, which were never
> made, owing to the failure of the drawers.[25]

Panic and ensuing depression tightened credit and made bankers
and merchants chary of accepting any but the best bills and
notes. By 1844, however, lending was becoming freer. Funds
were accumulating and seeking investment, *Hunt's Merchants'
Magazine* noted, as it reminded its readers of the tragedy which
followed the excesses of credit during the 1830's[26] and urged that
only short-term paper be discounted.[27] By the 1850's paper of all
kinds was again freely discounted. Although English funds no
longer sought investment in bank stocks, New Yorkers continued
to borrow from London "under a system of floating indebtedness,
conducted through the agency of bills of exchange at sixty days'
sight." Nor was each draft predicated on a specific shipment of
merchandise: "In the general ramifications of the money operations

[24] One such firm was J. L. & S. Joseph & Co., private bankers of New York.
A casualty of the panic, the firm listed among its assets over $2,500,000 in notes,
bills, and accounts in Southern markets. *Journal of Commerce*, Oct. 9, 1837, copied
in *Financial Register*, I (Nov. 8, 1837).

[25] April 22, 1837, copied in *Financial Register*, I (Oct. 25, 1837), 129. This is
part of an attack on Jackson's bank policy which the paper alleged was responsible
for the panic. The chain of results described goes on to include the buyers of the
Southern bills on the North (among them merchants in the South who owed money
in the North) and the consequent failure of Northern merchants who were not
paid because the bills their debtors had purchased were worthless.

[26] X (1844), 76-78.

[27] *Ibid.*, 564.

the amount of European acceptances of American bills is probably five or six times greater than the aggregate commercial transactions."[28] New York banks and note brokers discounted freely, the length of the notes accepted increasing until even 12-month notes were being discounted.[29] Although the panic in 1857 brought renewed conservatism and long notes were no longer discounted, the caution was temporary. In 1859 and early 1860, ample funds were available for discounting notes up to six months to run,[30] and although banks preferred notes of three months or less, exceptions were often made and longer notes discounted.[31]

Thus the cotton factor was able to draw upon the immense capital resources of New York and London, this in turn allowing him to supply the advances and credit needed by his planter customers. As a result, of course, the factor, like the planter he served, was in debt. It seems that this was obvious to most planters. Despite differences they might have with their factors, the planters rarely accused them of being responsible for low prices and high costs. Advice to stay out of debt, diversify the economy, establish direct trade, invest in manufacturing, and the like were not usually designed to allow Southerners to bypass the Southern cotton factor but rather to escape the clutches of what one Alabamian called the "foreign millionary operators," who, by lending their money, gained control of the South's most important crop.[32]

[28] George McHenry, The Cotton Trade (London, 1863), 179.

[29] Margaret G. Meyers, Origins and Development, Vol. I of The New York Money Market (New York, 1931), 54.

[30] Hunt's Merchants' Magazine, XLIII (1860), 72-73.

[31] J. S. Gibbons, The Banks of New York (New York, 1870), 60. A merchant with a 6-month bill which the bank thought very good was allowed to give his own note for 3 months, the bank holding the longer note for security. His note would be repaid in 3 months by discounting the original bill, which then would have only 3 months to run. Since Hunt's lists rates for longer bills as well as rates for unendorsed bills (single name) and bills from merchants "not well known," it is probably safe to assume that many who discounted did not bother to use the method Gibbons described.

[32] DeBow's Review, XXV (1858), 40-41. "Millionary," according to the Oxford English Dictionary, was a contemporary term meaning millionaire. For many Southerners concerned about sectional dependency, "foreign" meant simply non-Southern—either Northern or European.

CHAPTER FOURTEEN

Bankers in a Dependent South

Recognizing that Northern and foreign financial institutions were the South's creditors, many Southerners wondered why Southern banks could not wrest this power from them. In a speech before the 1855 Commercial Convention in New Orleans, Albert Pike of Arkansas expressed the frustration many reformers felt: "I have felt, though not a commercial man, that it was a shame that a thousand or two dollars cannot be raised here without being compelled to apply to some Liverpool agent."[1] Analogous to the criticism that Southern merchants were no more than peddlers of Northern goods was the charge that Southern banks were timid lackeys of Wall Street.

By the early 1840's the disastrous effects of overexpansion and bank speculation in cotton had virtually ended banking in Mississippi and Arkansas and had resulted in very conservative banking practices in the other cotton states. As the depression waned, however, the conservative practices of the Southern banks were criticized by many who saw that merchants and factors were forced to turn to outside agencies for their credit.

The products of Southern agriculture make outsiders rich, charged a Southerner in 1853. "Why should not the profits, by use of northern credit or capital, be enjoyed by our own people through whose hands these rich products pass, but merely as media or agents to enrich others?" he asked. Southerners could earn these profits if it were not for the "paucity of banking facilities" in the South and most especially in New Orleans. "Our merchants cannot convert the notes of their customers into money, or at least except to a limited extent. Their notes remain untouched in their portfolios until they mature. It requires a merchant of large capital to engage in such a business. . . ." He concluded by advocating a change in the Louisiana banking law.[2]

Here was the familiar lament—Southern dependency upon the North. Southern planters required credit and Southern banks were unable to supply enough to meet their needs; planters and merchants were forced to turn to the North. Conditions seemed to defy solution. A change in the Louisiana bank law so as to allow longer credits through the renewal of commercial notes—an action specifically prohibited by the law of 1842—suggested a return to an overexpansion of paper credit, the very menace which had impelled the law in the first place. The result was a dilemma that critics could not resolve.

In 1860, H. C. Cabell of Richmond, Virginia, condemned the New York banks for their practice of issuing loans on the basis of deposits without retaining a sufficient specie reserve, a practice, he noted, wisely avoided by Southern banks. He then went on to condemn the Southern banking system for its inability to meet the needs of Southern planters: Southern banks would not negotiate bills which did not have a ready sale in New York. He suggested that the South alter its banking system to "render it and the products of the South independent of the caprices, whims and follies, and misfortunes of Northern banks." His solution, however, was hardly a banking reform. He suggested that the Southern banks themselves negotiate bills independently of New York although he offered no way in which banks could do this without adopting the New York system of banking which he condemned. Instead he proposed the by now very familiar saw—direct trade with Europe.[3]

Southerners might complain about their banking laws and urge that bankers in the South break the connection with the North, but in truth the entire credit structure of the South required the connection. Whenever a financial or political crisis broke the connection, a complete paralysis gripped the cotton market in the South, illustrating the indispensable role of Northern banks in financing the cotton crop.

---

[1] *DeBow's Review*, XVIII (1855), 633.
[2] *Bankers' Magazine*, VII (1853), 468-69.
[3] *Hunt's Merchants' Magazine*, XLII (1860), 311-17, 323.

The crisis of 1837 and its aftermath produced a most serious derangement of the money market. "Our Cotton Market is in a most strange situation," reported the *New Orleans Price-Current* on April 15, 1837; "indeed, it might with propriety be said that we have none, as transactions are so nearly suspended." Demand, of course, was down, but so were prices. Yet those who might want to take advantage of low prices, the paper continued, could not buy, and the market was inactive. "This inactivity may be chiefly attributed, we believe, to the utter inability of buyers to raise funds, as the Banks are not purchasing either Sterling or Domestic Exchange."[4] The banks were not purchasing because they could not sell exchange: Bills were not being paid to the North and hence the market for domestic exchange dropped; foreign debts were not being paid and hence the market for foreign exchange had fallen in the North. The market was brought to a virtual standstill. Only those few with cash were able to purchase the crop in the South,[5] and many factors were therefore consigning the crop abroad in hopes of securing a sale elsewhere.[6] It was in this context that Southern banks, following Nicholas Biddle's initiative, attempted to offer relief by providing large advances with their own notes. Relief was temporary and resulted in even further monetary disturbance as much of the bank paper depreciated greatly.

Five years later conditions remained substantially the same. Indeed, depreciated bank notes added to the difficulties. Debts could not be collected except in depreciated currency at great discount; most factors were unwilling to sell for depreciated currency and thus bills could not be negotiated. Prices remained low and the market remained sluggish.[7] The coming year promised more of the same. The crop will soon be in, wrote the New Orleans factor Maunsel White in July 1842. "Those wishing to purchase must send the Silver or Gold for it, as nothing else will purchase. We are in the greatest confusion in consequence of the Currency."[8] As the season got underway, White's prognosis proved correct. The *New Orleans Price-Current* noted in September that

---

[4] See also the issue of Nov. 18, 1837.
[5] *New Orleans Price-Current*, May 6, 1837.
[6] *Ibid.*, May 20, 1837.
[7] *Ibid.*, June 11, 18, 1842.
[8] To Robert Shaw, July 9, 1842, Maunsel White Papers, Southern Historical Collection, University of North Carolina Library, Chapel Hill, N. C.

specie was flowing in from the North to buy the crop. For the moment the paper found this beneficial. Prices might remain low, but planters and merchants dealing on a specie basis "will find some compensation in the fact that their dollars are dollars in reality, and not the unsubstantial shadows that, in too many instances, have proved but barren promises."[9] A month later the same paper was not so sanguine. The cotton market "has continued to labor under great depression" not because there was no demand for cotton but because of "the scarcity of specie, the supply of which is totally inadequate to meet the wants of trade." Exchange was extremely difficulty to sell—"the very best Bills can rarely be disposed of." As a result, those who had specie were able to drive prices down.[10] The Louisiana cotton planter Bennet H. Barrow noted the effect in his diary: "the news [from] N. Orleans is really distressing[,] cotten [sic] selling from 4 to 6 ¢ cash[,] 7 ¾ to 8 on 30 & 40 days—all for the want of specie & not being able to negotiate Bills."[11]

The financial crisis of 1857 had similar results, although they were not as long lasting and Southern banks had not flooded the market with rapidly depreciating notes. Liverpool buyers were offering as much as 17 cents per pound for cotton in the Southern markets, to be paid, as was the usual custom, in sterling bills. Commercial difficulties in New York had greatly reduced the demand for these bills and instead of the usual premium paid for them in New York, the bills were being sold at a discount, sometimes as much as 10 percent or more during the early part of the season. Under such circumstances, Southern banks refused to accept sterling bills except at a great discount, and sales could not be made. New York bills were even more sharply discounted. The result was a severe decline in the price paid for cotton. Middling New Orleans cotton, for example, which opened at 16 cents in New York in September, by January fell to less than 9 cents and did not rise above 13 cents for the remainder of the season.[12] So long as the demand for foreign and domestic bills

[9] Sept. 1, 1842.

[10] Oct. 5, 1842.

[11] Entry of Oct. 11, 1842, "Plantation Diary of Bennet H. Barrow," Edwin Adams Davis (ed.), *Plantation Life in the Florida Parishes of Louisiana, 1836-1846 as Reflected in the Diary of Bennet H. Barrow* (New York, 1943), 275.

[12] *Hunt's Merchants' Magazine*, XLII (1860), 318; E. J. Donnell, *History of*

was down, Southern banks had either to refuse to discount them or to accept them only at a substantial discount.

The political crisis of 1860-1861 produced substantially the same effects on the South as did the earlier economic crisis. William Mure, the British consul at New Orleans, wrote that the political agitation had served to "obstruct the usual channels of Trade. . . . Importers and jobbers are unable to sell their stocks of goods, so that they cannot find the means of purchasing exchange to liquidate their Domestic and Foreign obligations. The Cotton Factors are unable to sell their produce, which the agents for Liverpool houses and Manchester spinners are ready to purchase, but are deprived of facilities of negotiating their bills of exchange. . . ."[13] In December 1860, *Hunt's Merchants' Magazine* noted "the loss of credit [in New York] growing out of political derangements." Payments were not being made from the South and therefore banks and other lenders in New York were reluctant to discount the longer-term paper predicated on the flow of exchange from the South.[14]

The financial center of the South was in the North. When Northerners did not supply the credit or specie to move the crop, when Northern bills were not in demand in the South, and when the sale of sterling bills for Northern remittances was down, cotton prices sagged and planters and merchants suffered. In 1857 a Southern newspaper raged: "Every failure, every swindle, every forging transaction at the North produces a convulsion in the money market there, and New York being the great monetary center of the country, it thrills and vibrates through every household in the South. There is not a planter in the South to-day who is not suffering from this very cause—suffering in credit, in character, and fortune."[15] The rage was impotent. The only suggestion

---

Cotton (New York, 1872), 470-74; Richard Manning Boykin, *Captain Alexander Hamilton Boykin* (New York, 1942), 91.

[13] To Lord John Russell, New Orleans, Dec. 13, 1860, printed in *Louisiana Historical Quarterly*, XIII (Jan. 1930), 32-33. See also entries of Nov. 17 and Nov. 29, 1860, *The Private Journal of Henry William Ravenel, 1859-1887*, ed. Arney Robinson Childs (Columbia, S. C., 1947), 39, 41.

[14] *Hunt's Merchants' Magazine*, XLIII (1860), 715-16. *Bankers' Magazine*, XV (1860), 419-21, took note of the general prosperity in banking circles but added that "the only speck in the horizon is the threat of secession in the South." The journal was confident that secession would not come and was sure that the interruption of the "current of commerce and finance" would be "only temporary."

[15] *Vicksburg True Southron*, copied in *DeBow's Review*, XXIII (1857), 658.

for change offered was direct trade with Europe in Southern ships, a suggestion which had been made repeatedly for twenty years to no avail.

The logic of the North-South financial relationship is clear enough. It was simply a matter of capital moving to where it was needed. If the Southern planter suffered when there was a dislocation in the nation's monetary center, he gained when the system was working efficiently, for from New York's vast capital resources—and the resources it was able to tap in Europe—came the credit necessary for the operation of the plantation system.

Northerners were quick to describe the benefits accruing to the South as a result of the resources made available by the North and to chide Southerners for their carping. "The growth of wealth in the cotton states may . . . be almost entirely traced to eastern capital," declared a contributor to a Philadelphia journal in 1837. "Everybody knows" that the planters secured supplies from the merchant on credit "in anticipation of the next year's crop" and "it is equally well known" that this credit could be given only because the merchant received his goods on credit from Northern merchants. "The wealth of the cotton growing states, it is manifest, is therefore greatly augmented by the borrowing of foreign capital, and the condemnation of so advantageous a policy, comes with bad grace from a cotton planter."[16]

The planter needed Northern capital resources, wrote another; his prosperity would disappear if he had to rely on "the small capital of the place of production." Nor could direct trade and the utilization of foreign capital help: "Without the intervention of the great capital and demand at New York, the producer would be entirely at the mercy of the buyer in whatever port abroad his cotton might land, and he would in no case find a greater economy than at present."[17]

The commercial supremacy of New York City was not a plot against the South, insisted the New York *Times* in December 1860, but arose because the city's "position, skill, industry and wealth" made it possible for it to "fulfill its duties better than any other agent." Enunciating the concept of comparative advantage

[16] *Financial Register*, I (Aug. 16, 1837), 63.

[17] [Samuel Powell], *Notes on "Southern Wealth and Northern Profits"* (Philadelphia, 1861), 24.

—although it did not use the term—the *Times* argued that New York was simply doing that for which it was best equipped, just as was the South by devoting itself to staple crop agriculture.[18]

Political economist Stephen Colwell noted that Southern planters had adopted the prevailing system of marketing cotton voluntarily. Coercion had not been necessary to get Southerners to accept a system from which they benefited. "A very large proportion of the money advanced on cotton, at all the places of delivery, comes from New York; and bills drawn upon cotton are transmitted thither, to reimburse advances." Even foreign bills were most profitably sold by Southerners in New York because "it is there that the importers of foreign goods are concentrated, and thence their remittances are made. There the buyers of exchange congregate, and there, of course, the best price can be obtained." Thus, the North-South economic relations were "a matter not only of convenience, but economy."[19]

Daniel Lord described the nation's interregional trading pattern, a pattern of mutual advantage to all sections:

> The proceeds of the Southern crops comes [*sic*] North simply *to pay Southern debts.* . . . Every year the value of merchandize going West over the Erie Canal, New York Central and Erie Railroads, exceeds that coming East over the same routes, by $100,000,000. This is a puzzle to many persons who do not reflect upon the course of trade in this country. They look upon the enormous excess of Western-found freight as proof of the extravagance or unsoundness of the West. It is simply the process by which that section gets pay for the products which it sells to the South. These debts Cotton pays. The Northern shipper takes it to Europe, brings back the proceeds, which are distributed by Northern merchants and factors to the creditors of the South, throughout the length and breadth of the land.[20]

[18] Dec. 7, 1860, as reprinted in Howard Cecil Perkins (ed.), *Northern Editorials on Secession* (New York, 1942), II, 567.

[19] [Stephen Colwell], *The Five Cotton States and New York* ([Philadelphia], 1861), 9-12. For a similar analysis by an English visitor, see James Robertson, *A Few Months in America* (London, 1855), 14. The same point was made in 1840 by a cotton buyer. See John T. Entz, *Exchange and Cotton Trade Between England and the United States* (New York, 1840), 16.

[20] *The Effect of Secession Upon the Commercial Relations Between the North and South, and Upon Each Section* (New York, 1861), 16.

TABLE 1. GENERAL STATEMENT OF BANK RESOURCES DATED

Area	Number of banks (incl. branches)				Capital		
	1845	1850	1858	1860	1845	1850	1858
Louisiana	28	25[a]	15	13	19,670,580	12,370,390[a]	22,800,830
Mississippi	—	1[a]	2	—	—	118,460[a]	1,110,600
Alabama	6	2[a]	6	8	11,856,484[c]	1,800,580[a]	3,235,650
Georgia	24	21	30	29	10,250,702	13,482,198	16,015,256
South Carolina	11	14[a]	20	20	11,065,668	13,213,031[a]	14,885,631
Tennessee	23	23[a]	45	34	8,284,929	6,881,568[a]	9,083,069
Arkansas	10	—	—	—	3,002,706	—	—
Total	102	86	118	104	64,131,069	47,866,227	67,131,036
New York	150	198	294	303	43,674,146	48,618,762	107,449,143
Massachusetts	103	126	173	174	30,020,000	36,925,050	60,319,720
Pennsylvania	48[b]	58	76	90	14,587,226[b]	17,926,222	25,691,439
Total	301	382	543	567	88,281,372	103,470,034	193,460,302

[a] 1851.
[b] Does not include Pennsylvania Bank of U. S.
[c] Includes non-specie-paying banks.
[d] Rate of increase, 1851-1860, is 44 percent.
[e] Rate of increase, 1850-1860, is 129 percent.
[f] Rate of increase, 1851-1860, is 51 percent.
[g] Rate of increase, 1850-1860, is 87 percent.

Although the rhetoric of the defenders of New York sometimes exhibited a smug condescension and implied that a beneficent city was graciously bestowing its capital resources on a dependent South, and although Southern defenders might argue that New York's wealth would disappear should the city be deprived of its ability to exploit the South, the core of the pro-New York argument was sound: The Northern and foreign money markets provided the capital which was unavailable in the South but which the Southern planter and farmer required.

A glance at banking statistics reveals the overwhelming resources of the Northern states (see Tables 1, 2, and 3). Throughout the 1840's and 1850's, the cotton states lagged far behind the Northern states of New York, Pennsylvania, and Massachusetts in banking, as measured by both capital and loans and discounts. On January 1, 1860 New York bankers reported loans and discounts amounting to over $200 million, almost twice the sum loaned by all the cotton states combined. Moreover, despite the proposals and resolutions by members of the Southern Commercial Conventions, the Southern position relative to the North deteriorated over the years. While nationally, loans and discounts by banks almost doubled during the last ante bellum decade, they increased by only 50 percent in the cotton states. The share of the cotton

Near January 1 for Selected Areas and Selected Years

Capital (cont.)	Loans and discounts				Area
1860	1845	1850	1858	1860	
24,496,866	18,417,669	19,309,108[a]	23,229,096	35,401,609	Louisiana
no returns	—	112,275[a]	393,216	no returns	Mississippi
4,901,000	15,132,251[c]	4,670,458[a]	5,585,424	13,570,027	Alabama
16,689,560	5,451,751	11,421,626	12,677,863	16,776,282	Georgia
14,962,062	14,440,112	23,212,330[a]	22,056,561	27,801,912	South Carolina
8,067,037	9,337,780	10,992,139[a]	13,124,292	11,751,019	Tennessee
—	2,352,617	—	—	—	Arkansas
69,116,525[d]	65,132,180	69,717,936	77,066,452	105,300,849[f]	Total
111,441,320[e]	70,793,354	107,132,389	162,807,376	200,351,332[g]	New York
64,519,200	48,770,975	63,330,024	92,458,572	107,417,323	Massachusetts
25,565,582	25,646,533[b]	39,430,145	49,149,323	50,327,157	Pennsylvania
201,526,102	145,210,862	209,892,558	304,415,271	358,095,812	Total

Sources:

1845: U. S. Congress, House, *Bank Returns*, 29th Cong., 1st Sess., House Exec. Doc. 226 (August 10, 1846), 1250-51.
1850 U. S. Congress, House, *Condition of the Banks Throughout & the United States*, 35th Cong., 1st Sess., House Exec. Doc.
1858: 107 (April 27, 1858) 326-29, 334.
1860: *Hunt's Merchants' Magazine*, XLIII (1860), 336.

states in total loans and discounts dropped from 19 percent to 15 percent from 1850 to 1860.[21]

It was not the cotton factor, then, nor the lack of sufficient energy on the part of Southern merchants, nor poor banking laws and practices that were responsible for the commercial dependence of the South. Southern wealth was invested predominantly in land and slaves, and the section lacked the liquid capital resources adequate for its credit needs. The experience following the 1837 crisis had shown the dangers to the economy when the Southern banks issued notes at will to move the crop, and thereafter Southern banks remained wisely conservative.[22]

[21] In a speech to the Southern Commercial Convention in New Orleans in 1852, James Robb argued that the South was not deficient in banking capital. He compared banking capital in New Orleans with that in Boston, New York, Philadelphia, and other cities on a per capita basis and concluded that the "constant subject of complaint that New-Orleans has an insufficient banking capital" was unfounded. DeBow, *The Industrial Resources, Etc., of the Southern and Western States* (New Orleans, 1853), II, 152-54; Herbert Wender, *Southern Commercial Conventions, 1837-1859* (Baltimore, 1930), 74-76. Robb's error arose primarily from his comparing banking capital in the *cities* of New Orleans, New York, etc. New Orleans had all the banks in Louisiana whereas New York, Pennsylvania, Massachusetts, and other Northern states had many banks outside their major cities. Moreover, Robb ignored the fact that Mississippi and Arkansas had virtually no banking resources at all and that the resources in other cotton states were meager.

[22] By 1860 banking in the cotton states had not reached 1837 levels. Total loans and discounts in the fall of 1837 exceeded $115,000,000 as compared to

The thesis that the cotton factor held the planter in debt bondage and was the real power behind the throne of King Cotton[23] is unfounded. The phrase reflects more of the anti-middleman rhetoric of its author than it does of the facts of Southern economic life. There is no evidence that factors forced planters to

TABLE 2. BANK RESOURCES FOR SELECTED AREAS, 1850 AND 1860

Area	Population	Bank capital (per capita)	Loans and discounts (per capita)
		1850	
Cotton states[a]	4,683,217	$ 10.22	$ 14.90
Louisiana	517,762	23.89	37.27
New York	3,097,394	15.69	34.58
Massachusetts	994,514	37.04	63.67
		1860	
Cotton states[a]	5,769,753	11.98	18.49
Louisiana	708,002	34.60	50.01
New York	3,880,735	28.71	51.62
Massachusetts	1,231,066	52.40	87.25

a S. C., Ga., Ala., La., Miss., Tenn., and Ark.

grow cotton and buy slaves. There was always a ready market for slaves and, except for the depression years of the early 1840's, prices tended upward. Slaveowners who desired to do so could have sold their slaves and invested the proceeds in cotton factorage firms. That planters did not do so is not the result of the machinations of the cotton factors. This is not to say that the

TABLE 3. DISTRIBUTION OF BANK LOANS AND DISCOUNTS FOR SELECTED AREAS, 1850 AND 1860

Year	Total loans & discounts	Percent in cotton states[a]	Percent in New York
1850	$364,000,000	19	29
1860	692,000,000	15	29

a S. C., Ga., Ala., La., Miss., Tenn., and Ark.

factor and the factorage system had no effect on Southern economic life. To view the factor as a kind of sinister back-room manipulator, however, is misleading, as it obscures his real influence, which was neither sinister nor detrimental.

$105,300,000 in 1860. (For 1837 figures see U. S. Congress, House, *Condition of State Banks*, 25th Cong., 2nd Sess., House Exec. Doc. 79 [Jan. 8, 1838], pp. 850-51; for 1860 figures see Table 1.)

23 The quoted words are Alfred Holt Stone's, "The Cotton Factorage System of the Southern States," *American Historical Review*, XX (April 1915), 562. Stone was a post-Civil War cotton planter. His article, a pathbreaking study, clearly reflects his antagonism toward the postwar merchant.

The factor played an important part in the organization of the marketing process for the South's chief crop. As the proprietor of a relatively stable enterprise with known and liquid assets, he was able to draw capital into the South, capital which was needed to finance and move the crop. Furthermore, his knowledge of price and market conditions and his skill in preparing cotton for sale served as an important aid to the planter who, often far from the market and busy with the affairs of the plantation, was ill-equipped to direct the sale of his produce. Through the factor's efforts the plantation was supplied and the products of the plantation sold. Bankers and storekeepers were adjuncts to the factor, helping to move capital and merchandise into the section and staple crops out to worldwide markets. They were not powers behind the throne but royal retainers, providing important services to the throne.

CHAPTER FIFTEEN

The Costs and Risks of Cotton Marketing

If the factors' services were important and necessary, this does not preclude the possibility that they took advantage of their strategic position and exploited the planters by overcharging them for their services. Indeed, the very importance of their services, combined with the fact that planters were seldom on hand to oversee their factors, suggests ample opportunities for such exploitation.

Marketing the crop was expensive. Insurance, transportation, storage, and commissions were the basic and minimum marketing charges paid by the planter. Those planters and farmers who sold locally to storekeepers or itinerant merchants could escape the direct assessment of these charges, but since local buyers had no option but to resell through a factor, the price they offered had to include the added expenses. Most of the ante bellum crop, however, was consigned by planters to factors and these charges were deducted directly from the planters' gross proceeds.

It is impossible to determine the exact total of these basic charges. Only the 2.5 percent commission charge for selling was, with few exceptions, consistently assessed.[1] Other charges varied from year to year and within each year. A heavy crop could put pressure on transportation facilities and force rates up; low water on the rivers would create a premium for rail transportation whereas ample river transportation would push rail rates down. Thus, for example, planter Eli Capell had 6 bales sold on January 20, 1848 and was charged by his factor $6.75 for "Cash Pd Frt &

RR Charges"; on February 10 the same factor sold 6 more bales of Capell's cotton and although these had almost identical weights as the first, only $3.00 was charged to "Cash paid Freight."[2] Still other matters complicate efforts to arrive at an exact figure for marketing costs. Storage and insurance fees mounted if cotton were held for any length of time. Bales injured in transit or poorly packed had to be repaired, labor and material costs being added to the marketing charges.

Given these variations, only a rough estimate can be made of marketing costs. A check of bills of sale in planters' papers and a number of estimates by contemporaries[3] puts minimum marketing costs at between 6 and 10 percent of the gross proceeds on sales. These figures are for a domestic sale in the market to which the cotton was first sent. Should a planter desire to reship to another market, costs, of course, went up.

Of the 6 to 10 percent assessed for marketing cotton, only the selling commission of 2.5 percent usually went directly to the factor, although, as will be shown, there were other opportunities for profit. It is fruitless to attempt to judge whether the 2.5 percent commission was excessive. This charge was standard throughout the country for selling merchandise[4] and had been traditional since the days of the colonial tobacco trade. Standard also was the 2.5 percent commission for buying, another significant item of income pocketed by the factor. During the ante bellum period there was little alternative to selling through factors and therefore little opportunity to escape the 2.5 percent commission for selling. There were alternatives, however, to buying through the factor; planters often purchased from local storekeepers, city merchants, and even directly from the North. Yet throughout the

---

[1] See Chapter V, above.

[2] Bills of sale by Gribble & Montgomery for Capell, New Orleans, Jan. 20, Feb. 10, 1848, Eli J. Capell and Family Papers, Merritt M. Shilg Memorial Collection, Department of Archives and Manuscripts, Louisiana State University, Baton Rouge, La.

[3] For a collection of such estimates see James L. Watkins, *The Cost of Cotton Production*, U. S. Department of Agriculture, Division of Statistics, Misc. Ser., Bull. 16 (Washington, D. C., 1899), 38-39, 41-42, 45-46. See also *DeBow's Review*, VII (1849), 436.

[4] See table of commission charges for New York in Robert Greenhalgh Albion, *The Rise of New York Port [1815-1860]* (New York, 1939), Appendix xx, 413.

ante bellum period, accounts of planters with their factors consistently carried a sizable number of items purchased by the factor with the 2.5 percent being charged. Had the practice been considered burdensome or had it considerably increased prices, it is reasonable to assume that it would have been discontinued.

Interest, charges for drawing, accepting, and negotiating bills must also be considered part of the factor's income, as well as a significant item in assessing costs of production. Interest on an advance on cotton sent to market would be deducted from the gross proceeds along with commissions and freight and therefore was a direct cost of marketing, whereas interest on an advance during the growing year was considered a cost of production. In either case, the charges were made on the planter's income by the factor, although, it should be remembered, not all of the interest charges ended up as profits in the factor's books because he, in turn, was usually paying interest on money he had borrowed.

The factor was also able to augment his income in other ways. Services such as storage, wharfage, drayage, insurance, repairs on bales, and, if necessary, shipping, were all arranged by the factor at the planter's expense, a system which a factor might turn to his advantage, as is illustrated in the testimony before a South Carolina court in 1855. One Felex Meetze of Columbia had gone deeply in debt to R. and J. Caldwell, local merchants, and was unable to repay the merchants. The Caldwells moved from Columbia to Charleston where they established themselves as cotton factors. They offered Meetze a contract to do all the drayage for the firm at a stipulated price. He accepted the offered contract and for "seven or eight" years hauled the Caldwells' cotton, handling on the average 20,000 bales a year. Meetze used part of the proceeds to pay off the old debt which he owed his employers.[5] Thus, what had seemed to be a bad debt and a sure loss to the merchants had been turned into a fully paid account through their ability to control the drayage business for the crop consigned to them. No evidence was given to show that the price paid to Meetze for drayage was higher than the competitive price in Charleston, nor was there any indication that anyone thought that the Caldwells' actions were illegal or even improper. Nevertheless, it is evident

[5] *Edmund G. Holmes v. R. & J. Caldwell & Co.*, 8 Richardson (S. C. Ct. App.), 247 (1855).

Cotton ready to be harvested
Courtesy of the National Cotton Council of America

An ante bellum cotton gin
From *Harper's Weekly*

An ante bellum cotton press
From *Harper's Weekly*

Carrying cotton for shipment from the plantation
From *Harper's Weekly*

A steamboat loaded with cotton
Courtesy of the State Historical Society of Missouri

that the ability to control the disbursement of business could benefit the factor.

Receiving the business of a busy factor could be most advantageous to a tradesman; withdrawal could mean disaster, as the same case illustrates. "The draying business," Meetze testified, "is generally done under contract; some kind of business may be easily got, but a contract is hard to get." Obviously a contract with a large factorage firm virtually guaranteed business and was desirable. Meetze was able to pay his debt, purchase equipment, and accumulate a profit for himself. Desiring to leave the business, he found a buyer in Edmund G. Holmes. Although Holmes was promised the factor's business, he was never given a contract and soon after he had purchased Meetze's equipment, the factor transferred his business to another drayage firm. Holmes was left with newly purchased wagons, horses, and other equipment, but with no cotton to haul. Clearly, under this system, a factor was in a position to demand special consideration in the form of lower prices or rebates from tradesmen with whom he dealt. If this lower price or rebate were not passed on to the planter, the factor could make a profit in addition to his proceeds from commissions and interest. How widespread this was is impossible to tell. Obviously, such practices would not be publicly disclosed.[6]

In some instances outright fraud might swell factor's profits. In a statement dated November 1835, the Liverpool Cotton Brokers' Association directed a complaint to Americans in the

---

[6] Available evidence does not support Stone's contention that the practice was a common one (Alfred Holt Stone, "The Cotton Factorage System of the Southern States," *American Historical Review*, XX (April 1915), 561). This conclusion is based on negative evidence, however, that is, the absence of widespread complaints. An article from the *Pittsburgh Daily Despatch*, reprinted in *Hunt's Merchants' Magazine*, XXVII (1852), 393, indicated that irregular practices were not confined to cotton factors: "Can a Commission Merchant in 'good and regular standing' in a Christian Church, go to a steamboat officer and bargain for the shipment of say 400 bbls of flour at *forty* cents per barrel, provided the steamboat officer will agree to fill up the bill at *fifty* cents per bbl.—so as to enable the merchant to make $40 over his legitimate commission, &c., off the confiding consignor or owner, who pays this forty dollars more than he need pay, if the whole transaction were straight forward and *bona fide?* Is this a 'fair business transaction?' Is it honorable or even honest? Is it not a mean fraud? We think so—yet it is done here, not occasionally, but constantly—by people affecting honor or even piety. A man who confides in them is made to suffer to the tune of five or ten cents per hundred on the freight which he entrusts to them for shipment, and steamboatmen must become parties to the fraud, or in the case of refusal, give place to those who will. . . . We have a host of witnesses to support our statements, if anybody doubts."

cotton trade concerning "the fraudulent practices in the packing of Cotton." The English importers complained that there was an increasing amount of false packing of cotton bales. Trash was being placed inside the bale to increase its weight. Some bales were not packed uniformly, "a plating or thin layer of good Cotton [being placed] on the two sides of the bale usually sampled, the inside being wholly composed of a very inferior quality." Often the difference in grade between the outside and inside layers was slight, "the obvious intention of which being to render the fraud more secure, by adding to the difficulty and uncertainty of detection." The statement noted that the practice often meant a loss to the buyer of as much as £3 or £4 per bale. Nor was such fraud confined to an occasional bale or two; the practice was growing and often "extended to whole parcels of one or two hundred bales in a lot."[7] Such behavior, of course, was not the factor's doing since the cotton was packed on the plantation. But if he winked at such chicanery, he along with the offending planter could often profit handsomely. Twenty-three years later a meeting of "cotton buyers and cotton brokers" sought "to redress certain abuses and grievances existing in connection with the cotton trade of New Orleans." Among the resolutions was one that stated that sellers should be "held responsible for any just reclamations for false packed cotton" and should indicate their responsibility on the invoice of sale.[8]

Although it is evident that the issue of falsely packed cotton remained alive throughout the ante bellum period, it is hardly likely that this was a major means of consistent profit-making by either factors or planters. Buyers would soon learn to avoid factors with a reputation for selling such cotton and factors to protect themselves would demand more care from their customers.

In the absence of factors' financial records it is not possible to determine precisely how profitable cotton factorage was. However, the continued existence of the system, the virtually unchanging schedule of charges assessed, and the persistence of some firms over long periods of time suggest that the enterprise was profitable yet reasonable in its charges. Nevertheless, the enterprise was not

[7] "To the American Chamber of Commerce," Liverpool, Nov. 6, 1835, as printed in *New Orleans Price-Current*, Feb. 20, 1836.

[8] Resolutions dated Oct. 29, 1859, printed in *Hunt's Merchants' Magazine*, XLII (1860), 105-106.

without its risks, as the distress and even ruin of many firms testify. Financial panic, crop failures, low prices, sharp competition, and poor judgment were but a few of the hazards cotton factors had to face.

The failure to receive the cotton on which they had advanced money was a fundamental risk taken by factors. Planters might hold back cotton on the plantation in the belief that in so doing a better price might be obtained. Should the factor be under obligations for the money he had already advanced to the planter, delay in receiving the crop might cause financial hardship. Cotton on hand could be sold but cotton on the plantation was beyond the factor's control and he could do little more than urge that the cotton be sent forward, perhaps adding the expert opinion that "we scarcely think you can get any better price by holding."[9] In times of financial crisis when prices were low and money was tight the problem became even more acute. Well aware that their hard-pressed factors would be forced into early sales to meet their obligations, planters sometimes held their cotton on the plantations to keep it out of their merchants' hands. An English cotton buyer in Savannah noted the problem in a letter to his Liverpool correspondent in April 1837: "There is no negotiating—nor in fact hardly any business going forward, the distress throughout the Country being so general as to affect the credit of almost every house engaged in business. . . . In Georgia & S. Carolina the planters are holding & many will continue to do so through the Summer— In Alabama they are building Sheds over their Cottons at the Landings on the Banks of the Rivers having no confidence in their Factors. . . ."[10] Again in 1857 there was a tendency to hold back cotton on the plantations. Reflecting the concern of local factors, an Augusta newspaper urged those planters who "have partially or wholly anticipated, by accommodations from their factors, the value of their crop" to send their cotton forward. Holding, the paper insisted, would only ruin the merchants and would fail to help the planters in any way.[11]

9 Reynolds, Byrne & Co. to Walker, New Orleans, Oct. 28, 1830, Zachariah Walker Papers, Mississippi Department of Archives and History, Jackson, Miss.

10 Godfrey Barnsley to John MacLellan & Co., Savannah, April 17, 1837, Barnsley v. MacLellan Copy Correspondence, Godfrey Barnsley Papers, Emory University Library, Atlanta, Ga.

11 *Weekly Constitutionalist*, Nov. 11, 1857.

Unfavorable weather conditions also prevented cotton from coming to market. Low water was a regular problem delaying cotton shipments on the rivers, a circumstance that could be expensive for both factor and planter. In April 1845 John C. Calhoun wrote that it was impossible to get advances from Mobile factors "in consequence of the heavy advances, which the factors had made to the planters whose crops had not come down from the low state of the river or other causes."[12] Sometimes only certain areas were affected, but at times a general lack of rainfall brought on near crisis. During the 1854-1855 season low water in the Gulf area rivers prevented shipments to New Orleans and Mobile. Factors who had advanced money to planters were pressed for payment before the crop was available for sale. Many firms were able to make their payments only with the greatest difficulty; others were forced to suspend payments for a time.[13]

Low water could have a very depressing effect on prices. Factors in the interior towns found buyers reluctant to make purchases when adequate transportation to the coast was not available. In November 1839, an Augusta factor informed his South Carolina customer that prices were very low in Augusta due in part to low water on the Savannah, which prevented buyers from shipping cotton to the coast. "We hope to see a change in favor of Cotton sellers as soon as the river rises so people can ship," he hopefully added.[14] When rain raised the water level, however, problems did not always end. Cotton would arrive in a rush; the great supply, and the need to sell quickly to meet due bills, would drive prices—and hence factors' commissions—down. To protect themselves, factors were reluctant to incur extensive liabilities where low water was a recurrent problem and preferred to deal with planters on the large rivers or in areas where railroads penetrated.[15] Even where railroads were available, cost remained a real problem.

---

[12] To Francis W. Pickens, Fort Hill, April 1, 1845, printed in *South Carolina Historical and Genealogical Magazine*, VII (Jan. 1906), 13.

[13] J. C. Lewis to Jones Fuller, Jan. 18, 1854, as quoted from Fuller Manuscripts in Charles S. Davis, *The Cotton Kingdom in Alabama* (Montgomery, Ala., 1939), 159; E. J. Donnell, *History of Cotton* (New York, 1872), 446.

[14] Baird & Rowland to John B. Bull, Augusta, Nov. 14, 1839, Bull-Morrow Papers, Georgia Historical Society, Savannah, Ga.

[15] *New Orleans Bulletin*, reprinted in *DeBow's Review*, XXIII (1857), 375. This provided an inducement to factors to support internal improvement activities, as will be shown below.

When rivers were low, railroads, free of riverboat competition, raised their rates. Planters and factors had to decide whether a shipment at higher rates would be as profitable as holding for lower river rates while paying added insurance and interest costs. The state of the market when the water level finally rose was a matter of conjecture, adding to the hazards and uncertainties faced by the factor.[16]

Rate variations and uncertainties in ocean transportation created other risks. Although the general tendency of ocean freight rates on cotton was downward,[17] there was a great variation in rates during the season and often between seasons as well. During the 1849-1850 season, for example, rates to Liverpool were 7/16 pence per pound on September 15 and as low as ⅛ on May 1.[18] Buyers and sellers had to take rates into consideration when arranging a sale or shipment abroad. A shortage of transportation might induce buyers to lower their offered prices so as to cover the extra costs and a factor then had to decide whether to sell at the lower price or hold awaiting a drop in freight rates. A temporary absence of shipping might create the same dilemma. Thus, in March 1831 a New Orleans factor informed his customer that "the scarcity of shipping" had brought the market to a virtual standstill. Buyers' offers were very low and the factor urged the planters to forego immediate sales "for if we are to force sales, it must be done at a very great sacrifice."[19] In short, factors had to weigh the costs of holding against the possible advantages of lower rates,[20] a risk

[16] In Dec. 1856, a New Orleans factor described the costs of holding cotton to a planter on the Red River: "Interest lost, and insurance paid, cost a quarter of a cent every month—Cottons that would now bring 11½, would have to bring 12¼ three months hence, to nett the same amount." R. W. Estlin & Co. to Peter T. Hickman, New Orleans, Dec. 2, 1856, Hickman-Bryan Papers, Joint Collection, Western Historical Manuscripts Collection, State Historical Society of Missouri Manuscripts, Columbia, Mo. Hickman's correspondence indicates that he faced this same problem many times. Usually his inclination was to hold, but his factors generally advised that he send his cotton to market at the higher railroad transportation rate.

[17] Douglass C. North, *The Economic Growth of the United States, 1790-1860* (Englewood Cliffs, N. J., 1961), 126-27, 258.

[18] *New Orleans Price-Current*, Sept. 7, 1850. The weekly edition of the *Price-Current* carried freight rates for the week. Each year in its "Annual Remarks" (published sometime around Sept. 1) the paper described the general tendency of rates for the previous season.

[19] Reynolds, Byrne & Co. to Walker, New Orleans, March 2, 1831, Zachariah Walker Papers.

[20] Obviously, buyers too would try to take advantage of lower rates to increase

made even more hazardous by the fact that while cotton was being held prices could fall because of reasons unrelated to shipping rates.

Numerous other hazards added to the risks taken by cotton factors. Since profits depended so largely on commissions, the factor had to make the best possible sale in what was often a violently fluctuating market. Slow communication, added to meager or often inaccurate information about both the size of the crop and the anticipated demand, posed grave problems for the factor who had to decide when to sell or hold as well as whether to sell locally or ship to the North or Europe. The experience of a number of New Orleans factors in the 1850-1851 season illustrates this problem. Bad weather led the factors to expect a short crop. Influenced by the judgment of Harry Hill, the head of Hill, McLean and Company, "the leading house in the trade in New Orleans at that time," factors and speculators ignored growing indications that the crop would not be short, as expected. Instead of selling they held out for higher prices. Cotton continued to arrive in New Orleans and those who decided to sell found prices declining. But others persisted in their belief that better prices could be had and refused to accept prices being offered by buyers in New Orleans. Instead, they shipped to the North and to Europe but found, contrary to their expectations, that prices in these markets were even more depressed. As a result, enormous losses were sustained by all who participated in this short-crop speculation.[21]

Like other businessmen, factors faced the risks of competition. Every major market and most of the lesser markets had cotton factors; in addition, as has been shown, numerous other merchants handled cotton as part of their business. The large numbers seeking consignments and the ease with which a planter could switch from one merchant to another led to vigorous competition for the planter's business. Factors advertised in directories and newspapers and sent agents and partners into the interior and into other markets in an effort to attract business. Sometimes more direct methods were used. An Augusta factor asked one of his

---

their profits and thus there was no guarantee that they would immediately raise their prices when shipping rates went down.

[21] *New Orleans Price-Current*, Sept. 1, 1851; Donnell, *History of Cotton*, 397.

customers to distribute some circulars in the neighborhood of his plantation, explaining that he was "not acquainted in your settlement."[22] Special favors were offered in return for business. A New Orleans factor offered to lend a planter $70,000 to buy land on the Red River: "As he would put 200 negroes on it . . . *we would like to make the payment for him, and take his business.*"[23]

Often factors personally went into the interior to solicit business. The Florida planter Bennet H. Barrow recorded such a visit in his diary: "Mr Warfield my Cotten [*sic*] merchant or 'Factor' came home with me last night. looking through the Country for buisness [*sic*]."[24] New planters could expect either a personal visit or a letter from a factor seeking his patronage.[25] Should a factor go out of business, his customers would be quickly approached by other enterprising merchants, as William Johnson learned when his New Orleans factor died: "The death of our personal & highly esteemed friend James Armour having deprived you of his services induces us to solicit a portion of patronage for ourselves," wrote Andrews and Brother of the Crescent City. "Test our zeal and we are sure you will give us your confidence," the letter promised.[26] A satisfied customer, however, could prove more helpful than a letter soliciting business. Johnson ignored the letter from Andrews and Brother, for a short time sent cotton to Black and Mure, and then, through the recommendation of a friend, gave his business to Washington Jackson and Company. "We are very much obliged to our mutual friend Doctr [*sic*] Jenkins—and much indebted to your self for the offer of your business," wrote Washington Jackson and Company.[27]

Factorage, then, could be profitable, but it was always a precarious business. The weather, the size of the crop, the state of the money markets in the North and abroad, the whims of

[22] John B. Smith to E. & J. Bull, Augusta, Sept. 21, 1827, Bull-Morrow Papers.

[23] J. M. Rhorer & Co. to P. T. Hickman, New Orleans, Jan. 7, 1860, Hickman-Bryan Papers.

[24] Entry of Oct. 31, 1838, printed in "Plantation Diary of Bennet H. Barrow," in Edwin Adams Davis (ed.), *Plantation Life in the Florida Parishes of Louisiana, 1836-1846 as Reflected in the Diary of Bennet H. Barrow* (New York, 1943), 135.

[25] Weymouth T. Jordan, *Hugh Davis and His Alabama Plantation* (University, Ala., 1948), 135.

[26] Andrews & Brother to Johnson, New Orleans, Oct. 7, 1843, William Johnson Papers, Mississippi Department of Archives and History, Jackson, Miss.

[27] Letter dated New Orleans, Jan. 23, 1844, *ibid*.

planter customers, and sharp competition—all were hazards the factor had to face. The cost to the planter for financing and marketing his crop was high, but only by modern standards. High costs reflected high risks. In the absence of a common currency, an organized central banking system, rapid and sure means of transportation and communication, and a cotton exchange, it would be difficult to conceive of a less expensive means to market the crop.[28]

[28] See Thomas P. Govan, "Banking and the Credit System in Georgia, 1810-1860," *Journal of Southern History*, IV (May 1938), 184; Ralph W. Haskins, "Planter and Cotton Factor in the Old South: Some Areas of Friction," *Agricultural History*, XXIX (Jan. 1955), 14.

CHAPTER SIXTEEN

Cotton Factorage and Southern Economic
Development: Conclusions

Commercial rivalry did not prevent factors in a particular market from joining together to advertise the virtues of their homeground. On the contrary, they often united to add their support to efforts to improve transportation facilities designed to divert trade from one market to their own or to tap new trading areas. Merchants were actively involved in the strenuous competition between Savannah and Charleston to control the markets in the South Carolina and Georgia backcountry. Charleston's attempt to divert this trade from the Savannah River resulted in the construction of a railroad from Charleston to Hamburg, a town across the river from Augusta. This move was matched by a later effort resulting in the construction of a Savannah to Augusta railroad. Active in the promotion of both these projects were the merchants of both ports as well as those in the interior towns which would be affected.[1]

Even New Orleans, supported by the nation's best natural waterway, moved into railroad construction in an effort to tap areas outside the Mississippi River region so as to prevent the trade of these areas from going elsewhere. In the railway boom of the 1850's in Louisiana, numerous factors—among them Glendy Burke, H. S. Buckner, Maunsel White—contributed their time, abilities, and money for the promotion of railway construction. Mobile and its merchants followed suit for similar reasons.[2] Thus, urban rivalry in the South, as elsewhere in the nation, provided an impetus for the expansion of transportation. And as elsewhere, urban merchants in the South, prominent among them the cotton factors, actively supported transportation improvements.

To be sure, railway construction in the South lagged far behind the North. When railroads were proposed and built, however, factors generally gave enthusiastic support. If their financial support was limited, this did not stem from lack of interest but from lack of funds. As James Robb, the Louisiana railroad promoter noted, the factors had little to spare after using their capital and credit to support the agricultural community.[3] But they supported Robb and others who favored government aid for railroad construction.

The principal aim of factors and other city merchants who supported internal improvements was to attract trade. Railroad promoters argued that by opening new areas to commercial production and by expanding demand through lower prices, railroads would bring prosperity to the cities and at the same time promote the development of towns in the interior.[4] To the extent that cheap and ample transportation has these effects, Southern development was delayed by the section's relatively small investment in railroads. Yet, the cotton factorage system cannot be blamed for inadequacies in Southern transportation, nor should it be blamed for the lack of urban development in the South.

The urban growth which characterized the North and West in

[1] Alexander Trotter, *Observations on the Financial Position and Credit of Such of the States of the North American Union as Have Contracted Public Debts* (London, 1839), 233; *Hunt's Merchants' Magazine*, XXIX (1853), 58-59; Ulrich Bonnell Phillips, *A History of Transportation in the Eastern Cotton Belt to 1860* (New York, 1908), *passim*; Charles S. Sydnor, *The Development of Southern Sectionalism, 1819-1848* (Baton Rouge, 1948), 267-70; Avery O. Craven, *The Growth of Southern Nationalism, 1848-1861* (Baton Rouge, 1953), 267-68; George Rogers Taylor, *The Transportation Revolution, 1815-1860* (New York, 1951), 77-78; Carter Goodrich, *Government Promotion of American Canals and Railroads, 1800-1890* (New York, 1960), 102-107, 116-20.

[2] DeBow, *The Industrial Resources, Etc., of the Southern and Western States* (New Orleans, 1853), II, 434, 439; John F. Stover, *The Railroads of the South, 1865-1900* (Chapel Hill, 1955), 8; Sydnor, *Development of Southern Sectionalism,* 272-73; Craven, *Growth of Southern Nationalism,* 268; Goodrich, *Government Promotion,* 158-60; Harry Howard Evans, "James Robb, Banker and Pioneer Railroad Builder of Ante-Bellum Louisiana," *Louisiana Historical Quarterly,* XXIII (Jan. 1940), 170-258.

[3] Evans, "James Robb," 207.

[4] See the "Address" prepared by a committee promoting a New Orleans Railroad Convention, held in 1852. DeBow, *Industrial Resources,* II, 435-54. The chairman of the committee which prepared the "Address" was Glendy Burke, a prominent New Orleans cotton factor.

the ante bellum period was not matched in the South. A list of the nation's fifteen largest cities in 1860 does not include the important ports of Charleston, Savannah, or Mobile, nor does it include any of the major inland centers such as Memphis, Natchez, Augusta, or Montgomery. Excepting border state cities, New Orleans is the only Southern city on the list.[5] Not only were Southern cities small, but they were also few in number, as an English traveler noted in 1856: "Every step one takes in the South, one is struck with the rough look of the whole face of civilization. The country is nowhere well cleared; towns and villages are few and far between, and even those which you see have an unfinished look. . . . Notwithstanding the rapid prosperity of the South, and especially of the Gulf States, during the last twenty years, they have, on the whole a very wild appearance."[6] Census figures

TABLE 4. URBAN POPULATION OF THE UNITED STATES, 1860, BY REGIONS

Region	Urban population	Percent urban
West South Central[a]	215,368	12.3
East South Central[b]	236,755	5.9
South Atlantic[c]	614,671	11.5
Total South	1,066,794	9.6
New England[d]	1,148,489	36.6
Middle Atlantic[e]	2,638,848	35.4
East North Central[f]	973,459	14.1
West North Central[g]	289,783	13.4
Total North & West	5,050,579	25.6

[a] Ark., La., Okla., Texas.
[b] Ky., Tenn., Ala., Miss.
[c] Del., Md., D.C., Va., Ga., N.C., S.C.
[d] Me., N.H., Vt., Mass., R.I., Conn.
[e] N.Y., N.J., Penna.
[f] Ohio, Ind., Ill., Mich., Wis.
[g] Minn., Iowa, Mo., N.D., S.D., Kan., Neb.
    Source: U. S. Department of Commerce, Bureau of the Census, *Sixteenth Census: 1940*, Vol. I, *Population* (Washington, D. C., 1942), 20.

support visitors' impressions. As Tables 4 and 5 indicate, the South in 1860 had fewer cities and, with the exception of Louisiana, a smaller percentage of its population urbanized than either the Northeast or the Northwest. Almost all of Louisiana's urban population was concentrated in New Orleans, the Crescent City containing over 90 percent of the state's urban population in 1860.

[5] Taylor, *Transportation Revolution*, 389, lists the following fifteen cities ranked in order of population for 1860: New York, Philadelphia, Baltimore, Boston, New Orleans, Cincinnati, St. Louis, Chicago, Buffalo, Newark, Louisville, Albany, Washington, San Francisco, and Providence.

[6] James Stirling, *Letters from the Slave States* (London, 1857), 177.

TABLE 5. URBAN POPULATION[a] OF THE UNITED STATES, 1840 AND 1860,
BY SELECTED STATES

State	1840			1860		
	No. of urban places	Total urban population	Percent urban	No. of urban places	Total urban population	Percent urban
Alabama	1	12,672	2.1	5	48,901	5.1
Arkansas	–	–	0.0	1	3,727	0.9
Georgia	4	24,658	3.6	9	75,466	7.1
Louisiana	2	105,400	29.9	4	185,026	26.1
Mississippi	1	3,612	1.0	5	20,689	2.6
South Carolina	2	33,601	5.7	2	48,574	6.9
Tennessee	1	6,929	0.8	4	46,541	4.2
Texas	2[b]	7,665[b]	3.6[b]	5	26,615	4.4
Pennsylvania	20	307,977	17.9	46	894,706	30.8
Massachusetts	24	279,454	37.9	57	733,209	59.6
New York	10	471,266	19.4	31	1,524,344	39.3
Ohio	9	83,491	5.5	36	400,435	17.1
Illinois	3	9,607	2.0	23	245,545	14.3
Indiana	3	10,716	1.6	17	115,904	8.6
Iowa	–	–	0.0	9	60,028	8.9
Michigan	1	9,102	4.3	13	99,701	13.3
Missouri	1	16,469	4.3	11	203,487	17.2

[a] 2,500 or more.   [b] 1850.
Source: U. S. Department of Commerce, Bureau of the Census, *Sixteenth Census:
1940*, Vol. I, *Population* (Washington, D.C., 1942), *passim*.

The failure of the South to develop large and thriving interior
cities is attributed by some to the domination of the factorage
system. Factors congregated in a few of the larger cities; the
easily available credit and large trading facilities they offered
provided competition which tended to eclipse nearby towns. In
1860, J. W. Dorr of the *New Orleans Crescent* took an extensive
trip through the Louisiana backcountry, reporting his experiences
as he went along.[7] In the course of his visits to the interior he
noted the effect of New Orleans on the business of the towns:
"Wherever the middling classes are a considerable proportion of
the population, there the country stores are numerous; where the
wealthy planters predominate, they are scarce, for everything the
planter does not raise on his estate he purchases in the city [New
Orleans], and there the planters' ladies go to do their shopping."[8]

This would seem to support the contention that the factorage
system tended to limit the development of cities in the South

[7] These articles have been reprinted in Walter Prichard (ed.), "A Tourist's Description of Louisiana in 1860." *Louisiana Historical Quarterly*, XXI (Oct. 1938),
1110-214.
[8] *Ibid.*, 1117.

TABLE 6. TOTAL POPULATION OF SELECTED STATES IN RELATION
TO POPULATION OF LARGEST CITY IN STATES, 1860

State	Total population	Population of largest city	Percent of total population in largest city
Alabama	964,201	29,258 (Mobile)	3
Arkansas	435,450	3,727 (Little Rock)	0.7
Georgia	1,057,286	22,292 (Savannah)	2
Louisiana	708,002	168,675 (New Orleans)	24
Mississipi	791,305	6,617 (Natchez)	0.8
South Carolina	703,708	40,522 (Charleston)	6
Tennessee	1,109,801	22,623 (Memphis)	2
New York	3,880,735	1,174,779[a] (N. Y. C.)	30
Pennsylvania	2,906,215	565,529 (Philadelphia)	19
Ohio	2,339,511	161,044 (Cincinnati)	7
Illinois	1,711,951	112,172 (Chicago)	6
Indiana	1,350,428	18,611 (Indianapolis)	1
Iowa	674,913	13,000 (Dubuque)	2
Michigan	749,113	45,619 (Detroit)	6
Missouri	1,182,012	160,773 (St. Louis)	13

[a] Includes five boroughs of present-day New York City.
Source: U. S. Department of Commerce, Bureau of the Census, *Sixteenth
Census: 1940*, Vol. I, *Population* (Washington, D.C., 1942), *passim.*

inasmuch as the large city seems to have deprived the interior
areas of the nucleus of potential towns, the local store. But this
tells only part of the story. Lewis E. Atherton has shown that
"the North and West, both on a population and an absolute
basis, had more stores and larger investments in these than did the
South."[9] The existence of New York, Philadelphia, Baltimore, and
Boston did not prevent the growth of an extensive network of

[9] *The Southern Country Store, 1800-1860* (Baton Rouge, 1949), 39-42. The
quoted words are on p. 42. Atherton's figures are for 1840. Unfortunately, the
censuses for 1850 and 1860 did not contain corresponding information. There is
no reason to suspect, however, that the generalization for 1840 would not hold
for later years as well.

stores in the North and West, nor did they prevent Cincinnati, St. Louis, Chicago, Buffalo, Louisville, and Albany from growing into large cities by 1860.

The point is even more obvious when it is noted that the largest Southern cities were no more dominant over their states in terms of population than were Northern and Western cities; indeed, they were often less so (see Table 6). Thus, for example, Mobile had only 3 percent of the population of Alabama whereas St. Louis contained 13 percent of Missouri's total population in 1860. Yet Alabama had only four other cities of 2,500 or more and Missouri had ten more. Even more striking is a comparison between New York and Louisiana. New York City had 30 percent of the state's population in 1860, but the state had thirty additional cities; New Orleans had 24 percent of the population of Louisiana and the state had only three other urban areas.

The differences in urban development between North and South arose not from the existence of the factorage system in the South but from a difference in effective demand. Even if all the planters had made all their purchases through city factors—which was not the case—more stores and towns would have arisen had there been a need for them, that is, had there been more customers ready to make purchases and carry on other business locally. But the great majority of Southerners who owned few or no slaves did not induce widespread urbanization in the South. Frank Lawrence Owsley has described their economic role: "A grazing and farm economy rather than a plantation economy was practiced by nearly all the non-slaveholders and by 60 to 80 per cent of the slaveholders. Farm economy meant a diversified, self-sufficient type of agriculture, where the money crops were subordinated to food crops, and where the labor was performed by the family or the family aided by a few slaves."[10]

Largely self-sufficient farmers may not have been poor,[11] but

[10] *Plain Folk of the Old South* (Baton Rouge, 1949), 134-35.

[11] Owsley's (*ibid.*) main contention, of course, was that nonslaveholders were not all "poor whites." Richard A. Easterlin, in his studies of per capita income in the United States, argues that the South did not lag behind comparable areas in the North. Thus, his estimates of per capita income in 1840 for the three Southern regions, South Atlantic, East South Central, and West South Central, are $55.00, $55.00, and $104.00, respectively. This compares with $51.00 for the West North Central (Iowa and Mo.), $46.00 for the East North Central. Both Southern and Western incomes, excepting the West South Central, were exceeded

they had less to spend than those who concentrated on money crops. In the aggregate, therefore, farmers in the South gave rise to a weaker demand than those in areas with a greater concentration on commercial agriculture. The planter class controlled most of the money income in the countryside, and because planters spent a large part of their money in the cities through their factors, the development of towns lagged. The culprit was not the factor but the nature of money income distribution. But this does not tell the whole story.

The lack of large towns and cities in the South was also a result of an overwhelmingly agricultural economy. Stanley Lebergott has estimated that 84 percent of the Southern labor force was employed in farming in 1860 as compared with only 40 percent so employed in the North and West.[12] The effect of this emphasis on agriculture was perceptively recognized in 1835 by a Yankee traveler in Mississippi:

> Towns in this state have usually originated from the location of a county seat, after the formation of a new county. Here the courthouse is placed, and forms the centre of an area which is soon filled with edifices and inhabitants. If the county lies on the river, another town may arise, for a shipping port, but here the accumulation of towns usually ceases. A county seat, and a cotton mart, are all that an agricultural country requires. The towns in this state are thus dispersed two or three to each county, nor so long as this is a planting country, will there be any great increase to their number, although in wealth and importance they may rival, particularly the shipping ports, the most populous places in the valley of the west.

---

by New England ($83.00) and the Middle Atlantic States, N. Y., N. J., Pa., Del., and Md. ($77.00). Richard A. Easterlin, "Interregional Differences in Per Capita Income, Population, and Total Income, 1840-1950," *Trends in the American Economy in the Nineteenth Century* ("Studies in Income and Wealth by the Conference on Research in Income and Wealth," Vol. XXIV [Princeton, 1960]), 73-140; cited data from Appendix A, Table, A-1, 97-98. See also the same author's "Regional Income Trends, 1840-1950," in Seymour E. Harris (ed.), *American Economic History* (New York, 1961), 525-47. These figures do not reveal income distribution nor do they differentiate money income from income in kind. Such information would be extremely useful for the matter at hand. Owsley's studies would suggest that a large part of Southern income was in kind and that money income figures would reveal gross distortions in distribution.

[12] Stanley Lebergott, "Labor Force and Employment, 1800-1960," *Output, Employment, and Productivity in the United States After 1800* ("Studies in Income and Wealth by the Conference on Research in Income and Wealth," Vol. XXX [New York, 1966]), 131.

In these towns are the banks, the merchants, the post offices, and the several places of resort for business or pleasure that draw the planter and his family from his estate.[13]

A glance at studies of the history of interior cities,[14] or at Southern business directories,[15] or at the impressions recorded by travelers when they visited cities[16] shows that Southern towns, for the most part, developed in response to the needs of an agricultural community. They were important as trading centers for the surrounding area, but few could boast any manufacturing development. Even New Orleans, the nation's fifth largest city in 1860, had only 3 percent of its population engaged in manufacturing, a proportion which fell below that of every one of the fifteen most populous cities that year, with the exception of San Francisco.[17] In short, Southern towns were mainly distribution points for manufactured goods produced elsewhere and did not benefit from the population and demand enjoyed by towns with manufacturing enterprises in the North and East. Again, it was not factorage that stifled urban growth, but rather the preponderance of agriculture.

The South was an agricultural section with most of its available capital invested in land, agricultural equipment, and slaves. Most manufacturing and commerce was left to Northerners, and, as a result, part of the profits of planting and farming was diverted to the North to pay for manufactured goods, transportation, insurance, and other commodities and services. The region also came to rely upon outside capital for the advances, loans, and credit required for agricultural production and marketing. The cotton factorage firms, as efficient commercial enterprises, were

13 [Joseph Holt Ingraham], *The Southwest. By a Yankee* (New York, 1835), II, 205.

14 See, for example, Clanton W. Williams, "Early Ante-Bellum Montgomery: A Black-Belt Constituency," *Journal of Southern History*, VII (Nov. 1941), 495-525; Martha Boman, "A City of the Old South: Jackson, Mississippi, 1850-1860," *Journal of Mississippi History*, XV (Jan. 1953), 1-32; Weymouth T. Jordan, *Ante-Bellum Alabama: Town and Country* (Tallahassee, 1957), 22-40.

15 [John P. Campbell (ed.)], *Southern Business Directory and General Commercial Advertiser* (Charleston, 1854), I, *passim*.

16 [Ingraham], *The Southwest*, II, 160, 169-70; Alexander Mackay, *The Western World or Travels in the United States in 1846-1847* (3rd ed., London, 1850), II, 211; James Robertson, *A Few Months in America* (London, 1855), 57; Robert Russell, *North America: Its Agriculture and Climate* (1857), as reprinted in Guy Stevens Callender, *Selections from the Economic History of the United States, 1765-1860* (Boston, 1909), 283-86.

17 Taylor, *Transportation Revolution*, 389.

The New Orleans docks before the Civil War
Courtesy of the State Historical Society of Missouri

The New Orleans docks about 1890

From *Tales of the Mississippi*, copyright 1955 by Ray Samuel, Leonard V. Huber, and Warren C. Ogden, reprinted by permission of Hastings House, Publishers, Inc.

A New Orleans rail terminal about 1890

From *Tales of the Mississippi*, copyright 1955 by Ray Samuel, Leonard V. Huber, and Warren C. Ogden, reprinted by permission of Hastings House, Publishers, Inc.

Unloading cotton at Memphis, Tennessee

From *Memphis Illustrated* (New York, 1892). Courtesy of Tennessee State
Library and Archives, Nashville

A modern cotton gin
Courtesy of the National Cotton Council of America

A modern compress and warehouse
Courtesy of the State Historical Society of Missouri

able to draw this capital into the South and to make it available to planters and farmers as the need arose.

Many in the South were concerned with their commercial and financial dependence on the North and efforts were made to alter their status. Some sought to develop a more diversified economy by encouraging manufacturing, railroads, and shipping; others considered plans to bypass Northern—and sometimes Southern— middlemen and to alter the banking structure of the South in order to cut marketing costs. Little came of these efforts. Diversification of the Southern economy depended upon adequate capital and a real desire for change. Both were lacking in the ante bellum South. For both economic and social reasons, agriculture remained the primary concern of ante bellum Southerners.

The cotton factor operated within this context; he neither created the environment nor can he be charged, to a greater degree than most other Southerners, with the responsibility for its persistence. On the contrary, he was often among those who sought to enlarge Southern facilities and change conditions. He was not, as some have thought, the villain but was rather a necessary part of the Southern economy. A more rounded economy, a system of free labor, and modern methods of trade might have benefited the South. That these changes did not come prior to the Civil War was not the fault of the cotton factor.

CIVIL WAR
AND AFTER

PART FOUR

Wartime Cotton Trade

Yankee Doodle, now, good-bye!
We spurn a thing so rotten;
Proud independence is the cry
Of Sugar, Rice, and Cotton

> —*Eastern Clarion* (Paulding, Miss., Oct. 18, 1861, as quoted in D. Clayton James "Mississippi Agriculture, 1861-1865," *Journal of Mississippi History,* XXIV (July 1962), 130.

*Those rampant cotton and sugar planters,
who were so early and furiously in the
field for secession, and who, after war had
commenced, were so resolved [at] burning
their cotton and destroying their sugar not
only did not burn and destroy in three
cases out of four, but a great many of
them, having taken the oath of allegiance
to the Yankees, are now raising cotton in
partnership with their Yankee protectors,
and shipping it to Yankee markets.*

> —"Cotton and Sugar Planter," reprinted
> in the *Mississippian* from the *Rich-
> mond Examiner*, undated clipping in
> Charles Clark and Family Papers,
> Mississippi Department of Archives
> and History, Jackson, Miss.

*Cotton is five cents a pound and labor of
no value at all; it commands no price
whatever. People gladly hire out their
negroes to have them fed and clothed.
... Langdon was for martial law and making the bloodsuckers disgorge their ill-
gotten gains. We, poor fools, who are
patriotically ruining ourselves will see our
children in the gutter while treacherous
dogs of millionaires go rolling by in their
coaches—coaches that were acquired by
taking advantage of our necessities.*

> —Mary Boykin Chesnut, A *Diary from
> Dixie*, ed. Isabella D. Martin and
> Myrta Lockett Avary (New York,
> 1905), 139.

While the secession crisis was occupying the political energies of the South, her merchants were marketing a cotton crop of almost four million bales and her farmers and slaves were preparing for the next crop which would, during the first summer of civil war, mature into an estimated four and a half million bales.[1] As usual, most planters were in debt to their factors, having anticipated the proceeds of their crops through advances, and many were already looking for credit to finance the next year's crop.

The crisis, however, had blocked the regular channels of commerce. Many Southern merchants were unwilling or unable to make remittances to their Northern creditors; buyers were unable to discount their bills except at ruinous rates. As prices tended downward, factors suddenly faced the specter of maturing bills, and many were unable to meet their obligations. "Quite a large number of our Factors have suspended and it is feared others may follow," wrote a New Orleans factor in December 1860. "The panic," he observed, "is infinately [sic] worse than that of 1857 on account of the uncertainty regarding political matters."[2] Failure to pay debts compounded the economic dislocation. Northern merchants, frightened by Southern talk of repudiation and by the introduction of stay laws in Southern legislatures, sought frantically to liquidate their Southern debts. Despite assurances by some Southerners and appeals to Southern honor, the fears of Northern merchants remained unallayed.[3]

The outbreak of war confirmed these fears. Financial relations were completely severed. Agents for Northern firms, intimidated by mobs, closed their offices in the South and went home.[4] The *New York Economist* resigned itself to the fact that remittances to the North had virtually stopped:

> At last the crash in commerce on the derangement in politics has come upon us. Hopeful merchants have tried to look cheerfully at the threatening clouds that have overhung our trade since November last, and traders generally have battled bravely against the overpowering march of events, refusing to believe that the political crisis could result so seriously as it has. At last, however, the worst fears are realized. We are launched on the sea of civil war; and trade is sternly summoned to contract its operations within the narrowest possible limits. . . . New York has in the Southern States debts that are to be counted by tens of millions; and, although large amounts of this indebtedness are daily falling due, yet scarcely a dollar comes to hand in liquidation. In the States actually seceded repudiation has, to a large extent, been adopted, and, where debtors are too honorable to directly repudiate, they yet refuse to remit until the close of the war.[5]

Other Northern papers responded with greater acerbity as they raged against the "robber-like depravity" of the "poor, ruined, demented and utterly demoralized South" which refused to pay its debts; and angrily they urged that a "just retribution" be militarily exacted from the "land of treason and Barbarism."[6] The South, of course, countered Northern claims with patriotic righteousness. Payment of debts or, indeed, any trade with the North

[1] James L. Watkins, *King Cotton* (New York, 1908), 30.

[2] Rhorer & Zunts to P. T. Hickman, New Orleans, Dec. 5, 1860, Hickman-Bryan Papers, Joint Collection, Western Historical Manuscripts Collection, State Historical Society of Missouri Manuscripts, Columbia, Mo.

[3] Philip S. Foner, *Business & Slavery* (Chapel Hill, 1941), 208-23. On Dec. 3, 1860 the *Daily Atlas and Bee* (Boston) expressed the hope and the expectation that Southern merchants would honor debts owed the North and repudiate the argument that these debts could go unpaid in case of war. Reprinted in Howard Cecil Perkins (ed.), *Northern Editorials on Secession* (New York, 1942), II, 564-67.

[4] William Howard Russell, *My Diary North and South* (Boston, 1863), 230-31.

[5] As copied in *DeBow's Review*, XXXI (1861), 93.

[6] *Daily Green Mountain Freeman* (Montpelier), May 17, 1861, reprinted in Perkins, *Northern Editorials*, II, 605-606.

was tantamount to betrayal. To allow trade or the payment of debts "would counteract the operations of war, and throw obstacles in the way of the public efforts, and lead to disorder, imbecility and treason."[7] Most debts went unpaid. When the war ended Southerners owed Northern merchants an estimated one hundred and fifty million dollars, most of it to New Yorkers.[8]

If the South was largely cut off from its market and its source of credit in the North and abroad, this did not mean, however, that internal trade in cotton ended. On the contrary, cotton continued to be grown and marketed in the South despite war, blockade, and Confederate attempts to curtail production. Its destination, however, was seldom the cotton mills of the North or Europe, but rather the remote warehouse or the hidden cotton shed on the plantation.

[7] *DeBow's Review*, XXXI (1861), 96-97.

[8] "Report of the Special Committee of the Chamber of Commerce of the State of New-York on the Confiscation of Cotton in the Southern States by the Government, April 27, 1865," printed in New York Chamber of Commerce, *Annual Report, 1864-'65* (New York, 1865), Pt. I, "Special Reports," 151-52; Foner, *Business & Slavery*, 218.

CHAPTER SEVENTEEN

Business, Not Quite as Usual

The severing of commercial relations between North and South caused disruption and hardship, but these disturbances, many felt, would be temporary. Indeed, some were sure that the war was a fortunate development. At last, the South would be able to break its dependence upon the North. If habit and indolence had sustained Southern dependency, the exigencies of war would bring a new day. In 1862, General Duff Green ecstatically proclaimed his millenial hopes:

> Do you not see in the manifestation of God's providence, in the progress of the slave-holding States, that He has committed to them, as a chosen people, an important and peculiar trust, connected with the spread of His gospel? . . . Do you not see that the tendency, if not the inevitable consequence of the pending war will be to give a unity of interest and of opinion, and a consequent permanence to the Government of the Confederate States, which, as their territory is sufficient to sustain a population of more than two hundred million, must in a few years give them a numerical strength greater than any other of the civilized nations of the earth?

Southerners, as God's chosen people, had only to take advantage of the opportunities which had been given them. His plan was simple enough and not unfamiliar. The South must establish a well-financed agency, backed by funds invested in Confederate securities, that would at once finance the South's cotton crop and also borrow funds from Europe necessary to finance direct trade.[1]

Others echoed these sentiments. Thomas J. Hudson, the president of the Cotton Planters' Convention, wrote that military victory to guarantee political independence was only the first step, a step that had to be followed by economic independence: "No more dependence upon Yankee brains or Yankee hands, is and must be the watchword of every true-hearted Southerner."[2] Peace could not mean a return to the status quo: "Political independence without commercial independence, will be an abstraction," wrote Louisiana Confederate Congressman John Perkins, in calling for discriminatory duties against the United States.[3] So as to show that change was already taking place, that Southerners had "all the energy, industry and ingenuity which is necessary to success, and are now showing it," DeBow began a series of articles which were to be a regular feature in his *Review*: "What We Are Gaining By the War."[4] The rise of home manufacturing and local industry which would make the South forever independent of the North were proudly described in these articles.

Thus direct trade, improved banking and commercial facilities, and local manufacturing were in the South's grasp, available as the fortunate byproduct of war. At the heart of all the rosy expectations was the fervent belief in the powers of King Cotton. Europe, many Southerners held, unwilling to be deprived of cotton, would force the blockade to be lifted and open up trade with the South.

Cotton factors shared these views. Even as they were forced to suspend payments and to refuse advances during the secession crisis, factors remained complacent in the expectation that Northern capital would soon be replaced by foreign capital, thus enabling the regular marketing procedure, after a short period of readjustment, to continue as usual. Such was the tenor of a long letter sent by Watt and Noble of New Orleans to all their customers in December 1860. "The political action of the Cotton States has caused great derangements in our Commercial and Monetary systems, and we think that it is manifest we must cut loose from New York and establish direct dealings with England

---

[1] "Commercial Importance and Future of the South," *DeBow's Review*, XXXII (1862), 120-34. Quoted words are on 133.
[2] Letter from Lamar, Miss., dated Dec. 11, 1861, printed *ibid.*, 161-62.
[3] *Ibid.*, 162.
[4] *Ibid.*, 158-60, 327-33.

and the continent of Europe," the letter began. The failure of New York to buy sterling bills as freely as usual had depressed cotton prices. Had New Orleans been trading directly with Europe, there would have been a ready market for sterling bills in the South and "cotton would now be selling freely at good prices, independent of the condition of things in New York or any other Northern city." Because of the disruption of trade, the firm announced that it was unable to pay drafts drawn on it. Suspension, however, would be temporary, lasting only until direct trade was established. "Our paper," is confidently asserted, "is good and will be paid in full." The letter closed on a note of patriotism: "Our hearts and souls are with the people of these States in their determination to maintain their rights; and we are willing to bear our share of the dangers and sacrifices necessary to the establishment of a Southern Confederacy and a direct trade with Europe."[5]

Factors had managed to sell most of the 1860 crop before hostilities closed the South,[6] but by this time a new crop was growing in the fields. Sale of the crop and repudiation of Northern debts had provided temporary financial relief for hard-pressed factors and merchants, but they still faced the problem of credit for the coming year. Advances on the new crop as well as debts carried over from prior years left planters deeply in debt to factors in the summer of 1861. In New Orleans alone, reported a committee of the Mississippi legislature in July 1861, "it is not an exaggerated estimate to say that over one hundred millions of dollars will fall due . . . within the next eight months . . . for which the growing and future crops are solemnly pledged."[7]

Ordinarily, of course, the crop would come forward in the fall and winter, would be duly sold, and the debt—or at least a good part of it—canceled. Now, however, there were no Northern and foreign buyers in the Southern markets and the blockade prevented

[5] Watt & Noble to "Dear Sir," New Orleans, Dec. 1, 1860, Stephen D. Heard Papers, Southern Historical Collection, University of North Carolina Library, Chapel Hill, N. C. This is a printed form letter obviously intended to explain and justify the firm's suspension to its customers and correspondents.

[6] *DeBow's Review*, Rev. Ser. I (1866), 99; James L. Watkins, *King Cotton* (New York, 1908), 30; (William Howard Russell, *My Diary North and South* (Boston, 1863), 230-31.

[7] Quoted in John K. Bettersworth, *Confederate Mississippi* (Baton Rouge, 1943), 97.

the factors from sending the cotton to the North or Europe. For the moment there seemed to be no reason to send the cotton to the cities. In July 1861, a circular signed by 130 New Orleans cotton factors advised planters "not to ship any portion of their crops of Cotton to this city, or to remove it from their plantations, until the blockade is fully and entirely abandoned, of which due notice will be given."[8] In the following months similar counsel came from Savannah, Mobile, Charleston, Memphis, and Augusta.[9] In each instance the basis for the advice was the same: vast accumulations of cotton that could not be sold because of the blockade created a fire hazard in the city; moreover, great stores of cotton in the cities were tempting inducements for Federal troops to attack in order to capture the staple.

Cotton factors, like other Southerners, optimistically expected an early end to the blockade. Certainly, they assumed, the need for the 1861 crop would bring European ships to Southern ports. The *Augusta Chronicle*, in urging planters to keep their cotton on the plantation, spoke of the blockade's being lifted by January 1862. Should all the area's cotton be in Augusta when the blockade was lifted, "the buyers would be the veriest bears, and the price would go down, down, with such a supply urgently seeking market, and all to the planter's loss."[10] With the blockade still holding in 1862, a writer in *DeBow's Review*, persisting in "an abiding faith in the potent influence of 'King Cotton,'" explained the delay in lifting the blockade as the result of a combination of deep-seated antislavery attitudes in Europe and slander spread by Northern newspapers "prompted by the most corrupt and venal government that ever disgraced a professedly civilized country." But King Cotton was forcing a change in European attitudes: "Six months ago the South had no friends, and now the North has none." Taking for granted the imminent lifting of the blockade, this writer and others debated whether Europeans should be allowed to buy all the cotton they needed immediately, some claiming that the South should punish them for their delay by withholding cotton.[11]

---

[8] *New Orleans Price-Current*, July 27, 1861.

[9] *Ibid.*, Aug. 17, 24, Oct. 5, 1861; *Augusta Chronicle*, as copied in *Hunt's Merchants' Magazine*, XLV (1861), 378. See also *ibid.*, 425.

[10] As copied in *Hunt's Merchants' Magazine*, XLV (1861), 378-79.

[11] *DeBow's Review*, XXXII (1862), 279-81. See also *ibid.*, 304-305.

Fantasies of judicial dispensations had to give way, however, to a more palpable and nagging reality: the South faced more immediate problems. It was already clear that the government needed funds to prosecute the war and that cotton on the plantation did not provide the food and manufactured goods that had usually been imported. Deprived of bills and notes predicated on cotton, the Confederacy was deprived of the basis for its circulating medium. To meet the altered conditions a dual program was attempted: cotton on hand would be used as the basis of a circulating currency, and efforts would be made to induce planters to switch from the production of cotton (and the other staple crops) to the growing of food.

The Produce Loan, passed by the Confederate Congress in May 1861, was designed to provide the government with money through loans. Proceeds from the sale of agricultural products were to be given to the government in return for 8 percent bonds. In a flurry of patriotic fervor, great amounts of cotton and other produce were pledged, but it was soon evident that without a market, there would be no proceeds. To solve this problem, the law was amended the following April to allow the produce itself to be given to the government in return for the bonds. Government cotton, it was thought, could serve as security for foreign loans. Not only would this provide the Confederate government with funds, but it would also serve as an added inducement to foreigners to break the blockade and come to the South to get their cotton. Despite the hoopla attending the loan and the initial enthusiasm, little was realized from it. Although the government came into legal possession of some cotton, the staple itself, for the most part, remained on the plantation. Only a small amount filtered through the blockade so as to provide the needed revenue. Some of the remainder was later confiscated, some was stolen, and a great deal was destroyed intentionally or through the exigencies of the war.[12] Clearly the Confederacy did not have the

12 W. P. Harris, "The Confederate Loan," *The Mississippian*, undated clipping from 1861 in Charles Clark and Family Papers; also clipping from *Mississippian*, dated June 7, 1861, *ibid.*; E. Merton Coulter, *The Confederate States of America, 1861-1865* (Baton Rouge, 1950), 164-70; Willard Range, *A Century of Georgia Agriculture, 1850-1950* (Athens, Ga., 1954), 50-51; Bettersworth, *Confederate Mississippi*, 100-105; Paul W. Gates, *Agriculture and the Civil War* (New York, 1965), 84-85, 105-106.

resources to offset the loss of Northern and European markets.

With imports from the North and West cut off, and with large numbers of Southern farmers conscripted for military service, the South's food needs soon became desperate. The cotton which many Southerners had seen as their trump card was soon regarded as a liability, draining manpower and land from food production. Although no effort was made to destroy the crop of 1861, which was already in the ground when war and blockade became a reality, strenuous efforts were made to substitute King Corn for King Cotton beginning with the 1862 growing season. To the Confederate Congress' urging of a voluntary limitation on cotton planting, the state governments, except for Louisiana and Texas, added the coercive restraints of a series of taxes on cotton produced over a given maximum. Although some planters flatly refused to cut back production and others were enticed by climbing prices to devote a part of their land to cotton growing, a combination of patriotism, state law, the blockade, and the devastation produced by war led to a marked reduction in cotton production beginning in 1862. The crop of 4,500,000 bales in 1861 (before efforts at reduction had begun) was reduced to about 1,500,000 in 1862, 450,000 in 1863, and 300,000 in 1864.[13]

Although steadily decreasing production, control of part of the crop by the Confederate government, and wartime destruction all decreased the volume and activity of the cotton market, it never became completely quiescent. Factors, storekeepers, and speculators continued to buy and sell. If the volume decreased considerably, the dollar value spiraled, as rapid price increases in the North were reflected in prices paid in the South. The war disadvantaged many, but those who risked the hazards of continued cotton trade could reap fortunes. At the end of the war, a stockpile of cotton became the means to wealth, as more than a few realized during the war.

[13] Coulter, *Confederate States*, 239-42; Watkins, *King Cotton*, 30; D. Clayton James, "Mississippi Agriculture, 1861-1865," *Journal of Mississippi History*, XXIV (July 1962), 130-31; Clement Eaton, *A History of the Southern Confederacy* (New York, 1954), 240-41; Bettersworth, *Confederate Mississippi*, 148-52; Charles W. Ramsdell, *Behind the Lines in the Southern Confederacy* (Baton Rouge, 1944), 88; Roger W. Shugg, *Origins of Class Struggle in Louisiana* (Baton Rouge, 1939), 180-81; Gates, *Agriculture and the Civil War*, 15-22, 30-33; U. S. Bureau of the Census, *Historical Statistics of the United States, Colonial Times to 1957* (Washington, D. C., 1960), 302.

Deprived of their regular sources of credit and having greatly extended themselves in loans, advances, and acceptances to planters, many factors were unable to survive the first years of war.[14] But the conflict did not destroy the factorage system. If some went bankrupt or suspended operations, others did not. Every market still had factors who attempted to meet the needs of their customers as they had during peacetime.

In Augusta, Georgia, for example, the firm of Heard and Simpson continued its factorage business throughout the war. Although the firm's correspondence obviously reveals the effects of war, the basic pattern of business remained unchanged. In July 1862, one N. C. Bacon wrote the factors that he was sending them 5 bales of cotton "which is my subscription to the produce loan of the Government." The merchants were asked to sell the cotton and buy the bonds, receiving the typical advice of planter to factor: "dispose of it in the way that will be the least trouble to you and most advantage to me."[15] Many customers asked that Heard and Simpson invest all or part of the proceeds of their cotton in Confederate bonds, but others requested that full proceeds be remitted in cash. Some, however, did not want their cotton sold; instead, they sent it to the factors with instructions to store it.[16] When sales were made, the procedure followed was the same as always: a 2.5 percent commission and expenses of transportation and other costs were deducted from the gross proceeds.[17] Hundreds of invoices for purchases of various items indicate that the factors were supplying their customers with plantation necessities in much the same manner as they had before the hostilities, although the

[14] Shugg, *Origins of Class Struggle*, 194; M. B. Hammond, *The Cotton Industry* (New York, 1897), 294. By early 1862, every Southern state had passed stay laws to protect debtors. For a discussion of these laws see Gates, *Agriculture and the Civil War*, 326-40. If factors, as a result of these stay laws, could not press for the collection of debts owed them, neither could they be harassed by their creditors. Most of the debt protected by stay laws was probably carried over until the end of hostilities. As will be shown, many factors rendered accounts in 1865 for debts contracted in 1860-1861. Those with additional resources could continue business during the war, whereas others, with fewer resources, had to suspend or curtail business.

[15] To Heard & Simpson, n.p., July 1, 1862, Stephen D. Heard Papers.

[16] A note dated July 1, 1863 lists over 3,000 bales of "Cotton in Ware House" held for some twenty-four people. *Ibid.*

[17] "Cotton Book No. 5," *ibid.*, contains letterpress copies of account sales by Heard & Simpson, 1860-1863.

variety of the items available, of course, was much more limited. Even personal favors continued to be asked and granted: "I want a silk dress for my Daughter," wrote storekeeper W. H. Sims in September 1863. "She expects to be married soon, consequently I want to give her a silk." Wartime shortages made it impossible for the factors to buy a silk dress, but they did manage to locate some material which Sims accepted as a suitable substitute.[18]

Judging by the extent of correspondence, it is clear that Heard and Simpson's business diminished during the war. It is equally clear, however, that factorage in Augusta, and elsewhere in the eastern Confederacy,[19] continued on a limited scale throughout the war years. The same was true in the West, although the early capture of New Orleans by Federal troops opened outside markets to that city, markets that were unavailable to the blockaded East. Wealthy, Unionist planter Stephen Duncan of Mississippi dealt with his regular New Orleans factors right through both Confederacy and occupation. Significantly, both his factors had branch houses in the North and in Europe which handled a large portion of Duncan's business. One of the factors, William E. Leverich, rendered an account on April 21, 1862 just a few days before New Orleans was bombarded and taken, in which he showed that he had accepted drafts, paid bills, and loaned money to Duncan on notes that would not fall due until 1862 and 1863.[20] When in April 1864 Duncan calculated the value of his estate, he listed stocks and bonds held by H. L. and C. P. Leverich (the New York firm with whom he had dealt before the war) along with cotton in the South and in Manchester.[21] At the same time, Duncan was dealing with another of his prewar factorage houses, Washington

[18] Letter lated La Grange, Sept. 28, Oct. 3, 1863, *ibid.*

[19] See a/c sales by Lundes & Lapsley for a/c of estate of R. H. McFaddin, Selma, Ala., Oct. 3, 1863, Johnston-McFaddin Papers, Southern Historical Collection, University of North Carolina Library, Chapel Hill, N. C.; Johnson & Harrold to Mr. W. E. Sanders [Americus, Ga.], Sept. 19, 1861, Harrold Brothers Papers, Emory University Library, Atlanta, Ga.; John Colcock to James Gregorie, Limeston Springs, Oct. 17, 1863, Gregorie-Elliott Papers, Southern Historical Collection, University of North Carolina Library, Chapel Hill, N. C. The last letter describes sales of cotton in Columbia, Augusta, and Macon, Ga., all of which the writer claimed netted more than sales would in Charleston.

[20] Duncan Special a/c in a/c with Leverich, New Orleans, April 21, 1862, Stephen and Stephen, Jr., Duncan Papers, Louisiana Department of Archives, Louisiana State University, Baton Rouge, La.

[21] Schedule of Estate, April 1864, in Journal, 1861-1870, *ibid.*

Jackson and Company. Occupation did not disturb the relationship; it merely meant that Duncan could again sell in New York
and Liverpool and collect money being held for him in Liverpool
from his 1861 crop.[22]

Not all Southerners were willing (or able) to send cotton to
New Orleans after the city fell in April 1862. Nevertheless, some
factors seemed to have aided their old customers. Mississippian
Charles Clark—a general in the Confederate army and later (1863-
1865) Confederate governor of Mississippi—dealt with the New
Orleans factorage firm Fellowes and Company before the war and
continued to do so even after New Orleans was occupied. In July
1862, several months after New Orleans had fallen, Fellowes and
Company rendered an account current to Clark. It was a typical
factor's account showing drafts accepted, supplies purchased,
interest charged, commissions assessed, and proceeds from the sale
of produce. The account showed a debt owed by Clark of more
than ten thousand dollars.[23] Another account, rendered by the
same firm in December 1865, showed that on February 15, 1862
(two months before the capture of New Orleans) the factor had
presented Clark with an account showing a debt of $6,033.24.
On that day, $6,000 in cash had been paid and the small balance
carried over. The 1865 account also indicated that in the fall and
winter of 1862-1863 the factor had paid bills and advanced cash to
Clark and others to a total of over $2,500, none of which had been
repaid as of December 1865.[24] Although neither account indicated
sales of cotton for Clark—proceeds shown on the 1862 account
are for the sale of hay—it is clear that Clark's prewar factor continued to provide him with services and loans throughout both
Confederate and Federal rule of New Orleans, even though he
probably did not receive cotton to sell.[25]

The fall of New Orleans brought newcomers into the factorage
business. Thomas W. Knox noted that the older merchants

22 Journal for Carlisle Plantation and Journal, 1861-1895, *ibid*.

23 Clark in a/c current with Fellowes & Co., New Orleans, July 15, 1862,
Charles Clark and Family Papers, Mississippi Department of Archives and History,
Jackson, Miss.

24 Clark in a/c with Fellowes & Co., New Orleans, Dec. 1865, *ibid*.

25 There is no indication of payment of the $10,000 owed as indicated on the
July 1862 account; it does not appear on the Dec. 1865 account. The first entry on
the 1865 account is dated Aug. 1862. The first bill was probably paid when the
account was rendered in July 1862.

"found themselves crowded aside by the ubiquitous Yankees" who followed the army into New Orleans:

> In '63 and '64, New Orleans could boast of more cotton factors than cotton. The principal business was in the hands of merchants from the North, who had established themselves in the city soon after its occupation by National forces. Nearly all cotton sent to the market was from plantations leased by Northern men, or from purchases made of planters by Northern speculators. The patronage naturally fell into the hands of the new possessors of the soil, and left the old merchants to pine in solitude. The old factors, most of them Southern men, who could boast of ten or twenty years' experience, saw their business pass into the hands of men whose arrival in New Orleans was subsequent to that of General Butler.[26]

Thus the factorage system continued throughout the war years. Recognition of this, however, is only part of the story of cotton marketing during the Civil War. Business could not be completely "as usual" if only because most of the cotton remained in the South. More important questions must be asked: Who bought the cotton? What happened to that which was purchased? Answers to these questions not only help to illuminate the wartime marketing system but also shed light on immediate postwar developments.

In October and November of 1862, a British merchant, W. C. Corsan, traveled through the South, visiting the Confederate areas as well as New Orleans, then under Federal occupation. His firm had had extensive dealings with "many Southern merchants, from or of whom we had heard almost nothing since the commencement of the civil war," and the purpose of his visit was "to ascertain whether our old friends were living or dead, and solvent or ruined."[27]

Stopping first at New Orleans, Corsan found trade with the interior cut off and commerce at a standstill. Investigation convinced him, however, that the war had not brought total ruin to the merchant community. On the contrary, many had made large profits which they had safely invested:

[26] *Camp-fire and Cotton-field: Southern Adventure in the Time of War* (New York, 1865), 394, 396. Knox had leased a plantation on the Mississippi and he visited New Orleans to sell his crop.

[27] [W. C. Corsan], *Two Months in the Confederate States, Including a Visit to New Orleans Under the Domination of General Butler* (London, 1863), 6.

So long as transit with the interior was possible, a brisk trade had gone on, and the stocks of groceries and dry goods especially had been almost entirely sold out at enormous prices in Confederate money. These funds, as fast as they accumulated, had been despatched by the hands of trusty agents into the interior, and invested in sugar or cotton, at eight to ten cents per pound, on the plantations. As a rule, only such lots of cotton were purchased as either were then, or could easily be, removed from twenty-five to fifty miles from the river, road, or railway. It was considered prudent, also, not to have in any case more than fifty bales stored in one place. The result of all this was, that all the principal houses in the city had realized very large fortunes, and invested the bulk in cotton, at about threepence sterling per pound.[28]

Since the average New York price for cotton at the time was over sixty-seven cents and the average Liverpool price over twenty-two pence,[29] the British merchant and his readers easily appreciated the potential fortunes cached in the South.

Moving into Confederate territory, Corsan discovered similar conditions. At Jackson, Mississippi, he found most of the stores had closed but not before merchants had sold out their wares at "immense profits." Mobile merchants seemed to be a more enterprising lot, making regular trips into the interior to buy goods which they then resold in the Alabama port at enormous profit. Surpluses were carefully invested in state, bank, railway, or Confederate bonds "or in cotton, at about fifteen to twenty cents per pound." The cotton was "stored far away from any water-course, road, or railway, and never more than twenty-five bales in one place."

In Charleston he noted that most of the prewar merchants did not participate in the lucrative blockade-running: "The regular resident merchants had, I found, sold out their stocks long ago, closed their stores, invested their money in plantations, cotton, scrip, gold, or sterling exchange, removed their families into the interior, and remained behind watching events." This procedure, he concluded, had been very profitable: "I could hear of no house which had not done well." In Petersburg, Virginia, the same story was repeated. Most of the merchants had " 'sold out' and

[28] *Ibid.*, 25-26.
[29] Watkins, *King Cotton*, 30.

'realized,' which means they have made their fortunes and put it
[*sic*] where it is safe."[30]

The validity of Corsan's observations is certainly open to question. As a creditor, he was undoubtedly anxious to find his customers in sound financial condition. Moreover, since much of his
information seems to have come second hand—he is never really
clear about his sources—he may have been unduly influenced by
those who were strenuously complaining about speculation, high
prices, and profiteering. On the other hand, his tone is not one
of condemnation or even disapproval. Though critical of slavery,
he was sympathetic to the South, feeling that the Confederacy
probably could hold out, forcing the North to grant independence.

Although the British merchant's portrait is undoubtedly exaggerated there is, nevertheless, adequate evidence that many fortunes
were made in the South during the war, often in precisely the way
Corsan described. A few general examples from various parts of
the section may serve to introduce a more detailed description of
the methods by which fortunes were amassed.

An official guide to the city of Charleston, published in 1875,
contained a laudatory sketch of a prominent firm in the city,
George W. Williams and Company. Williams, along with a
partner, had opened a wholesale grocery business in Augusta in
1842; ten years later he started a second house in Charleston.
Both firms prospered until they closed in 1862. The war did not
ruin Williams, however. On the contrary, "so judiciously was the
capital invested, as to leave more than a million of dollars with
which to begin business at the termination of the war."[31]

Edmund Richardson of New Orleans was the subject of another
laudatory biographical account, "based exclusively upon information obtained directly from himself" and published in 1883.
Starting as a clerk in a country store, the article notes, Richardson
soon went into business for himself. When the Civil War
began, he owned several country stores, five plantations on the
Mississippi, and was also a partner in a New Orleans factorage

---

[30] [Corsan], *Two Months in the Confederate States*, 110-11, 132-33, 150. The
Britisher also noted that gold, like cotton, had been hoarded and hidden away by
individuals and firms throughout the South. *Ibid.*, 242. On the hoarding of specie
by New Orleans merchants see Thomas Ewing Dabney, "The Butler Regime in
Louisiana," *Louisiana Historical Quarterly*, XXVII (April 1944), 505.

[31] Arthur Mazyck, *Guide to Charleston* (Charleston, [1875]), 143-45.

firm. Although the war brought financial hardship and loss to the prosperous merchant-planter, it by no means meant his total ruin. "In the Fall of 1865 he attempted to reorganize his places for planting, and with five hundred bales of cotton saved from the general wreck, reopened his commission house in New Orleans."[32] At the prevailing prices in 1865, these 500 bales were worth about seventy to one hundred thousand dollars or more.

Merchants in the Southeast also maintained their share of wealth. In his tour of the South after the war, Whitelaw Reid met a number of the leading personages of Savannah, among whom was Charles Green, "a noted British merchant, of many years' residence" in the city. "Mr. Green is among the wealthiest inhabitants; has made more money out of the war than any one else, unless Savannah rumor greatly belies him." Reid added that Green professed to be a Union man, but the Northern visitor doubted that Green's unionism was of long standing.[33]

An Augusta merchant candidly described his financial standing at the close of the war in a letter to one of his creditors: "I have under the blessing of a kind Providence managed to squeeze through and pay a debt of fifty five thousand dollars at one hundred cents on the dollar at the close and have cash over enough to make all purchases cash for both stores. I bo[ugh]t my associate Mr Salisbury out & he left for the north early in the war— . . . I did an enormous trade all through the war—I was prosperous and last year I was worth in then New York valuations (mostly cotton) between four and five hundred thousand dollars."[34]

Prosperous wartime trading, profits judiciously invested, cotton hidden and saved—these are the recurring themes in the histories of those who saved themselves from ruin. To these must be added others—trade with the enemy, fraud, and theft. In all these activities cotton assumed a leading role. If the war had proved that King Cotton's power was far from absolute, it did not topple him from his throne, and many found it advantageous to continue to serve him.

[32] "Edmund Richardson," in Latham, Alexander & Co., *Cotton Movement and Fluctuations, 1876 to 1883* (New York, 1883), 41, 43.

[33] *After the War: A Southern Tour, May 1, 1865, to May 1, 1866* (London, 1866), 152.

[34] A. H. Jones to Henry Lee Reynolds, Augusta, Oct. 3, 1865, Henry Lee Reynolds Papers, Southern Historical Collection, University of North Carolina Library, Chapel Hill, N. C.

CHAPTER EIGHTEEN

Blockade-Running and Trade with the Enemy

Southern trade with the outside world continued throughout the war despite Federal blockade and Confederate restrictions.[1] Both sides were of two minds concerning this trade. Although the Federal government recognized the strategic value of an effective blockade, it also recognized the need for cotton in Northern mills. Similarly, the Confederacy, after it became clear that the blockade would not be broken, saw that trade could help to supply the South with needed food and military supplies. At the same time, merchants and speculators were well aware of the potential profits arising from the sale of cotton in the North and Europe. Both governments at first prohibited trade with the enemy and then tacitly permitted it while attempting to regulate it to their own advantage. The Federal government tried to restrict the flow of gold into the South, while the Confederates attempted to make all sales in the valuable metal which could then be used to buy needed military supplies. Late in the war, the Confederate government itself took an active part in the trade, with government agents selling cotton for gold to meet the needs of the Confederacy. Both government agents and private merchants shipped cotton over the border into Mexico, through the lines into the North, and through the blockaded ocean ports.

Complicating matters was the fact that neither government maintained complete control over the trade. The confusion of war, inadequate legislation along with poor enforcement of existing legislation, and the connivance of corrupt officials allowed for an extensive trade between the belligerents, at times, perhaps, to the disadvantage of both governments' war efforts, but usually to the profit of private enterprisers.

With the price of cotton rising steadily in the North and in Europe and with shortages and inflation afflicting the South, the profit opportunities in blockade-running were manifest. Two successful trips out of three through the Federal blockade would earn investors 500 to 1000 percent on their money, a prospect that drew not only Southerners but also foreigners and even Northerners into the trade.[2] But the venturesome blockade-runners were seeking profits first and benefits to the Confederate war effort second—or not at all. Attempts by the Confederate government to outfit its own blockade-runners or to guarantee a portion of the space on private runners for government imports and exports met only limited success.

Efforts by the Confederate government to use the cotton trade to aid the war effort in effect often led to private aggrandizement as Confederate agents, buying and shipping cotton for the government, found it possible to turn a personal profit while in government employ. Confederate enthusiast and editor, J. D. B. DeBow, while serving as a government representative, sent enough of his own cotton through the blockade to accumulate some six thousand dollars in the Bank of Liverpool. Additional profits went into Confederate government securities, some of which he used to buy homes in Richmond and Columbus (Mississippi) and land

[1] Unless otherwise indicated, the discussion of the general features of this trade is based on the following: John K. Bettersworth, *Confederate Mississippi* (Baton Rouge, 1943), 147-87; Charles W. Ramsdell, *Behind the Lines in the Southern Confederacy* (Baton Rouge, 1944), 58-60, 106-11; Clement Eaton, *A History of the Southern Confederacy* (New York, 1954), 250-51; A. Sellow Roberts, "The Federal Government and Confederate Cotton," *American Historical Review*, XXXII (Jan. 1927), 262-75; E. Merton Coulter, "Commercial Intercourse with the Confederacy in the Mississippi Valley, 1861-1865," *Mississippi Valley Historical Review*, V (March 1919), 378-95; E. Merton Coulter, "Effects of Secession upon the Commerce of the Mississippi Valley," *Mississippi Valley Historical Review*, III (Dec. 1916), 275-300; E. Merton Coulter, *The Confederate States of America, 1861-1865* (Baton Rouge, 1950), 286-95.

[2] For a discussion of the profitable blockade-running activities of a Southern businessman, see Thomas Robson Hay, "Gazaway Bugg Lamar, Confederate Banker and Business Man," *Georgia Historical Quarterly*, XXXVII (June 1953), 113-28; Edwin B. Coddington, "The Activities and Attitudes of a Confederate Businessman: Gazaway B. Lamar," *Journal of Southern History*, IX (Feb. 1943), 17-24.

in Mississippi, Louisiana, and Texas.[3] Trade into Mexico offered similar advantages. Long after the war had ended, a Confederate lady recalled that during the Civil War her planter husband "had contracts to move Government cotton to the [Mexican] frontier, which afforded him opportunities to move his own."[4]

Occupation of the South opened markets closer to home. At the same time, however, the disruption and uncertainties created by invading troops menaced the safety of cotton in the fields, stored on the plantations, or en route to market. Plantations with growing crops often were abandoned and cotton sheds or remote hiding places left unguarded as Federal troops moved into an area. Markings on bales were easily changed, making theft a simple matter. Around the staple there whirled a maelstrom of conflicting interests. While Yankee speculators—civilian and military—along with Southern marauders sought the valuable cotton, planters tried to protect and market their property and Confederate army officers attempted to burn all cotton that might fall into Union hands.

The first of the Southern cotton markets opened to trade were New Orleans and Memphis, occupied in 1862. These cities gave Southwestern planters nearby markets for their cotton and many could not resist the opportunity to use them. James Lusk Alcorn, the Mississippi planter, keen in sensing political winds and adapting to them, was quick to take advantage of economic opportunity as well. In late November 1862 he wrote from his plantation, Mound Place in Coahoma County, that he was selling his cotton to Northern buyers who paid in greenbacks. He informed his wife that he planned to stay on the plantation until he got all his cotton out and sold. He had other plans as well. Confederate money could be purchased by the sackful in Memphis for greenbacks; he planned to buy some for later use in purchasing land in Confederate territory.[5] Less than a month later, he reported his progress: "I have been very busy hiding & selling my cotton. I have sold in all one hundred & eleven bales. I have now here ten

[3] Otis Clark Skipper, *J. D. B. DeBow, Magazinist of the Old South* (Athens, Ga., 1958), 170.

[4] Eliza McHatton-Ripley, *From Flag to Flag* (New York, 1889), 77.

[5] To Mrs. Amelia Alcorn, Mound Place, Nov. 25, 1862, printed in P. L. Rainwater (ed.), "Letters of James Lusk Alcorn," *Journal of Southern History*, III (May 1937), 198-99.

thousand dollars in paper (Greenbacks) and one thousand dollars in gold." He added that he still had cotton unsold from which he hoped to realize $20,000 more "if I escape the burners."[6]

Profit-seekers in the occupied cities did not wait for business to come to them. Buyers or their agents scoured the countryside in search of cotton. Stephen Duncan, who sold cotton from his own Mississippi plantations through factors in New Orleans, also served as an agent for one "Martin of Liverpool." Using Natchez as his base of operations, Duncan purchased cotton at the plantation for cash, the planter agreeing to hold and protect the cotton until called for and then to ship it at his own expense to Natchez. At times Duncan provided funds to others to buy the cotton for him, paying 2.5 percent commission for this service. During the first half of 1863, Duncan purchased over eleven hundred bales in this manner at an average cost of about fifty-five dollars per bale.[7] Potential profit margins were immense since the average price being paid for cotton during the 1862-1863 season in New Orleans was over two hundred and thirty dollars per bale.[8] If potential profits in this trade were high, so too were the risks, as Duncan well knew. Among the wartime losses he recorded in his journal were eighty mules and over one hundred bales of cotton "stolen by Rebels."[9]

Trading opportunities also drew enterprising merchants and speculators to Memphis. Charles A. Dana, who with Roscoe Conkling and George W. Chadwick had organized a business to trade in cotton through occupied Memphis, described the scene

[6] To Mrs. Amelia Alcorn, Mound Place, Dec. 18, 1862, *ibid.*, 201. Alcorn was successively a Whig, a secessionist, and then a Republican of changing degrees of radicalness. The editor of his letters noted that Alcorn was very successful in his Civil War and postwar operations; eventually he owned some twelve thousand acres of delta land producing twelve to eighteen hundred bales per year. *Ibid.*, 197.

[7] Numerous receipts signed by planters, dated variously early 1863, Stephen and Stephen, Jr., Duncan Papers, Louisiana Department of Archives, Louisiana State University, Baton Rouge, La. Some receipts show Duncan to be the buyer; others indicate that Dunbar Hunt or G. L. Mandeville purchased the cotton for Duncan. A receipt signed by Mandeville, dated May 2, 1863 shows his commission charges.

[8] *DeBow's Review*, n.s. I (1866), 203.

[9] Entry for Dec. 21, 1864, Journal, 1861-1895 and a/c, July 1, 1863 to Jan. 1, 1865, Journal, 1856-1865, Stephen and Stephen, Jr., Duncan Papers. These purchases were only a small part of extensive cotton operations by Duncan. In April 1864 he reckoned his value in cotton, cash, and bills receivable at over one million dollars. Schedule of Estate, April 1865, Journal, 1861-1870, *ibid.*

when he arrived in late 1862. "The mania for sudden fortunes made in cotton," he wrote, had brought a hoard of speculators to the city. Even the army was "corrupted and demoralized" by the frenzied search for cotton: "Every colonel, captain, or quartermaster is in secret partnership with some operator in cotton; every soldier dreams of adding a bale of cotton to his monthly pay."[10]

The Federal authorities vacillated in their policies concerning the trade out of Memphis. Free trade with Confederate areas brought needed cotton to the city, but it also helped to supply the Confederacy with gold. Attempts to limit the movement of gold and important supplies into the Confederacy were evaded by smuggling. As a result, orders closing the trade completely were relaxed and then rescinded because of the need for cotton.[11] Wavering policies increased the risks but did not end speculative ventures by businessmen eager to secure cotton from the surrounding countryside.

One such enterprising businessman was a Southerner, Robertson Topp, who represented "a party of capitalists" in Memphis. Unwilling to risk going into the countryside themselves, the "capitalists" (otherwise unidentified) offered to finance Topp's purchases and pay him one-sixth of the net proceeds of the cotton when delivered and sold in Memphis. His backers had six boats plying the Mississippi and Tallahatchie rivers and a store of bagging, rope, and plantation supplies which Topp could offer planters selling cotton to him. Topp instructed an associate to go into the neighborhoods where large crops were growing and "engage every crop you can." Planters willing to sell would receive supplies and cash for their crops when they were delivered "to me at some point on the Missi[ssippi] or else on [the] Tallahatchie when that stream is up and boats running." He added that his backers could also supply him with Confederate money should any cotton be available for that currency.[12] Topp's contacts reached all the way to Wash-

---

10 To Edwin Stanton, Memphis, Jan. 21, 1863, as printed in Charles A. Dana, *Recollections of the Civil War, with the Leaders at Washington and in the Field in the Sixties* (New York, 1898), 17-18.

11 Joseph H. Parks, "A Confederate Trade Center under Federal Occupation: Memphis, 1862-1865," *Journal of Southern History,* VII (Aug. 1941), 289-314.

12 To Rowan Bridges, [place illegible], Sept. 12, 1863, Robertson Topp Papers, Burrow Library, Southwestern at Memphis, Memphis, Tenn. Topp explained that his backers were among a few in Memphis who had legal permission to ship supplies

ington and London. In April 1864 he received an unsigned letter written on House of Representatives stationery. His correspondent advised him that he expected special orders to be issued him to buy cotton and ship supplies in the Memphis and Vicksburg areas and he urged Topp to get to Memphis "as quickly as steam could carry you." In the meantime, the correspondent was planning a trip to New York "for Capital." He added that "an arrangement can be made with Brown & Brothers for all the money needed."[13]

The story at Memphis was repeated a few months later at Vicksburg. Thomas W. Knox recalled that as the Federals approached Vicksburg, many planters and overseers in the area abandoned the plantations, often with the crop standing in the fields. General Grant authorized contractors to pick and sell the crop, provided they hired and fed Negro workmen and gave one-half of the proceeds to the government. "There was no lack of men to undertake the collection of abandoned cotton on these terms, as the enterprise could not fail to be exceedingly remunerative," wrote Knox. Old cotton, that is, cotton grown and baled in previous years, was not supposed to be handled by the contractors, but this regulation did not prevent many of them from doing so. Speculators frequently went into the countryside buying and stealing cotton which was then shipped out as part of the new crop. Knox noted that the best land yielded about a bale to a bale and a half to the acre, but contractors "were sometimes able to show a yield of ten or twenty bales to the acre," the excess, of course, being stolen or purchased cotton from previous years.[14]

Not all planters in the vicinity of Vicksburg abandoned their crops to Northerners. Ignoring pleas to switch to food production, many had continued to grow cotton to be smuggled through the lines or held for sale to speculators who accompanied Northern troops as they moved towards the beleaguered city.[15] Once the city had fallen, it, like Memphis, became a trading center for cotton, greenbacks, Confederate money, and gold.[16] In the backcountry

---

into Confederate territory. See also I. Fowlkes to Topp, Memphis, Oct. 20, 1863, *ibid.*

[13] Unknown person to Topp, Washington, D. C., April 10, 1864, *ibid.*

[14] *Camp-fire and Cotton-field, Southern Adventure in the Time of War* (New York, 1865), 307-309.

[15] Peter F. Walker, *Vicksburg: A People at War, 1860-1865* (Chapel Hill, 1960), 133-35.

[16] *Ibid.*, 214-20.

thieves and burners contested with planters, merchants, speculators, and government agents for control of the area's cotton. "I have seen cotton taken where the right was clear & unequivocal in favour of the party forced to give it up," complained a Mississippi planter in reference to the confiscating activities of Federal agents. He maintained that much of the confiscated cotton never found its way into government storehouses but was stolen.[17]

Again and again the advance of Federal troops brought cotton sales, speculation, and theft. When General Nathaniel P. Banks led a force up the Red River, he was followed by a swarm of speculators carrying rope and bagging and eager to lay hands on any available cotton. Much of the prize was put to the torch by retreating Confederate troops, but a portion remained for the speculators. They were allowed to buy what they could from the planters and then ship it back to New Orleans for resale. Confederate-owned cotton, of course, was to be confiscated by the army. Invoking this regulation, troops often seized cotton on the pretense that it belonged to the government and then promptly turned it over to eager speculators.[18]

Noting this trade with the enemy in the West, the *Richmond Examiner* savagely attacked the turncoat planters: "When it is remembered that the secession movement was inaugurated by the cotton population of the South, that the Confederate Government is conducted almost exclusively under the auspices of cotton states men, even to the extent of proscribing other important and as patriotic classes, these shameful transactions of mercenary cotton planters on the flats of the Mississippi appear still more strange and reprehinsible [sic]. If the secession Government is to be used as a private tart of cotton men, the infamy of the treachery of these cotton planters becomes the more black."[19]

[17] C. M. Vaiden to Wm. L. Sharkey, Vaiden, Miss., July 25, 1865, William L. Sharkey Papers, Mississippi Department of Archives and History, Jackson, Miss. Vaiden was complaining in this letter that Federal agents were requiring him to substitute his own cotton for that which he had been holding for the Confederate government, but which he claimed had been stolen.

[18] Richard Hobson Williams, "General Banks' Red River Campaign," *Louisiana Historical Quarterly*, XXXII (Jan. 1949), 132-37; H. L. Landers, "Wet Sand and Cotton—Banks' Red River Campaign," *ibid.*, XIX (Jan. 1936), 154, 166-76; G. P. Whittington, "Rapides Parish, Louisiana—A History," *ibid.*, XVII (Oct. 1934), 746-47.

[19] "Cotton and Sugar Planter," *Richmond Examiner*, as copied in the *Mississippian*, undated clipping in Charles Clark and Family Papers.

Planters in the East were no more eager to burn their cotton and refuse dealings with the Yankees than those in the West. The capture of Savannah also precipitated a wild scramble for possession of the cotton. As speculators and merchants rushed to gain control of the staple, the army and the treasury agents on the scene bickered over the disposition of the coveted article. Corruption was rife. Confederate cotton would often become transformed into private cotton (and thus be available for sale) while privately owned stocks might be seized as Confederate cotton, only to change once again into private cotton when it came time to ship.[20] When Charleston came under Federal domination, it became a ready market for cotton of every description, including that which was stolen. "Robberies are of daily occurrence," wrote Henry William Ravenal in his journal. He noted that a number of merchants were "buying all the cotton the negroes can steal & carry to them. Every body is losing cotton, cattle, hogs & sheep."[21]

Always dangerous, Southern wartime trade with the outside world was often illegal and usually considered unpatriotic. Thus, although the excitement and opportunities for profit drew some into blockade-running and trade with the enemy, many shunned such business and condemned those who put personal profit above the needs of their country. Others, whose patriotic scruples might have been less exacting, were never given the opportunity to take part in the lucrative trade inasmuch as large parts of the cotton areas were not opened until the last months of war. Whether from patriotism or lack of opportunity, most Southerners were not involved in trade with the outside world. Nevertheless, the needs of cotton growers and the hope of future profit in cotton did support a vigorous internal trade during the war.

[20] George Winston Smith, "Cotton from Savannah in 1865," *Journal of Southern History*, XXI (Nov. 1955), 495-515.

[21] Entry of Wed., Aug. 23, 1865, Arney Robinson Childs (ed.), *The Private Journal of Henry William Ravenal, 1859-1887* (Columbia, S. C., 1947), 250.

CHAPTER NINETEEN

Internal Trade and Speculation

Not since the Revolutionary War had there been an inflation like that which gripped the Confederacy. With the regular sources of food and manufactured goods cut off by Federal law and blockade, prices for these goods would be expected to rise. The added demands of war compounded the problem, while relief was blocked by the failure of the government to institute effective price controls. More important than the Confederate government's inability to maintain ceilings on prices were its monetary policies, which provided the greatest single impetus to runaway inflation. Government printing presses—Confederate, state, and local—poured currency into the economy at a rate far greater than any productive increases in the Confederacy. With more and more dollars seeking a limited supply of goods, prices rose sharply as the war progressed. Moreover, since rapidly rising prices discouraged holding funds, velocity increased sharply also. Aggravating the problem was the gradual constriction of territory in which Confederate money was used, as victorious Federal troops occupied the South.[1]

Such conditions made the Confederacy ripe for speculation, price manipulation, and extortion. Indeed, as prices spiraled, consumers blamed their plight on speculators who were said to be using the war to grow rich at the expense of their neighbors.[2] Demands that prices be regulated and that the military "put a stop to the extortions of greedy speculators"[3] rarely distinguished between those who manipulated prices and overcharged for essentials and those who merely advanced their selling prices in an effort to maintain a normal profit margin in a highly inflationary market. Farmers blamed merchants, city people blamed farmers, and both blamed manufacturers for rising prices. The onus of speculator and swindler often fell indiscriminately on anyone who had something to sell. Undoubtedly there were those who did take advantage of shortages to charge exorbitant prices for their goods; and there were others who were able to manipulate the currency to their advantage.[4] Yet, to see the Confederacy as the victim of a small group of avaricious predators hides both the overwhelming significance of the overexpansion of the money supply in creating inflation, as well as the fact that most merchants, farmers, and manufacturers were trying to protect investments and profits rather than to fleece an unfortunate and helpless population. Planters and farmers continued to need aid in the form of supplies and credit from factors and storekeepers, and merchants, in turn, had to find ways to stock their shelves in an inflation-ridden and blockaded South.

Ironically, the commodity in which there was most speculation was least affected by inflation. Until the last months of the war, cotton prices in the South increased slowly,[5] lagging far behind price increases in other commodities. Yet cotton was grown, sold, and resold throughout the war,[6] and so long as the blockade lasted

[1] For a brilliant discussion of the effect of the increase in the money supply on the Confederate economy see Eugene M. Lerner, "Money, Wages and Prices in the Confederacy," *Journal of Political Economy*, LXII (Feb. 1955), 20-40, reprinted in Ralph Andreano (ed.), *The Economy Impact of the American Civil War* (Cambridge, Mass., 1962), 11-40. A good description of inflation and its effects in the Confederacy may be found in E. Merton Coulter, *Confederate States of America, 1861-1865* (Baton Rouge, 1950), 219-38.

[2] Bell Irvin Wiley, *The Plain People of the Confederacy* (Baton Rouge, 1943), 40-41, 65-66.

[3] Entry of April 4, 1862, in Arney Robinson Childs (ed.), *The Private Journal of Henry William Ravenel, 1859-1887* (Columbia, S. C., 1947), 133.

[4] Occupation of the western Confederacy provided opportunities for speculation in currency. Henry William Ravenel explained how such financial maneuvers drove prices up: "Merchants from the West, who have bought up Confed notes in New Orleans, Memphis, Nashville & other places occupied by the enemy, at a discount, have been attending the sale of cargoes in Charleston, & have run up prices to such figures as to place them beyond the reach of ordinary means." Entry of Sept. 30, 1862, *ibid.*, 156-57. As has already been noted, James Lusk Alcorn and Robertson Topp bought Confederate money very cheaply in Memphis after the occupation.

[5] See Coulter, *Confederate States of America*, 220.

[6] Lerner's statement that "King Cotton was begging for buyers in southern markets" during the war is an overstatement, as will be shown. His major argument that cotton prices rose much more slowly than did prices of other commodities is

every sale was completely speculative. Largely unavailable to the consuming market, it became increasingly valuable in New York and Liverpool even as its price in the South rose gradually. (See

TABLE 7. COTTON PRICES PER POUND IN NEW YORK AND LIVERPOOL, 1860-1865

Season	New York (cents)			Liverpool (pence)		
	Lowest	Highest	Average	Lowest	Highest	Average
1860-1861	10	22	13.01	6½	11⅝	8.50
1861-1862	20	51½	31.29	12¼	29	18.37
1862-1863	51	92	67.21	20	29¼	22.46
1863-1864	68	189	101.50	21½	31¼	27.17
1864-1865	35	182	83.38	13	26	19.11

Source: James L. Watkins, *King Cotton* (New York, 1908), 30.

Table 7.) It took no great foresight to see that control of cotton would mean a fortune when the war ended or the blockade lifted. Nonperishable under ordinary conditions, it could be stored until the war was over. There were dangers, of course. Hidden cotton could be discovered and stolen. Confederate authorities might burn cotton as their troops retreated to prevent its falling into Federal hands. Federal armies might confiscate it as contraband of war. Despite these dangers, however, there was a brisk trade in the South throughout the war, as those with funds and daring to match sought control of the staple. Not only did speculators, with an eye on the war's end, attempt to buy cotton, but so too did many who, seeing the rapid decline in the value of Confederate money, sought the ownership of cotton for the greater security and stability it might bring them.

Both the risks and dangers as well as the day-to-day business activities of a typical Southern merchant during wartime may be followed in the records and correspondence of H. R. Johnson and Company of Americus, Georgia.[7] From their store in the small town in the southwestern part of the state, Henry Johnson and Thomas Harrold served the surrounding territory throughout the war, dealing with planters and farmers, storekeepers and factors, and anyone else who wanted to buy, sell, ship, store, or otherwise deal in cotton and other commodities. The firm had been orga-

---

correct and well taken. "Money, Prices and Wages . . . ," in Andreano, *The Economic Impact*, 18.

[7] The following analysis is based on the extensive Harrold Brothers Papers, Emory University Library, Atlanta, Ga., and unless otherwise indicated all letters cited are from this collection. Although its name was changed several times, the firm itself lasted until the 1940's. Its postwar activities are treated below.

nized during the last ante bellum decade and had operated as a
typical country store, supplying neighboring planters and farmers
with goods and buying and shipping cotton for customers. From
Thomas Wood and Company of New York the Americus firm had
received groceries which it had sold on commission and to Thomas
Wood had gone cotton to be sold in New York.[8]

War and blockade, of course, cut the Americus firm's ties with
New York, but the store remained open and shelves were stocked
from Southern sources. Wholesalers in Macon, Columbus, Augusta, and Atlanta provided bagging, rope, sugar, coffee, whiskey, and
other items,[9] but other sources were used as well. Often local
farmers would be approached directly. In March 1862, for example,
Johnson and Company arranged with one William Mize "to
purchase Bacon[,] Corn &c for the Americus Market." Mize, with
$500 in cash provided by the storekeepers, was to buy produce
from farmers and planters and haul it to the Americus store. His
compensation would be one-half the net profits after resale.[10]
Another type of agreement, in this case directly with a local farmer,
brought flour into the store. The storekeepers agreed to pay a debt
owed by one Chesley D. Clegg and to accept payment later in
produce: "The said Clegg will bring in about 600 to 800 or 1000 Lbs
good family flour at 12½ [cents] per 100 Lbs to pay his note."[11]

Barter was still another means to stock the store. With money
depreciating, many farmers and merchants preferred cotton (which
was appreciating in value) to cash for goods they offered for sale.
A Virginian wrote that he had purchased salt and wanted to trade
it for cotton: "I do not wish to sell it for money at all," he
concluded.[12] Similarly, a Macon merchant asked that Johnson and
Company sell his customer's tobacco but added that he wanted
the proceeds in cotton, not money.[13]

In the course of its business, H. R. Johnson and Company came
into possession of several plantations. Either purchased or taken

---

[8] See Chap. VII, above.

[9] Hundreds of receipts for supplies purchased in these cities may be found in the
Harrold Brothers Papers.

[10] Johnson & Co. agreement with Mize, Americus, March 26, 1862.

[11] Johnson & Co. agreement with Clegg, Americus, Aug. 15, 1862. By this agreement, of course, the Americus storekeepers were giving the farmer an advance on
his wheat crop.

[12] D. G. Thomas to Johnson & Co., n.p., Va., June 20, 1862.

[13] H. R. Jewett to Johnson & Co., Macon, Aug. 6, 1862.

over from defaulting planters, these plantations seem to have been a new aspect of the storekeepers' business. Johnson, on a visit to Macon, suggested that they be advertised in the paper and rented for a part of the crop grown—a procedure that would help to supply the store—but added "you had best ask some planter for advice" on terms.[14]

Purchases from other merchants and from local farmers and planters, in addition to keeping the store well stocked, could also provide speculative profits as prices soared. Holding for the rise, a legitimate and sometimes profitable venture in peacetime, became almost a sure thing in the midst of rampant inflation, even if the legitimacy and morality of such practices might be questioned during wartime. The advice sent Henry Johnson by a Macon merchant in the early summer of 1862 illustrates the opportunities available: "Let me advise you to buy up what flour you can. It is rappidly [sic] advancing. Superfine is now selling here at $16—and Holders look for $20– in a short time."[15]

Although the buying and selling of food and supplies were important,[16] even more important was the firm's cotton business. The storekeepers bought, sold, and stored cotton on their own and as agents for others, numbering among their customers factors, storekeepers, planters, speculators, and even Confederate army officers. One aspect of their cotton business was ordinary factorage: Necessary goods were supplied to planters and their cotton was sold upon delivery for the regular 2.5 percent commission.[17] But factorage was only part of an active and extensive cotton business carried on by the Americus firm.

In connection with its store, H. R. Johnson and Company owned and operated a public cotton warehouse in Americus where

[14] Johnson to Johnson & Co., Macon, Oct. 17, 1864.

[15] F. J. Champion to Johnson, Macon, June 11, 1862. Champion felt it was lack of confidence rather than an oversupply of currency which was causing inflation: "If Stonewall Jackson gains a few more victories our People will have more confidence in Confederate money."

[16] In addition to making purchases for their store, Thomas and Uriah B. Harrold, his son, bought wool and corn for the Confederate government. They were paid a commission for this service. See numerous receipts signed by U. B. Harrold, agent for Capt. A. M. Allen, dated variously, 1863; A. B. Adams to Thomas Harrold, Macon, May 3, 11, 17, etc., 1864; wool purchase vouchers signed by Thomas Harrold.

[17] For typical examples see Johnson & Harrold to W. E. Sanders, [Americus], Sept. 19, 1861; John W. Jordan, Jr. to Johnson & Co., Smithville, Feb. 7, 1865.

merchants and speculators from various markets kept their cotton. Americus proved to be a relatively safe place for cotton—it was outside the line of Sherman's march—and cotton buyers from various points in Georgia and elsewhere utilized the Johnson and Company warehouse during the war.[18] Owners hoped that such cotton, insured and protected, would be held safely until it could be shipped. Even the Bank of Memphis, long after the city of Memphis had fallen to Federal troops, held cotton in storage in Americus—and elsewhere—regularly paying storage, insurance, and taxes on the stored cotton.[19]

Johnson and Company were also cotton buyers, purchasing the staple on order for shipment elsewhere or for storage in Americus. Again, some who hired the storekeepers to buy cotton for them were intent on a long-term investment. Writing from Alabama in the late summer of 1862, U. B. Harrold informed his father that a Mr. Bray from Eufaula wanted Johnson and Company to buy cotton for him. Bray, he added, wanted "to continue buying as he gets money on hand and wants the cotton for permanent investment to ship when the war is over."[20] Whereas Bray felt cotton stored in the countryside was safer and expected Johnson and Company to buy of planters who would agree ·to hold the cotton on their plantations,[21] other buyers requested the storekeepers to store it in their warehouse in Americus.[22] In either case, the aim was to hold the cotton in safety until the blockade was lifted.[23]

[18] James Yonge to Thomas Harrold, Macon, Sept. 10, 1864; McCallie & Jones to Johnson & Co., Macon, Oct. 10, 1864; H. R. Johnson to Johnson & Co., Macon, Oct. 19, 1864.

[19] W. C. McClure to Johnson & Co., Berzelia, Ga., Aug. 30, 1864. McClure was cashier of the Bank of Memphis and this letter informed the Americus merchants that he would be in Americus soon "to pay Storage Taxes &c &c on 91 Bales Cotton stored in your Warehouse owned by the Bank of Memphis." The bank also had cotton in the Price & Black Warehouse in Americus and probably elsewhere as well. See, W. C. McClure to Johnson & Co., Augusta, Oct. 8, 1864. It appears that McClure was traveling about the South looking after the bank's affairs.

[20] To Thomas Harrold, Eufaula, Ala., Aug. 10, 1862.

[21] In the same letter informing his father of Bray's wishes, the younger Harrold announced that he had arranged an option on part of the crop of a General Bivins who had agreed to hold the cotton on his plantation after sale.

[22] Hiram Roberts to H. R. Johnson, Savannah, Nov. 29, 1862.

[23] When the war ended and transportation facilities became available, Johnson & Co. received numerous requests that cotton being held in the firm's warehouse be delivered to its owners or forwarded for them to New York. See Horne & Caldwell to Johnson & Co., Macon, Aug. 9, 1865; R. W. Cubbedge to Johnson

Other speculators were more energetic, buying cotton in several markets and moving it around in ways they thought most profitable. Such were the brothers James and George Yonge of Augusta. Correspondence with the brothers began in September 1864 when James wrote from Macon: "I would like to hear from you about prices of cotton down your way say any where along the line of South Western R Road as far as Albany. I am frequently buying Cotton but have no correspondent in your Section."[24] An agreement was made, for three weeks later Yonge wrote that he wanted Johnson and Company to buy cotton for him. He informed the Americus merchants that he had telegraphed his brother in Augusta for funds and that the money should be in Americus shortly.[25] The brothers were also buying in Macon through Charles Day, a merchant there, while Day, in turn, filled part of the Yonges' order by having Johnson and Company buy in Americus.[26] Cotton purchased in Americus for Yonge was held there until December 1864, when Yonge wrote asking that Johnson and Company send his cotton to Macon consigned to Day.[27]

For their services as buyers, H. R. Johnson and Company charged a commission of 2.5 percent on the gross purchase price, adding to this, of course, any added expenses such as storage, insurance, and taxes should they be incurred.[28] On such terms Johnson and Company purchased extensively for factors, interior merchants, and speculators of all kinds throughout Georgia.[29] Nor were these activities by the Americus merchants extraordinary; many others were doing the same thing in other markets. "I am anxious for the sake of the Party who sent me this order to fill it well and I would like a portion of it bought in your market," wrote a Macon merchant in a typical letter accompanying an order for Johnson to buy cotton.[30]

The Americus storekeepers did more than act as agents for

& Co., Macon, Oct. 3, 1865; S. Waxelbaum to Johnson & Co., Macon, Oct. 5, 8, 1865.

[24] James Yonge to Thomas Harrold, Macon, Sept. 10, 1864.

[25] *Ibid.*, Sept. 30, 1864.

[26] Charles Day to Johnson & Co., Macon, Nov. 24, 1864.

[27] James Yonge to Johnson & Co., Augusta, Dec. 30, 1864.

[28] Hiram Roberts to H. R. Johnson, Savannah, Nov. 29, 1862; Johnson & Co. to Roberts, Americus, Dec. 2, 1862; Roberts to Johnson & Co., Savannah, Oct. 17, 1864.

[29] See the company Letter Books for numerous examples.

[30] F. J. Champion to H. R. Johnson, Macon, Dec. 26, 1861.

others. Not only did they serve as factors, warehousemen, and commission merchants, but they also purchased and sold cotton on their own account or in joint account with others. Agreements were sometimes made with those who had cotton to sell to haul it to the warehouse in Americus.[31] On other occasions the cotton purchased was stored elsewhere: "We have 15 Bales at Brown's Station stored in S. Denton's store," Johnson wrote a prospective buyer in early 1864.[32]

Although Johnson and Company undoubtedly considered some of their cotton purchases as long-term investments, much of what they bought was resold, the proceeds, in turn, being used to buy still more. Their correspondence reveals that they kept abreast of price developments in the interior markets as well as in Savannah and were always ready to buy or sell their cotton should an advantage present itself. Visits to surrounding markets along with business connections with other merchants provided information and allowed for sales and purchases throughout the state. One of the many reciprocal arrangements Johnson and Company had with other merchants was with the venerable Savannah factorage firm, Robert Habersham and Sons. The two firms bought and sold on order for each other and in addition they sometimes pooled their resources to buy on joint account for resale in both Americus and Savannah. A brief analysis of their voluminous correspondence during the last year of war may serve to illustrate the methods used in this cotton trade as well as the special problems created by the war.

In the fall of 1864 Habersham was holding a large quantity of Johnson and Company's cotton in Savannah. Habersham himself felt "gloomy," a condition which would grow as the enemy drew nearer. He noted, however, that the general feeling in the city was that the market would soon improve: "Many people are buying & storing Cotton here under the impression that it will be higher before long."[33] Some of these buyers were buying in anticipation of the imminent end of the war—Atlanta had already fallen—but Habersham warned darkly that cotton left in the city might be

[31] See, for example, agreement between James H. Raven and Johnson & Co., Americus, May 19, 1864.

[32] Johnson & Co. to John B. Ross, Americus, Feb. 11, 1864. See also, E. M. McDonald to Johnson & Co., Cuthbert, Ga., Oct. 28, 1865.

[33] Robert Habersham & Sons to Johnson & Co., Savannah, Sept. 28, 1864.

seized by the government and lost by its owners.[34] Habersham continued to hold Johnson's cotton throughout November, awaiting the expected rise.[35] In the meantime in Americus, Johnson and Company was holding cotton owned jointly by the two firms. The Savannah factor offered the opinion that "quick profits no doubt are the best in these days of so much uncertainty," but left the disposition of the Americus cotton to Johnson: "Sell as you see fit."[36] By late November the Savannah factor was pressed for funds to meet his obligations to planter customers: "Please remit us all the funds you can spare. We are very much in need of money having most pressing calls from our Planting friends. With regard to the Joint a/c Cotton we would not invest anything more, and certainly would be glad to realize what we have already, but you must act in the matter as you see proper, being better able to judge."[37]

It was not until December 1 that Habersham began selling Johnson and Company cotton in Savannah.[38] Within two weeks some two hundred and seventy thousand dollars' worth had been sold[39] but there were still hundreds of bales left in the Savannah factor's warehouses. A final report from Savannah, dated three days after the city had fallen, noted the sale of 200 more bales.[40] In Americus, Habersham's cotton remained unsold. Correspondence with Savannah was cut off, but William Neyle Habersham of the Savannah firm had fled to Augusta and continued writing to the Americus storekeepers. No longer feeling the "pressing calls from our Planting friends," he no longer wanted to realize cash on his Americus holdings: "At present would rather hold on to our Jnt a/c Cotton & am not anxious to realise." Habersham suggested that any excess funds being held in Americus for him be invested in cotton, but he left the final decision on buying and selling to Johnson and Company.[41]

[34] *Ibid.*, Oct. 4, 1864.
[35] *Ibid.*, Nov. 4, 21, 1864.
[36] *Ibid.*, Oct. 31, 1864.
[37] *Ibid.*, Nov. 21, 1864.
[38] *Ibid.*, Dec. 1, 8, 1864.
[39] *Ibid.*, Dec. 14, 1864.
[40] *Ibid.*, Dec. 31, 1864.
[41] Wm. Neyle Habersham to Johnson & Co., Augusta, Jan. 9, 1865. Wm. Neyle noted that he left Savannah in a hurry, leaving company records behind. Other members of the firm apparently stayed in the city to protect their remaining cotton. *Ibid.*, Jan. 7, 1865.

By this time Habersham was near hysteria. He complained from Augusta that he was out of touch with business "& in confusion," unable to "have any business ideas." Repeating rumors of indiscriminate confiscation of cotton by the occupying troops in Savannah, in the same letter he confusedly urged Johnson and Company both to sell out all his cotton and to buy more but concluded by leaving all final decisions to the Americus merchants, promising he "will be perfectly satisfied with what you do."[42]

Not all merchants dealing in cotton succumbed to such hysteria. Johnson and Company continued to receive orders to buy and sell cotton from men with whom they had dealt throughout the war. The Americus storekeepers, too, remained calm. In mid-January 1865, Henry Johnson, then in the Confederate army, wrote his partner Thomas Harrold that he was very happy to hear that their cotton in Savannah had been sold "for I had given it up at lost." He then offered calm advice to his associate: "The only suggestion I have to make, is to reinvest in Cotton as soon as possible. . . . I'm in hopes that we will be furloughed by the first of next month, so that I can help you in purchasing Cotton."[43]

[42] *Ibid.*, Jan. 18, 1865. See also Habersham to Johnson, Augusta, Jan. 21, 23, 1865.
[43] H. R. Johnson to Thomas Harrold, Doeter Town, Ga., Jan. 19, 1865.

CHAPTER TWENTY

Profits Realized—and Profits Lost

Speculation resulting in high income and cotton sales at high prices did not automatically insure large profits when the war ended. A vast accumulation of Confederate money in April 1865 was just so much paper. One way to protect profits was to invest Confederate currency in safer paper or in specie. "The safest investment is Sterling [bills]," Habersham wrote to H. R. Johnson and Company in late September 1864, and the Savannah factor offered to buy them, adding, however, that others were well aware of their value and therefore their cost would be high.[1]

When Habersham sold over a quarter of a million dollars worth of Johnson's cotton in December 1864, he faced the crucial problem of what kind of funds to remit. With the war all but over, the Confederate money, which, Habersham later wrote, was delivered in bushels when the sale was made,[2] had little value. Recognizing this, Habersham had arranged for part of the payment to be made in personal notes, the value of which would depend upon the postwar economic condition of the one who gave them, and in state bonds and state bank notes. He also tried to convert the Confederate currency he received into bank notes. This was a costly proposition; in one instance he was forced to pay five dollars in Confederate money for each dollar in Alabama bank notes.[3] Apparently, state bonds were not entirely acceptable to the Americus merchants, for they immediately sought to convert the bonds into better paper, sending the younger Harrold to Columbus and using James Yonge of Augusta, with whom the firm had had previous dealings, to sell off the bonds.[4] But, as H. R. Johnson had suggested, the best investment would be in cotton.

Henry Johnson was not the only one who recognized that control of cotton could mean a fortune when the war ended. As has already been indicated, from the very start of the war planters and merchants had stored cotton awaiting the end of the blockade and the resumption of trade. The opening of Memphis and New Orleans had meant that a few might, if they desired, get their crops to market, but by early 1865 it had become clear to many that soon the entire South would be open to trade. As the Confederate armies collapsed, those who had cotton stored away began to get it ready to bring to market. Eager merchants in the North and in Europe made preparations to receive cotton at prices sometimes reaching as high as $1.80 a pound. Alert to opportunities, many Southerners had planted cotton early in 1865, but it was the old cotton, hidden away, which was of immediate concern. When a Liverpool cotton firm sent an investigator into the South in an attempt to determine how much cotton was available, his report was heartening to a cotton-starved world. A Northern journal happily reported his conclusion: "He says there is plenty of cotton to be seen in out of the way places, and all of it awaiting facilities for transportation to market; and he believes that there is plenty more still hidden away."[5] The journal predicted that as much as four million bales would be found "hidden in remote places or buried in underground *caches* throughout the South."[6] Less optimistic but more accurate were the figures offered by the *Commercial and Financial Chronicle*. In the summer of 1865 the journal estimated that some two million bales were hidden away and another million and a quarter bales were growing in the fields.[7]

1 Robert Habersham & Sons to Johnson & Co., Savannah, Sept. 28, 1864, Harrold Brothers Papers, Emory University Library, Atlanta, Ga.

2 Wm. Neyle Habersham to Johnson & Co., Augusta, Jan. 7, 1865, *ibid.*

3 Robert Habersham & Sons to Johnson & Co., Savannah, Dec. 1, 8, 14, 17, 31, 1864, *ibid.*

4 U. B. Harrold to Thomas Harrold, Columbus, Ga., Jan. 9, 1865; James Yonge to Johnson & Co., Augusta, Jan. 20, 1865, *ibid.*

5 *Hunt's Merchants' Magazine*, LIII (Aug. 1965), 225.

6 *Ibid.*

7 I (July 8, 1865), 51. Henry Hentz, a leading New York cotton merchant at the time, later recalled that there were about two million bales in the South when the war ended. "Reminiscences of the Cotton Trade of Old," New York *Times*, Dec. 29, 1890, as reprinted in *Cotton and Finance* (New York), I (Nov. 30, 1912), 396. Exact figures are impossible to determine. Much was destroyed by

With prices high, it was clear that possession of cotton was the means to a fortune. But mere ownership—or even possession—did not guarantee that profits could be realized. The cotton had to be found and brought safely to market—no easy task in a desolated, disorganized, and occupied South. It had to be protected from theft, confiscation, and, before the war was completely over, from Confederate torches. Even if the entire marketing process were carried on legally—which it was not—the problems were myriad. The establishment of legal ownership, a matter which caused little concern in normal times, became a problem of great moment as the war ended. Whitelaw Reid wrote from Mobile just after the war that over one hundred and twenty thousand bales, "which captured records showed to be the property of the Rebel Government" (and thus liable to confiscation) were in private hands in the Mobile region. Some of the holders of this cotton, he reported, claimed to have purchased it from the Confederate government and therefore, they argued, they had legal ownership. Others maintained that they had a moral right to the cotton they held because they had been forced to subscribe to the cotton loan; confiscation of their cotton, they reasoned, would mean that they were being penalized for what they had done under duress.[8]

As important cotton markets fell to Federal troops, the policy adopted by the occupying troops became crucial. Shortly after the capture of Savannah, its apprehensive merchants urged President Lincoln to prevent the confiscation of their property. "At all the interior depots the policy of the restored federal rule at Savannah is narrowly watched," the Chamber of Commerce wrote the President in January 1865, "and the confiscation of a few thousand bales of cotton at Savannah will jeopard the great stocks throughout the country." Retreating Confederate General William J. Hardee did not destroy Savannah cotton stores, the President was reminded, "because he believed private property would be respected." Confiscation of cotton in Savannah, the Chamber warned, would mean that cotton still in Confederate hands would be immediately destroyed, a circumstance which would have a

---

both plan and accident, even as the war drew to a close; some hidden cotton had been ruined. In general, the dislocation in the immediate aftermath of war prevented accurate accounting.

[8] *After the War: A Southern Tour, May 1, 1865, to May 1, 1866* (London, 1866), 207.

profound effect on the North as well as the South. The President was reminded of the large debts owed the North by Southerners; cotton "is now the only means the owners have of discharging their suspended obligations to their northern creditors."[9] A resolution passed by the Savannah Chamber of Commerce at the same time as its letter to Lincoln was drafted called upon the President to reopen trade from Savannah "as early as convenient," a move which would serve "as a sure means of drawing free supplies of cotton and other produce from the interior."[10]

The concern, of course, was not that Confederate government cotton would be confiscated, but that private owners would lose their stocks. Unsettled conditions and high cotton prices offered tempting opportunities for fraud. The methods used were simple enough, varying only slightly from practices in Mobile described by H. M. Watterson to President Andrew Johnson in October 1865. Agents of the federal government, he charged, would seize cotton from private parties on the pretext that it was Confederate government cotton. The agent would then ship it "to a *private consignee*," who would sell it as private cotton and the proceeds would be divided among all involved, except, of course, the swindled planter.[11] Although charges of fraud were undoubtedly exaggerated, there is no question that fraud was rife and constituted a real danger to those who owned cotton and desired to bring it to market as the war drew to a close.[12]

Still another menace to stored cotton came from retreating Confederate troops. Confederate commanders, even in the final months of the war, were often reluctant to allow cotton to fall into Federal hands. Thus, for example, in January 1865, the Confederate commanding general of the Augusta area wrote factor Stephen D. Heard, who operated a warehouse in Augusta, that all cotton stored in the vicinity had to be removed or burned to

[9] Savannah Chamber of Commerce to President Abraham Lincoln, Savannah, Jan. 24, 1865, as reprinted in New York Chamber of Commerce, *Annual Report, 1864-'65* (New York, 1865), Pt. I, 83.

[10] Resolutions of Savannah Chamber of Commerce, Jan. 24, 1865, reprinted *ibid.*, 82-83.

[11] Letter dated Mobile, Ala., Oct. 3, 1865, as printed in Martin Abbott (ed.), "The South as Seen by a Tennessee Unionist in 1865: Letters of H. M. Watterson," *Tennessee Historical Quarterly*, XVII (June 1959), 152.

[12] See E. Merton Coulter, *The South During Reconstruction, 1865-1877* (Baton Rouge, 1947), 6-9; Richard W. Griffin, "Cotton Frauds and Confiscations in Alabama, 1863-1866," *Alabama Review*, VII (Oct. 1954), 265-76.

prevent its being seized by the enemy.[13] In an attempt to protect his cotton, Heard shipped some of it to Wilmington, North Carolina,[14] where it was again ordered to be moved, this time to Florence, South Carolina. Florence seemed no safer and Heard's representative there, fearful that the cotton might be lost, decided to sell it for Confederate money.[15]

The hazards and difficulties involved in moving cotton from its interior hiding places after the war can be illustrated from the experiences of Henry Lee Reynolds, a Mobile hardware merchant.[16] Soon after the war began Reynolds fled to the North, but his partners, Jack P. Richardson and James C. Reynolds (a nephew) remained in the South. Although isolated from his business during the war, Reynolds managed to come into possession of cotton that was stored in the interior. Early in 1865 this cotton began to trickle out from the interior, and, as it appeared, Reynolds' associates had it shipped to New York or Liverpool for sale.[17]

Reynolds' cotton did not come to market easily. Much of it had to be found and removed from its hiding places, often a difficult and dangerous task. In May 1865, Reynolds decided to go South himself in an attempt to facilitate the removal. He went to New Orleans, where, with the help of an influential father-in-law, he managed to receive an army pass to go to Mobile.[18] From May until September 1865, Reynolds was in Mobile while several of his associates and employees were out scouring the countryside for his cotton. One M. F. Berry wrote from Enterprise that he had found some of the cotton, discovered that other bales had been stolen,

13 B. D. Fry to Heard, Augusta, Jan. 21, 1865, Stephen D. Heard Papers, Southern Historical Collection, University of North Carolina Library, Chapel Hill, N. C.

14 Wm. R. Utley to Heard, Wilmington, N. C., Feb. 13, 1865, *ibid.*

15 *Ibid.*, New York, Sept. 29, 1865. All was not lost for Heard in this transaction. Utley reported that the Confederate currency was "invested . . . in gold for you at 80 for 1."

16 All the citations in the following discussion are from the Henry Lee Reynolds Papers, Southern Historical Collection, University of North Carolina, Chapel Hill, N. C.

17 William C. Reynolds to H. L. Reynolds, Mobile, Jan. 10, 1865; J. C. Reynolds to W. C. Reynolds, Enterprise [Ala.], Jan. 11 [1865]; L. Jaquelin Smith to H. L. Reynolds, New York, Jan. 15, 1865; Alfred C. Reynolds to H. L. Reynolds, Mobile, May 12, 1865; a/c sales of 5 bales of cotton for a/c of H. L. Reynolds by Degan, McGinnis & Wilson, New York, July 22, 1865.

18 Stephen P. Hill to Maj. Gen. Nathaniel P. Banks, Washington, D. C., May 4, 1865; Pass No. 688 issued Reynolds by Head Quarters, Department of the Gulf, New Orleans, May 15, 1865.

and that he would continue looking. Searching for what many considered speculator's cotton was unpopular and hazardous in 1865. "I understand that I have been threatened," Berry reported in early July. "I may be bushwacked, but I know I am right and will go ahead," he decided.[19]

Reynolds' partner, Jack P. Richardson, had traveled as far as Memphis on his cotton-hunting expedition. At the end of August he reported his successes and failures—and frustrations. He had already seen several planters who had been holding cotton for Reynolds and he planned to see more. In the meantime, he had succeeded in getting some cotton to Memphis only to have it held up by a local cotton agent who claimed the staple belonged to the Confederate government and therefore would be confiscated.[20] Richardson persisted in his efforts; in early September, after Reynolds had left Mobile for New York, an associate reported that 132 bales had finally been released in Memphis.[21]

Stored cotton was in constant danger of being stolen. In July, a Shubuta, Mississippi, planter holding some of Reynolds' cotton penned an anxious letter urging that the bales be removed. Unless the cotton was taken away soon, he could not be responsible for its safety "as they are stealing it every night." To protest the thefts was to invite reprisals—"a man might . . . get his house burned," he complained. "The returned soldiers are determined to have govt and Speculators [sic] Cotton and if they cannot get that to take other cotton and it appears impossible to have it stopped."[22] Threats might not have always been necessary to get planters to release cotton. One of Reynolds' nephews hunting cotton in Mississippi reported that he was regularly informed that the cotton sought had been stolen. He added that he suspected that sometimes the planter who was supposed to be holding the cotton was a party to the theft.[23]

Reynolds' associates continued to search for his cotton. Although

---

[19] To H. L. Reynolds, Enterprise, June 10, July 8, 1865. Berry's relationship to Reynolds is not clear from the correspondence. He mentioned in his letters finding cotton belonging to others and might possibly have been an agent, hired to find property not only by Reynolds but by others who had cotton stored on plantations. His determination in the face of danger could mean that he was paid a percentage of the proceeds of the cotton found rather than a straight salary.

[20] To H. L. Reynolds, Memphis, Aug. 31, 1865.

[21] W. C. Reynolds to H. L. Reynolds, Mobile, Sept. 9, 1860.

[22] J. D. Nixon to H. L. Reynolds, Shubuta, Miss., July 14, 1865.

[23] W. C. Reynolds to H. L. Reynolds, Mobile, Sept. 9, 1865.

some cotton did appear, other stocks were forever lost. As late as December 29, 1865 James Reynolds was still in the countryside seeking cotton and attempting to get planters who owed money to Reynolds to pay their bills.[24] The correspondence does not reveal how much—if any—profits Reynolds finally realized. He did accumulate enough, however, to form a partnership in the general commission business in New York with Jacquelin Smith while William C. Reynolds, with the help of his uncle, reorganized the Mobile firm under his own name.

Although the Civil War separated the South from its cotton market and from its source of credit, it did not end trade in cotton. Production was curtailed and much was destroyed by war, but enough remained to maintain a lively commerce. Most planters and merchants were probably ruined by war, but there were many who benefited. If there were economic and even physical dangers to be faced in the Civil War cotton trade, there were enough potential benefits to induce many to participate. Those with cotton after the war ended could command the cash and credit needed for economic reconstruction. Those without cotton had to rely on those who had it. Both groups were important elements in the immediate postwar Southern economy. Changes in cotton-marketing procedures following the war were in part a product of their interaction.

[24] *Ibid.*, Sept. 9, 25, Nov. 18, Dec. 29, 1865.

PART FIVE

Economic Reconstruction

*[The] flow of capital to the Southern States
is progressing in a daily increasing current.
And judging from present evidence, the
people have saved from the general ruin
more cotton, more tobacco, more naval
stores, more of their various produce of all
kinds, than had been supposed possible.*

—Commercial and Financial Chronicle,
I (Sept. 23, 1865), 387.

*When the planter was an owner of slaves,
and had along with that ownership and
fund of property now swept away, an unlimited control over the labour necessary
to bring his crop into market, he enjoyed
great credit in the river towns and seaports. This is now gone.*

> —Robert Somers, *The Southern States
> Since the War, 1870-1871* (New York,
> 1871), 241.

*The changes which have taken place in
the marketing of the cotton crop of the
southern states during recent years have
been of such importance as very largely to
revolutionize the business. The changes
referred to have not been confined to the
handling of the crop proper, but have
affected things from before planting to
the point of consumption.*

> —*Bradstreet's*, XIII (April 10, 1886), 226.

*The local storekeeper is dignified by the
name of merchant, and, although the
town in which the store is situated may
only be populated by five white people,
seven niggers and a yellow dog, he is also
mayor, postmaster, tax collector, and may
be owns the cotton gin in addition to
dispensing hardware, dry goods, boots,
shoes, groceries, buggies, and fertilizers.*

> —C. P. Brooks, *Cotton* (New York, 1898),
> 242.

While politicians wrangled over such matters as the legal status of the defeated Confederacy, the relative roles of the Congress and the President in determining when the Southern states should re-enter the union, and other aspects of political reconstruction, most Southerners faced more immediate and mundane problems. The Southern soldier returning to plantation, farm, and town had to begin his life anew, and the former slave, now ostensibly free, had to find his place in the economy. The adjustment to free labor was but one of many problems that had to be solved if new crops were to be planted and if destroyed or neglected businesses rebuilt.

Confederate losses were staggering. An estimated quarter of a million men lost their lives and thousands more returned home maimed in body and spirit. Inflation and investment in state and Confederate securities wiped out millions of dollars of Southern wealth while the devastation wreaked by invading armies and marauders destroyed many millions more. James L. Sellers has estimated that Southern wealth declined by 43 percent between 1860 and 1865 and this figure excludes the value of slave property lost. And to these material losses must be added the less tangible but equally important losses arising from the disorganization of established institutions and uncertainty about the future.[1]

Political problems were vexing and of great importance, but they could be deferred for weeks, months, and even years. Economic problems were more pressing. Planters, farmers, and ex-slaves often needed food, clothing, seed, and tools before farms could be rebuilt and new crops planted, and for many without personal resources credit became an immediate necessity. Merchants and bankers, eager to supply this need and anxious to revive, rebuild, or expand their businesses, sought to renew relationships with customers, North and South. And, amidst the disruption and desolation, those who had ambitions beyond a return to their former status looked about for fresh opportunities.

[1] "The Economic Incidence of the Civil War in the South," *Mississippi Valley Historical Review*, XIV (Sept. 1927), 179-91; J. G. Randall and David Donald, *The Civil War and Reconstruction* (2nd ed.; Boston, 1961), 517-18, 531-32, 543-47; E. Merton Coulter, *The South During Reconstruction, 1865-1877* (Baton Rouge, 1847), 1-6, 13-21; R. H. Woody, "Some Aspects of the Economic Condition of South Carolina after the Civil War," North Carolina Historical Review, VII (July 1930), 346-64.

CHAPTER TWENTY-ONE

The Return of King Cotton

In June 1865, a leading New York commercial journal reported with obvious approval that "President Johnson appears to be sincerely desirous of pacificating the late insurgent parts of the country, and reopening them to the healing influences of commerce and private enterprise as soon as possible." The reopening of trade with the South and the easing of restrictions were wise and necessary moves as anyone who understood the "great part that commerce has always played in burying national animosities, and in ever advancing the true interests of civilization and progress" would appreciate, the journal noted enthusiastically.[1]

Other journals muted the patriotic note and stressed the economic advantages of renewed North-South relations; Northern merchants were reminded that Southerners had saved great quantities of their staple crops during the war, and that the marketing of these products warranted Northern support.[2] Indeed, if Southerners were to discharge their prewar debt—certainly the first step in reopening normal trade between the sections—stocks of accumulated staples had to be brought safely to market, argued a committee of the New York Chamber of Commerce in April 1865.[3]

High cotton prices and the possibility of immediate profit were encouragement enough to induce a scramble among cotton merchants—and would-be cotton merchants—North and South. A Southern friend of Augusta factor Stephen D. Heard who had managed to find his way to New York after the fall of Richmond reported widespread cotton speculation in the city. "Cotton *fever awful*," he wrote and, adding that he would soon return South, offered his friend some advice: "hold on to your Cotton dont let any one frighten or swindler [*sic*] you or your friends out of it."[4]

The guns of war had hardly stilled before North-South business relations were rebuilt. "Every one is leaving for the North who can," noted W. H. Tison, the senior partner of a Savannah factorage firm, in mid-1865. Secessionist principles were already forgotten, he complained; "in another year if the South were able they would patronize the North as formerly." His complaints did not blind him to practical realities, however, for his letter, penned to his junior partner, W. W. Gordon, who had already left for the North, also contained some hardheaded business advice: "Visit around our old friends in N. York and see what can be done."[5]

What had to be done was clear enough. Southerners needed money and credit—to buy and ship cotton, to stock stores and warehouses with supplies, and to advance to merchants who had (or could get) cotton and other valuable merchandise. Northerners were eager to make their money available; high prices and an active market promised good profits for those who moved quickly. "Money is offered freely by N. Y. or Northern houses," wrote Tison, and his letters mentioned sums ranging from $3,000 to $250,000 in gold and greenbacks which were being sent South for investment in cotton.[6] For Tison the lesson was obvious. He too planned a trip to the North after which "if there is no change in cotton and I have money offered to me in New York [I] may return here [Savannah] to purchase cotton."[7]

---

[1] *Hunt's Merchants' Magazine*, LII (June 1865), 443. The journal, however, was not completely sanguine in its expectations: "Some time, however, will necessarily have to elapse before our old relations with these sections of the country can be re-established. Meanwhile a good deal of lawlessness will prevail, and capital will be frightened away." *Ibid.*, 448.

[2] *Commercial and Financial Chronicle*, I (Sept. 23, 1865), 387.

[3] "Report of the Special Committee of the Chamber of Commerce of the State of New-York on the Confiscation of Cotton in the Southern States by the Government," April 27, 1865, printed in New York Chamber of Commerce, *Annual Report, 1864-'65* (New York, 1865), Pt. I, "Special Reports," 151-52.

[4] W. L. Davis to Heard, New York, May 10, 1865, Stephen D. Heard Papers, Southern Historical Collection, University of North Carolina Library, Chapel Hill, N. C.

[5] Letter dated Savannah, July 6, 1865, Gordon Family Papers, Southern Historical Collection, University of North Carolina Library, Chapel Hill, N. C. Tison provided Gordon with a list of people he should see in New York.

[6] To W. W. Gordon, Savannah, July 20, 22, 1865, *ibid.*

[7] *Ibid.*, July 22, 1865.

While some Southerners hurried North, Northern firms sent their representatives into the South. Some, such as George Y. Barker, a partner in the New York commission firm of Adolphus C. Schaefer and Company, came to work out business relationships with Southern merchants, offering return commissions and the right to draw advances on any cotton consigned to them.[8] Others came with gold and greenbacks and, joined by Southern merchants, ventured into the interior to buy cotton for shipment to New York, allowing their Southern partners a share of the profits.[9]

The mails also served to renew old relationships. A Liverpool merchant responded to a letter from Charleston merchant, R. Dewar Bacot, informing the Southerner that he was "very glad" to hear from him and "trust[s] with you that our renewed Correspondence may be of mutual benefit." These pleasantries disposed of, the English merchant immediately placed an order for cotton with Bacot. In this as in subsequent orders, Bacot was given permission to draw on the Liverpool firm for cotton purchased.[10] Similarly, H. R. Johnson and Company of Americus, Georgia, opened business relations with R. R. Graves and Company of New York. The New York firm offered to share selling commissions on "any consignments of cotton you may influence to us." In addition, Graves sent cash to be used both to advance to planters who agreed to send cotton to him and to finance outright purchases by Johnson and Company on joint account with the New York firm.[11]

Backed by Northern funds, buyers scoured the countryside in

[8] Schaefer & Co. to Heard, New York, Aug. 12, 1865, Stephen D. Heard Papers. Heard had already sent some cotton to Watts, Crane & Co. of New York. Wm. H. Stark to Heard, Savannah, July 20, 1865. After Barker's visit, however, Heard seems to have used Schaefer & Co. for all his New York business. The relationship lasted for about a year, until a business disagreement led to severed relations.

[9] "Col May left here in a buggy with two good horses & a Yankee partner in pursuit of Cotton. . . . His wife told me that she sat up till 12 oclock at night sewing bags for his gold." W. H .Tison to W. W. Gordon, Savannah, July 22, 1865, Gordon Family Papers, Southern Historical Collection. See also *ibid.*, July 20, 1865.

[10] Wm Klingender to R. Dewar Bacot, Liverpool, Nov. 18, Dec. 9, 16, 1865, Bacot-Huger Collection, South Carolina Historical Society, Charleston, S. C.

[11] R. R. Graves to Johnson & Co., New York, July 1, Aug. 9, 10, 19, 22 (telegram), 28, Sept. 4, 6, 9, Oct. 10, Dec. 31, 1865, Johnson & Co. to Graves & Co., Americus, Aug. 30, 1865, U. B. Harrold to Johnson & Co., New York, Sept. 20, 1865, Thomas Harrold to Johnson & Co., n.p., Aug. 29, 1865, Harrold Brothers Papers, Emory University Library, Atlanta, Ga.

search of cotton that had been stored and hidden during the war. "From what I can learn the whole country is flooded with cotton buyers & speculators," wrote Tison in July 1865. Noting the absence from Savannah of several of his acquaintances, he decided that "they are out buying cotton for some Yankee."[12] Stephen D. Heard and H. R. Johnson and Company, supported by the resources of New York merchants, hired and financed storekeepers and speculators to make purchases for them while others offered their services in return for shared profits or commissions.[13]

By the end of the year, most of the wartime crop seems to have found its way to market and the flow of funds from the North slackened. When in mid-November, Adolphus C. Schaefer and Company offered financial aid to H. R. Johnson and Company, the Americus merchant answered that he had already made arrangements with R. R. Graves and Company to whom he had shipped 1,500 bales in August, September, and October. He was preparing another shipment of 500 bales. "After these lots are shipped we do not know of much more that we can control & there will soon be a large falling off in the shipments from South West Georgia," Johnson advised.[14]

The Civil War had shown that the power of King Cotton was not as great as many Southerners had supposed. But the first months of peace also made it clear that the king's powers were ample enough to produce a rapid economic reunion between erstwhile enemies. And indeed it was well that its powers were viable. Funds moving into the South to buy cotton or pay for the shipment of cotton to the North and Europe allowed merchants, storekeepers, and planters to begin the reconstruction of their economic life. Planters who had saved cotton found that with the proceeds they could buy food and clothing and hire men to

[12] W. H. Tison to W. W. Gordon, Savannah, July 20, 1865, Gordon Family Papers, Southern Historical Collection. See also *ibid.*, July 22, 1865.

[13] For examples see W. C. Darden to Heard, West Point, Ga., July 24, 1865, W. H. Sims to Heard, La Grange, Ga., Aug. 21, 1865, F. A. Frost to Heard, La Grange, Sept. 22, 1865, Stephen D. Heard Papers; W. G. White to Johnson & Harrold, n.p., Aug. [?], 1865, L. B. Fite to Harrold & Co., Nashville, Sept. 11, 1865, Harrold Brothers Papers.

[14] Johnson & Co. to Schaefer & Co., Americus, Nov. 13, 1865, *ibid.* In fact, Johnson & Co. did continue to make purchases in December; facilities offered by Graves apparently were considered adequate.

work their land. Mrs. Chesnut described in her diary in May 1865 the relatively bright outlook of two such lucky planters: "J. H. Boykin was at home . . . to look after his own interests, and he, with John de Saussure, has saved the cotton on their estates, with the mules and farming utensils and plenty of cotton as capital to begin on again."[15] At the same time, storekeepers such as Henry Johnson and Thomas Harrold found that profits from cotton enabled them to make purchases from Northern merchants to restock their shelves.[16] Visitors and other observers noted a brisk trade in Northen goods of all kinds as Northern merchants sent large shipments to Southern stores or came themselves to sell their merchandise.[17]

Although capital moving into the South to market the old crop helped to promote some economic rehabilitation, it was but a fraction of what the war-devastated South needed. The sale of about two million bales of cotton in 1865 grossed an approximate four hundred million dollars,[18] but only a portion of this remained in the South after charges were assessed for transportation, interest, commissions, and other expenses. Many planters owed debts to their factors and other merchants, debts which had gone unpaid and had been accumulating interest for as long as five years. Southern merchants in turn were deeply obligated to Northern firms. Both growers and merchants required new loans, but indebtedness had first to be eliminated, a difficult task for those who had not managed to save valuable commodities during the war.

High prices in 1865 induced a number of Northerners to invest

[15] Mary Boykin Chesnut, A Diary from Dixie, ed. Isabella D. Martin and Myrta Lockett Avary (New York, 1905), 387.

[16] See invoices from New York firms (Potter & Williams, Pinchot, Warren & Co., Lake & McGreery, and others) dated variously, Aug., 1865, Harrold Brothers Papers.

[17] Sidney Andrews, The South Since the War (Boston, 1866), 365-66; Whitelaw Reid, After the War: A Southern Tour, May 1, 1865 to May 1, 1866 (London, 1866), 375; F. W. Loring and C. F. Atkinson, Cotton Culture and the South Considered With Reference to Emigration (Boston, 1869), 69-70. In Dec. 1865 a Mobile hardware merchant complained of active competition; there were already seven other hardware dealers in Mobile and still another, backed by New York credit, was about to open. W. C. Reynolds to H. L. Reynolds, Mobile, Dec. 6, 1865, Henry Lee Reynolds Papers, Southern Historical Collection, University of North Carolina Library, Chapel Hill, N. C.

[18] See George Ruble Woolfolk, The Cotton Regency (New York, 1958), 76.

directly in cotton production. In September 1865 Henry William Ravenal recorded in his journal that "the first contract I hear of for the cultivation of cotton next year, is one which Mr James Lagare is making with E M Bruce & Co (representing some Northern capitalists) to cultivate his lands with 100 labourers, to receive $5000 for his own services, $1000 for an overseer, & ⅓ of net profits &c—."[19] Another South Carolinian reported that a planter had received a pardon and the return of his land and had "a proposition made him by a Yankee" to advance money necessary to get back into production in return for "a share of the crop," a proposition which the planter "has under consideration."[20] A Georgian wrote that Northern money was available, but he could not bring himself to borrow from the Yankees. Yet he was well aware that he had to borrow from some source if he were to continue work on his land.[21]

While some planters fretted over a Yankee liaison, other Southerners worked out proposals for more long-range and impersonal aid from the North. A few even put their states' rights opinions behind them long enough to suggest federal aid. In 1867 the merchants and factors of Charleston urged Congress to advance funds to Southern planters in need. One Charleston merchant, enthusiastically caught up in the suggestion, reported that the government had agreed to advance money through factors, the planters "to give the Government a lien on their crops."[22] Such expectations were unfounded; by and large the federal government offered little financial aid.[23] Indeed, the cotton tax

[19] Entry of Sept. 25, 1865, in Arney Robinson Childs (ed.), *The Private Journal of Henry William Ravenal, 1859-1887* (Columbia, S. C., 1947), 257.

[20] Mrs. S. L. Haskell to Sophie Haskell, Home Place, Nov. 16, 1865, Langdon Cheves Collection, Haskell Papers, South Carolina Historical Society, Charleston, S. C.

[21] James Peter Baltzelle to Lucien Barnsley, Woodlands, Ga., Feb. 10, 1866, Barnsley Collection, Archives Division, Tennessee State Library and Archives, Nashville, Tenn.

[22] John Colcock to James Gregorie, Charleston, Dec. 29, 1867, Gregorie-Elliott Papers, Southern Historical Collection, University of North Carolina, Chapel Hill, N. C.

[23] Some indirect government aid was given to the South. For example, mail service was restored, although it took two years before the service equaled that of 1860. E. Merton Coulter, *The South During Reconstruction, 1865-1877* (Baton Rouge, 1947), 195. Some of the section's railways, rebuilt by Federal forces after capture during the war, were returned to their Southern owners after the war. John F. Stover, *The Railroads of the South, 1865-1900* (Chapel Hill, 1955), 50-52.

(2.5 cents and later 3 cents per pound), not repealed until 1868, added to the cotton planters' postwar burdens.

Immediately after the war a group of Southerners sought to induce large-scale private loans to planters. The American Cotton Planters' Association, organized in New York City on September 28, 1865, proposed to raise funds to support the resumption of cotton growing in the South. The plan called for long-term loans (five years) from Northern and foreign factors and capitalists. Planters would pay 10 percent per annum on the money advanced, give a mortgage on their plantations, a lien on movable goods purchased and on the crop, and, in addition, would promise to send the crop grown to the factor making the loan. The leaders of the association corresponded with some Northern and European firms and individuals, but nothing came of the proposed venture.[24]

Northerners, too, were concerned about the rebuilding of the cotton industry in the South and many saw the need for large-scale financial investments. On November 27, 1865 the Boston Board of Trade considered a series of resolutions dealing with Southern economic rehabilitation. Recognizing the section's need for capital to "develop industry . . . [and] to increase the production of their staples, and especially of cotton," the resolutions called upon the federal government to "aid forthwith in sustaining and organizing such protection of the laboring classes now in the Southern States as cannot be reached by private capital."[25] A supporter of the resolutions conceded that Northern private capital was already moving into the South, but, he insisted, unsettled conditions discouraged investment on a scale necessary to return cotton production to normal. Delay was dangerous because large cotton exports were needed in the nation's balance of international payments schedule. In the absence of adequate private investment, he concluded, government aid was required.[26] The Boston group

[24] Mary Wilkin, "Some Papers of the American Cotton Planters' Association, 1865-1866," *Tennessee Historical Quarterly*, VII (Dec. 1848), 335-61, VIII (March 1949), 49-62.

[25] Boston Board of Trade to New York Chamber of Commerce, Boston, Nov. 28, 1865, printed in New York Chamber of Commerce, *Annual Report, 1865-'66*, Pt. I, p. 67.

[26] Edward S. Tobey, *The Industry of the South: Its Immediate Organization Indispensable to the Financial Security of the Country* (Boston, 1865), *passim*. This work contains the Boston Board of Trade resolutions and Tobey's speech in support of them.

passed the resolutions unanimously and then sent them to the New York Chamber of Commerce for its consideration.

New York merchants were of a different mind. On the advice of its executive committee, the New York Chamber of Commerce unanimously rejected the proposals of the Boston merchants. Perhaps because they felt government aid would lessen their own opportunities in the South,[27] the New York merchants argued that the matter had best be left to "the promptings of personal interest to bring about the desired results." Any government interference beyond the maintenance of law and order "would mar rather than facilitate increased production of cotton," the New York group insisted. Attesting to the efficacy of private enterprise was the evidence that the South was "already attracting . . . the capital requisite to produce a fair crop of cotton for the coming season."[28]

The position taken by the New York merchants prevailed. Neither government aid nor large-scale, long-term private loans on the pattern envisioned by the Cotton Planters' Association were forthcoming, despite the obvious need and repeated pleas by Southern leaders.[29] In the absence of aid on a massive scale, the cotton trade returned to familiar channels. Significant changes had already begun to affect the trade, but these changes were not the result of planning, private or public. Indeed, at first they were quite invisible, and when new methods did become clear and dominant, planters and merchants were surprised at the result. In the meantime, planters and merchants returned to the familiar, prewar methods of marketing and financing the cotton crop—the cotton factorage system.

[27] For a discussion of New York, Boston, and Philadelphia rivalry, see Woolfolk, *The Cotton Regency, passim.*

[28] Report of Executive Committee of New York Chamber of Commerce, Jan. 4, 1866, printed in New York Chamber of Commerce, *Annual Report, 1865-'66,* Pt. I, p. 70.

[29] "If those who desire that the South shall raise a *large* cotton crop will establish cotton banks in the Southern cities to aid the planter—one in New Orleans, for example, with a cash capital of $20,000,000 to loan on cotton expectations, as our local banks did before the war, they will do more to ensure an ample cotton crop than by all the conventions they can assemble or resolutions they may pass." *New Orleans Prices Current,* as copied by *DeBow's Review,* n.s. I (1866), 198. See also *ibid.,* 548.

CHAPTER TWENTY-TWO

The Resurrection of the Cotton Factorage System

The return of King Cotton after the Civil War brought back also his chief retainer, the factor. In every major cotton market in the South many names, long familiar in the factorage business before the Civil War, began to reappear in advertisements and in planters' correspondence. Some had maintained "business as usual" relations throughout the war and merely continued on into the postwar period. Others were rebuilding a business interrupted by the war. But there were others, relative newcomers, who, sensing new opportunities, pooled their resources and began business. In any case, the postwar factor, whether a novice or a practiced businessman, initially functioned much as he had during the prewar period.

Like his ante bellum predecessor, the postwar factor had to be skilled in selling cotton and in buying the planters' supplies. But initially, prices were high and selling a relatively simple matter. Moreover, the shortage of goods in Southern markets along with high prices made purchasing less a matter of searching for the best buy and more a question of having the funds with which to purchase. The most important function of the postwar factor became his ability to supply the credit cotton growers needed. The difference between success and failure for those who sought to rebuild the factorage system immediately after the war rested on their ability to secure capital. Wartime profits, hoarded cotton, business or family ties with Northern capital sources or with owners of cotton in the South, success in getting planters and farmers to repay old bills—all these could be the means to fill the cotton growers' most pressing need—credit. Those who had these opportunities and took advantage of them resurrected the cotton factorage system in the postwar South.

In truth, of course, the cotton factorage system had never completely died. Although many factors did not survive the first year after secession, others, as has already been shown, continued to serve their customers during the war, often adding to their businesses purchases on their own accounts, warehousing services, and financial and commodity speculation. For such firms the transition to peacetime factorage was a relatively simple matter.

Augusta factor Stephen D. Heard's wartime trade proved invaluable at the war's end. His own cotton, some of which was safely stored in West Point, Georgia,[1] along with that sent by merchants with whom he had dealt during the war, allowed Heard to have cotton on its way to New York by July 1865.[2] His New York merchants supplied advances on the cotton shipped, divided commissions with him, and, in addition, sent funds to advance to owners or to make outright purchases.[3] Profits from these transactions apparently were adequate enough to provide a foundation for Heard's future business. Although in 1870 references in the firm's correspondence show Heard to have become less active because of poor health, his son, who by 1868 had joined the firm, continued to serve the needs of cotton growers in the Augusta area well into the 1870's.

In Savannah, the name Habersham had long been associated with cotton factorage.[4] One of the largest firms in the city on the eve of Civil War, Robert Habersham and Sons was active

[1] In addition to his warehouse in Augusta, Heard along with William C. Darden operated a warehouse and commission business in West Point, Ga. See Copy of Petition to Troup County Superior Court in case of Stabler & Cole vs. Heard & Darden, March 27, 1866, Stephen D. Heard Papers, Southern Historical Collection, University of North Carolina Library, Chapel Hill, N. C. The case involved a dispute over cotton stored by the plaintiffs in 1863.

[2] J. L. Morris to Heard, West Point, July 17, 1865 and Wm. H. Stark to Heard, Savannah, July 20, 1865, *ibid.*

[3] Adolphus C. Schaefer & Co. to Heard, New York, Aug. 12, 1865, and regular letters from Schaefer & Co. thereafter, *ibid.* Other merchants offered Heard similar arrangements. See P. P. Clements to Heard, Baltimore, Dec. 22, 1865, *ibid.*

[4] As early as 1823 planters were sending cotton and rice to be sold by R. & J. Habersham in Savannah. See R. & J. Habersham Papers, Georgia Historical Society, Savannah, Ga.

throughout the war buying and selling on planters' and merchants' accounts as well as on its own. Again, as with Stephen D. Heard, the firm's wartime business became the foundation for its postwar success. Two aspects of this business proved decisive—the firm's ownership of cotton at the close of the war and its ability to maintain its relationship with some of its wealthy prewar and wartime customers. One such wartime customer was H. R. Johnson and Company of Americus, Georgia. When the war ended, the Americus firm was holding a large quantity of cotton owned jointly by the two companies. Habersham also seems to have had cotton in Savannah, for by July 1, 1865 the firm had already established a business connection in New York. A letter on that date authorized the Americus firm to use its discretion in deciding when to ship the cotton jointly owned and added that any other cotton shipped would be sent on to New York for sale "and [we] have not a doubt we can advance what you may want on it."[5] By October, Habersham was announcing sales of cotton from Americus.[6] Anxious to increase shipments from Johnson and Company, the Savannah factor wrote in December that "we are perfectly willing to divide commissions with you in any Cotton you influence to us." Johnson accepted the offer, shipping some of his customers' cotton to Habersham, drawing advances on the Savannah factor, and dividing selling commissions with him.[7]

By December 1865 Habersham had also re-established connections in England. He had decided to give up his prewar merchant in Liverpool, Brown, Shipley and Company, who, he felt, had become "rather too large a House for Cotton" and had arranged instead to work through Robert Hutchinson, "who attends personally to all Sales & will do justice to any business." Hutchinson had agreed to return 1 percent of his commission on cotton shipped to him through Habersham, and the Savannah merchant, in turn, offered to divide this 1 percent with H. R. Johnson and Company on all the Americus firm's Liverpool shipments.[8]

5 Robert Habersham & Sons to Johnson & Co., Savannah, July 1, 1865, Harrold Brothers Papers, Emory University Library, Atlanta, Ga.

6 Robert Habersham & Sons to Johnson & Co., Savannah, Oct. 20, 1865, *ibid.*

7 Robert Habersham & Sons to Johnson & Co., Savannah, Dec. 16, 1865, Feb. 19, 1866; a/c current of R. Habersham & Sons with Johnson & Co., [Savannah], April 13, 1866, *ibid.*

8 Robert Habersham & Sons to Johnson & Co., Savannah, Dec. 16, 1865, *ibid.* Habersham noted that Hutchinson had long experience in the cotton business: "He

In addition to the invaluable connections with H. R. Johnson and Company, Habersham also retained the custom of some of the largest planters in the area. Thus, for example, the Savannah factor, having handled the personal accounts and business affairs of the wealthy Telfair family before the war, continued these services during and after the war as well.[9] Similarly, George Noble Jones, another customer of long standing, continued to entrust an extensive business in cotton to Habersham after the Civil War.[10]

A wartime business, however, was no guarantee that a factor would emerge in 1865 with ample funds to meet the needs of his customers. John Colcock of Charleston, for example, sold cotton during the war and often reinvested the profits from his transactions.[11] With the war's end, however, profits had disappeared. In the fall of 1865, Colcock's nephew and partner wrote that he was "making every effort . . . to raise money enough to go to Charleston & see what we can do towards resuming our old business there." So discouraged was he "by accounts received from those who have been down for the same purpose" that he indicated he might be ready to "pocket my Southern feelings & work faithfully for a Yankee."[12] A small loan in the spring of 1866 averted this catastrophe, but the business of John Colcock and Company never prospered. Specializing in sea-island cotton when prices were low and production decreasing, the firm was perpetually short of cash resources. Requests from planters for as little as $100 had to be turned down. The firm nevertheless did manage to limp along for a number of years by borrowing from Charleston banks and from New York capitalists.[13]

---

was educated here as a merchant & we knew him near Thirty years ago, buying Cotton here for A Low & Co."

[9] These accounts for the ante bellum, wartime, and postwar periods may be found in the Telfair Family Papers, Georgia Historical Society, Savannah, Ga.

[10] See correspondence from Habersham to Jones, dated variously 1866-1871, George Noble Jones Papers, Georgia Historical Society, Savannah, Ga.

[11] Colcock to James Gregorie, Limestone Springs, Oct. 17, 1863, April 12, 1864, Gregorie-Elliott Papers, Southern Historical Collection, University of North Carolina Library, Chapel Hill, N. C.

[12] R. H. Colcock to James Gregorie, Limestone Springs, Oct. 8, 1865, *ibid.*

[13] Note signed by Colcock for loan of $4,000 from Charles T. Lowndes & Co., Charleston, March 21, 1866; a/c sales of 8 bags Sea Island cotton by Colcock & Co. for a/c of James Gregorie, Charleston, May 29, 1867; John Colcock to James Gregorie, Charleston, July 15, 22, Dec. 19, 26, 1867, Feb. 4, 11, 15, March 15, 19, 26, April 9, 1868, April 20, 1869; Chas. M. Rose to James Gregorie, New York, May 19, 1868, *ibid.*

For some prewar factors, the coming of peace brought the task of rebuilding a business that had been largely inactive during the war. Such was the problem faced by the venerable Savannah firm of Tison and Gordon.[14] As he looked about in Savannah during the summer of 1865 and noted sourly the rush of profitable speculative activity by others, Tison lamented his condition: "I am here living on bacon & rice without one dollar to go to market. . . . I staked all on the Confederacy and all is gone. No one will lend me a dollar & my lands will not sell unless I sell for a much less value than they are worth. What will become of me."[15] Two weeks later he complained of lost opportunities. "You & I could have recovered all that we had lost during the war in the past two months," he wrote to his junior partner. "But it is not for us to make money this easily."[16]

But all was not lost for the firm despite Tison's pessimism. Tison's junior partner, W. W. Gordon, was married to the only daughter of Colonel John H. and Juliette Kinzie of Chicago and through his wife he had come into possession of valuable properties in the Northern city. When the war ended, Gordon left immediately for Chicago. He, at least, was not penniless. Nor was Tison content to indulge his self-pity. Instead, he went to New York in search of old friends and money with which to purchase and ship cotton. In August 1865, he wrote Gordon (in Chicago) from New York asking the younger man to meet him in the Empire City "so that I may introduce you to such of my friends as may be yet in business."[17]

Back in Savannah in early November, Tison was no longer bemoaning his fortune. The firm had returned actively to the cotton business, buying and selling, offering advances, and shipping to New York.[18] Gordon had returned from Chicago only to leave immediately for the interior to purchase cotton for the firm. Business was improving and the younger man decided to remain in cotton factorage in Savannah. In the early spring of 1866 he

[14] Upon his graduation from Yale in 1854, W. W. Gordon became a clerk in the Savannah factorage firm, Tison & Mackay. Two years later he became a partner in the firm, then renamed Tison and Gordon.

[15] W. H. Tison to W. W. Gordon, Savannah, July 6, 1865, Gordon Family Papers, Southern Historical Collection, University of North Carolina Libary, Chapel Hill, N. C.

[16] *Ibid.*, July 20, 1965.

[17] *Ibid.*, New York, Aug. 1, 1865.

[18] *Ibid.*, Savannah, Nov. 7, 1865.

wrote to his agents in Chicago that "I have concluded to continue in business in this City [Savannah] and shall have therefore use for all the money I can command."[19] Thus a combination of the credit one partner was able to command through his old contacts in New York and the funds available from the Chicago property holdings of the other partner had made it possible for the firm of Tison and Gordon to survive the Civil War in Savannah.

Ownership of cotton along with accommodating creditors allowed Edmund Richardson to reopen his factorage house in New Orleans after the Civil War. The owner of country stores in Brandon, Canton, Morton, and Newton, Mississippi, Richardson in 1852 had become a partner in the New Orleans factorage firm of Thornhill and Company. When the blockade closed New Orleans, Thornhill and Company had debts of some half a million dollars and had extended credit widely to its planter customers. With the war's end, Richardson set out to collect old debts and to rebuild his factorage business. As the proprietor of five plantations and owner of some five hundred bales of cotton, he was able to settle with his creditors, paying half his debt in cash and receiving twelve months to repay the rest. His credit re-established, he was able to provide services to his customers, and within a year he was successful enough to pay off his entire debt and accumulate additional capital as well. By the 1880's Richardson's firm, Richardson and May, was reported to be the largest cotton commission house in the United States. His other interests included 17,000 acres in cotton growing, insurance, country stores, and cotton-seed oil milling.[20]

In Richardson's case the ownership of cotton at the war's end had aided him in securing the credit necessary to resume business. Direct ownership of cotton, however, was not always required. Merely having access to cotton stores put a factor in an enviable position. Those whose customers were able to pay old debts in cotton had the basis for a postwar business, as may be illustrated in the case of John Watt and Company of New Orleans. In December 1860 planters Mr. and Mrs. F. N. Richey had borrowed

[19] Tison & Gordon to Baird & Bradley, Savannah, March 24, 1866, *ibid.* In later years the firm's property served as collateral for loans from local and Northern banks. Tison to Gordon, Baltimore, Sept. 9, 1869, New York, Aug. 30, 1870; Gordon to Tison & Gordon, New York, Oct. 26, 1869, July 30, 1870, *ibid.*

[20] "Edmund Richardson," in Latham, Alexander & Co., *Cotton Movement and Fluctuations, 1876 to 1883* (New York, 1883), 41-43.

$2,815.68 from Watt and Company for one year at 10 percent interest. When the war ended this note (and many others like it in Watt's books) was still unpaid. Watt and Company sent letters to those who owed the firm money indicating that James S. Prestidge, "our friend, lawyer and agent" was "intrusted with the settlement in the country of our business. . . ." Because of accumulated interest, Mrs. Richey's debt had grown to $4,286.82. Prestidge negotiated a settlement with Mrs. Richey whereby she was to repay the debt with cotton shipped to Watt and Company. This Mrs. Richey did and within a year Prestidge wrote that matters were finally "arranged . . . satisfactorily between us. . . ." He added that he hoped Mrs. Richey would continue to ship her cotton to Watt and Company, promising "to give satisfaction" if she did. Apparently the settlement caused no bitterness, for Mrs. Richey did indeed ship more of her cotton to the re-established New Orleans firm.[21]

And so it was in every major cotton market in the South. Factors well known to the planting community reopened their businesses to the postwar trade. Some acquired new partners and others brought sons into the business, but planters would have no difficulty recognizing familiar names in the business cards which began to reappear in the press and in the postwar commercial directories.[22] Some of the well-known names never reappeared as bankruptcy, illness, and death claimed their toll. But there were others who took the places of those who left the trade.

New men, alert to the opportunities in factorage and able to secure the necessary backing, joined the ranks of the old-timers

[21] Note dated, Mississippi, December 29, 1860, and signed: F. N. Richey and N. Richey in favor of John Watt & Co.; John Watt & Co. to Mrs. Nancy Richey, New Orleans, Oct. 15, 1865, Dec. 25, 1866, Jan. 9, 1867; James S. Prestidge to Nancy Richey, Vicksburg, June 14, 1866, Brookhaven, Oct. 12, Nov. 7, 1866, Mrs. Nancy Richey Papers, Mississippi Department of Archives and History, Jackson, Miss.

[22] For further examples see John M. Cooper & Co., *Directory for the City of Savannah, to which is added, A Business Directory for 1860* (Savannah, 1860), 172-73; N. J. Darrell & Co., *Savannah City Directory for 1867* (Savannah, 1867), 24-25; T. M. Haddock (comp.), *Haddock's Savannah, Ga., Directory, and General Advertiser* (Savannah, 1871), 357-59; [Andrew Morrison], *Industries of New Orleans* (New Orleans, 1885), 63, 75, 94, 128, 135; Andrew Morrison (comp.), *New Orleans and the New South* (New Orleans, 1888), 46, 104; U. S. Congress, Senate, Committee on Agriculture and Forestry, *Report . . . on Condition of Cotton Growers*, 53rd Cong., 3rd Sess., Report 986 (1895), I, 227, 236.

in the major cotton markets. Many could boast previous mercantile experience and a familiarity with the cotton trade. Thus, in the case of McFerran and Menefee, "Commission Merchants, Cotton Factors, and Manufacturer's Agents for the Sale of Bale Rope and Bagging," the opening of their business in Cincinnati in October 1865 was simply a matter of re-establishing an old business in a new place. Before the war the firm had been located in Louisville, Kentucky, and in their advertising circular the factors made it clear that they were not newcomers to the cotton business: "We feel assured that with our past experience in the sale of this Staple we can render satisfaction to those shipping to us."[23]

Similarly, in Savannah, J. F. Wheaton, before the war a partner in Wilder, Wheaton and Company, in September 1865 gave his experience—but not his name—to a new concern, F. W. Sims and Company. The advertising circular of the new firm indicated that it would be a "General Commission and Forwarding Business" and would buy and sell cotton on commission. In a personal letter soliciting the business of an interior merchant, Sims explained that cotton sales could be arranged in various markets at the seller's choice: "We have made arrangements in Augusta to have a representative there and any Cotton consigned to us to be forwarded to New York will be forwarded for *one* Commission of fifty cents per bale for our attention in Augusta and Savannah."[24]

Establishment of a new firm, of course, required capital and the means to secure credit. For those who had profited from the war, these requirements presented no problem. George W. Williams and Company, for example, began with more than a million dollars. A wholesale grocer in Charleston and Augusta before the war, Williams used his profits to reopen his grocery business in 1865 and also to establish cotton factorage houses in both Charleston and New York.[25]

Few had a million dollars at the end of the war and most new firms started much more modestly. Early in 1866, Eustace Golsan

[23] Circular from McFerran & Menefee, Cincinnati, Oct. 14, 1865 in Harrold Brothers Papers.

[24] Circular from F. W. Sims & Co., Savannah, Sept. 1865; F. W. Sims to Thomas Harrold, Savannah, Sept. 26, Oct. 3, 1865, *ibid*. Sims, listed on the company letterhead as a former newspaperman, probably provided the working capital, and therefore the name, for the new firm.

[25] Arthur Mazyck, *Guide to Charleston* (Charleston, S. C., [1875]), 143-48.

left his Autaugaville, Alabama, home for New Orleans, where, with a Louisianian, J. Y. Sanders, he organized Golsan and Sanders, "Cotton Factors, and General Commission and Forwarding Merchants," promising, according to the firm's letterhead, "Special attention given to Receiving and Forwarding, as well as to the Purchase of Merchandise and Supplies for Planters and Country Merchants." Golsan was not untutored in the cotton trade. His father, H. L. Golsan, had been a country storekeeper in Autaugaville during the last two decades before the Civil War[26] and he, along with two other sons, continued his business as "Cotton Buyers and Dealers in Groceries" in the postwar period. Soon after his son had organized the New Orleans firm, the elder Golsan offered some fatherly advice: "be careful of your credit dont try to overeach [sic] in your business . . . & recollect let your associations be with & of the best business men & merchants shaking others off. be content with a small business for the present. patience & perserverance [sic] overcometh & accompliseth [sic] all things. Sell cotton &c as high as any. buy goods as low as any. let the Bank & Insurance offices be right that you do business with."[27]

Aid of a more concrete sort also came from the Autaugaville store. Indeed, cotton purchased by the elder Golsan and his sons formed the core of the first business conducted by the new firm in New Orleans.[28] In addition, the Alabama merchants did their best to drum up business for Golsan and Sanders. "Send me 50 or 100 of your cards," wrote Robert W. Golsan while on a buying trip to Vernon, Alabama in May 1866.[29] "I have been doing everything for you I can & will continue to do so," he assured his brother in a later letter.[30] Other relatives offered similar aid. Carews and Company, storekeepers in Autaugaville and cousins of the younger Golsans, sent some of their own cotton and induced a few of their customers to send consignments to Golsan and

---

[26] See their bills receivable and bills payable for the ante bellum years, Golson Brothers Papers, Department of Archives and Manuscripts, Louisiana State University, Baton Rouge, La. In the following discussion, all letters cited are from this collection.

[27] J. H. Golsan to Golsan & Sanders, Autaugaville, Nov. 7, 1866.

[28] Robert W. Golsan to Golsan & Sanders, Vernon, Ala., May 26, 1866; J. H. Golsan to Golsan & Sanders, Autaugaville, June 2, 1866; H. L. & R. W. Golsan to Golsan & Sanders, Autaugaville, July 14, 1866; and numerous other similar letters during 1866.

[29] To Golsan & Sanders, Vernon, May 26, 1866.

[30] Robert W. Golsan to Eustace Golsan, Autaugaville, July 31, 1866.

Sanders in New Orleans.[31] Eustace Golsan himself returned to Autaugaville during the summer of 1866, visiting friends and relatives in an attempt to solicit business for the firm.[32]

While Golsan was bringing in business from Alabama, Sanders solicited consignments from his native state. Although less successful than Golsan, Sanders did manage to attract some trade from Louisiana planters and merchants.[33]

Thus the fledgling firm was launched largely on the basis of business supplied by relatives, friends, and neighbors. Sanders left the firm in May 1867, but Eustace Golsan, along with his brother Robert, who became his partner after Sanders' departure, continued. Gradually, and amidst great difficulties, the firm grew,[34] but the bulk of the business in the early years came from those areas in Alabama where the Golsans had personal influence.[35]

The difficulties encountered by the Golsans in their new factorage firm were not uncommon among those attempting to resurrect the cotton factorage system. Investment opportunities in railroads, housing, and other Northern and Western enterprises along with the sharp decline in cotton prices from the abnormal wartime highs diverted potential investment from the South. The failure of the immediate postwar crops to meet expectations, bringing ruin to many planters, factors, and other investors, and the general political uncertainty in the reconstruction South added to the burdens of those seeking credit. As a result credit was often limited, and many firms, new and old, failed.[36]

[31] Carews & Co. to Golsan & Sanders, Autaugaville, June 7, Aug. 20, Sept. 3, Oct. 17, 1866; J. D. Cory to Golsan & Sanders, Autaugaville, Aug. 21, 1866.

[32] See his letters to Sanders from Alabama during July.

[33] Frank M [illegible] to Sanders, Rosedale Plantation [near New Iberia, La.], May 21, 1866; Braxton King to Sanders, Franklin Parish, La., May 26, 1866; Albert Johnston to Sanders, Lagas Bridge, La., June 2, 1866; A. H. Curry to Golsan & Sanders, Sicily Island, La., April 11, 1867.

[34] By the summer of 1867 the firm seemed about to fail. New customers had to be turned away because advances could not be given. Robert Golsan to Eustace F. Golsan, [New Orleans], July 23, 1867; Thomas W. Hutchinson to E. F. Golsan & Co., Pensacola [Fla.], July 22, 1867; E. F. Golsan & Co. to Thos. W. Hutchinson, [New Orleans], July 25, [1867]. Conditions improved in the fall when cotton began to come to market, and the firm survived although it is clear from the surviving correspondence that it was never highly profitable.

[35] This becomes abundantly clear from an investigation of their Letter Book, 1866-1867, which contains letterpress copies of all outgoing correspondence.

[36] *Hunt's Merchants' Magazine*, LVI (1867), 354, LIX (1868), 22-23; F. W. Loring and C. F. Atkinson, *Cotton Culture and the South Considered with Reference to Emigration* (Boston, 1869), 158-59.

Nevertheless, the system survived, generally operating as it had in the ante bellum period. The factor sold cotton, purchased supplies, provided credit, served as a banker, and in numerous other ways fulfilled the role which tradition had assigned him. Like his prewar counterpart, the factor numbered among his customers planters, storekeepers, and speculators, and, again, as in prewar times, some factors speculated in the staple on their own account. A few typical examples of postwar factorage in various Southern markets may serve to illustrate the continuity of the institution.

Planter Eli J. Capell grew cotton in Mississippi throughout the war.[37] However, his plantation diaries, which give detailed descriptions of the day-to-day work on his land, make no mention of marketing these crops until July 1865, when Capell recorded, "I started two teams to Woodville with *twelve* Bales of Cotton which belongs to R Pritchard N.O."[38] This was only the first of many 1865 shipments to Pritchard, who became Capell's New Orleans cotton factor.[39]

Arrangements with the factor had undoubtedly been made much earlier. The two men had had a long-standing business relationship. Throughout the 1850's Capell had consigned a part of his crop to factorage houses in which Pritchard was a partner; indeed, Pritchard had sold some of the planter's cotton as late as July 1861.[40] Although there is no record of wartime sales, the two men continued their association. On at least two occasions in 1864 Pritchard visited the Capell plantation[41] and it was on these or other visits that the New Orleans merchant purchased cotton from Capell which the Mississippian then held on his plantation. With

[37] Plantation Diary, 1861; Plantation Diary, 1862; Plantation Diary, Jan.–June 1863; Plantation Diary, June 1863–April 1866, Eli J. Capell Plantation Diaries and Record Books, Louisiana Department of Archives and Manuscripts, Louisiana State University, Baton Rouge, La.

[38] Entry of Wed., July 19, 1865, Plantation Diary, June 1863–April 1866, *ibid.*

[39] Capell recorded that he made additional shipments on July 26, Oct. 11, Oct. 25, and Dec. 19, 1865. See entries for these dates in Plantation Diary, June 1863–April 1866, *ibid.*

[40] See "Sales of Cotton Accounts" and "Accounts Current" from Carroll, Pritchard & Co. and Pritchard & Flower, dated variously 1853-1861, Eli J. Capell Papers, Louisiana Department of Archives and Manuscripts, Louisiana State University, Baton Rouge, La.

[41] Entries for May 11 and May 31, 1864, Plantation Diary, June 1863–April 1866, Eli J. Capell Plantation Diaries.

this cotton—and presumably more stored elsewhere in the country —Pritchard began his postwar business. In June 1865 he wrote Capell: "I would be glad if at your earliest convenience you could ship the 12 B/C purchased of you that I may be able to realize upon same & help those who wish to do business with me."[42] It was in response to this letter that Capell started the first 12 bales to Woodville in July.

In the years that followed, Capell consigned his cotton to R. Pritchard (or successor firms) in New Orleans. When a sale was made the factor rendered an account which, except for the date, was identical to an account sale of ante bellum times. From the gross sale price the factor deducted charges for freight, insurance, drayage, storage, weighage, brokerage, and a commission of 2.5 percent.[43] Letters and accounts show that the factor sent supplies on order, honored drafts which Capell drew on him to pay for goods purchased from other merchants in New Orleans, and also provided the planter with cash. Annual accounts were balanced by sales of cotton and by drafts drawn on other New Orleans firms, among them factors, indicating that Capell was sending cotton to more than one merchant, as had been his custom before the war.[44]

As before the Civil War, factors offered their customers the option of a European sale: the postwar pattern duplicated the practice initiated in the early nineteenth century. Thus, for example, sea island planter Henry Sanford dealt with Fraser and Dill, cotton factors and commission merchants of Charleston, and through them with Baring Brothers in Liverpool. Fraser and Dill supplied the plantation on credit as ordered by Sanford or his overseers and forwarded the cotton to Liverpool, paying all expenses of shipping. Once the cotton was on its way to Liverpool, the factors reimbursed themselves by drawing against it. After selling the cotton, Baring Brothers remitted the proceeds to San-

---

[42] Pritchard to Capell, New Orleans, June 16, 1865, Eli J. Capell Papers.

[43] Pritchard to Capell, New Orleans, March 21, 1867; accounts of sales of cotton by Pritchard & Bickham, New Orleans, dated variously, 1869-1871; a/c of sales of cotton by Bickham & Moore, New Orleans, Nov. 10, Dec. 17, 1879, *ibid.*

[44] Bills of sale from various New Orleans merchants (commission merchants, dry goods, tannery, druggists, grocers, hardware, etc. for Capell account, May 1867); "Drafts for 1866 & 67" (list kept by Capell showing drafts drawn on Pritchard in favor of the merchants from whom he purchased); accounts current, Pritchard & Bickham with Capell, 1870-1871, 1871-1872, 1872-1873, 1877-1878, *ibid.*

ford's account in New York, and the Charleston factors then drew upon this account to balance their books.[45]

Newcomers followed the same ante bellum business methods. Advances were offered, supplies provided, and cotton sold locally or, through business associates, in the North and abroad. E. F. Golsan and Company, for example, sold cotton through William B. Reynolds and Company, Boston; Gholson, Walker and Company, Liverpool; and Ware, Murphey and Company, New York, in addition to selling in their home market, New Orleans.[46]

Selling cotton, buying supplies, and providing credit were the most important functions of the factor before and after the Civil War, but as the planter's representative in the market place, the factor was called upon to handle other business as well. The familiar ante bellum services continued after the Civil War. Factors aided in the movement of funds by collecting bills of exchange;[47] they added their endorsements to planters' and merchants' notes so that these notes could be more readily discounted in the banks;[48] and they attended to other business and personal matters of their customers.[49]

When Edward King visited New Orleans in the 1870's, he described a scene reminiscent of the 1840's and 1850's:

> In the American quarter, during certain hours of the day, cotton is the only subject spoken of; the pavements of all the

[45] Fraser & Dill to Sanford, Charleston, March 5, March 9, May 13, 1869; Baring Bros. to Sanford, Liverpool, April 3, Nov. 9, 1869, London, Nov. 6, 1869; W. H. Trescott to Fraser & Dill, Hazelwood, S. C., March 11, 1869, Henry Shelton Sanford Papers, General Sanford Memorial Library, Sanford, Fla.

[46] See Letters from these firms, 1871, Golsan Brothers Papers. Letters to these firms may be found in the company Letterbook, 1871, *ibid.*

[47] Thomas H. Allen & Co. to Burrus, Memphis, Jan. 14, 1884, John C. Burrus Papers, Mississippi Department of Archives and History, Jackson, Miss.; Lyrette & Co. to Golsan & Sanders, Mobile, June 26, 1866; J. A. Memgay to Golsan and Sanders, Mobile, June 29, 1866; LeGrand, Allen & Manley to Golsan & Sanders, Montgomery, Feb. 1, 14, April 19, 1867, Golsan Brothers Papers.

[48] W. H. Tison to W. W. Gordon, Savannah, June 15, 1870; George Walter to W. W. Gordon, Savannah, June 17, 1870, Gordon Family Papers, Southern Historical Collection.

[49] Factor Stephen D. Heard was asked by a customer to invest the proceeds from the sale of his cotton. He suggested that Heard look into the possibility of investing in stocks or in gold but in the end left the decision up to the factor, asking only that the money be used to provide interest and that it be available when needed. Wm. H. Bonner to Heard & Son, White Plains, Ga., July 27, Aug. 4, 1868, Stephen D. Heard Papers. More modest was the request of another of Heard's customers. R. W. Wolten sent a railroad ticket to the factor asking that he secure a refund for him. Washington, Nov. 22, 1869, *ibid.*

principal avenues in the vicinity of the Exchange are crowded with smartly-dressed gentlemen, who eagerly discuss crops and values, and who have a perfect mania for preparing and comparing the estimates at the basis of all speculations in the favorite staple; and young Englishmen, whose mouths are filled with the slang of the Liverpool market; and with the skippers of steamers from all parts of the West and Southwest, each worshiping at the shrine of the same god.

From high noon until dark the planter, the factor, the speculator, flit feverishly to and from the portals of the Exchange, and nothing can be heard above the excited hum of their conversation except the sharp voice of the clerk reading the latest telegrams.[50]

If there is a familiar ring to King's description, there is also something startlingly different: the Exchange, the arriving telegrams, and, above all, the feverish excitement.

That the pace and mode of commerce had changed was noted—and sometimes lamented—by those who remembered the prewar trade. Robert Somers, after a visit to Savannah in 1870, wrote that the cotton business in that city was so competitive "as to astonish the older merchants."[51] A merchant of long experience in the cotton trade found postwar conditions completely disconcerting: "I have neither inclination or talent and believe I am now too old for business as now conducted."[52] The cotton trade had become "much more harrassing," he explained on another occasion. The telegraph, which brought news from all over the world "three times a day or oftener," required merchants to be constantly alert and able to move with dispatch. Where before the war "we could act for a day, now a transaction in cotton has to be completed in half an hour or an hour or something may arise to mar it."[53]

The increase in the pace of business was simply a reflection of other, more profound, changes in the cotton trade, changes which to old-timers in the trade seemed unethical. "My own opinion is that half the city is rotten to the core," was W. H. Tison's sour

[50] *The Great South* (Hartford, Conn., 1875), 50-51.
[51] *The Southern States Since the War, 1870-1871* (New York, 1871), 79.
[52] Barnsley to unstated person, Woodlands, Ga., Sept. 15, 1869, Godfrey Barnsley Papers, University of Georgia Library, as quoted by Coulter, *The South During Reconstruction,* 219.
[53] Barnsley to Julia [his daughter], New Orleans, March 9, 1870, Barnsley Collection, Archives Division, Tennessee State Library and Archives, Nashville, Tenn.

comment concerning the failure of a Savannah firm.[54] In letter after letter to his partner, Tison complained of the departure from traditional business methods and bemoaned his inability to adjust to new conditions.[55] At the end of June 1870, he wrote that he could not continue. "I have lost all love for money—And you must expect to take entire charge & control of our business on your return for I am grown unfit. . . . I must withdraw from business . . . I must I must."[56]

Despite his complaints, Tison remained in the factorage business as did hundreds of others in the South. Yet, complaints were not without foundation. King Cotton's retainer had returned after the Civil War, but he sat uneasily at his master's side.

[54] To W. W. Gordon, Savannah, June 23, 1870, Gordon Family Papers, Southern Historical Collection.

[55] To W. W. Gordon, Lallanza, Italy, Sept. 23, 1868, Gordon Family Papers, Georgia Historical Society, Savannah, Ga.; to W. W. Gordon, Sweet Springs, West Virginia, Aug. 19, 21, 24, 31, 1869, New York, Sept. 6, Savannah, Dec. 3, 1870, Gordon Family Papers, Southern Historical Collection.

[56] To W. W. Gordon, Savannah, June 30, 1870, *ibid.*

CHAPTER TWENTY-THREE

The Decline of Cotton Factorage

Paradoxically, at the very time that the cotton factorage system was being resurrected, signs of its decline could be noted.[1] A combination of technological changes that had begun to affect the cotton even before the Civil War added to the social and economic changes following the war gnawed at the very foundations of the system. Each of the major functions of the factor—salesman, buyer, and supplier of credit—was gradually replaced by other, more efficient agencies, and as this occurred, cotton factorage tended to disappear. Efforts by factorage firms to remain viable in the face of the changes only insured the eventual collapse of the system.

Two of the factor's key functions, that of seller and of supplier, were undermined by technological change in the form of improved transportation and communication links between the interior South and the outside world. Even before the Civil War, transportation improvements had begun to change the direction of cotton movements and the nature of cotton factorage in some areas of the South. By the 1850's, as has been shown, planters in western Georgia and northern Alabama found that the railroads offered them a number of new markets for their crops. The Atlanta and West Point, the Georgia, the Western and Atlantic, and the Memphis and Charleston (and connecting lines), along with the traditional river routes, connected the area with markets on the Atlantic (Charleston, Savannah, and Norfolk), on the Gulf (Mobile, New Orleans, and Pensacola), or in such widely scattered interior points as Augusta, Macon, Montgomery, or Memphis. As a result, comparative prices in the various markets, rather than the availability of transportation, began to determine the direction of cotton movements. The competitive dangers involved in this easing of transportation restrictions in turn dictated accommodative efforts by the factors. To secure or maintain their business, factors began to buy cotton in the interior. They financed local merchants, many of them itinerant, who were instructed to buy up as much of the local crop as they could and then to ship it to them.[2]

Such practices adumbrated the eventual disintegration of factorage. Not only were factors departing from their traditional role as sellers by becoming buyers as well, but local merchants were beginning to control a portion of the crop. Later, when local buyers no longer needed the financial assistance of the factors and were able to resell their cotton directly to the consumers or to exporters, factorage would become superfluous.

The possibility of direct shipments from the interior to a consuming or foreign market would aid in this development. The beginnings could be seen in the establishment of the so-called overland route to the North on the eve of the Civil War. A portent of the future was reported in a Memphis newspaper in the spring of 1860: "The first direct shipment of cotton from Memphis to Liverpool, by the Northern or overland route, was made on Saturday last. The shipment consisted of three hundred bales. It will be taken to Pittsburg by water, thence to New York via the Pennsylvania Central Railroad, and to Liverpool by the usual means of transportation, there to be sold on account of the Memphis shipper."[3] A year later a Buffalo paper reported cotton shipments from Memphis to Boston by a direct, west-to-east route. The cotton had traveled by river to Cincinnati and then by rail to Boston. "This is cheaper than it can be shipped down the Mississippi to New-Orleans, and thence by vessel, and the difference in time is about thirty days in favor of the Northern route."[4] Initially,

---

[1] The following discussion appeared in a somewhat different form as "The Decline of Cotton Factorage After the Civil War," *American Historical Review*, LXXI (July 1966), 1219-36.

[2] See Chap. VIII, above.

[3] *Memphis Bulletin*, as reprinted in *New Orleans Price Current*, April 25, 1860.

[4] *Buffalo Commercial*, as reprinted in *Hunt's Merchants' Magazine*, XLIV (June 1861), 782-83. The paper added that "a small portion is brought all the way by rail, but the rates on this are a little higher."

only a relatively small amount of cotton was involved in the overland route. Of the last crop marketed before the Civil War, only 143,424 bales were sent in a northerly direction, crossing the Ohio River at various points and making connections with the east-west trunk lines in the North. The amount, when compared to the total crop, was slight, but it had risen steadily over the previous years.[5]

When the cotton trade was fully reopened in 1865, the impact of earlier developments in transportation began to be felt more profoundly. In 1865-1866 more than two hundred and ten thousand bales moved to Northern markets via the overland route. By 1869-1870 the number exceeded three hundred and fifty thousand bales and in the crop year 1879-1880 well over one million bales out of a total crop of over five and a half million bales used this route. Overland traffic had increased from 2.3 percent of the total crop in 1859-1860 to over 19 percent in 1880. Of the total amount of cotton going to Northern cities in 1880 via overland and coastwise transportation, some 44 percent went via the overland route; of that portion of the total crop used by Northern manufacturers, about 72 percent went overland. In the early post bellum years, some of the cotton moving in this northeastern direction traveled part of the way on the Ohio River, but gradually all-rail routes came to predominate. Thus, receipts by river at Cincinnati in 1870 exceeded one hundred and forty-six thousand bales, almost 42 percent of that taking the overland route, but a decade later river receipts at Cincinnati had dropped to about seventy-six thousand bales, less than 7 percent of the overland total.[6]

East-west railroads south of the Ohio River were also drawing increasing amounts of the crop to the Atlantic ports. In 1859-1860, 24.3 percent of the cotton crop left the South via the Atlantic ports; in 1879-1880 the proportion going to the Atlantic had risen to 36 percent.[7] In part, this increase resulted from the fact that more cotton was going to the older, traditional cotton markets of

[5] Joseph Nimmo, Jr., *Report on the Internal Commerce of the United States . . . 1881*, 46th Cong., 3rd Sess., House Exec. Doc. 7, Pt. 2, p. 187. The increase given is as follows: 1857-1858—9,624; 1858-1859—85,321; 1859-1860—108,676; 1860-1861—143,424.

[6] *Ibid.*, 187-88, 192; Joseph Nimmo, Jr., *Report on the Internal Commerce of the United States . . . 1879*, 45th Cong., 3rd Sess., House Exec. Doc. 32, Pt. 3, p. 127.

[7] Nimmo, *Report, 1881*, 182. See also *Bradstreet's*, VII (March 3, 1883), 134.

Charleston and Savannah. But these ports had to share the postwar business with other growing Atlantic ports. Norfolk, for example, which before the war had received only a few thousand bales, most of which had been produced in the immediate neighborhood, became in the postwar years a major cotton market. The Norfolk and Western and the Seaboard and Roanoke railroads, completed on the eve of the Civil War, through their connections with other lines, opened the Western cotton lands to the Virginia port. By 1875 Norfolk received almost four hundred thousand bales and a decade later receipts approached the half-million mark.[8]

Railroads were obviously changing the pattern of cotton movements, diverting cotton from the Gulf ports which had been pre-eminent when river transportation was the most important means to market.[9] But the railroads did more than change trade patterns; they altered the entire nature of the Southern trade. The railroads not only gave sellers the option of several of the older markets but opened hundreds of new markets. Cotton marketing moved inland, away from the huge markets on the coast that traditionally had handled the crop. W. H. Tison noted the change when he visited Selma, Alabama, in 1870 and saw cotton being purchased there for New York delivery. The cotton was sampled, classed (that is, graded according to color and staple length), and compressed, the whole procedure being "done . . . in Sea Port & business like manner."[10]

The services of a sea port factor were totally unnecessary; the entire marketing process was handled in Selma. The cotton Tison saw being purchased for New York delivery might have been shipped to one of the seaports, but a factor did not have to handle it there. When Robert Somers visited Charleston in November 1870 he found cotton exports from the city growing, but the cotton was "giving little return to the town itself" because much of it was

[8] Wm. F. Switzler, *Report on the Internal Commerce of the United States* . . . *1886*, 49th Cong., 2nd Sess., House Exec. Doc. 7, Pt. 2, pp. 93-97.

[9] In the early postwar years, the changes in routing disrupted traditional methods of estimating crop movements. Statistics from the major Southern ports no longer provided sufficiently accurate information. "The routes of transportation have so materially changed that former methods of estimating the consumption are no longer reliable," noted *Hunt's Merchants' Magazine,* LIX (Dec. 1868), 415. See also *ibid.,* LX (April 1869), 78.

[10] To W. W. Gordon, Selma, Jan. 26, 1870, Gordon Family Papers, Southern Historical Collection, University of North Carolina Library, Chapel Hill, N.C.

simply passing through on its way to other markets. Buyers, he explained, were going "over the heads" of Charleston factors and merchants by making their purchases in the interior.[11] Somers watched the procedure in Memphis in February of the following year. Spinners' representatives were buying cotton in Memphis for shipment to Liverpool, a procedure made possible by the "establishment of *through* bills of lading by the various railroad companies in connection with the ocean steamship lines from New York."[12]

Cotton traveling on such through bills of lading was merely transferred from railroad car to ship and then continued on its way. Even this was expedited: in Norfolk, for example, "railway cars run out on the wharves, where the largest of merchant vessels may lie alongside and receive the bales directly into their holds."[13] Traditionally, cotton arriving in the ports had been in the form of "gin bales" and before transfer aboard ship had been recompressed into smaller, higher density bales so as to diminish their bulk. But, beginning in the early 1870's, powerful cotton compresses were built in the interior. This not only obviated recompression at the ports but also allowed railroad cars to double their previous capacity, thereby lowering freight rates.[14]

The railroad, through bills of lading, and improved cotton compresses were moving cotton-buying into the interior, thereby undermining the old cotton factorage system. Another technological innovation, the improvement of communications, accompanied and hastened the shift. The telegraph, the transatlantic cable, and later the telephone put merchants in every market in almost instantaneous touch with one another. Cotton prices in Liverpool and New York could be known in minutes not only in New Orleans and Savannah, but, as the telegraph expanded inland along with the railroad, in hundreds of tiny interior markets. Robert Somers noted while in Memphis that an English buyer

[11] *The Southern States Since the War, 1870-1871* (New York, 1871), 45.

[12] *Ibid.*, 259-60. "The ports of Norfolk, Va., Wilmington, N. C., Charleston, S. C., and Savannah, Ga., are not to any considerable extent cotton markets. The cotton which passes through these ports consists largely of direct shipments made from the interior points throughout the South to Northern seaports or manufactories in the Northern States, by means of arrangements entered into between railroads and ocean steamer lines." Nimmo, *Report, 1879*, 125.

[13] Switzler, *Report, 1886*, 93.

[14] Joseph Nimmo, Jr., *First Annual Report on the Internal Commerce of the United States (1877)*, 44th Cong., 2nd Sess., House Exec. Doc. 46, Pt. 2, p. 143; Edward King, *The Great South* (Hartford, Conn., 1875), 231.

could watch the movement of prices, judge his needs, and then place his order directly, via the telegraph, to Memphis. He could raise or lower his offered price at a moment's notice.[15] The result was obvious. The seller had no need of the expert advice of the factor concerning possible price movements and other market information. In the interior statistics were received regularly and posted for all to see and judge.[16]

Ineluctably the trend toward interior buying and direct shipments to the manufacturer increased. The 1880 census, in its cotton production survey, chronicled the shift: Reports from county after county in the cotton South announced that local cotton marketing was pronounced and increasing. Every town, indeed, virtually every stop on the railroad, had become a market where the grower could sell his crop.[17]

The Southern railroad boom of the 1880's[18] continued the process; by pushing deeper into the interior the railroad opened still more markets. Bradstreet's Southern correspondents reported the effect. A South Carolinian wrote that in his state "better

15 The Southern States, 260.

16 The great market at Liverpool was also bypassed. John Crosby Brown, himself a merchant connected with various firms bearing his name, firms which had been very active in the cotton business, described the change:

"Communication between the Old and New Worlds by cable, successfully established in 1866, revolutionized trade between the two countries, leaving the Liverpool merchants connected with that trade without their usual occupation. In fact, the necessity for the intervention of merchants gradually ceased. Manufacturers in England, France and Germany bought their cotton by cable on samples previously sent to them from various places of shipment, i.e., New Orleans, Mobile, Charleston, Savannah, Galveston, Memphis, and other inland towns. Samples were sent to them from brokers and merchants in these cities, oftentimes accompanied by a firm offer price. These they could examine carefully in their own offices, make their selection for the style of goods they desired to manufacture, and cable either the acceptance of the offer or a counteroffer, with authority, usually arranged through some banker, to draw against shipment. As a consequence warehouse property in Liverpool, largely built for cotton storage, and which had heretofore brought a good return to the owners, was for a time empty, and its value greatly diminished. Consignments of cotton and other produce to Liverpool for sale practically ceased, and to a great extent manufactured goods for shipment to this country, which had heretofore been attended to by Liverpool merchants, were shipped directly by the manufacturers to the buyers in the United States on a through bill of lading. The old mercantile firms which were the pride of Liverpool soon disappeared." A Hundred Years of Merchant Banking (New York, 1909), 123.

17 Eugene W. Hilgard, "Report on Cotton Production in the United States," in U. S. Department of the Interior, Census Office, Tenth Census (1880) (Washington, D.C., 1884), V, VI, passim.

18 John F. Stover, The Railroads of the South, 1865-1900 (Chapel Hill, 1955), 190-93.

markets are now open in country towns by reason of foreign buyers sending agents to the interior." From Alabama came the report that "cash buyers were in every neighborhood, crops were bought up promptly and shipped direct to the mills and export." And a Texas correspondent noted that "cotton that was formerly sent to commission merchants to be held is now bought by contractors, and goes direct to New England or abroad." The journal found that there were 164 interior cotton markets in the Southern states in 1885.[19]

By this time it was clear that cotton marketing had altered considerably from prewar days. In 1886 *Bradstreet's* devoted a long article to the "Changes in Marketing the Great Staple."[20] The basic change the journal's correspondents discovered was that interior buying had become "general throughout the South about the year 1875," a development which the editors traced to the railroad and the telegraph. As a result, the business of the old port-city markets was undermined. "The sending of cotton buyers into the interior, shipping cotton they buy on through bills of lading, avoiding heavy charges at the ports, has cut considerably into business formerly exclusively enjoyed by those ports," the article noted. Nor had the process ended. Competition among buyers "leads them every year to go further into the country, and each year sees the remote producer and the mills or exporters brought closer together." Facilitating inland buying and direct shipments were the "new compresses of great power in towns which formerly sent their cotton half pressed to the ports."

A New England correspondent traced the effects of the change on his section. Until recently the cotton mills had had resident agents in the large port markets who purchased cotton from factors on order from the mills. These agents were given general orders concerning price and quality, but final decisions were "left to their own judgment." This had now largely been abandoned. Mill buyers, the correspondent explained, dealt with brokers who had representatives throughout the Southern interior: "The telegraph is used freely, and the buyer knows hour by hour what

---

[19] XI (Feb. 14, 1885), 99-100. The listing showed the 164 towns to be broken down by states as follows: N.C., 19; S.C., 28; Ga., 17; Ala., 19; Miss., 20; La., 6; Texas, 34; Ark., 6; Tenn., 15. See also B. F. O'Neal to editor, Bellevue, La., Feb. 22, 1885, XI (March 7, 1885), 156.

[20] XIII (April 10, 1886), 226-27.

cotton can be had for in each of the interior and seaboard markets. He names a price to any mill man who is in need of cotton, and if he receives an order he telegraphs forthwith to his southern correspondent to make a trade. The staple thus being secured a bill of lading is issued." English buyers, the correspondent added, now utilized the same procedure.

Bradstreet's writers predicted that interior buying would continue to grow. Their predictions were borne out. By the turn of the century the Industrial Commission reported that more than half the crop (55.4 percent in 1897-1898) was received in thirty interior markets. From these markets the crop moved directly to the consuming markets. Factorage expenses "once considered legitimate are no longer a feature of the movement of this crop." Although 50 percent of the crop still left the country through New Orleans, Galveston, and Savannah, these cities served merely as expediters of cotton already bound for the mills on through bills of lading. Local markets—"almost any town of any consequence"—had adequate cotton compresses, were in telegraphic communication with the North and Europe, receiving hourly reports of prices all over the world, and from them cotton could be shipped anywhere on through bills. "This system tends to dispense with the middlemen," the article flatly concluded.[21]

Postwar factors soon became acutely aware of the competition from inland buyers. Stephen D. Heard, the Augusta factor, for example, found himself in competition with his own business correspondent in New York. A member of the New York firm of

---

[21] U. S. Industrial Commission, *Report . . . on the Distribution of Farm Products* [Vol. VI of the commission's reports] (Washington, D.C., 1901), 150-52, 167-69, 173, 181-83. For a contemporary description of interior cotton sales see William D. Kelley, *The Old South and the New* (New York, 1888), 129-30. The same developments which undermined the pre-eminence of the port markets in the South affected the New York market also. Hopkins, Dwight & Co., New York commission merchants, wrote a Senate investigating committee that cotton sales in New York had declined sharply because of "the growth and development of interior markets and the ability of cotton buyers in comparatively small towns in the interior to handle shipments of cotton from their points directly to the mills in the United States, or directly to Europe, upon through bills of lading at rates of freight that are but little, if any, more than the rates from these interior points to New York." U. S. Congress, Senate, Committee on Agriculture and Forestry, *Report . . . on Condition of Cotton Growers,* 53rd Cong., 3rd Sess., Report 986 (1895), I, 485. Whatever cotton continued to go to New York was usually intended to cover futures contracts. "New York don't do what is known as a factorage business very much," a Memphis cotton buyer told the same committee. *Ibid.,* I, 128. For additional, similar testimony see *ibid.,* 474, 477, 479, 483.

Adolphus C. Schaefer and Company had visited the South in 1865 and arranged a business connection with Heard. In return for any cotton Heard influenced to be sent to Schaefer, the Augusta factor was to receive a rebate of 1 percent on the selling commission. Thus began a typical Southern factor-New York merchant relationship. But the traveling New Yorker was not content with this arrangement. Instead, he went further inland to the smaller markets and visited some of Heard's customers (or potential customers) offering them the same arrangement as he had with Heard. One of Heard's old customers in West Point, Georgia, wrote that the Schaefer partner had visited that town and had informed one of the merchants there that "if he would ship his cotton through direct he would save the one pr cent you were getting out of the firm."[22]

Through bills of lading had not yet been initiated in the area and many of those who were interviewed by the New Yorker shipped their cotton to Schaefer and Company via Augusta and Stephen D. Heard. When Heard requested his return commission on such cotton he was refused by the New York firm; the company argued that these were not Heard's customers. "The Cotton *was sent to you, with orders to ship it to us*. You had no discretion or influence in the matter,"[23] the New Yorkers expostulated. This provoked a sharp retort from Heard. He found Schaefer's letter "couched in language evidently intended to add insult to injury," language "characteristic" of those "who have no scruples as to the means used to obtain money from others." Angrily, Heard decided to forego his commissions, and, enclosing a check for the balance he owed, concluded that "our business acquaintance must end."[24]

Severing business relations might assuage Heard's ruffled feelings, but it did not solve the problem. Local planters and merchants *could* deal directly with New York and receive a rebate on the commission besides. And once through bills of lading were established—as they very quickly were—Heard would not even be called upon to handle the cotton as it went through Augusta. He would have to offer similar terms or lose the business. This was

[22] W. C. Darden to Heard, West Point, Ga., Oct. 23, 1865, Stephen D. Heard Papers, Southern Historical Collection, University of North Carolina Library, Chapel Hill, N.C.
[23] Schaefer & Co. to Heard, New York, Aug. 15, 1866, *ibid.*
[24] Heard to Schaefer & Co., Augusta, Aug. 31, 1866, *ibid.*

made abundantly clear in a letter from planters in West Point at the beginning of the 1867 marketing system: "We will probably make some two hundred and fifty bales Cotton this year on our plantations, and will probably buy some, and we want to make an arrangement with some house in your city to ship to . . . but we think that 2½ per cent commissions is more than the planter can afford to pay . . . if you are willing to receive our shipments and deduct half the commissions let us hear from you at once."[25]

Faced with this competition, the postwar factor had to adjust to new conditions or be driven out of business. One way, open especially to the factor in the interior, was to become a buyer himself, filling orders from spinners and shipping direct. In the early summer of 1870 Heard's new New York merchants, Austell, Inman and Company, wrote that "some of our spinning friends" were making purchases in the South for direct shipment to the North. The New York firm promised to do its best "to influence some of them to invest in Augusta." Heard was urged to make his charges "as light as possible as orders will seek points where they can be filled cheapest."[26]

Ironically, in buying for spinners, the factor hastened the decline of the factorage system because the buying department of a factorage house competed against the commission department. In trying to fill his orders, the factor—or agents he hired—scoured the countryside looking for cotton to buy and, in so doing, added to the number of interior buyers who were slowly destroying the commission business.[27] Usually the buying department, if success-

[25] Bass & Johnson to Heard, West Point, Aug. 29, 1867, *ibid.* See also F. W. Sims & Co. to Thomas Harrold, Savannah, Sept. 26, 1865, Harrold Brothers Papers, Emory University Library, Atlanta, Ga.

[26] Austell, Inman & Co. to Heard & Son, New York, May 2, 1870, Stephen D. Heard Papers.

[27] Even before the Civil War, competition had led factors to finance buyers in the interior in return for their business. This custom was revived and expanded after the war to meet the renewed and keener competition. For typical examples see R. W. Reid to W. H. Tison, Monticello, Fla., Aug. 12, 1867; Tison to W. W. Gordon, Savannah, Aug. 14, 1867, Oct. 23, 1869, April 18, 1870, Selma, Ala., Jan. 26, 1870, Gordon Family Papers, Southern Historical Collection; Gordon to Tison, Savannah, Sept. 18, 1875, Gordon Family Papers, Georgia Historical Society; W. C. Darden to Heard, West Point, Ga., Sept. 3, 1867; M. S. Glass to Heard, Kidran, Ga., Dec. 10, 1869; McDowell & Crain to Heard, Hoganville, Ga., Sept. 24, 1867, Stephen D. Heard Papers; Godfrey Barnsley to Wm. Duncan, New Orleans, June 14, 1869; Godfrey Barnsley to M. Menlove, New Orleans, June 24, 1869, Barnsley Collection, Archives Division, Tennessee State Library and Archives, Nashville, Tenn.

ful, became more important and gradually absorbed the commission business.[28] Planters soon discovered that factors, anxious to fill purchase orders, would buy cotton at the going market rate, thus saving the grower the cost of commission charges.[29]

While improved transportation and communication were undermining the factor's role as cotton seller, these same improvements were eliminating also his responsibilities as a plantation supplier. Railroads that took cotton out of the South from remote interior markets also brought food and manufactured goods from the West and the Northeast directly to Southern village stores. When Whitelaw Reid visited the South immediately after the Civil War, he found New Orleans to be the center for the distribution of Western provisions in the Mississippi valley. As he traveled from New Orleans to Natchez he noticed that the boat made frequent stops at plantations where supplies, purchased in New Orleans, were dropped off. He found this to be a remarkable example of Southern conservatism, for the goods he saw being delivered had been carried from the North past these same plantations on the way to New Orleans only to return "with double freights and

[28] See William Hustace Hubbard, *Cotton and the Cotton Market* (New York, 1925), 137-38.

[29] Hilgard, "Report on Cotton Production," *Tenth Census* (1880), VI, 325. Tradition and law dictated that without the owner's permission a factor could not buy cotton that was consigned to him for sale; that is, the buying business and the commission business were supposed to be kept separate. (See Chap. VI, above.) After the Civil War, as buying by factors became more common, the separation of the two functions became more important. Some stoutly maintained that they did no buying at all. L. S. Lake, a Memphis cotton factor, told a Senate investigating committee that he never bought cotton: "Our business prevents that, because it would confuse us, and our patrons would object to my confusing the cotton purchased by myself with the other business." Senate Committee on Agriculture and Forestry, *Condition of Cotton Growers*, I, 191. Most did not confine their business to selling, however. As late as 1925, a Federal Trade Commission investigation undertaken as a result of a Senate resolution of June 7, 1924 found the buying of cotton consigned to them to be one of the abuses practiced by factors. The charges were strenuously denied by the factors of New Orleans who, in their reply, listed the legal safeguards planters had against this abuse. Federal Trade Commission, *Cotton Merchandising Practices*, 68th Cong., 2nd Sess., Senate Doc. 194 (1925); *Spot Cotton Trade of New Orleans*, 68th Cong., 2nd Sess., Senate Doc. 207 (1925). Despite law and tradition, it is probable that factors, feeling the pinch of competition, resorted to buying cotton consigned to them. Caution had to be exercised, however. See, for example, Tison & Gordon to Mr. C. J. Miller, Savannah, March 17, 1875, Letter Book, 1872-1876, Gordon Family Papers, Georgia Historical Society, Savannah, Ga. The Savannah factors proposed that Miller buy a shipment of 85 bales of cotton coming to them for sale, the purchase to be made for Tison & Gordon "as a speculation" with their money. Miller was cautioned to manage the matter "very delicately": "Don't mention any names in Telegraphing and dont Telegraph to us."

double commissions." When he inquired of planters why this method was used, the typical answer was that "Mr. So-and-so, in New Orleans, has sold all his cotton or sugar, and purchased all his supplies for the last ten or twenty years, and he doesn't want to be bothered making a change."[30]

Conservatism, however, would not sustain a system made obsolete by improved transportation. In 1877, Henry G. Hester, secretary of the New Orleans Cotton Exchange, described the changed trade relations between New Orleans and the West. The Crescent City never recovered from the disruption of trade during the Civil War, he wrote. Goods from the West bound for Europe or Eastern cities no longer passed through New Orleans but went directly, via the railroads, to the Eastern areas of the country for consumption or export. Even the bulk of the Southern trade was lost: "Twenty years ago the entire States of Louisiana, Texas, Mississippi, and Alabama, and large portions of Arkansas, Tennessee, and Georgia, obtained their supplies of provisions, breadstuffs, groceries, and even dry goods, from New Orleans. This was largely the case even ten years ago, but now the local trade is confined to Louisiana, Southern Texas, and only small portions of Mississippi, Alabama, Georgia, Florida, and Arkansas. Railroads leading down from the West have penetrated in every direction and touched the Gulf coast at several points. Little by little they have drawn shipments away from the river."[31] The experience in the other port cities was the same. By 1870 Charleston and Savannah had ceased to be ports of entry for Western goods. No longer were goods traveling down the Mississippi and coastwise to these Atlantic ports for distribution in the interior; instead, Western produce moved directly from the Northwest to central Georgia, Alabama, and Tennessee via the railroads.[32] Mobile suffered the same fate. Alabama was no longer dependent upon its port: "The railroads receive the commerce of the interior and carry it, east or west, beyond the State, and return the incoming trade."[33]

With Western goods available in the interior, it was no longer

[30] *After the War: A Southern Tour, May 1, 1865, to May 1, 1866* (London, 1866), 475.
[31] Nimmo, *First Annual Report* (1877), 168-69.
[32] Switzler, *Report, 1886,* 374.
[33] *Ibid.,* 444.

necessary for the cotton grower to look to a factor in the ports to make purchases for him. Merchandise from the Northeast, manufactured goods, and foreign imports also bypassed the factors. The trend was already evident on the eve of the Civil War. The Boston and Southern Steamship Company advertised in July 1860 that "THEY WILL FORM A CONNECTING LINE WITH THE SOUTH CAROLINA RAILROAD and goods will be forwarded to all ports in the Southern and Southwestern parts of the country, by that and connecting roads, at through rates of freight, relatively as low as by any other steam line whatever."[34]

In 1869, the nation's leading commercial journal reported that Southern buyers from the "minor villages, the corners and cross roads," places "unknown in Northern markets" before the war, "now deal directly with the North." In addition, the journal continued, commercial travelers "go from New York and Philadelphia, and from the manufacturing towns, and solicit direct trade with those with whom business was formerly done by the intervention of the Southern jobber or merchant."[35]

With buyers and suppliers on hand deep in the interior, two of the factor's services had become less important. The factorage system, nevertheless, did not disappear overnight. Many continued sending cotton to factors to be sold on commission simply because they needed the credit facilities factors offered. A Grenada, Mississippi, correspondent for *Bradstreet's*, while noting the growing trend towards interior selling, added: "The only obstacle in the way of all the cotton being sold to local buyers is the lack of capital with which to make the crop without drawing from New Orleans, where planters get advances on agreement to ship one bale of cotton for every $10 advanced."[36]

The familiar ante bellum credit pattern can be seen in letter after letter in the papers of postwar factors requesting supplies on credit and pledging cotton in return. The following is typical:

> I am planting on a small scale and have no merchant   I was
> fortunate enough to have means almost to purchase my sup-

[34] Boston *Shipping List*, July 4, 1860, as quoted in Edward Chase Kirkland, *Men, Cities, and Transportation* (2 vols.; Cambridge, Mass., 1948), II, 178.

[35] *Hunt's Merchants' Magazine*, LXI (Nov. 1869), 364. See also Nimmo, *Report*, 1881, 77.

[36] XIII (April 10, 1886), 226. The editors indicated that numerous other correspondents in the South had made the same report.

plies for the present year. Consequently have applied to none as yet.

But as you are in the commission business and willing to assist me a little I will send you my crop.

The assistance I want is small one coil of rope & one Role [sic] of Bagging one Barrel of flour & one Barrel Mess Pork also one bank of twine If my arrangements suit you pleas [sic] forward soon If not let me hear from you.[37]

But again, if the need for credit helped to perpetuate the factorage system, it also contributed to its decline. The need did not diminish, but alternatives to the resources of the factor appeared: credit facilities, like the markets, moved inland.

In part, the shift was a result of transportation developments that allowed growers to make their purchases locally. Most of the credit advanced by the ante bellum factor had been in the form of supplies and luxuries ordered by the planter during the year with payment not due until the crop was sold. As postwar growers began to get their supplies locally, they began also to get their credit locally. A second and closely related reason for the shift inland of credit facilities arose from the social revolution produced by the emancipation of the slaves. When slaves became tenants they had to find the means to feed and clothe themselves and to provide themselves with the supplies needed to plant a crop. Local merchants stood ready to provide these facilities. As local credit became available, the factor's domination of this aspect of cotton marketing weakened.

Paradoxically, however, many of the conditions that would ultimately destroy the factor's role as creditor at first helped to resurrect cotton factorage in the ante bellum period. Tenants lacked the financial resources to grow a crop and, like the planters of old, had to find means to secure supplies on credit. Unlike the planter, however, the tenant owned no land and had few tools and other possessions to serve as security for a loan. All he usually possessed was his labor power and the skill required to grow cotton. These "possessions" were transformed into loan security by lien laws passed by every Southern state after the Civil

[37] Braxton King to J. Y. Sanders, Franklin Parish, La., May 26, 1866, Golsan Brothers Papers, Department of Archives and Manuscripts, Louisiana State University, Baton Rouge, La. Many similar letters may be found in this collection, the Stephen D. Heard Papers, and in the Gordon Family Papers, Southern Historical Collection.

War. Creditors could get a prior lien on any cotton grown to the extent of the credit advanced. With this as his security, the planter-landlord often stipulated in his agreements with his tenants that he would supply them with certain necessities or would aid them in securing such supplies. But the planter, himself, rarely had the financial resources to give such aid, and he turned, as he had before the war, to his cotton factor.

In return for the right to sell the crop controlled by the planter-landlord, the factor was willing to extend the credit requested. Often a planter would open a store on his land from which tenants could receive supplies on credit, paying their bills in cotton at the end of the season. The process can be followed typically in the records of Eli J. Capell, who owned the Pleasant Hill Plantation in Amite County, Mississippi. His daybook showed income and expenditures on his plantation beginning in 1849. Entries for the ante bellum period are ordinary planter-slaveowner business records listing dealings with his New Orleans factors and with other merchants. After the war, entries begin to refer to "the Store." While Capell carefully kept his plantation account separate from the store account, the separation was merely a bookkeeping arrangement. He owned both and profited from both. At the same time his postwar entries show dealings with R. Pritchard and later Pritchard and Bickham, the New Orleans factors to whom he sent his cotton to be sold and from whom he received goods on credit to stock his store.[38]

Local storekeepers, warehousemen, and speculators also turned to the factors for credit. In 1866, for example, a Wetumpka, Alabama, firm, Seaman and Brothers, wrote Golsan and Sanders, New Orleans cotton factors, requesting an "accommodation" of "Six or Eight hundred dollars" in groceries and other merchandise. The Wetumpka firm indicated that they were rebuilding their warehouse and promised to "throw some business to your hands during the season." The New Orleans factors agreed to furnish the merchandise but stipulated very firm conditions: Golsan and Sanders were to "be the sole Factors & Merchants for Seaman & Bros in New Orleans," and "every possible consignment for sale

[38] Daybook, 1849-1876, Eli J. Capell Plantation Diaries and Record Books, Louisiana Department of Archives and Manuscripts, Louisiana State University, Baton Rouge, La.

or for forwarding together with all orders that Mess[rs] Seaman & Bros can in any way influence" were to be sent to the New Orleans firm.[39]

Factors soon discovered that their new-found business lacked the stability of ante bellum factorage. Competition was one problem. Just as the factor as cotton seller had to meet the competition from local buyers, so too did the factor as creditor face local competition. Despite any arrangements to the contrary, planters, tenants, and merchants began to get supplies on credit and to dispose of their crop (or part of it) close to home. A letter from a Mound Bayou, Mississippi farmer to his New Orleans factor illustrates this new source of competition: "I shiped [sic] you 4 Bales Cotton in Janry last and would have sent you 8 bales—but I owed Mr. F. M. Miller here—and give him 2 Bales—And I bought a Mule and gave 2 Bales in payment for it—So you can understand the reason you did [not] get the 8 Bales—You must not think hard of me disappointing you but I could sell the Cotton here for 13 cents—without any expence [sic]—and had to do it to pay my debts— . . ."[40] When a Mobile paper reminded planters of "the great importance of sending forward their cotton to those factors making advances," it was obviously reacting to this new problem. Numbers of planters "have shipped their crops to other houses, or sold it on the plantations, and left the factor to get his money the best way he can." If the practice continued, the paper warned, it will become impossible for "the honest planter to get aid when he needs it."[41]

The charge of dishonesty often went wide of the mark. The decision to sell locally was usually made on the basis of the probable profit margin. Interior buyers could meet or even exceed prices being realized by factors' sales because they could save the cost of factors' commissions. Thus, Seaman and Brothers in Wetumpka, after promising in July 1866 that they would send all their cotton to Golsan and Sanders in New Orleans, in October wrote that they

---

[39] Seaman & Bros. to Golsan & Sanders, Wetumpka, June 21, 1866; E. F. Golsan to Seaman & Bros., Autaugaville, July 9, 1866, Golsan Brothers Papers. For a similar request made of a Savannah factor, see Geo. Walter [an employee of Tison & Gordon] to W. W. Gordon, Savannah, June 9, 1871, Gordon Family Papers, Southern Historical Collection.

[40] G. E. Thomas to E. F. Golsan & Co., Mound Bayou, Feb. 24, 1871, Golsan Brothers Papers.

[41] *Planters' and Exchange Prices Current*, Nov. 16, 1867.

were withholding their cotton from the New Orleans firm because "there is not any margin between this place & N[ew] O[rleans]."[42]

The factors were caught in a dilemma. If they withheld credit, they would lose the only remaining basis for their services. Yet if they continued to grant credit, they had no guarantee that cotton would come to them for sale. One solution was to deal directly with the growers (rather than storekeepers) and to take a lien on the growing crop. Stephen D. Heard of Augusta, for example, began requesting such liens of his customers in the 1870's,[43] as did other factors elsewhere.[44]

But the factor was at a distinct disadvantage if he chose to do business in this way. The competition was more than he could withstand. Local merchants had the advantage of being able to display their merchandise to their customers, while a distant factor had to sell goods on order, requiring from the grower both a period of self-denial and the ability to write. Moreover, the local merchant was on the scene and could see that cotton came to him as arranged; a distant factor could not give this close supervision. W. H. Tison, obviously remembering his old ante bellum business, complained bitterly of his post war dealings with small farmers.[45] The alternative, as Tison put it, was to deal with "merchants of the first class." Writing in August 1870, he noted that Harrold, Johnson and Company, storekeepers of Americus, Georgia, were among his firm's largest customers and added that he would be willing to lend the Americus firm money without security in hopes of getting some of their business, this with full knowledge that other factors were also lending Harrold, Johnson and Company large sums for the same purpose.[46]

Thus as cotton growers turned increasingly to local merchants for credit, the factor, in order to retain his cotton business, was forced to concentrate on merchants rather than planters. In 1893, it was noted that the largest and most profitable factorage business

[42] Letter dated Wetumpka, Oct. 11, 1866, Golsan Brothers Papers.

[43] See Stephen D. Heard Papers, *passim*.

[44] This is readily apparent from correspondence in the Golsan Brothers Papers and the Gordon Family Papers, Southern Historical Collection.

[45] To W. W. Gordon, Sweet Springs, W. Va., Aug. 21, 1869, Gordon Family Papers, Southern Historical Collection.

[46] To W. W. Gordon, Saratoga, Aug. 8, 24, 1870, *ibid*. In the earlier letter Tison expressed some misgivings about extending unsecured loans, but in the second letter he dismissed these misgivings completely.

was with interior merchants.[47] Ironically, therefore, as the factor's business waned in the face of interior competition, much of what business he continued to retain served to support and, indeed, to encourage his competition. At the same time, interior merchants became less dependent upon the credit facilities offered by the factor. Goods from the North, which now came directly to the storekeepers, were usually made available on credit. A traveling salesman representing a firm of New York hardware merchants recalled how he was required "to extend very long credits to almost every buyer" when he went South after the Civil War. Payment was taken in notes of four to eight months, the due date usually timed to the period when cotton was ready for marketing. Even then, it was often necessary to carry a customer over an entire year until the next crop was mature.[48]

Other wholesalers provided similar credit facilities to the country storekeepers. By 1880 credit from the North had become so widespread that conservative voices were counseling restraint. *Bradstreet's* complained that easy credit given to the local merchant allowed him to extend credit unwisely to Southern consumers.[49]

The interior merchant's control of cotton, moreover, opened new avenues of credit. Local banks would lend funds to established merchants and would discount bills of lading and crop lien notes; this paper could easily be rediscounted in the larger banks in the cities, North and South.[50] New York bankers and merchants continued their practice of advancing funds on cotton consigned to them or to their European correspondents.[51]

[47] H. S. Fleming, "In Our Cotton Belt," *The Cosmopolitan*, XIV (March 1893), 546.

[48] Edward P. Briggs, *Fifty Years on the Road: The Autobiography of a Traveling Salesman* (Philadelphia, 1911), 30, 34. See also Thomas Clark, *Pills, Petticoats and Plows: The Southern Country Store* (Indianapolis, 1944), 109-23.

[49] II (April 7, 1880), 5.

[50] Somers, *The Southern States*, 45, 147, 184; Hubbard, *Cotton and the Cotton Market*, 139-41; *Bradstreet's*, I (Oct. 22, 1879), 1; Nimmo, *Report, 1879*, 148; Robert Goodwyn Rhett, *Charleston, An Epic of Carolina* (Richmond, Va., 1940), 321-22. The *Commercial and Financial Chronicle* (along with other commercial journals) regularly carried advertisements of Southern bankers not only from the larger cities but also from such places as Talladega, Selma, Montgomery, and Eufaula, Ala.; Americus, Columbus, and Macon, Ga.; Vicksburg, Mississippi; and Wilmington, N.C. See, for example, XI (Nov. 12, 1870), 611. Often these firms indicated a willingness to buy and sell cotton and usually they advertised that they had a New York "correspondent" from whom credit facilities were available.

[51] See, for example, the advertisements of Williams & Guion and R. T. Wilson & Co. in *Hunt's Merchants' Magazine Year Book, 1871* (New York, 1871), ix.

Thus, as his business grew, the local merchant became increasingly independent of the factor. Conversely, as the factor's business declined, so too did his ability to command funds he needed to give credit. Cotton on hand or to come had been the valuable security on which the ante bellum factorage system had rested. Less cotton meant less credit which in turn led to less business.

In the face of competition arising from profound social and technological changes, the cotton factorage system, momentarily resurrected after the Civil War, gradually disappeared. Many firms, some of them with long and distinguished records in the business, simply disintegrated. Others adjusted their business to new conditions by becoming buyers or furnishing merchants themselves or by taking on other economic activities. The Golsan brothers, for example, in an effort to build up their business, speculated in the futures market[52] and served as agents for a Northern cotton gin manufacturer.[53] Many factors became manufacturers or distributors of fertilizer, selling the material—usually guano—on credit to planters, merchants, and farmers.[54] Such business diversification might serve to keep a factorage firm solvent, but at the same time it undermined the cotton commission business on which the ante bellum system had rested.

By the end of the century, C. P. Brooks wrote that "the consignment of cotton for sale has almost died a natural death."[55] Ten years later another cotton analyst wrote that only "a small percentage, comparatively, consign cotton to reliable commission merchants."[56] Nevertheless, despite reports of its early demise, the system continued to hold on, albeit tenuously. Factorage had steadily declined in importance in the cotton trade, a merchant wrote in 1925, "and, today, it is a question whether he [the factor]

[52] See correspondence to and from Ware, Murphy & Co., New York, dated variously, 1871, Golsan Brothers Papers.

[53] See agreement with Du Bois & Co., June 2, 1871, *ibid.*; also correspondence with Albertson & Douglass Machine Co. (of New London, Conn.), June-Sept. 1871, *ibid.*

[54] *Commercial and Financial Chronicle*, XVI (April 5, 1873), 464; *Bradstreet's*, III (Jan. 15, 1881), 20, V (Jan. 14, 1882), 22, (April 1, 1882), 197, (June 24, 1882), 388. Pelzer, Rodgers & Co., listed in a Charleston directory as "the largest cotton factors in the city," also managed the Atlantic Phosphate Co., a fertilizer firm. Arthur Mazyk, *Guide to Charleston* (Charleston, S. C., [1875]), 161, 170-71. Stephen D. Heard was also in the fertilizer business. In March 1871, for example, he was notified by the railroad agent in Augusta that his 16 carloads of guano had arrived. J. R. Preston to Heard & Son, March 6, 1871, Stephen D. Heard Papers.

[55] *Cotton* (New York, 1898), 242.

[56] T. S. Miller, *The American Cotton System* (Austin, Texas, 1909), 103.

will not disappear altogether."[57] A textbook published in 1938 reported the existence of factors in the South but found their numbers continuing to decline.[58]

Today, in Memphis and in other markets, a visitor will still find a few firms calling themselves factors, but the use of the word is somewhat misleading. In time the very term lost its former meaning. The factor had performed a multitude of services, not the least of which had been financing the growing and marketing of the crop. This method of financing had become less and less typical and gradually the term "factor" had come to be applied to any merchant who received cotton for sale on commission even though in most cases the other services—supplier and creditor—were not provided.[59]

By the 1880's it was clear that an entirely new pattern had emerged in the cotton trade. Most growers now sold their crop immediately after it was picked to the plantation or crossroads village store where they had received supplies, clothing, and other goods on credit during the year. Into these villages came buyers representing foreign firms or New England spinners or simply speculating on their own account. Gradually, however, a new pattern of buying arose also. *Bradstreet's* noted the development in 1886. The opportunities for profit in speculation had brought "a great many irresponsible persons" into the cotton-buying business. These people were being weeded out as consumers increasingly sought out the more responsible buyers who would guarantee the quality of the cotton to be delivered.[60]

Bradstreet's prognosis proved correct. Cotton buying became concentrated in the hands of a relatively few large European and American firms. These firms, known in the cotton trade as merchants, had representatives in virtually every market—often using the services of storekeepers and ginners—who bought cotton for them at given prices. The cotton was assembled in a number of given towns where the merchants had huge warehouses to store it while they awaited orders from consumers all over the world. An order would send the proper grade on a through bill directly

---

[57] Hubbard, *Cotton and the Cotton Market*, 136. Hubbard Bros. were New York cotton merchants.

[58] Harry Bates Brown, *Cotton* (2nd ed., New York, 1938), 438.

[59] Federal Trade Commission, *Report . . . on the Cotton Trade*, 68th Cong., 1st Sess., Senate Doc. 100, Pt. I, p. 29.

[60] XIII (April 10, 1886), 226-27.

to the consumer. By the turn of the century a small number of large firms, American and European, dominated this business. In 1904 Frank and Monroe Anderson along with Will Clayton organized Anderson, Clayton and Company, soon to become the largest cotton merchants in the world. By 1921, twenty-four firms with annual sales of 100,000 bales or more handled 60 percent of the American cotton crop.[61]

Still another new element in postwar cotton marketing was the futures system, the buying and selling of contracts for cotton to be delivered at a later date. Its effect on postwar factorage was apparent. On the one hand, futures trading provided new opportunities for speculation, opportunities that often proved attractive to factors faced with dwindling consignments; on the other hand, futures trading allowed hedging, a device which removed the speculative risk from cotton trading and thereby helped to support the factor's chief competitor, the interior merchant.

Like other postwar developments, the futures system had its roots in ante bellum times. In its simplest form it merely involved the sale of goods before they arrived in the market. Merchandise purchased in one market for shipment to another might be sold and resold several times before it finally arrived at its destination, a process which would become especially common during periods of great price fluctuation. Speculators quickly learned that contracts for future delivery of commodities did not have to be based only on specific goods en route. Sometime between the time of sale and the delivery date, they could effect a settlement through the purchase of goods in the market or by a cash payment. Such time contracts in grain were in use in the Chicago Board of Trade as early as the 1850's, becoming even more common during the Civil

[61] Senate Committee on Agriculture and Forestry, *Condition of Cotton Growers,* I, 35, 131, 158; U. S. Congress, Senate, Committee on Agriculture and Forestry, *Extracts from Hearings before a Subcommittee . . . Pursuant to . . . A Resolution to Investigate the Recent Decline in Cotton Prices,* 70th Cong., 1st Sess. (Washington, D.C., 1929), 3; Federal Trade Commission, *Report . . . on Agricultural Income Inquiry: Part I—Principal Farm Products* (Washington, D.C., 1938), 31, 313; Beverly Smith, "King Cotton Himself," *The American Magazine,* CXXV (April 1938), 18-19, 62-68; "Will Clayton's Cotton," *Fortune,* XXXII (Nov. 1945), 137-47, 231-38, (Dec. 1945), 159-63, 231-42; Ellen Clayton Garwood, *Will Clayton: A Short Biography* (Austin, Texas, 1958), 78-95; George Joubert, Jr., "Marketing Louisiana Red River and Mississippi River Delta Cotton," (unpublished M.A. thesis, Louisiana State University, 1954). Messrs. Eric Catmur and Albert O'Hare of the Memphis cotton buying firm of George H. McFadden & Bro., Inc.—one of the largest in the world—were generous of their time and energy in explaining the conduct of their business to me.

War. Indeed, so extensive had these practices become, that the Chicago Board in October 1865 adopted rules and regulations governing the futures trade.[62]

Similar developments took place in the cotton trade. The sale of cotton en route (or "cotton to arrive," as it was termed) was a feature of both the Liverpool and New York markets before the war, but as a speculative venture, it never reached the proportions of the sale and resale of actual cotton on hand. The wartime cotton famine, however, provided an immense stimulus to the "cotton to arrive" business. Those who managed to secure cotton found they could sell it profitably in a rapidly rising market before it actually arrived, and the result was an active speculative trade in cotton to arrive in New York and Liverpool. With the war's end, this business continued and expanded. The Atlantic cable allowed for purchases in the South well in advance of delivery and trading in cotton in transit expanded accordingly. Like their counterparts in grain, cotton speculators began to sell cotton for future delivery which at the time of sale they did not own. Manufacturers, anxious to secure cotton at a known price in the future without having to buy and store all their required cotton in advance, purchased contracts that would guarantee them delivery of the cotton at a later date at an agreed-upon price.[63]

By 1868, futures sales were a regular feature of the cotton market and journals began to report both futures sales and "spot" (actual cotton on the spot) sales.[64] Profit possibilities inevitably attracted speculators in growing numbers not only in New York and Liverpool but in the Southern markets as well. Factors and other merchants in the South were quick to adopt this new form of speculation, although some did not find it congenial. In the summer of 1869, Godfrey Barnsley wrote of "the gambling system . . . so extensively practised last season." Moreover, he complained,

[62] U. S. Department of Agriculture, *Marketing: The Yearbook of Agriculture—1954* (Washington, D.C., [1954]), 324-25; Morton Rothstein, "The International Market for Agricultural Commodities, 1850-1873," in David T. Gilchrist and W. David Lewis (eds.), *Economic Change in the Civil War Era* (Greenville, Del., 1956), 68-70.

[63] E. J. Donnell, *History of Cotton* (New York, 1872), 614; U. S. Commissioner of Corporations, *Report . . . on Cotton Exchanges* (Washington, D.C., 1908) Pt. I, 39-42; Stanley Dumbell, "The Origin of Cotton Futures," *Economic History*, I (May 1927), 259-64.

[64] Dumbell, "The Origin of Cotton Futures," 266; Commissioner of Corporations, *Report on Cotton Exchanges*, 40.

there was already evidence that the new system would continue: "one German House in N. York is said to have already sold 10,000 bales for winter delivery on the Continent."[65] As the season got underway, Barnsley bitterly observed that "the whole business in the staple seems to be assimilating to that of the stock market," but in spite of his reservations, he concluded that "if we are to do any business it appears as if we must go with the current."[66] In late September he wrote an English firm, James Finlay and Company, proposing a "moderate . . . business between N. Orleans and your port [which] might be made profitable through the telegraph, selling 'to arrive' when a margin could be realized." Finlay and Company refused Barnsley's offer, but another firm, R. Lockhart and Dempster, accepted a similar offer in early 1870.[67] Clearly, however, Barnsley was unhappy with futures trading. When the New Orleans Exchange was organized he refused to join because "its main object . . . is to foster sales of 'Futures'—which I look upon as gambling transactions."[68]

While Barnsley was arranging speculation in cotton to arrive, W. W. Gordon was negotiating an outright futures agreement in Savannah:

> The following agreement is this day [August 14, 1869] made between Tison & Gordon and Quentell Nisbet & Co. all merchants of this city. Tison & Gordon agree to deliver to Quentell Nisbet & Co at Savannah in the month of December next sellers option One Hundred (100) Bales of Upland Cotton for which Quentell Nisbet & Co agree to pay Tison & Gordon Twenty Six Cents per pound said cotton to class "Average Good Ordinary." In the event of any dispute arising between the contracting parties as to the classification of the cotton offered by Tison & Gordon the matter shall be submitted to some disinterested and competent third person for decision.[69]

Unlike a cotton to arrive transaction, this agreement was not based on any particular batch of cotton; it merely stipulated that cotton of a certain kind be delivered in the future. Gordon's senior

[65] To Ashbridge Smith & Co., Woodlands, Aug. 16, 1869, Barnsley Collection.

[66] To T. M. Rooker, Woodlands, Sept. 1, 1869, *ibid.*

[67] Barnsley to James Finlay & Co., Woodlands, Sept. 26, 1869; Barnsley to John R. Reid, New Orleans, Feb. 26, 1870, *ibid.*

[68] To "My dear Sir," New Orleans, Feb. 10, 1871, *ibid.*

[69] Gordon Family Papers, Southern Historical Collection. See also agreement dated Savannah, Aug. 17, 1869 between Tison & Gordon and Knoop Hannemann & Co., *ibid.*

partner, W. H. Tison, could not bring himself to participate in such futures speculation. He asked that Gordon risk his own personal funds on the venture as "I believe I prefer to hold off from such operations."[70] He was not, however, averse to sales of cotton in transit, as is indicated in a proposal to his partner in September 1869: "I think that your market [Savannah] & that of Albany are so depressed that prices will not go lower. And that there is quite a margin between us & Li[ver]pool so as to telegraph & sell to arrive."[71]

The objections to futures transactions by men such as Barnsley and Tison were not based merely on their conservative reluctance to try something new. Barnsley had had a bitter experience in the purchase of corn in transit: "I once contracted for a cargo of corn in N[ew] O[rleans]—the sellers offered an inferior quality which was refused. I sued and got judgment for $3500—parties failed, and never recovered a cent and lost the law expenses."[72] While such problems were being raised by the more cautious cotton traders, others felt it best to try to control and regulate the growing trade in futures since there seemed little likelihood that the new methods would be abandoned. As a result, in 1869 the Liverpool Cotton Brokers' Association established a series of rules regulating futures sales; the following year the New York Cotton Exchange was organized and in 1871 the New Orleans Exchange was opened, both of them with rules governing futures trading.[73]

Speculation, then, had brought about the establishment of regulated futures exchanges. Yet, if most transactions were made with an eye to speculation, some were arranged to avoid speculation. Cotton merchants found that they could avoid speculative risk by buying and selling futures contracts in conjunction with the purchases and sales of cotton, the process becoming known as "hedging." New York cotton merchant, Arthur R. Marsh, credited John Rew, a Liverpol merchant, with the insight that led to the establishment of hedging:

[70] To W. W. Gordon, Sweet Springs, W. Va., Aug. 21, 1869, *ibid.*
[71] *Ibid.*, Baltimore, Sept. 22, 1869.
[72] To T. M. Rooker, Woodlands, Sept. 1, 1869, Barnsley Collection. See also Barnsley to James Clunas, New Orleans, Dec. 28, 1869, *ibid.*
[73] Dumbell, "The Origin of Cotton Futures," 262-64; Department of Agriculture, *Marketing*, 325-26; New York Cotton Exchange, *Cotton and Cotton Futures* (New York, 1960), 15-17.

In 1868 or 1869, Mr. Rew saw that the newly laid Atlantic
Cable made it possible for a cotton merchant in Liverpool to
ascertain with unheard-of quickness the price at which actual
cotton could be bought in the Southern States, and the approximate date at which it could be shipped to England. He saw
also that if the price that was being bid in Liverpool for "cotton
to arrive" was high enough to enable him to buy the cotton in
the South and sell contracts for this same "cotton to arrive"
in Liverpool, two or three months later, he could enter into the
transaction with entire safety, as when his cotton reached Liverpool, he could either deliver it to the parties to whom he had
sold the contracts; or, if some spinner was willing to pay a
higher relative price than the holder of the contracts had
agreed to pay, he could buy back his contracts and sell the cotton to the spinner with the larger profit to himself. Here was
a method, then, by which Mr. Rew or any other importer of
cotton into Liverpool could relieve himself of the great risks
attending the handling of a commodity which had become
highly speculative, and go serenely about his business of importing cotton into Great Britain, able to make a fair profit
on every importation, and yet always able to work on a much
narrower margin than any of his old-style competitors, because
they were carrying the merchant's risk, with its alternate profits
and losses, while he had only profits.[74]

In short, hedging involved offsetting each transaction in cotton
with an opposite transaction in futures contracts; that is, cotton
purchased would be balanced by the sale of a futures contract and
cotton sold, by the purchase of a contract. Should prices change,
the gain in one transaction would be balanced or cancelled out by
a loss in the other, thus obviating the risk inherent in a fluctuating
market.[75]

Thus futures trading added to the forces undermining the
commission business in cotton. Some factors were drawn into
speculation, while others joined the exchanges and became brokers.
In either case, the commission business usually was subordinated
to the newer activities. At the same time, cotton merchants, by
utilizing the hedging features of the trade, could buy and accumu-

[74] The Economic Position of the New York Cotton Exchange and its Relation to
the Cotton Trade (New York, 1907), 5-7. See also Dumbell, "The Origin of Cotton
Futures," 264-67.

[75] For a good discussion of hedging, see Alston Hill Garside, Cotton Goes to
Market (New York, 1935); Alonzo Bettis Cox, Cotton: Demand, Supply, Merchandising (Austin, Texas, 1953).

late large stocks of cotton relatively safely, thereby encouraging the growth of large firms buying and storing cotton in the interior for direct shipment to consumers.

When the Civil War ended, King Cotton reascended his throne and for a while the old marketing system returned with him. But changed conditions doomed the old ways. Even as the postwar factorage system struggled to regain its ante bellum position, new forces tended to undermine the factors' hegemony in cotton marketing. Slowly, but steadily, factors were replaced in the cotton trade by furnishing merchants, merchant-buyers, and a new breed of speculators. King Cotton had found new retainers.

CHAPTER TWENTY-FOUR

The Furnishing Merchant

In the early pages of *The Hamlet*, William Faulkner introduces Will Varner, a leading personage of Frenchman's Bend, "the chief man of the country":

> He was the largest landholder and beat supervisor in one county and Justice of the Peace in the next and election commissioner in both, and hence the fountainhead if not of law at least of advice and suggestion. . . . He was a farmer, a usurer, a veterinarian; Judge Benbow of Jefferson once said of him that a milder-mannered man never bled a mule or stuffed a ballot box. He owned most of the good land in the country and held mortgages on most of the rest. He owned the store and the cotton gin and the combined grist mill and blacksmith shop in the village proper and it was considered, to put it mildly, bad luck for a man of the neighborhood to do his trading or gin his cotton or grind his meal or shoe his stock anywhere else.

A conversation with a prospective tenant succinctly reveals Varner's business methods:

> "What do you rent for?"
> "Third and fourth," Varner said. "Furnish out of the store here. No cash."
> "I see. Furnish in six-bit dollars."
> "That's right," Varner said pleasantly. . . .
> "I'll take it," he said.[1]

In a few words the novelist touches the essence of the furnishing merchant system in the post bellum South. As landlord, store-keeper, and creditor, the country merchant became the most important economic power in the Southern countryside.

According to Thomas D. Clark, their most perceptive student, the postwar country stores "were symbolic of the creation of a new southern economic system from the wreckage of the old. Perhaps no other institution more clearly embodied so much of the intimate story of the New South."[2] Clark did not exaggerate. Indeed, the institution was more significant in the New South than the facts Henry Grady and his followers observed. It involved more people and was more widely characteristic of post bellum Southern life. But the emphasis on the new should not obscure the fact that the furnishing merchant system was heavily freighted with remnants of the ante bellum South—the factorage system, the country store, and slavery. As a system of financing and marketing the crop, it resembled previous institutions serving the same functions; as a social organization, it bore the direct influence of the slave society that preceded it.

The legal supports for the furnishing merchant system were the crop lien laws passed by Southern legislatures in the years immediately following the Civil War. The essence of all these laws was the same—in return for credit, the farmer gave a lien on his unplanted or growing crop. By advancing credit, usually in the form of supplies, clothing, and luxuries rather than cash, the lender acquired prior rights on all the cotton produced by the borrower. C. Vann Woodward has called the lien system "one of the strangest contractual relationships in the history of finance."[3] Yet, few who had participated in prewar cotton financing would find it unfamiliar. Essentially, the lien system was a codification of the ante bellum factorage system which had prevailed mainly under common law and tradition. Throughout the ante bellum period factors advanced credit on the security of the growing crop, usually relying

[1] William Faulkner, *The Hamlet* (New York, 1965) 5, 8-9. The novel, published in 1940 as the first in a trilogy, depicts the fall of Varner and his replacement by Flem Snopes. Less amiable and infinitely more evil than Varner, Snopes retains the same general methods in the business he succeeds in wresting from its owner.

[2] *Pills, Petticoats and Plows: The Southern Country Store* (Indianapolis, 1944), 22. Scholarly and amusing, this study covers all phases of the post bellum store's activities.

[3] *Origins of the New South, 1877-1913* (Baton Rouge, 1951), 180.

on the planters' promises to consign the cotton to them but sometimes requiring a signed agreement to that effect. State courts
generally ruled that factors advancing supplies had certain prior
rights on the crop consigned to them even in the absence of a
written agreement to that effect;[4] but it was ante bellum tradition
rather than law which dictated that cotton be sent to the factors
providing advances. Traditional safeguards gave way to legal strictures, but the essence of the relationship remained. The manifest
similarities between factorage and the lien system led Charles
Nordhoff to observe that he could see no difference between the
Georgia lien law which he condemned and the same "evil" which
he had observed in operation in Louisiana "in slavery times."[5]

Whereas the word of a gentleman had usually sufficed to secure
the ante bellum factor for his advances, postwar factors began to
expect the legal safeguards of the lien system—even from gentlemen. When a Colonel Remington sought an advance of $8,000
from his factor, Tison and Gordon, W. H. Tison insisted that the
colonel offer adequate security. "The day is past & gone for such
[unsecured] credits," he observed. "It is those persons whom we
have most confidence in who have betrayed us."[6] Some planters
seem to have had little difficulty making the transition. "I most
certainly did not suppose you would advance supplies simply on
my *promise* to pay," a planter explained when his New Orleans
factor inquired about security for the advance he had requested.[7] In
his letter asking for an advance from Stephen D. Heard "to make a
crop," a Georgia planter added: "I will pledge myself to send you
my entire crop of cotton if you will furnish me with 1000 lbs
bacon & 250 bushls of corn & give you a Lean [sic] on the crop."[8]

Other planters were unhappy with the new system. One of
Heard's new customers refused to give the lien requested. He was

[4] See Chap. IV, above.

[5] *The Cotton States in the Spring and Summer of 1875* (New York, 1876), 109.
See also *Bradstreet's*, IV (Nov. 9, 1881), 322; Roger W. Shugg, *Origins of Class
Struggle in Louisiana* (Baton Rouge, 1939), 110; M. B. Hammond, *The Cotton
Industry* (New York, 1897), 107-109.

[6] To W. W. Gordon, New York, July 2, 1869, Gordon Family Papers, Southern
Historical Collection, University of North Carolina Library, Chapel Hill, N. C. See
also Tison to Gordon, Saratoga Springs, July 9, 1869, *ibid.*

[7] Burrus to Harris Parker & Co., n.p., Dec. 15, 1883, John C. Burrus Papers,
Mississippi Department of Archives and History, Jackson, Miss.

[8] James N. Lynch to Heard, Eatonton, Jan. 25, 1867, Stephen D. Heard Papers,
Southern Historical Collection, University of North Carolina Library, Chapel Hill,
N. C.

emphatic, if not very explicit, in his objections: "My opposition to giving the Lien does not arise from any mistrust in yourselves, nor from any desire to take the least advantage of you, but it is a fixed determination on my part never to give a Mortgage or Lien as long as there is a shadow of a chance to get along without it."[9] Another customer, one from prewar days, was insulted when asked to give a lien on his crop. He found it very "strange" that, after having dealt with Heard for fifteen years, the factor suddenly desired a lien on his crop for goods furnished. "I would say to you that my word is my bond and as for giving a lean [sic] I dont feel disposed to do so."[10]

But the lien system soon prevailed, not because the Southern planter's word had become less secure but because his property had become less valuable. He no longer owned slaves, and land values had dropped sharply after the Civil War. Moreover, the growth of tenancy meant most dealings were with cotton growers who had virtually no possessions at all; a tenant did not even own the little acreage on which he proposed to plant. The lien system thus arose not as a conspiracy to exploit the farmer—although as time went on it would be hard to convince many farmers of this—but in response to an immediate need. With land next to valueless and with little else to secure loans, the lien laws guaranteed that the one thing the cotton grower did have (or would have in the future)—cotton— would be used to repay the loan. Such a scheme, it was hoped, would induce those with means to lend the necessary funds to those who lacked the resources to get into production.[11] Thus, when the Mississippi legislature entitled the state's lien law an "Act for Encouraging Agriculture,"[12] the aim was not to hide a vicious scheme behind a pleasant euphemism. Postwar legislatures thought the lien laws would indeed encourage the rebuilding of agriculture. Naturally enough, the means proposed to achieve this goal resembled the methods used so successfully before the war.

Although the lien system resembled the factorage system, it

[9] John D. Munnerlyn to Heard & Son, Waynesboro, Ga., May 6, 1870, *ibid.*
[10] C. E. Barefield to Heard, Burke County, Ga., May 13, 1870, *ibid.*
[11] See U. S. Congress, Senate, Committee on Agriculture and Forestry, *Report . . . on Condition of Cotton Growers,* 53rd Cong., 3rd Sess., Report 986 (1895), I, 294, 310; Rupert B. Vance, *Human Factors in Cotton Culture* (Chapel Hill, 1929), 63; E. Merton Coulter, *The South During Reconstruction, 1865-1877* (Baton Rouge, 1947), 194.
[12] Quoted in Woodward, *Origins of the New South,* 180.

was also different. For one thing, the scale of business was vastly changed. The number of people directly involved increased whereas the individual transactions were usually small, so small as to have been beneath the interest of all but a few of the prewar factors. The change came as a result of emancipation and the rise of tenancy, the most important economic consequence of which was the altered nature of the demand. In the ante bellum period, as *Hunt's Merchants' Magazine* put it in an 1869 article describing business changes in the South since the war, "the planter . . . [had been] a sort of small jobber, or large retail dealer who provided for those dependent upon him everything they needed in the way of clothing, food, shoes, medicines, &c."[13] But the ante bellum planter was a "retail dealer" of a very peculiar kind: his "customers" had no choice concerning their "purchases"; and his aim was to keep his "sales" to a minimum. Emancipation destroyed this peculiar form of business. It left a propertyless and penniless group of ex-slaves faced with the necessity of providing food and clothing for themselves and their families. Here was a potential market of a more conventional sort. The artificial barriers imposed by slavery—the natural economic desire of the slaveowner to keep his expenses down—were removed; the freedmen now constituted a demand limited only by their income and the manner in which they chose to spend it. The failure to institute a wage labor system and the consequent growth of tenancy[14] increased this potential demand. The tenant, be he sharecropper or renter, not only had to provide for his personal needs and wants but also had to buy supplies required to plant a crop. The crop lien system served to turn the potential demand into a real one and the institution of the furnishing merchant arose to exploit the new market.

The furnishing merchant system differed from factorage in still another way. The storekeeper often took legal possession of the cotton on which he had a lien. Unlike the factor who merely served as the grower's agent in seeking out a sale, the storekeeper ordinarily

[13] LXI (Nov. 1869), 363. The same article may be found in *Commercial and Financial Chronicle*, IX (Oct. 23, 1869), 519.

[14] *Commercial and Financial Chronicle*, IX (Sept. 4, 1869), 294-95; *Hunt's Merchants' Magazine*, LXI (Oct. 1869), 271-74; Sir George Campbell, *White and Black* (London, 1879), 307; Hammond, *The Cotton Industry*, 124-25; Francis B. Simkins, "The Problems of South Carolina Agriculture After the Civil War," *North Carolina Historical Review*, VII (Jan. 1930), 56-57; Fred A. Shannon, *The Farmer's Last Frontier* (New York, 1945), 83-89; Coulter, *The South During Reconstruction*, 76-79.

bought cotton sent him to satisfy the terms of the lien. Sometimes a merchant stipulated that the cotton on which he had a lien be sold to him. Indeed, James Moffatt, who had a store in Troy, Tennessee, bought his customers' cotton while still in the fields. His lien agreements typically stated that customers had "this day sold to Moffat & Sons . . . Cotton now growing" at the "customary price when delivered," any proceeds exceeding the amount advanced to be paid the grower in cash.[15] G. W. Bennett gave the customers of his Cheneyville, Louisiana, store more choice. The grower was required "to deliver his entire crop of Cotton for the year" to Bennett but had the option of selling the staple to Bennett, or, if dissatisfied with the storekeeper's price, of allowing Bennett to ship it elsewhere to be sold.[16] A slightly different agreement was that made by William Henry Woods and Company, who supplied a Georgia farmer, John Cromley, with fertilizer on credit and took a lien on his crops, "growing or to be grown" during the current year. The farmer had the choice of a cash settlement or "paying . . . in Low Middling Cotton, at (15) cents per pound, well and securely baled."[17]

Even if he were not obligated to sell his cotton to his furnishing merchant, the farmer often felt it to be to his advantage to do so. Edward King noticed that the storekeeper could "often pay the planter and his cooperating freedmen a much higher price for cotton than the market quotations seem to warrant," the profits from his sales during the year easily absorbing the little extra money he paid out.[18] Moreover, shipments away from local markets meant additional costs for transportation, insurance, and commissions. As improvements in transportation and communications brought buyers deep into the interior, growers found these costs increasingly redundant and tended to avoid them.

Thus, unlike the ante bellum planter, the postwar grower seldom

[15] For numerous examples, all in much the same language, see "Journal" (Vol. 73), James Strong Moffatt Papers, Archives Division, Tennessee State Library and Archives, Nashville, Tenn.

[16] See a group of agreements made between Bennett and his customers in Ledger, 1859-1871, George W. Bennett Papers, Department of Archives and Manuscripts, Louisiana State University, Baton Rouge, La.

[17] Agreement between Woods & Co. and Cromley, n.p., March 14, 1872, printed in Chester McArthur Destler (ed.), "The Post-Bellum South: Some Letters and Documents," *Georgia Historical Quarterly*, XLVI (March 1962), 84.

[18] *The Great South* (Hartford, Conn., 1875), 53. See also *Bradstreet's*, XIII (April 10, 1886), 226.

delayed the sale of his crop. Instead of employing a factor to seek out the best sale in the South, the North, or in Europe, postwar growers usually sold their cotton quickly, ordinarily to the nearest buyer. They lacked the financial independence as well as the ability to secure the credit required to delay a sale. As a result, within a few weeks after his cotton was ginned, the farmer or tenant had usually sold his crop. The nearest buyer was ordinarily a merchant in the local town. The smallest towns might have but a single buyer, the local furnishing merchant, whereas the larger towns had a number of furnishing merchants, along with factors, speculators, and representatives of the buying firms. "To sell the cotton was a simple operation," William D. Kelley noted after a trip South in the 1880's. The grower came to town with his crop, often unginned, and within hours he sold it, purchased a supply of store goods, and was on his way home.[19]

If the credit arrangements associated with the furnishing merchant system showed the influences of the ante bellum factorage system, the scale and methods of business resembled that of the old country store. Like those of ante bellum times, the postwar stores carried a general line of merchandise; stocks of farm supplies and tempting luxuries were prominently displayed. "M. Faler & Co.," the letter head of a Hazlehurst, Mississippi, store advertised, "Dealers in Dry Goods, Clothing, Hardware, Boots, Shoes, Groceries, Bagging, Ropes, Ties, Etc."[20] The "Etc." usually included everything from mules to ribbons. And all was available on deferred payment after the farmer or tenant went through the simple process of giving the merchant a lien on the crop he proposed to plant.

The services offered by the country storekeeper were as varied as the goods which lined his shelves. In addition to supplies, the merchant sold food, clothing, and tools along with tobacco, whiskey, and other luxuries. Since few small farmers and tenants could afford to own gins and compresses, use of this machinery

---

[19] South Carolina, State Board of Agriculture, *South Carolina: Resources and Population; Institutions and Industries* (Charleston, S. C., 1883), 162, 193; William D. Kelley, *The Old South and the New* (New York, 1886), 129-30; U. S. Industrial Commission, *Report . . . on the Distribution of Farm Products* (Washington, D. C., 1901), 166-67; C. D. Brooks, *Cotton* (New York, 1898), 244; Harry Bates Brown, *Cotton* (2nd ed.; New York, 1938), 444-45.

[20] M. Faler and Company Papers, Mississippi Department of Archives and History, Jackson, Miss.

was usually available, for a price, at the store.[21] Storekeepers also advanced money to pay mail order bills, doctor bills, church contributions, taxes, and other expenses. Should a customer have a surplus of funds, the storekeeper would hold the money in safe-keeping for him.[22]

The storekeeper did not confine his business to those who had given him liens on their crops. Often, substantial planters availed themselves of his services. Thus, H. R. Johnson and Company of Americus, Georgia, in addition to serving as furnishing merchants for local farmers and tenants, also acted as factors for local planters, making commission sales in Americus and elsewhere for customers who consigned cotton to them. In return for consignments, the Americus firm advanced cash to planters and paid their bills, including wages of farm workers.[23] Planters who continued to deal with factors in the coastal cities found local merchants willing to act as receiving and forwarding agents,[24] to advance funds, and endorse and discount drafts.[25] Often planters paid the wages of hired hands in scrip which could be used only at a given store, a practice which widespread opposition and state legislation failed to end.[26]

Accounts were settled at the end of the year after the harvest. Cotton and other produce were taken to balance the books, or, if the cotton was not sold to the advancing merchant, the farmer paid cash after selling his crop elsewhere. Farmers many times found work at the store after their crop was brought in and for their services—hauling, ginning, and marking cotton, for example—re-

---

21 South Carolina State Board of Agriculture, *South Carolina: Resources and Population; Institutions and Industries*, 38, 589-90; *Bradstreet's*, XIII (April 10, 1866), 226. Store records and advertisements often indicated that there was a gin on the premises.

22 Clark, *Pills, Petticoats, and Plows*, 79, 98-99.

23 See receipts, invoices, and accounts in box labeled "Bills and a/c Receivable," Harrold Brothers Papers, Emory University Library, Atlanta, Ga.

24 See letters to E. F. Golsan & Co. of New Orleans from Kenneth Baillio and Pitre & Carriere, both of Washington, La.; Norwood Bros., Jefferson, Texas; and Fellows & Co., Camden, Ark., dated variously in the 1870's, Golsan Brothers Papers, Department of Archives and Manuscripts, Louisiana State University, Baton Rouge, La.

25 C. A. Walton & Co. to Mrs. Richey, Vicksburg, Jan. 29, 1867, Mrs. Nancy Richey Papers, Mississippi Department of Archives and History, Jackson, Miss.

26 Campbell, *White and Black*, 341; Ernest Lyon, "The Colored Man in the South: His Present Condition and Future Prospects," *The Independent*, XLVII (March 7, 1895), 298-99; Clark, *Pills, Petticoats and Plows*, 78-79; George Brown Tindall, *South Carolina Negroes, 1877-1900* (Columbia, S. C., 1952), 99-100.

ceived credit on their accounts.[27] Store goods commonly had two prices, a lesser price being charged for cash purchases. Few farmers had the cash, however, and most paid the credit prices—what Faulkner's Snopes called purchases with "six-bit dollars." Usually interest charges were not assessed separately; such costs were buried in the inflated credit prices. Estimates of what these interest charges would have been if figured separately, range from 30 to 110 percent.[28]

The furnishing merchant system changed little over the years. New products made their appearance, transportation and communication facilities improved, bookkeeping methods became a bit more sophisticated—but the system as a whole remained virtually unchanged. The description given by *Hunt's Merchants' Magazine* in 1869 differed little from that in the famous report, *The Collapse of Cotton Tenancy*, published almost seventy years later.[29] In fact, the business of the furnishing merchant differed little from that of the ante bellum storekeeper. Both were general merchants providing goods on credit; both numbered small farmers among their most important customers; and both took cotton and other merchandise in payment of debts.

Reflecting this continuity in the history of the country store was the fact that many of the postwar storekeepers were ante bellum merchants who had survived the war. A few, like H. R. Johnson and Company of Americus, Georgia, had maintained an active business throughout the war; when the conflict ended, the firm had ample resources to continue commercial activities on a large scale.[30] Other ante bellum storekeepers continued on a less

[27] For examples see "Ledger, 1871-1872," George W. Bennett Papers; "New Cotton Book," James Strong Moffatt Papers; H. T. T. Dupree Plantation Account Books, Mississippi Department of Archives and History, Jackson, Miss.; Drane and Dupree Papers, also in Mississippi Department of Archives and History; Account Book of Henry Strong, microfilm copy of MSS in Arkansas History Commission, Department of Archives and History, Little Rock, Ark. *passim*; S. G. Burney Ledger, Mississippi Department of Archives and History.

[28] Woodward, *Origins of the New South*, 180-81; Hammond, *The Cotton Industry*, 153-55; Shannon, *The Farmer's Last Frontier*, 91-92; Thomas D. Clark, "The Furnishing and Supply System in Southern Agriculture Since 1865," *Journal of Southern History*, XII (Feb. 1946), 28.

[29] *Hunt's Merchants' Magazine*, LXI (Nov. 1869), 363-65; Charles S. Johnson, Edwin R. Embree, and W. W. Alexander, *The Collapse of Cotton Tenancy* (Chapel Hill, 1935). See also Rupert B. Vance, *Human Geography of the South* (Chapel Hill, 1932), 177-204, 261-74.

[30] See letters from Johnson & Co. to R. R. Graves & Co. in Letter Book, July 29, 1865–Jan. 15, 1866, Harrold Brothers Papers.

elaborate scale. In Montroy, Arkansas, for example, Henry Strong reopened his store after the war, adding the local sharecroppers to his clientele of small farmers.[31] Still other prewar merchants, bankrupted by the war, were able to recoup their losses and re-establish their businesses by taking advantage of changing economic conditions. Whitelaw Reid noted an example of this process when he visited the Georgia Sea Islands in 1865. He stopped at a group of stores dubbed by Federal officers, "Robbers Row." The storekeepers enjoyed an active trade with freedmen and occupying Federal troops, earning in the process "fabulous" profits. Reid recorded how one of the merchants had made a fortune: "He was a bankrupt merchant, honest, but penniless. He believed the fall of these islands would open a field for handsome trade, and came down, as a sailor, to see for himself. Returning, he told his creditors what he had seen; and they had faith enough in him to make up for him a stock of goods, which he sold out immediately, at such a profit as to enable him to make subsequent purchases on his own account. He has paid off every dollar of his indebtedness, and is a wealthy man."[32]

New opportunities, of course, brought newcomers into the furnishing merchant business. When Robert Somers visited the South in 1870-1871, he reported that "much of the storekeeping business is conducted by sharp, active young men of Jewish aspect" who had been "sent down by firms in New York and other large towns to sell goods at a profit of 100 to 200 per cent. to the more impoverished class of planters, and to advance money on cotton at the approach of the picking season at as much interest as they can extort."[33] Although others also noted the influx of Jewish merchants into the South after the war,[34] it should be noted that many of the Jewish storekeepers had been in business during the ante bellum period.[35] Nor did Jews dominate the furnishing merchant business. Most storekeepers were indigenous.

Charles H. Otken charged in his angry polemic, *The Ills of the South*, that the furnishing merchants, a "moneyed tyranny" that

[31] Account Book of Henry Strong, *passim*.

[32] *After the War: A Southern Tour, May 1, 1865, to May 1, 1866* (London, 1866), 122-24.

[33] *The Southern States Since the War, 1870-1871* (New York, 1871), 151. See also 198.

[34] Coulter, *The South During Reconstruction*, 202-203.

[35] This conclusion is based on the names listed in Southern business directories.

reduced "its victims to a coarse species of servile slavery," were those who had accumulated vast fortunes through wartime speculation. These were Southerners, exempted from military service because of age or because they secured substitutes. Before the war these men "were worth nothing, or at best a few thousand dollars," but speculation in cotton during the war left them rich at its termination and they were able to dictate credit terms to poverty stricken planters and farmers.[36]

Otken's explanation was simplistic. Wartime speculation, as has been shown, was often a means to a fortune; indeed, when the war ended, there was a rush into the storekeeping business. "Every body seemed to have the merchant fever," wrote a North Carolinian reporting the opening of eight new stores in the little town of Oxford by the fall of 1865.[37] But not all storekeepers began business with resources garnered during the war. Many others, often with limited means and experience, seized opportunities to open country stores.

One of these was George W. Bennett of Rapides Parish, Louisiana, who in 1871 opened a store on the road between Cheneyville and Bunkie, Louisiana.[38] Apparently there was little more than his store in the immediate vicinity. The post office address on his early letters was Cheneyville; only later, after the store acquired a post office, was the locality dignified with the name, Bennettville. Bennett began his business with little capital, receiving his initial financing from New Orleans merchants. His first letter to a New Orleans factor, Tate and Company, contained $100, an order for supplies, and a promise to pay the balance on his order in sixty days. His plans were modest, his education obviously limited: "I have recently commence buisness on a small scael. your Firm was recomended to me by my freinds. If you will do my business on as good terms as any one else, I will continue to favor you with my patronage. my terms are cash altogether. What few goods I want will meet payments promply."[39]

Bennett did not intend to limit his patronage to Tate and

---

[36] *The Ills of the South* (New York, 1894), 8-11.

[37] A. R. Burwell to William Henry Burwell, Richmond, Va., Sept. 23, 1865, Wm. H. Burwell Papers, Southern Historical Collection, University of North Carolina Library, Chapel Hill, N. C.

[38] The following discussion is based on the George W. Bennett Papers, an extensive collection running to 50 volumes and covering the years 1871-1917.

[39] Bennett to Tate & Co., Cheneyville, La., April 21, 1871, *ibid.*

Company, for a week later he dispatched a letter to another New Orleans firm, Stevens and Seymore. Again he enclosed some cash with his order—this time only $10—and asked for three or four months to pay the balance.[40] A week later he wrote still another firm, New Orleans cotton factors Renshaw Cammack and Company, offering his future business in return for an order of supplies on credit. Two weeks earlier he had told Tate and Company that he was doing a cash business only, but to Renshaw Cammack he indicated that he was "furnishing a few industrus [sic] hard working Freedman [sic] this year on their Crop."[41] Apparently all three of the firms agreed to his terms, for in the next few months Bennett wrote a series of letters to each of them, ordering more supplies and making small remittances, but never paying up any bill completely. As the cotton harvest began, Bennett pressed his factors for more aid. In early September he wrote Renshaw Cammack that "an honest hard working freedman" had offered "to do business with me." "If you will send Two Bbls. Port & one sck Coffee, I can ship you that much more Cotton."[42] In addition to credit in the form of supplies, Renshaw Cammack also gave Bennett permission to draw on them for cash; four days later, he sent Tate and Company a draft on Renshaw Cammack as part payment on his bill.[43] Thus far, neither firm had received any cotton from Bennett.

His first shipment went to Renshaw Cammack on September 26.[44] Shortly thereafter, he wrote the New Orleans factor for a cash advance "to buy Cotton with."[45] A few days later, Tate and Company received its first shipment. Bennett indicated that he had purchased the three bales being sent for $212.40, and he asked the factor to hold the cotton if he were unable to sell at a profit. "I have to work hard for what little I get & am not able to loose [sic] anything."[46]

Such was the beginning of a small furnishing merchant in rural Louisiana. Starting with a little cash and the support of a few New Orleans merchants, Bennett began a business which was to

40 Bennett to Stevens & Seymore, Cheneyville, April 27, 1871, *ibid.*
41 Bennett to Renshaw Cammack & Co., Cheneyville, May 2, 1871, *ibid.*
42 Letter dated Cheneyville, Sept. 11, 1871, *ibid.*
43 Bennett to Tate & Co., Cheneyville, Sept. 15, 1871, *ibid.*
44 Bennett to Renshaw Cammack & Co., Cheneyville, Sept. 26, 1871, *ibid.*
45 Bennett to Renshaw Cammack & Co., Cheneyville, Oct. 9, 1871, *ibid.*
46 Bennett to Tate & Co., Cheneyville, Oct. 13, 1871, *ibid.*

last well into the twentieth century. He furnished local farmers and tenants on credit, receiving produce, especially cotton, in payment. In addition, he bought cotton outright for cash when local growers brought their crops to the gin which he operated in connection with his store. In the early years, numerous New Orleans merchants and factors supplied him with goods for his store, carrying his bill until cotton he owned was sent to the Crescent City to be sold.

What happened on the road to Cheneyville, was repeated in remote areas throughout the South. Thomas Clark has described the phenomenon: "Thus it was that buried in bends of the rivers, hidden behind mountains, perched on rises of ground besides bayous, and strung along thousands of miles of virtually impassable roads grew hundreds of villages and towns, each one originally no more than a single store building. They were places such as Shoe Heel, Emmalena, White Oak, Sawdust Valley, Dewey Rose, Talno, Ball Ground, Cerro Gordo, Merrilton, Tyrus, Piney Woods, Yocna, Chorique and Who'd-a-Thought-It known only to the natives, the drummers, Dun and Bradstreet, country politicians and postal inspectors."[47] When the Census Office made its massive survey of cotton production in 1880, the importance of the country stores in financing and marketing the cotton crop became clear. With few exceptions, the furnishing merchant system prevailed in the cotton areas of every Southern state.[48]

Here, then, of course, was the basic difference between the pre- and postwar stores. Although the ante bellum store had been an important economic agency in the Southern countryside, in terms of cotton marketing it had always been an adjunct of the factorage system, extending that system into the hinterland to small farmers and planters. The postwar store in contrast served not to extend the factorage system, but to undermine it. The growing number of postwar stores was a reflection of the fact that, as Edward King put it, "the whole character of the cotton trade has been gradually changing since the war."[49]

[47] *Pills, Petticoats and Plows*, 27. See also Francis B. Simkins, "The Solution of Post-Bellum Agricultural Problems in South Carolina," *North Carolina Historical Review*, VII (April 1930), 214-15; Vance, *Human Factors in Cotton Culture*, 63.

[48] Eugene W. Hilgard, "Report on Cotton Production in the United States," in U. S. Department of the Interior, Census Office, *Tenth Census* (1880) (Washington, D. C., 1884), V, VI, *passim*.

[49] *The Great South*, 53.

While ante bellum factorage and storekeeping influenced the credit and business relationships associated with the furnishing merchant system, many of the social relationships connected with the system reflected the influence of slavery. This is especially clear in the operations of the plantation stores—stores initially organized by the planters themselves in an attempt to solve the new problems associated with a free labor force. Released from slavery but never provided with the resources to maintain himself, the Negro after the Civil War was forced to turn to the planter class for aid. With the wage-labor system that grew up in the first few years after the war arose the plantation stores. An Italian visitor, entertained in New Orleans in 1867 by Edmond J. Forstall, banker, cotton merchant, and planter, noted these stores and something of their significance: "Before the war his [Forstall's] numerous slaves lived under a patriarchal regime. He provided most of their food and looked after their welfare. . . . In former days he had an immense capital tied up in slaves, which were always a precarious investment. . . . Now he pays his laborers a dollar a day in store orders, with which they are able to purchase food and clothing at his plantation store. Accounts are balanced weekly."[50] If Forstall was relieved of his "precarious investment," his former slaves probably found their freedom under such arrangements more apparent than real. Their tasks were the same as they had been under slavery; food and clothing continued to come from the master through his store.

Even when cash, rather than store orders, was paid the workers, circumstances often varied but little. Whitelaw Reid witnessed a payday at one of the many plantation stores he saw on his Southern travels. The Negro workers were paid in cash, but, the planter informed Reid, half of their monthly wages was withheld until the crop was finally sold so as to discourage the workers from leaving before the end of the year. From the half which was paid was first deducted the cost of purchases made by the workers on credit at the plantation store during the month. Some of the Negroes received nothing. Many had ended the month in debt to the planter, but they were never informed how much they owed. Secrecy was necessary, the planter explained, to keep the debt-

---

[50] Giulio Adamoli, "Letters From America, 1867," printed in *Louisiana Historical Quarterly*, VI (April 1923), 274.

[51] *After the War*, 525-30, and *passim*.

ridden Negroes from running away.[51] Again, freedmen who worked all month, received food and clothing from the planter at his store, and then were informed that their purchases balanced their wages, probably could see little meaning in their free status.

Freedmen might find their condition reminiscent of slavery, but planters usually discovered the store to be a good source of profit. "Many planters keep stores for niggers, and sell 'em flour, prints, jewelry and trinkets, and charge two or three prices for everything," a Louisiana planter told J. T. Trowbridge in 1865.[52] "We keep a store here," the overseer on a wage-labor plantation informed Edward King, "and, Saturday nights, most of the money they [the Negro workers] have earned comes back to us in trade."[53]

Gradually, wage labor gave way to various forms of tenancy, but the plantation stores usually remained, and new ones sprang up. Now the planter had become a furnishing merchant for his tenants. When Charles Nordhoff visited the South in 1875, he found plantation stores in Arkansas, Louisiana, Mississippi, and Georgia[54] —and they existed elsewhere as well.[55] His description of the operation of one of these stores clearly indicated that planter and furnishing merchant had been united in a single person:

> The planter keeps on the place a store at which renters may buy their supplies, and where they get a moderate credit. He also keeps a cotton-gin and a grist-mill, for the use of which he makes a charge; and he takes care to get his year's rent out of the first of the crop. In practice, furthermore, the planter finds it necessary to ride daily through his fields to see that the renters are at work, and to aid them with his advice. During the winter, he hires them to chop wood for his own use, and to split rails and keep up the fences.[56]

The records of Mississippi plantation owner Eli J. Capell illustrate both the transformation from wage labor to tenancy and the transition of planter to furnishing merchant. Capell's agreements with his tenants stipulated that he would supply the land, work animals, and heavy tools such as wagons and plows, while the tenant supplied the small tools—axes and hoes—and fed and

[52] *A Picture of the Desolated States; and the Work of Restoration, 1865-1868* (Hartford, Conn., 1868), 392.
[53] *The Great South*, 298.
[54] *The Cotton States*, 38, 70, 84, 106.
[55] Hilgard, "Report on Cotton Production," *Tenth Census* (1880), V, VI, *passim*.
[56] *The Cotton States*, 38.

clothed himself. Expenses of repairing and maintaining the gin, sheds, wagons, and plows, as well as the cost of feeding the work animals, were to be divided equally between tenant and landowner. This was a typical sharecropping agreement,[57] yet the language employed was often that used in wage-labor agreements. The sharecroppers were referred to as "laborers"; the cost of tools lost by the laborers "shall be deducted from their wages"; failure to live up to the agreement meant the laborers "shall be subject to be discharged and forfeit all wages due." The so-called wages, however, were simply a share of the crop: "The crops produced shall be divided equally between said proprietor [Capell] and said laborers, subject to the privilege of the proprietor for advances made to the laborers."[58]

The "advances" referred to were provisions and luxuries supplied on credit by Capell from his store.[59] At the end of the year when books were balanced, Capell's tenants rarely had much owing them. Indeed, they often ended the year in debt to Capell, as did one Judge Scott and his partners in 1870. Scott was the head of a "company" of three men who worked together and shared expenses and profits. In 1870, the company raised 5 bales of cotton which netted $259.58. Capell first deducted his half share as landlord— $129.79. From his tenants' half he deducted $15.10 for their share of repairing the gin, ginning the cotton, and supplying bagging and ties. This left Scott's company with $114.69, or $38.23 each for the year's work. But this income had already been spent at Capell's store. Capell recorded the three men's "Store a/c" which came to $166.22 for the year, and laconically closed the account: "Bal now due me by Scott is $51.53."[60]

As both landlord and furnishing merchant, the postwar planter was in a position to reap huge profits. A Mississippi planter boasted that when he rented his land to former slaves he was able to receive

[57] Legally, a tenant and a sharecropper are different. Strictly speaking, a tenant is one who pays a fixed rent—in money or, perhaps, in a given amount of produce— and then is free to grow what he likes on the land. A sharecropper agrees to grow certain crops which he then divides with the landowner. In practice, there was little difference between the two. Both grew cotton and both turned to the furnishing merchant for credit. See Shannon, *Farmer's Last Frontier*, 88-89.

[58] Articles of agreement between Capell and laborers, Jan. 21, 1868, Eli J. Capell Papers, Louisiana Department of Archives and Manuscripts, Louisiana State University, Baton Rouge, La.

[59] Daybook, 1849-1876; Daybook of Sales, 1886-1887, *ibid.*

[60] Statement of Judge Scott's a/c, 1870, *ibid.*

an annual income from his land "amounting to nearly its full value." In addition, he furnished renters supplies from his store, receiving a lien on their crops. "Now, my little piece here aint more than a couple of hundred acres," he concluded, "but it's paying me more than double what it did when I 'worked' fifty 'niggers' on it."[61]

A planter who rented out his lands and then opened a store to furnish his tenants had, of course, become a merchant as well as a landowner. Often, however, the movement toward uniting the two callings came from the other direction as well, as merchants began to acquire land. Charles Otken charged that the nefarious operation of the credit system allowed merchants to take land from farmers and planters. "Some merchants took land because they could not help themselves," he admitted, but many others, with a "strong hankering to become large landowners," conducted their business in such a way as to fulfill their dreams.[62] The implication of conspiracy notwithstanding, Otken did correctly recognize the tendency for furnishing merchants to become landlords.

In the first place, not all planters were successful in their efforts to rent out parcels of their land and to open a store. The Davis family of Alabama, for example, was unable to hold on to its plantation. Left with no resources but land after the war, they tried to rebuild their fortunes through various forms of tenancy, agreeing to provide workers on their land with supplies on credit. To get these goods, the Davises had to give mortgages on their land as well as crop liens to secure a local merchant. The ventures were never profitable, and each year the merchant appropriated part of the land through a mortgage foreclosure. Finally, in 1901, the last two hundred acres were lost.[63]

Efforts to protect landowners by law were unavailing. In Georgia, for example, the lien law first passed in 1866 restricted its provision to landlords. Except in 1873 and 1874, when the law was temporarily extended to include all merchants, only a landlord supplying his tenants could get a legal lien on a tenant's crops. Unless the landlord was financially independent, however, the law offered

---

[61] [Robert W. Andrews], *The Life and Adventures of Capt. Robert W. Andrews of Sumter, South Carolina* (Boston, 1887), 67.

[62] *Ills of the South*, 38.

[63] Weymouth T. Jordan, *Hugh Davis and His Alabama Plantation* (University, Ala., 1948), 160-68.

scant protection. The landlord supplied the tenant, but then he had to turn to the merchant to supply himself. Before granting the aid, the merchant required a guarantee from the landlord, usually in the form of a mortgage. In case of default, the land could be taken in foreclosure proceedings.[64]

Even in those places where the lien law allowed tenants to give liens directly to the merchant, the storekeeper might demand that the landowner also assume responsibility for the advance given his tenant.[65] In February 1883, for example, a tenant on John Burrus' plantation in Bolivar County, Mississippi, wrote his landlord that his furnishing merchant had repossessed his mule and wagon and that he was unable to get these necessities returned so as to be able to get back to work "without your aid or Endorsement." Burrus was forced to give this aid before a Mound Landing merchant, W. E. Ringo and Company, would furnish the tenant. The dangers in such an arrangement became apparent when accounts were rendered in early 1884. After the tenant's cotton was sold he had a debt of over $700. "We could not advance him this year unless under a similar arrangement with you as last year," Ringo and Company warned.[66]

The homestead exemptions were another method used to protect landowners, especially the small farmers. Under these laws, land and other property up to a given value were exempt from foreclosure by creditors.[67] These laws, too, offered little protection. Lenders simply required borrowers to waive these rights before they extended the loans.[68]

Thus, while some planters were becoming storekeepers, others were losing their lands to storekeepers. The plantation itself often remained intact, although in many places the ante bellum planters

[64] Enoch Marvin Banks, *The Economics of Land Tenure in Georgia* (New York, 1905), 46-51; Senate Committee on Agriculture and Forestry, *Condition of Cotton Growers*, I, 305.

[65] See Somers, *The Southern States*, 243; John D. Hicks, *The Populist Revolt* (Minneapolis, 1931), 41-42.

[66] W. W. Rife to Burrus, Bolivar Lndg., Miss., Feb. 10, 1883; Jacob Cade to Burrus, Hollygrove Plantation, Feb. 21, 1883; Ringo & Co. to Burrus, Mound Landing, Jan. 4, Feb. 18, 1884; a/c of J. C. Cade with Ringo & Co., Mound Landing, Feb. 18, 1884, John C. Burrus Papers.

[67] Campbell, *White and Black*, 369; Francis Butler Simkins, *The Tillman Movement in South Carolina* (Durham, N.C., 1926), 222-23.

[68] For examples, see contracts drawn up by Bennett in Ledger, 1859-1871, George W. Bennett Papers; agreement between William Henry Woods & Co. and John Cromley, March 14, 1872, in Destler, "The Post-Bellum South," 84.

had lost ownership to a new landlord class drawn from the ranks of the merchants.[69] But this is only part of the story of the movement of the merchant into the landlord class. The very valid contention that the plantation continued to exist after the Civil War must be seen in connection with an equally significant phenomenon: acreage devoted to cotton increased over five times from 1866 to 1930.

In 1866, cotton producers harvested over seven and a half million acres of cotton; by 1870, over nine million acres were devoted to cotton; in 1880, the figure had increased to almost sixteen million acres; in 1890 a total of almost twenty-one million acres of cotton were grown. By the turn of the century cotton acreage was up to almost twenty-five million and still increasing; in the next two decades the figure had risen to over thirty-four million acres, and in 1930, over forty-two million acres of cotton were harvested in the United States.[70] If most of the ante bellum plantations were not broken up and sold to independent farmers, here, at least, were millions of acres available to the small farmer.

When new lands were opened to cotton production, the furnishing merchant system spread to new areas. Here, too, as in the older areas, many merchants became landlords, as is shown by the expansion of tenancy in the South. In 1880, over 36 percent of the South's farms were run by tenants; by the turn of the century this figure had risen to almost 50 percent, by 1935 to over 60 percent. No respecter of race, tenancy involved more whites than Negroes; indeed, tenancy rose more rapidly among whites. Some 55 percent of the South's tenants in 1900 were white; by 1935, whites composed over 60 percent of the section's tenants. Most of the South's tenants were concentrated in the cotton-growing areas.[71]

[69] See Edgar T. Thompson, "The Natural History of Agricultural Labor in the South," in David Kelly Jackson (ed.), *American Studies in Honor of William Kenneth Boyd* (Durham, N.C., 1940), 147; Woodward, *Origins of the New South,* 179; Shugg, *Origins of Class Struggle,* 248-49.

[70] U. S. Bureau of the Census, *Historical Statistics of the United States, Colonial Times to 1957* (Washington, D. C., 1960), 301-302. Only a very small part of this acreage was outside of the South. See U. S. Department of Agriculture, Agricultural Marketing Service, *Statistics on Cotton and Related Data, 1920-1956* (Washington, D. C., 1957), 11.

[71] Johnson, Embree, and Alexander, *Collapse of Cotton Tenancy,* 4-5; Bureau of the Census, *Historical Statistics of the United States,* 278-79; Department of Agriculture, *Yearbook of Agriculture, 1940* (Washington, D. C., 1940), 888-91; Theodore Saloutos, *Farmer Movements in the South, 1865-1933* (Lincoln, Neb., 1964), 236-37.

As acreage and tenancy grew so too did the landholdings of the furnishing merchants. Brief announcements in the press regularly told of impending foreclosures by merchants. "The short cotton crop, coupled with the low price of cotton, has placed the farmers in a very poor condition financially, and the country merchants [are] foreclosing a great many trust deeds," a Southern correspondent commented briefly in *Bradstreet's* in 1883.[72] These announcements, as common as they were, did not tell the whole story. Many tracts passed unnoticed by newspapers and journals into the hands of merchants with the farmer remaining on this land, now a tenant rather than a landowner.

Technological innovation and the end of slavery produced a remarkable social transformation in the South after the Civil War. If cotton remained the section's chief crop and main occupation (and preoccupation), the social relations surrounding cotton planting and marketing gradually changed, as William Faulkner so clearly chronicles in his novels. He described the rise of the merchants, new men such as the Varners and the Snopeses; he depicted the decline and decay of the old aristocracy, the Compsons and the Sartorises. But at the same time he recognized that from the ranks of the old came the new. Such was Jason Compson, who "competed and held his own with the Snopeses who took over the little town following the turn of the century as the Compsons and Sartorises and their ilk faded from it."[73]

[72] III (Feb. 24, 1883), 116. See also Senate Committee on Agriculture and Forestry, *Condition of Cotton Growers*, I, 143-46, 289, 297; Clark, "Furnishing and Supply System," 43.

[73] William Faulkner, "Appendix: Compson, 1699-1945," in *The Sound and the Fury* (New York, 1946), 16-17. The novel was first published in 1929. The "Appendix" was written later by Faulkner and first apeared in *The Portable Faulkner*, ed. Malcolm Cowley (New York, 1946).

PART SIX

Cotton Marketing
and the Economy

"Next year we'll buy a farm," we said,
My wife and I when newly wed;
But next year came, and next, and next,
And always we were sore perplexed
To find enough to square the store
And get a start for one year more.

> —E. E. Miller, "The Cropper Speaks," as
> reprinted from *The Forum,* in Clar-
> ence Poe, "The Farmer and His Fu-
> ture," W. T. Couch (ed.), *Culture in
> the South* (Chapel Hill, 1935), 323.

Having once mortgaged his crop for sup-plies to his merchant, the farmer was prac-tically the slave to that merchant. Under the declining price of cotton his crop would barely pay his lien. He was thus left dependent for the next year's supplies on his merchant, who charged him what he pleased.

> —Henry W. Grady, *The New South* (New York, 1890), 178.

The merchants, who advance plantation supplies, have replaced the former masters and have made peons of them and of their former slaves.

> —George K. Holmes, "The Peons of the South," *Annals of the American Academy of Political and Social Science*, IV (Sept. 1893), 267.

The merchant is virtually forced to exploit the tenant if he is himself to survive.

> —Charles S. Johnson, Edwin R. Embree, and W. W. Alexander, *The Collapse of Cotton Tenancy* (Chapel Hill, 1935), 31.

Merchants . . . were only functional parts of the whole ineffective scheme of produc-tion and credit.

> —Thomas D. Clark, *Pills, Petticoats and Plows: The Southern Country Store* (Indianapolis, 1944), 323.

Southern farmers did not have to be told that economic reconstruction did not bring them prosperity. As early as 1884, Tom Watson was advising farmers in the South "to put on your armour, & man the walls" to fight the "danger which threatens."[1] Even Henry Grady paused in his paean to the New South to note problems in Southern agriculture.[2] By the 1890's, Southern farmers were in revolt and their problems gained national recognition. A rash of articles, books, and official investigations, all tried to describe and explain the causes and to prescribe cures for the depressed state of Southern agriculture.[3]

Suggested cures had little effect or, at best, had only a temporary effect. Southern agriculture remained in a chronic state of poverty and distress. And, if Southern farmers were poor, then the section itself was poor. Even before the Great Depression had made its influence felt, the South, as Thomas D. Clark has put it, "had fallen behind the nation in every positive statistical category."[4] Indeed, President Franklin Delano Roosevelt's statement in 1938 that "the South presents right now the nation's No. 1 economic problem" would have been accurate in virtually any year after the Civil War. Poverty, C. Vann Woodward has noted, was "a continuous and conspicuous feature of Southern experience since the early years of the Civil War."[5]

The key to Southern agriculture—and hence, to Southern poverty—was cotton, for from the Civil War to World War II, cotton was, by far, the chief crop. In 1929, cotton provided Southern farmers with almost half their total cash receipts;[6] in 1938, half the section's farmers had no other crop from which to draw cash income.[7] Moreover, hundreds of thousands of merchants, bankers, buyers, speculators, salesmen, fertilizer dealers, distributors of plows, mules, and hoes—all owed their livelihood, or a part of it, at least, to cotton.[8] Cotton was king: Southern economic fortunes were closely tied to the fortunes of this monarch.

[1] C. Vann Woodward, *Tom Watson, Agrarian Rebel* (New York, 1938), 128.

[2] See Henry W. Grady, "Cotton and Its Kingdom," *Harper's Magazine,* LXIII (Oct. 1881), 719-34; Grady, *The New South* (New York, 1890), 172-79, 219-30. Despite his concern, Grady was optimistic. As will be shown, he felt that the problems were being solved.

[3] Some of the books and articles were angry polemics, whereas others were attempts at scholarly analysis. These works, as well as an investigation undertaken by the Senate Committee on Agriculture and Forestry, are treated in detail below.

[4] *The Emerging South* (New York, 1961), 22. For some of these statistical categories see Clarence Poe, "The Farmer and His Future," in W. T. Couch (ed.), *Culture in the South* (Chapel Hill, 1935), 325-28.

[5] *The Burden of Southern History* (Baton Rouge, 1960), 17.

[6] William B. Hesseltine and David L. Smiley, *The South in American History* (2nd ed.; Englewood Cliffs, N. J., 1960), 587.

[7] U. S. National Emergency Council, *Report on Economic Conditions of the South* (Washington, D. C., 1938), 45.

[8] *Ibid.,* 46.

CHAPTER TWENTY-FIVE

An Agrarian "New South"

When the Civil War ended, Northern merchants hopefully looked to a resumption of the remunerative Southern trade. In October 1865, the *Commercial and Financial Chronicle* of New York reported that that city's trade with the South was improving, although it warned that 1860 levels had not been reached and might not be equaled "for years" because of the "exhaustion of the country and want of cotton."[1] Nevertheless, the journal was optimistic. A month later it argued that capital shortages would not hold back cotton production because the prospect of "handsome profits" would induce "Northern capitalists" to make funds available. "The planters have always been able to borrow upon the prospective crop; and their character for commercial honor, together with the high profits of planting, will enable them to do so still."[2]

There were problems, of course, for the Southern trade did not immediately reach the level of 1860. But the difficulties, many insisted, were political, not economic. *Hunt's Merchants' Magazine* sounded this theme in early 1866: "In order that we may develope [*sic*] the wealth of the South, all political questions must be settled, so that peace and security may become universal." The South needed capital and Northerners were anxious to invest it, but they would not do so, the journal concluded, "so long as the States are under semi-military rule."[3] As the elections of 1866 drew near, *Hunt's* reiterated its warnings: "Our merchants have not deemed it prudent to extend credit to . . . [the South] until political affairs become more settled," declared the journal in October 1866.[4] The advent of radical reconstruction and a downturn in the economy confirmed the fears of those who looked for an early return of normal North-South economic relations. *Hunt's* traced the general postwar recession in part, at least, to the failure of the North to resume normal trade with the South. Again, the problem was political rather than economic. Rebuilding the South would bring a "call for new supplies of goods, machinery and implements, which in due time would contribute largely to the national supply of products, and help forward the process of general recuperation." Northern capital was ready to move South to rebuild the section "but very naturally halts until it is apparent what is to be the future relation of the seceded States to the central Government."[5] Such sentiments were echoed by Secretary of the Treasury Hugh McCulloch[6] and repeated endlessly in New York commercial journals.[7]

Yet, even as they expressed their concern over radical reconstruction policies, representatives of Northern merchants found reasons to remain optimistic. As early as 1866, *Hunt's Merchants' Magazine* noticed that the nature of the Southern trade was changing. The South now bought "less of the fine, costly descriptions . . . and also a much smaller proportion of the very common materials which in former times were required for clothing the slaves." The former planters were unable to afford the more costly goods and the Negroes, free to purchase as they pleased, were "able to clothe themselves with better fabrics."[8] For the first time the Negro had become a real customer; his buying power, it was expected, would increase the demand for goods. The result "will be a change in the class of goods required, but the aggregate value . . . should border closely on that of former times."[9] By 1869, *Hunt's* was almost jubilant in its optimism: "The general business of the South, which was small at the end of the war, has steadily increased, and is

---

1 I (Oct. 14, 1865), 486.
2 *Ibid.* (Nov. 11, 1865), 612.
3 LIV (March 1866), 172-74.
4 *Ibid.*, LV (Oct. 1866), 310.
5 *Ibid.*, LVI (March 1867), 172.
6 See his report of Nov. 30, 1867, printed *ibid.*, LVII (Dec. 1867), 453-54.
7 For typical examples see *ibid.*, LVIII (Feb. 1868), 121-24; *Commercial and Financial Chronicle*, VI (Jan. 18, 1868), 70-71.
8 LV (Oct. 1866), 309-10.
9 *Commercial and Financial Chronicle*, V (Aug. 10, 1867), 167.

assuming large dimensions, while it is in a more healthy condition than ever before . . . the vastly increased number of independent 'customers' in the Southern States enhances the demand for goods both in quantity and variety. At the same time the demand for the finest class of goods is increasing. The new wants and methods of trade are the direct outgrowth of the new system of labor."[10]

Optimistic voices were heard even in the war-devastated and occupied South. The South had natural wealth of "inestimable value," wrote J. D. B. DeBow in October 1865, and economic rehabilitation would come quickly if the section took steps "*to induce an influx of population and capital from abroad.*"[11] In a similar vein, a correspondent for a New Orleans newspaper argued that if the freedmen were "induced or compelled to work" and if Northern capitalists provided credit, the South would soon raise a good cotton crop.[12] Political developments in Washington, however, dampened DeBow's enthusiasm somewhat. He found "an intense feeling of disappointment and chagrin" among Southerners who "perceive a disposition in the national councils to humble and degrade them." Like the Northern merchants, he concluded that economic rehabilitation was being blocked by the political activities of the "radical party."[13]

Despite disappointment over political developments, optimism persisted. The ante bellum planter, a Georgian wrote, spent his profits "to buy more land and more negroes"; he made his purchases in the large cities and spent his surpluses in Europe or at the fashionable watering places, with the result that towns, churches, and schools were never built. Now, however, the Negroes had money to spend and towns and stores were growing up where earlier none existed.[14] Another Georgian predicted that the South, freed from the debilitating limitations of slavery, would prosper and soon even exceed the North in wealth: "The cotton & sugar crops will enrich the South and as surplus capital cannot now be invested in

---

[10] LXI (Nov. 1869), 364. Also, *Commercial and Financial Chronicle*, IX (Oct. 23, 1869), 519.

[11] DeBow to Gov. Perry of South Carolina, New York, Oct. 12, 1865, printed in *DeBow's Review*, rev. ser. I (Jan. 1866), 8.

[12] *New Orleans Price Current*, as reprinted *ibid.* (Feb. 1866), 197-98.

[13] *Ibid.* (March 1866), 332-33.

[14] F. W. Loring and C. F. Atkinson, *Cotton Culture and the South Considered With Reference to Emigration* (Boston, 1869), 16-17. This book, designed to bring capital and migrants to the South, undoubtedly overstated the extent of Southern optimism in the 1860's.

negroes, and land useless without laborers, the varied resources are likely to be developed and in half a century unless war prevent, the South will be wealthier than the North."[15] Similarly, a Mississippian reported that Southern Negroes had money and "consume on a much larger scale than formerly," making "the business of supplying them" a new and lucrative enterprise.[16]

Even the two disastrous crop years which followed the war did not dim optimism. On the contrary, adversity, some insisted, helped remove the main impediments to Southern economic progress. At the start of the 1868 crop season, a Mobile paper congratulated the planter community for its "comparative freedom from debt." The losses of the 1866 season had led merchants to refuse to give large advances on cotton during 1867, and planters, therefore, had been forced to curtail expenses and to grow their own food. As a result, profits would not be drained out of the South to pay for imports from the North.[17] *Hunt's* regarded this as the first step toward the financial independence of the South, "foreshadowing the ultimate abolition of the system of credit upon which the whole production and trade of the South has usually been conducted."[18]

Economic independence was the first step toward prosperity for the South and increased influence in national affairs, wrote a Mobile factor in 1868. The step was easily taken, he argued, if the planters would give up their "vain attempt to prosper in the production of Cotton, to the neglect of all other products." He urged diversified agriculture, a vast expansion of the railroad network, and the establishment of manufactures in the South. The results of such a program would be revolutionary: "If by a concert of action, the Southern people would produce all they consume, and only sufficient Cotton for their own use, it would revolutionize the financial and political condition of this country, and make us masters of the situation. It would do more good towards *proper* reconstruction than all the speeches and resolutions that an army of demagogues could publish in a century."[19]

[15] Godfrey Barnsley to George Barnsley, Woodlands, Ga., Aug. 17, 1869, Barnsley Collection, Archives Division, Tennessee State Library and Archives, Nashville, Tenn.
[16] Loring and Atkinson, *Cotton Culture and the South*, 75.
[17] *Merchants' Exchange Prices-Current* (Mobile), Sept. 1, 1868.
[18] LIX (Oct. 1868), 291.
[19] "October Circular" of S. J. Murphy & Co., Mobile, Oct. 15, 1868, Johnston-McFaddin Papers, Southern Historical Collection, University of North Carolina

These were the advance prophets of Gradyism, the heady doctrine of the 1880's which proclaimed the arrival of the "New South." Diversified agriculture, industry, and, above all, energy would transform the South. Although the leaders of the New South movement paid homage to the old South by proclaiming the glories of the good old days and wheeling out Confederate War heroes,[20] it was the new which interested them, the desire to emulate the North, or, as Henry Watterson put it, to "out-Yankee the Yankee." Grady was ecstatic in his description: "For twenty-five years the industrial forces of the South have been at work under the surface. Making little show, experimenting, working out new ways, blocking up old ways, peering about with the lamp of experience barely lit, digging, delving, struggling, until at last the day has come, and independence is proclaimed. Now watch the change take place with almost comical swiftness!"[21]

The rhetoric of the New South movement reigned supreme in the 1880's. Opposition was largely inarticulate and usually ignored.[22] Even Tom Watson momentarily gave in to the optimistic fervor of the times.[23] The movement, however, was not mere rhetoric. When Charles Nordhoff visited the South in 1875, he saw new towns being built "almost everywhere" he went. With

---

Library, Chapel Hill, N. C. See also *DeBow's Review*, rev. ser. I (April 1866), 428-29.

[20] "I accept the term, 'The New South,' as in no sense disparaging to the old," said Henry Grady in his famous speech at Delmonico's Restaurant in New York on Dec. 22, 1886. "Dear to me, sir, is the home of my childhood and the traditions of my people. I would not, if I could, dim the glory they won in peace and war, or by word or deed take aught from the splendor and grace of their civilization—never equalled and, perhaps, never to be equalled in its chivalric strength and grace. There is a New South, not through protest against the old, but because of new conditions, new adjustments and, if you please, new ideas and aspirations." "Henry Grady: The New South, 1886," ed. Thomas D. Clark, in Daniel J. Boorstin (ed.), *An American Primer* (Chicago, 1966), I, 468. The Old South, as C. Vann Woodward has perceptively noted, was "one of the most significant inventions of the New South." *Origins of the New South, 1877-1913* (Baton Rouge, 1951), 154-55.

[21] Henry W. Grady, *The New South* (New York, 1890), 270.

[22] Excellent descriptions of the New South movement may be found in Woodward, *Origins of the New South*, 142-74 and the same author's *Tom Watson, Agrarian Rebel* (New York, 1938), 113-28. In addition to Grady's works already cited, contemporary examples of the rhetoric of the movement are M. B. Hillyard, *The New South* (Baltimore, 1887); William D. Kelley, *The Old South and the New* (New York, 1888); A. K. McClure, *The South: Its Industrial, Financial, and Political Condition* (Philadelphia, 1886); Wilbur Pisk Tillett, "The White Man of the New South," *Century Magazine*, XXXIII (March 1887), 769-76.

[23] Woodward, *Tom Watson*, 119.

slavery gone, he explained, Southern capital was no longer locked up in labor and had become available for urban growth.[24] Whatever the reasons, towns did spring up in the South and so also did

TABLE 8.   URBAN AND RURAL POPULATION, FOR UNITED

| Year | United States | | | North[a] |
	Urban	Rural	Percent Urban	Urban
1860	6,216,518	25,226,803	19.8	5,050,579
1870	9,902,361	28,656,010	25.7	8,150,168
1880	14,129,735	36,026,048	28.2	11,568,656
1890	22,106,265	40,841,449	35.1	17,684,179
1900	30,159,921	45,834,654	39.7	24,076,196
1910	41,998,932	49,973,334	45.7	32,050,402
1920	54,157,973	51,552,647	51.2	40,179,824

[a] Me., N.H., Vt., Mass., R.I., Conn., N.Y., N.J., Penna., Ohio, Ind., Ill., Mich., Wis., Minn., Iowa, Mo., N.D., S.D., Neb., Kan.
[b] Del., Md., D.C., Va., W.Va., N.C., S.C., Ga., Fla., Ky., Tenn., Ala., Miss., Ark., La., Okla., Texas.

industry. Old railroad lines were repaired and extended and new ones were built; the tobacco industry became mechanized and grew, stimulated by the new popularity of cigarettes; Birmingham, born out of a cotton field, became a center for steel manufacture; and cotton textile mills began to dot the Southern Piedmont. Indeed, the South seemed to be becoming Yankeeized, and the future seemed boundless.

Urban growth and the development of manufactures in the South was a fact; but any description of these changes should not obscure the more basic fact that the New South remained rural and largely agricultural. As Table 8 clearly indicates, the post-Civil War Southern population was more rural than both the North's and the nation's. By 1900 the Northern population was more than half urban, whereas the South remained 82 percent rural. Moreover, all the cotton states, with the exception of Louisiana, were even less urbanized than was the South as a whole.[25] The section lagged similarly in manufacturing. In 1900, for example, the South had 16.4 percent of the manufacturing establishment in the country with a capital value of only 9.7 percent of the total national figure.

[24] *The Cotton States in the Spring and Summer of 1875* (New York, 1876), 23.
[25] For state-by-state figures see U. S. Department of Commerce, Bureau of the Census, *Sixteenth Census of the United States: 1940*, Vol. I, *Population, passim.*

With 12.3 percent of the wage earners, the section's manufacturing plants produced only 9.1 percent of the country's total value of manufactures. More significant is the fact that over the years the

STATES, NORTH, AND SOUTH, 1860-1920

North—Continued		South[b]			
Rural	Percent Urban	Urban	Rural	Percent Urban	Year
14,640,405	25.6	1,066,794	10,066,567	9.6	1860
17,129,673	32.2	1,496,579	10,791,441	12.2	1870
20,302,862	36.3	2,016,735	14,499,833	12.2	1880
22,133,207	44.4	3,261,326	16,766,733	16.3	1890
23,303,503	50.8	4,420,885	20,102,642	18.0	1900
23,706,713	57.5	6,622,658	22,766,672	22.5	1910
23,502,021	63.1	9,300,055	23,825,748	28.1	1920

Source: U.S. Department of Commerce, Bureau of the Census, *Sixteenth Census of the United States: 1940*, Vol. I, *Population* (Washington, D. C., 1942), 20.

South's position in manufacturing relative to the rest of the nation changed very little. Thus, although Southern manufacturing expanded and grew after the Civil War, its rate of growth never exceeded that of the rest of the nation, and manufacturing in the South remained in 1900, and in 1930, in much the same relative position as in 1860.[26]

Most Southerners, then, remained untouched by urbanism and industrialism; yet, the New South movement gained wide acceptance. In a word, Southerners accepted the Yankee rhetoric and outlook even in the absence of Yankee industry. This has led some students to seek an explanation of the movement in political or ideological rather than in economic developments. Wilbur J. Cash, for example, found the movement to be merely a new tactic in the older sectional struggle: a strong South would be better able to cope with and withstand the North. Ideologically, he concludes, the movement had more that was old than new in it.[27] C. Vann Woodward, rejecting the idea that an industrial revolution in the postwar South caused those changes "in outlook, institutions, and particularly in leadership" which "*did* take place," has argued that

[26] Gilbert C. Fite and Jim E. Reese, *An Economic History of the United States* (2nd ed.; Boston, 1965), 363; Woodward, *Origins of the New South*, 140; William H. Nicholls, *Southern Tradition and Regional Progress* (Chapel Hill, 1960), 27-28.
[27] *The Mind of the South* (Garden City, N. Y., 1956), 185-91.

the source of these changes can be found only by looking "beyond the limits of economic history."[28]

Yet, if economic history does not reveal the whole story, it does, nevertheless, provide a great deal of insight into the New South movement. Although there was no industrial revolution in the South, there were significant changes in agriculture and trade, changes which supported a new class in the postwar South. More-over, members of this new class were urban oriented even when they were not urban dwellers.

Although the New South did not become urbanized in terms of census classification, the number of towns and villages increased enormously as compared with the ante bellum period. But it is important to understand the character of these towns. For every Birmingham and Durham there were hundreds of cities, towns, and villages that depended for their existence on agriculture rather than industry. Vicksburg, for example, which in prewar days had languished in the shadow of nearby New Orleans, gained independent stature after the war. In the decade 1860-1870 its population grew from 4,591 to 12,443, an increase of 171 percent.[29] Its new prominence, the town's Chamber of Commerce explained in an 1870 circular addressed "to the Cotton Spinners of Europe and America," arose from changes in the cotton trade "as a result of the late war." Like numerous other prewar towns, Vicksburg had experienced rapid growth because of the "vastly increased number of cultivators of the soil" who, unlike the few major planters of old, "prefer to buy and sell at the near instead of the distant markets." Consumers of cotton were urged to make their purchases in Vicks-burg which, the Chamber advertised, was ideally located in the center of good cotton country, had ample transportation and facilities for handling the staple, and offered abundant banking and exchange resources.[30]

Here, then, was an ante bellum town, now grown larger and more prosperous. It had more bankers and merchants and its industry—transportation, communication, storage, compresses, gins, and the like—had expanded. But its commerce and industry alike

[28] *Origins of the New South*, 140-41.

[29] Bureau of the Census, *Sixteenth Census: 1940*, Vol. I, *Population*, 568.

[30] "Circular of the Chamber of Commerce of Vicksburg to the Cotton Spinners of Europe and America," reprinted in *Hunt's Merchants' Magazine*, LXIII (Sept. 1870), 230.

depended not on manufacturing, but on the cotton trade. The same story could be repeated for other ante bellum towns.[31] The following table shows the population increase of some of the leading cotton markets for the decade ending 1870.

Selma	104.1 percent increase
Montgomery	19.7
Little Rock	232.2
Augusta	23.2
Macon	31.1
Shreveport	110.4
Natchez	37.0
Memphis	77.8
Galveston	89.1[32]

This, however, is only a part of the picture. Many of the old towns as well as the new ones which were springing up never reached "urban" status; indeed, some even escaped the notice of census takers computing the number of towns in a state. An official publication of the state of South Carolina described this phenomenon and assessed its significance:

The census of 1880 counts one hundred and five towns in the State. [Of these, only 6 were designated as "urban."] This count, however, includes only a small proportion of the lesser villages and trading settlements which are increasing with great rapidity, and are effecting marked changes in the social and industrial condition of the population. The growth of the larger towns has been set back by the destruction and losses attendant upon the war, and by the radical revolution it effected in the industries of the State, disturbing all the established methods of trade. But along the lines of railways, and every where in the rural districts, there has been a remarkable increase in the number of establishments engaged in trade. The cross-road store has become an important factor in the organization of labor and in the distribution of wealth. . . . The thirty-three thousand plantations of 1860 are divided out among ninety-three thousand small farmers in 1880. Wholly

[31] See Edward King, *The Great South* (Hartford, Conn., 1875), 265-66; Emory R. Johnson, *et al.*, *History of Domestic and Foreign Commerce of the United States* (Washington, D. C., 1915), I, 279-80; *Bradstreet's*, XIII (April 24, 1886), 263; U. S. Congress, Senate, Committee on Agriculture and Forestry, *Report . . . on the Condition of Cotton Growers*, 53rd Cong., 3rd Sess., Report 986 (1895), 1, 120-21.
[32] Bureau of the Census, *Sixteenth Census: 1940*, Vol. I, *Population, passim*.

occupied by their struggle with the soil and the seasons, these small farmers, of necessity, intrust their trading interests to the care of the country storekeeper. And thus the cross-roads store stands again, as stood formerly the Indian trading post, a pioneer in a new industrial departure. The blacksmith, the wheelwright, and the trial justice settle near them, and when two or three stores are gathered together, churches and schools are opened, and a town which, from its very commencement, has instantaneous communication through the telegraph with every corner of the globe, is admitted into the great fellowship of cities, and takes its growth.[33]

Instead of the 105 towns counted by the census, the report listed 493, adding a warning that even this was an incomplete list. In these towns 4,645 stores with an estimated investment of over forty million dollars had annual sales of about one hundred fifty million dollars.[34]

This was the New South's most significant "urban" development —the crossroads town, which the census, if it noted its existence at all, would simply designate as rural nonfarm. Perhaps one may smile at the reporter's enthusiasm, at his calling a town that was so small that census takers did not see it, a part of the "great fellow-ship of cities." Yet, in a very important sense, this was not an overstatement. These little towns were not only in close and easy communication with their larger counterparts, they were micro-cosms of large cities. Their merchants and bankers were country cousins to the merchants and bankers of the large cities. They adopted many of the same methods, faced many of the same problems, and, it should elicit no surprise, shared a similar outlook with their big city cousins. In a word, a town-oriented middle class had emerged in the New South.

With obvious elation, A. K. McClure, an active partisan of the New South movement, described the members of this class in Atlanta, the leading city in what he called the "Empire State of the South." There was little about the city to remind one of the Old South, he wrote. "The young men are not the dawdling, pale-faced, soft-handed effeminates which were so often visible in the nurslings of the slave." On the contrary, the intelligent and

[33] South Carolina State Board of Agriculture, *South Carolina: Resources and Population; Institutions and Industries* (Charleston, S. C., 1883), 659-60.
[34] *Ibid.*, 660-61.

active young men of Atlanta were the "foremost missionaries in the new civilization in the South." True, they had not forgotten their fathers and they paid homage to their accomplishments, but they had no desire to emulate or resurrect the past. "Instead of discussing the old plantation times 'before the wah,' they talk about railroads, factories, the tariff, the schools, the increase of crops, and the growth of wealth and trade." Indeed, he noted, these men would be Republicans had the Southern branch of that party not been merely "a mixture of sectionalism and plunder."[35]

The furnishing merchants were a significant part of this middle class. Their stores served as the base for varied economic activities, as enterprising merchants found the time, the energy, and, from their profits, the resources to enlarge and expand their businesses and to invest in new ventures. The reason for this was not simply that postwar merchants, once freed from the enervating effects of slavery, were more energetic; more important was the fact that changes in the cotton-marketing system in the post bellum South offered opportunities that were not available in prewar days. The decline of cotton factorage transformed the storekeeper from an adjunct to the seaport factors to the pivotal figure in cotton marketing and financing, and the development of interior purchasing, shipment on through bills of lading, and the futures system opened the way to new economic ventures for them.

Typical of the new business methods were the activities of storekeepers H. A. Busick of Morton, Mississippi, D. W. Busick of Brandon, Mississippi, and J. R. Stevens, merchant and bank president of Huntsville, Alabama. To their business of furnishing local farmers, the storekeepers added extensive speculation on the futures market. They bought and sold futures contracts, sometimes as a partnership and sometimes on their individual accounts, on the New Orleans exchange, through Richardson and May, and on the New York exchange, through Latham, Alexander and Company.[36]

---

35 *The South*, 58-62.

36 H. A. Busick & Co. to D. W. Busick, Morton, Miss., Sept. 4, 1871; H. A. Busick & Co. statement, Jan. 1–July 31, 1871, Morton, Miss., Sept. 4, 1871; Richardson & May to D. W. Busick, New Orleans, May 15, May 31, July 28, Aug. 29, 1883; statements of purchase & sale [by Richardson & May] for a/c of Stevens and Busick, New Orleans, May 15, July 28, Aug. 29, Sept. 12, 1883; Stevens to D. W. Busick, Huntsville, May 31, Aug. 21, 26, 1883, July 14, 1884; Richardson & May to Stevens, New Orleans, May 31, 1883 (telegram); Stevens and Busick in a/c with Latham, Alexander & Co., New York, May 1, 1884, D. W. Busick Papers, Mississippi Department of Archives and History, Jackson, Miss.

Even more varied were the activities of H. R. Johnson and Company of Americus, Georgia. As has already been shown, the Americus storekeepers bought and sold cotton, furnished some local farmers, and acted as factors for others. As early as 1865 they became the agents of the Southern Transportation Company in their town, a position which authorized them to issue bills of lading on goods to be shipped from Americus to Baltimore, Philadelphia, New York, Boston, and other cities.[37] At the same time, the Americus storekeepers were actively engaged in gold speculation.[38] By 1877, their letterhead indicated that in addition to their grocery and commission business, they sold fertilizers, ran a cotton warehouse, and were the local agents for the Mutual Life Insurance Company of New York. As time went on, their records show, they extended their interests into real estate, lumber, building supplies, and hardware.

When merchants bought land or foreclosed mortgages and became landlords, they did not become planters in the prewar sense. Land worked by tenants was just another form of investment, the tenants merely a new group of customers. When the reverse process took place, that is, when planters opened stores to serve their tenants, the result was the same. The ante bellum planter had then become a businessman. His income derived from his store, his gin, his compress, and only indirectly by way of rents, from his land. Such planters, even when they lived in the country, had become town-oriented in their economic pursuits.[39]

Not all planters, of course, became merchants. But even those who eschewed the merchant's calling often found nonagricultural outlets for their financial surpluses. Stocks and bonds drew the investments of some Southern planters,[40] but it was the futures

---

[37] C. E. Evans to Johnson & Co., Macon, Nov. 6, 1865, Harrold Brothers Papers, Emory University Library, Atlanta, Ga.

[38] Mitchell & Smiths to Johnson & Co., Oct. 19, 21, 1865, *ibid.*

[39] C. P. Brooks, *Cotton* (New York, 1898), 110-16; Sheldon Van Auken, "A Century of the Southern Plantation," *Virginia Magazine of History and Biography*, LVIII (July 1950), 372; Benjamin Burks Kendrick and Alex Mathews Arnett, *The South Looks at Its Past* (Chapel Hill, 1935), 109-10, 112; Edd Winfield Parks, "Southern Towns and Cities," in W. T. Couch (ed.), *Culture in the South* (Chapel Hill, 1935), 501-503.

[40] See, for example, Thos. F. McGehee to Heard, M——[?] City, Ga., Feb. 5, 1866; Daniel Dickson to Heard & Son, Sparta, March 6, 1871, Stephen D. Heard Papers, Southern Historical Collection, University of North Carolina Library, Chapel Hill, N. C.

markets which seem to have been most attractive as the telegraph put planters in instantaneous touch with brokers on the New Orleans and New York exchanges. Members of the exchange would usually have representatives in the larger Southern towns; factors often accepted these agencies as a means of augmenting their declining commission business.[41] Both planters and factors were drawn into futures speculation soon after the exchanges were opened. The methods and the excitement may be seen in the speculations in 1871 of a Washington, Georgia, planter, B. W. Heard. The planter, obviously a neophyte, began his purchases through his cotton factor, Stephen D. Heard, but an unsteady market, repeated requests for margins, and the real possibility of a serious loss led him to the offices of the New York brokers, Inman, Swann and Company, where he could oversee his speculations personally. After a harrowing few weeks, the futures market rallied and he was able to sell out his contracts at a small profit. "I have gained some experience & suffered a devil of an amount of anxiety," he confessed. In the same letter, he asked that his factor sell his cotton, get his bank statement, and collect his railroad stock dividends for him.[42] Clearly, cotton planting was playing a minor part in the Washington planter's economic activities.

For the New South enthusiasts these new economic activities were a sign of progress. "The 'gentleman idler' has lost caste in the South; he is an institution of the past," proclaimed Wilbur Tillett in 1887.[43] Of course, not all could make the change. "Our Sons are all working hard and have many difficulties to encounter," sadly wrote a South Carolinian. "One comfort we have [is that] so many of our best people are poor now we feel almost proud of our poverty," she concluded.[44] Many of these people lost their land

[41] Senate Committee on Agriculture and Forestry, *Condition of Cotton Growers*, I, 89.

[42] Inman, Swann & Co. to Heard & Son, New York, March 6, 1871; B. W. Heard to Heard & Son, Washington, Ga., March 7, 1871, New York, Aug. 21, 1871; B. W. Heard to Inman, Swann & Co., Washington, Ga., May 15, 1871; Inman, Swann to B. W. Heard, New York, May 19, 1871, Stephen D. Heard Papers. Extensive correspondence between Heard and Inman, Swann during the 1870's reveals that the New York brokers sold cotton in New York for Heard and his customers and also bought and sold futures contracts for Heard's private account and for a number of Heard's customers.

[43] Tillett, "The White Man of the New South," 769-76.

[44] Sophie L. Haskell to Mrs. Charlotte Grinshaw, Home Place, Abbeville, S. C., June 18, 1876, Langdon Cheves Collection, Haskell Papers, South Carolina Historical Society, Charleston, S. C.

and became tenants.[45] Others, clinging to an idealized past and unwilling to accept the new, found themselves, as the historian John Spencer Bassett and the novelist William Faulkner have suggested, in the backwaters of history.[46]

The economic transformation brought with it political changes. When the Montroy, Arkansas, storekeeper Henry Strong became a justice of the peace in 1878,[47] he was doing what many other merchants and storekeepers were doing. In a word, to their economic pre-eminence, the post bellum Southern middle class added political domination. As two careful scholars have put it, the political "center of gravity in the South was shifting from country to town."[48] This was reflected in party politics. Visitors to the South after the war noticed that the old prewar conflict between Whig and Democrat was still very much alive, although it was often hidden behind the facade of a single party, the Democrats.[49] C. Vann Woodward, who has most closely investigated this phenomenon,[50] observed that the old Whigs and their followers were not the prewar planter Whigs but were spokesman "for much the same type of economic interests as the Republicans—railroads, industries, business enterprise of one kind or another."[51]

The social origins of this group are less important than the social and economic position it held in the post bellum period. Planters who had become storekeepers, cotton merchants, speculators, and investors in railroads and cotton mills could not be distinguished

[45] This fact was often lost sight of by New South propagandists who celebrated the break-up of the plantations and proclaimed the rise of an independent yeomanry. See Woodward, *Origins of the New South*, 175-76 and Roger W. Shugg, *Origins of Class Struggle in Louisiana* (Baton Rouge, 1939), 274-313.

[46] Bassett, "The Industrial Decay of the Southern Planter," *South Atlantic Quarterly*, II (April 1903), 107-13. For Faulkner's point of view, see especially *The Sound and the Fury* and *Sartoris*.

[47] Account Book of Henry Strong, microfilm copy of MSS in Arkansas History Commission, Department of Archives and History, Little Rock, Ark. Strong kept his judicial records in the same account book in which he recorded his store business, his lien contracts, and other affairs; this was the same book in which he kept his prewar business records.

[48] Kendrick and Arnett, *The South Looks at Its Past*, 109-10. See also Frank Tannenbaum, *Darker Phases of the South* (New York, 1924), 123, 125-26.

[49] Sidney Andrews, *The South Since the War* (Boston, 1866), 135-36; Charles Nordhoff, *The Cotton States in the Spring and Summer of 1875* (New York, 1876), 15, 37, 42, 92. See also Robertson Topp to A. H. Douglass, J. T. Latham, R. D. Baugh, Memphis, Aug. 8, 1870, Robertson Topp Papers, Burrow Library, Southwestern at Memphis, Memphis, Tenn.

[50] See especially *Reunion and Reaction* (Garden City, N. Y., 1956), chap. ii, "The Rejuvenation of Whiggery," 23-53.

[51] *Ibid.*, 42.

from those who had begun as merchants and only later accumulated land. Both represented a new business outlook.[52]

But, if townsmen came to dominate the political and economic life of the New South, their towns were not the result, for the most part, of an industrial revolution. Nor was the outlook of the townsmen based simply on the desire to emulate the successful men in the North or, as Ben Tillman put it, to "say 'Me too,' every time the New York *World* and Grover Cleveland grunts [*sic*]."[53] Rather, most towns arose as a result of changes in the organization of agricultural production, primarily changes in the financing and marketing of cotton. On the ruins of slavery and the plantation system a new business class had arisen, and its members, although only rarely industrialists, had much in common with the business classes in the North.

[52] Of course, planters and factors in the ante bellum period sometimes invested surplus funds in railroads and other industrial enterprises, but this was the exception rather than the rule. As Thomas D. Clark has put it, "Young men of the ante-bellum South looked forward to professions of law, medicine and the ministry, or to running a plantation; their sons now found clerking a gentlemen's trade." *Pills, Petticoats and Plows: The Southern Country Store* (Indianapolis, 1944), 27.

[53] Speech of Senator Benjamin Tillman at South Carolina Day at the Atlanta Exposition in 1895, printed in *The Cotton States and International Exposition and South, Illustrated* (Atlanta, 1896), 135.

CHAPTER TWENTY-SIX

The Farmer's Quest for Economic Independence

To Henry Grady and his followers the South was well on its way to recovery after the disaster of Civil War. Prospects for the future seemed unlimited. To be sure, there were some signs of trouble. Grady himself lamented the undue emphasis on cotton to the exclusion of other agricultural products, an emphasis, he claimed, that left the farmer helplessly in the hands of a usurious merchant.[1] Similarly, in early 1871 a Louisiana newspaper warned that Southern farmers would never be prosperous so long as they concentrated their entire effort on cotton growing: "How can an agricultural people be prosperous who pay double the conventional interest on large sums of money, and pay cash to distant farmers for nearly everything they consume?"[2] Grangers in Americus, Georgia, charging that farmers "had been 'gouged' by rings and combinations," in 1874 organized their own commission house so as to "cope with the established houses of the city and section, in the purchase of supplies and other things needful to planters."[3] And the Census Office's cotton survey in 1880 described an expansion of tenancy and an increase in the number of debtors.[4]

For most observers, however, the cloud of doubt and trouble was small and foretold not a storm, but the passing of bad times. Even as they lamented the problems, they discovered signs of change that blunted their criticism. Grady found evidence of the growth of crop diversification and improvements in the methods of growing and shipping the crop and concluded optimistically that problems were being solved.[5] Indeed, the very evils themselves were producing change. The "better class of farmers" disapproved of and shunned the furnishing merchant system because it encouraged "extravagant spending" and tenantry, concluded an analysis by the South Carolina State Board of Agriculture.[6] For the Americus Grangers, the organization of a farmers' commission house was the first step in the right direction: "The farmers have it in their power to be free, if they will but act in concert, as the merchants do." William B. Dana concluded his study in 1878 by noting that Southern planters were raising more food on their farms and becoming more independent of the money lenders, while sharecropping was gradually giving way to wage labor.[7]

With the coming of the Alliance movement and the Populists, and stimulated also by the depression of the 1890's, the cheerful and optimistic voice of the New South was interrupted by more pessimistic tones. The sorry state of cotton producers received national attention. Chronic difficulties that had long been ignored or explained away by cheerful prognostications were now illuminated in the fierce light of polemical and political publicity. In 1895 a committee of the United States Senate, after a long and extensive investigation, told the nation what cotton growers had long known. Cotton prices were not high enough to bring a profit to the producer and they were even then continuing to drop. Insolvency, suffering, and discontent plagued the cotton farmers of the South, the committee concluded.[8]

Critics often directed their main fire against the furnishing merchant. Here was an enemy close at hand and easily identifiable; here was the usurer, overcharging for what he sold and underpaying for what he bought. Editors and political leaders never tired of

[1] Henry W. Grady, "Cotton and Its Kingdom," Harper's Magazine, LXIII (Oct. 1881), 722-23; Grady, The New South (New York, 1890), 172-79.

[2] Planters' Banner (Franklin, La.), March 1, 1871. See also Robert M. Davis, The Southern Planter, the Factor and the Banker (New Orleans, 1871), 4-5.

[3] "An Address to Planters and Grangers," Americus, Sept. 24, 1874. (Copy in Harrold Brothers Papers, Emory University Library, Atlanta, Ga.)

[4] Eugene W. Hilgard, "Report on Cotton Production in the United States," in U. S. Department of the Interior, Census Office, Tenth Census (1880) (Washington, D.C., 1884), V, VI, passim. See also a similar discussion by Bradstreet's Southern correspondents, XI (Feb. 14, 1885), 99.

[5] The New South, 219-30.

[6] South Carolina: Resources and Population; Institutions and Industries (Charleston, 1883), 32.

[7] Cotton from Seed to Loom (New York, 1878), 159.

[8] U. S. Congress, Senate, Committee on Agriculture and Forestry, Report . . . on Condition of Cotton Growers, 53rd Cong., 3rd Sess., Report 986 (1895), I, iii-iv.

excoriating this parasite in their midst.[9] When the Farmers' Alliances were organized, members expressed their antagonism and distrust of the merchants—indeed, of all middlemen—by specifically excluding them from membership.[10] Writing in 1942, Ben Robertson recalled the cotton farmers' animosity toward the merchant in the South of his youth. "They were usurers and thieves, and we fought them and the bankers behind them in our counties, in our states, at Washington, and at every national convention of the Democratic Party."[11] The attack against the merchant even found its way into the scholarly *Annals of the American Academy of Political and Social Science* with a blistering article by George K. Holmes: "The merchants, who advance plantation supplies, have replaced the former masters and have made peons of them and of their former slaves."[12]

Often attack against the merchant was set in the wider perspective of an assault on the crop lien system upon which he thrived. Indeed, the two were inseparable in the minds of many, as is illustrated in the passionate jeremiad of Charles H. Otken, which begins simply as an onslaught against the merchant but which ends as a denunciation of the entire system:

> Robust honesty is still in the land, but it is timid and passive. It is shackled by environments. About 300 farmers are, on an average, at the mercy of one man. Year in and year out, for a quarter of a century, this submission has endured. There is no money in the country, save during the winter months. All those who have dealings with the farming class, rendering to them valuable and necessary service, are involved in these impoverished circumstances. Enterprise is stunted. Progress is choked. Whatever is of the highest value to the country, relating to its material advancement, its intellectual and moral elevation, is depreciated and throttled by this ruinous method.[13]

Less emotional was the economist M. B. Hammond, who

[9] Thomas D. Clark, *Pills, Petticoats and Plows: The Southern Country Store* (Indianapolis, 1944), 315-16.

[10] Hallie Farmer, "Economic Background of Southern Populism," *South Atlantic Quarterly*, XXIX (Jan. 1930), 89-90; Theodore Saloutos, *Farmer Movements in the South, 1865-1933* (Lincoln, Neb., 1964), 75-76.

[11] *Red Hills and Cotton* (New York, 1942) 83.

[12] "The Peons of the South," IV (Sept. 1893), 265-74. The quoted words are on 267.

[13] Charles H. Otken, *The Ills of the South* (New York, 1894), 25.

published the results of his study in 1897. For Hammond, the enemy of Southern progress was the crop lien system, not its chief actor, the local merchant. After carefully demonstrating the exorbitant charges assessed by the merchant, he concluded that the merchant himself should not be blamed. Given an iniquitous system, high prices were a necessity to compensate for the great risk of supplying landless, propertyless cotton tenants on credit.[14]

Critics of the lien system charged that it led to overproduction and, as a result, low prices, and at the same time prevented crop diversification and encouraged inefficient and therefore more expensive production methods. The heart of the problem, Otken explained, was that cotton farmers bought all they needed on credit. "Men in debt, want money," and the Southern farmer knew "that cotton is the only crop that will bring money." He therefore neglected every other crop in an effort to grow more cotton. The result was tragic. The food that he did not grow had to be purchased, increasing his debts; his emphasis on cotton growing increased the supply, lowering prices and making payment of debts impossible. Each year the cycle was repeated and each year the tragic results became more far-reaching.[15]

Since the furnishing merchant derived part of his profits from selling food and other supplies, he made no effort to convince farmers to curtail the cotton crop in favor of corn or meat production.[16] On the contrary, the merchant prevented crop diversification by refusing to advance credit on any crop but cotton.[17] Nor did those farmers who dealt with factors fare any better. Before he would give an advance, the factor often required a contract stipulating that the farmer would send him a certain number of bales to sell, a Georgia farmer told the Industrial Commission in 1899. Even if the farmer failed to raise the minimum promised, he had to pay the commission on the entire number agreed upon. Should the farmer object, his credit would stop.[18]

[14] M. B. Hammond, *The Cotton Industry* (New York, 1897) 153-56.

[15] Otken, *The Ills of the South*, 56. Other critics made the same point. See, for example, Hammond, *The Cotton Industry*, 156-57; Senate Committee on Agriculture and Forestry, *Condition of Cotton Growers*, I, 294, 299, 317.

[16] Otken, *The Ills of the South*, 57.

[17] Senate Committee on Agriculture and Forestry, *Condition of Cotton Growers*, I, 299, 317, 415; Holmes, "Peons of the South," 266-67.

[18] U. S. Industrial Commission, *Report on Agriculture and Agricultural Labor* (Washington, D.C., 1901), 47.

Whereas some critics of the lien system argued that it caused overproduction of cotton, others attacked its tendency to encourage inefficient production. For some the basic problem stemmed from the fact that the Negro had become a tenant rather than a wage earner. The head of the Alabama State Grange declared that when the ex-slaves received credit they refused to work for wages, and landowners were forced "to rent to the labor on their lands or turn it out to the commons." Having rented out his land, the owner moved to town and left production unsupervised.[19] This unsupervised labor was inefficient and destructive, explained another Alabamian: "Under this system the farm lands are rented to thriftless negro tenants, who mortgage their crops to merchants in the villages and towns for supplies to raise them. Neither the owner of the land or the merchant exercise any control or management over the growing of the crops, or very little, if any. The results of this system has [sic] been the waste of the farm lands, the destruction of the improvements upon them, and the cultivation of cotton, with very inferior methods of culture, to the practical exclusion of all other crops."[20] Some observers noted that the Negro was not responsible for the unfortunate circumstances in which he found himself. Since he seldom owned land and was able to rent only small plots, it was well-nigh impossible for him to promote efficiency even if he were so inclined, Holmes observed.[21] Ernest Lyon noted too that the Negro tenant was often cheated by the merchant and was powerless to do anything about it.[22]

Neither the special problems faced by the Negro tenant nor the recognition by some that the inefficiency of tenant production was not confined to the Negro[23] weakened the general argument that methods of cotton production were notoriously inefficient in the postwar South. Such was the analysis of the historian Ulrich B. Phillips in a sharply reasoned article published in 1903. He argued that capable and experienced managers had fled their lands, thereby

[19] Senate Committee on Agriculture and Forestry, *Condition of Cotton Growers*, I, 310; see also 415.

[20] *Ibid.*, I, 314.

[21] "Peons of the South," 270-71.

[22] "The Colored Man in the South: His Present Condition and Future Prospects," *The Independent*, XLVII (March 7, 1895), 298-99.

[23] See Senate Committee on Agriculture and Forestry, *Condition of Cotton Growers*, I, 294.

shirking their leadership responsibilities and leaving production in the hands of the incapable.[24]

The futures market was the target of still other critics seeking an answer to the South's economic problems. Witness after witness testified before the Senate Committee on Agriculture and Forestry that the futures system was a curse on the cotton grower because it allowed speculators and manipulators to depress cotton prices. Since spot cotton prices were related to the prices of futures cotton, the ability of wealthy speculators to manipulate the market through their large-scale purchases and sales of "fictional" cotton lowered the prices paid to the grower.[25] Defenders argued that the futures system actually helped the farmer and all who dealt with him. First of all, it brought more buyers into the market, which tended to force prices up. More important, however, the system allowed buyers and consumers to hedge to protect themselves against violent changes in the spot market. With this protection, buyers could operate on a smaller profit margin and, as a result, growers benefited by getting higher prices than they would have received had the buyer been forced to shoulder the additional risk.[26] The champions of the futures system did not carry the day in the committee rooms. The majority of the committee sided with the opponents of the futures system, roundly condemning it as a gambling device that interfered with the operation of the laws of supply and demand. Brokers, speculators, and buyers, the committee decided, all profited by a system that brought economic hardship if not downright penury to the cotton farmer.[27]

The majority report of the Senate committee found two additional factors responsible for low cotton prices. Clearly reflecting the charges of the agrarian radicals of the time, the report denied that overproduction caused low prices. Instead, the report main-

[24] "The Economics of the Plantation," *South Atlantic Quarterly*, II (July 1903), 231-36. Although he emphasized the "ignorance" and the "indolence" of most Negro farmers, Phillips recognized there were "unenterprising" whites as well. For similar analyses see Holmes, "Peons of the South," 272-74; John Hyde and James L. Watkins, *The Cost of Cotton Production*, U. S. Department of Agriculture, Division of Statistics, Miscellaneous Series, Bulletin 16 (Washington, D.C., 1899), 62-63.

[25] Senate Committee on Agriculture and Forestry, *Condition of Cotton Growers*, I, 1, 3, 55-57, 87, 93-94, 147, 152, 170, 176, 181-82, 185, 190, 218-19, 222-23, 227-28, 234-36, 239, 241-43, 412, 415.

[26] For representative samples of the testimony of defenders of the futures system see *ibid.*, I, 8-10, 15-16, 99-100, 166-67, 206-207, 230, 447-52, 474-75, 480, 484.

[27] *Ibid.*, I, viii-xx.

tained, the culprits were the tariff and the demonetization of silver. The levy on imported cloth decreased the foreign demand for raw cotton and the tariff on manufactured goods raised the cost of cotton production. Most important, however, the demonetization of silver caused a shortage of money and, consequently, low prices.[28]

Quite the opposite were the conclusions of a study undertaken by the Department of Agriculture in 1897. "The principal cause of the decline in the price of cotton since 1890 is overproduction," the report, issued in 1899, declared flatly.[29] More significant was the report's contention that although the price of cotton had fallen in the two decades after 1876, the cost of production had decreased at an even sharper rate. Basing its analysis on answers to questionnaires sent to planters, the reports of its county correspondents in the ten principal cotton states, and the wholesale prices of plantation supplies (including food and clothing), the report concluded that the average price of cotton fell 24 percent from 1876-1896 while the average cost of production fell 36.4 percent.[30] When the costs of production were broken down, the results were even more startling: "With one exception—that of flour—there has been a reduction in every article enumerated, and, . . . with the exception of coffee, salt, cotton gins, and mules, the percentage of reduction is greater than the percentage of reduction in the price of cotton."[31]

Such facts seemed totally at odds with the well-known deterioration of the condition of cotton growers over the period. Resolution of the seeming contradiction was, however, obvious enough; costs of production had been based on wholesale, not retail, prices. Even though wholesale prices had dropped very sharply, the grower had not benefited. The conclusion was inescapable: "So great had been the reduction in the wholesale cost of plantation supplies that the conclusion seems reasonable that if that reduction has not inured to the advantage of the planter the fault is chargeable to the conditions of the retail trade."[32] Although its language was more restrained, the conclusions of the Department of Agriculture study

28 *Ibid.*, I, v-viii, xxi-xli.
29 Hyde and Watkins, *The Cost of Cotton Production*, 65.
30 *Ibid.*, 56-58.
31 *Ibid.*, 59-60.
32 *Ibid.*, 61.

paralleled those of Otken, Holmes, and other critics of the furnishing merchant and the crop lien system. Potential profits to the grower were siphoned off by the merchant.

Both angry farmers and objective agricultural analysts could recognize the problems, but critics had few constructive solutions. For some, the problems defied solution. A South Carolinian explained that the "Reform party" of his state had promised to repeal the dread lien law but could not, for the result would have been general economic ruin. Merchants could not be expected to lend money without security and poor farmers had no security other than their cash crop. To do away with the lien law would injure both the poor farmer and the merchant.[33]

Most critics, however, claimed to see a way out of the morass of debt and low prices. The nostrum most frequently suggested was crop diversification. Its benefits seemed obvious. To diversify would mean to reduce cotton acreage with a consequent drop in production; a diminished cotton supply would bring higher cotton prices. Furthermore, farmers who grew their own food would not have to buy it on credit and thus they could escape the clutches of the merchant. Here was a familiar panacea, offered repeatedly to ante bellum planters and now resurrected to solve the problems of post bellum cotton growers.

Critics of all persuasions ended their discussions with a plea for diversification. New South leader Henry Grady had seen it as the means of solving the South's agricultural problems in 1881.[34] Otken concluded his fiery condemnation of the merchant and the lien system by suggesting crop diversification.[35] Holmes offered the same solution and even held out hope to the Negro if he would follow the advice "to shun the storekeeper" by practicing economy and diversification.[36] Both Senate and Department of Agriculture investigators came to the same conclusion.[37] Even merchants sometimes claimed to see benefits in crop diversification. In 1895, for example, a St. Louis cotton factor self-righteously explained that

---

[33] Senate Committee on Agriculture and Forestry, *Condition of Cotton Growers*, I, 294.

[34] "Cotton and Its Kingdom," 724.

[35] *Ills of the South*, 63-64.

[36] "Peons of the South," 268-74.

[37] Senate Committee on Agriculture and Forestry, *Condition of Cotton Growers*, I, xliv; Hyde and Watkins, *The Cost of Cotton Production*, 61-66.

he had "always urged . . . that a farmer or planter should first raise all the articles . . . which are required upon the farm."[38]

Not only was diversification a remedy for the South's ills, but it also recommended itself as a cure that could be self-administered. Indeed, it had to be self-administered. Success, Otken noted, depended primarily upon the farmer himself. He would have to forego the pleasures that credit buying might bring and so achieve his independence from the furnishing merchant. "The remedy for this state of things is severe economy, earnest self-denial, and a fixed determination to buy for cash. Two years of self-denial and economy will enable the majority of the Southern white people to buy on a cash basis."[39] Holmes denied the need for legislation, insisting that the farmer could solve his own problems through individual effort.[40] Many felt that the bitter medicine of self-denial had to be swallowed whether the farmers liked it or not. Since cotton prices were low, farmers would be unable to meet their obligations to their merchants. The merchants would then have no choice but to curtail further advances and the farmer, faced with the specter of starvation, would plant food crops. Diversification would result, and, *ipso facto*, Southern agriculture would again flourish. A writer in the *Nation*, ignoring completely the trend toward tenancy, saw an independent yeomanry emerging from the Souther farmer's plight. Merchants who foreclosed on land were finding it impossible to sell in large tracts and were forced to sell small units at low prices. This, he argued, was attracting a large number of farmers into the South, a "fact [which] assures a careful cultivation of the soil up to the point of diminishing returns."[41] Even the Senate Committee on Agriculture and Forestry, admitting that worldwide remonetization of silver and a reduction of the tariff were unlikely, was reduced to the hope that bankruptcies would extinguish old debts and make it possible for the debt-free grower to work under the higher-priced dollar.[42]

---

[38] Senate Committee on Agriculture and Forestry, *Condition of Cotton Growers*, I, 25.

[39] Otken, *Ills of the South*, 30.

[40] "Peons of the South," 274.

[41] Jesse F. Stallings, J. C. C. Black, Charles J. Boatner, and Hernando D. Money, "Industrial Condition of the Various Southern States," *The Independent*, XLVII (March 7, 1895), 303-305; Wyatt Collier Estes, "Effect on the South of the Low Price of Cotton," *Nation*, LXI (Sept. 12, 1895), 186-87; Senate Committee on Agriculture and Forestry, *Condition of Cotton Growers*, I, 13.

[42] Senate Committee on Agriculture and Forestry, *Condition of Cotton Growers*, I, xliv.

However plausible diversification sounded, it was, in reality, a fantasy. The depression did not bring relief; on the contrary, it deepened the problems by swelling the ranks of the tenants. Advice to practice self-discipline in order to achieve independence from the merchant was ignored—and for good reason. A farmer near starvation was being told to tighten his belt. A tenant who owned nothing was being asked to grow a food crop for which he had neither seed nor land. And, presumably, the landlord was expected to supply land to a tenant who was cutting back on his cash crop, the only means he had to pay his rent. The ultimate goal might be less cotton at higher prices with food supplies grown on the farm, but most farmers lacked the ability to take the first step. Since most borrowing was for consumption, it was hardly reasonable to expect poverty stricken farmers to forego such borrowing even if land and equipment were available.[43] Self-help was clearly not the way out. Southern farmers were caught in a trap from which they could not extricate themselves. And they did not. Higher cotton prices after the turn of the century brought increased production, a greater reliance on the cash crop, and a rise in tenancy. (See Table 9.) When, in 1938, in the midst of another depression, a government agency investigated conditions in the South, it

TABLE 9. SOUTHERN FARMS BY TENURE OF OPERATOR, COTTON PRODUCTION, AND PRICE, 1880-1930

Item	1880	1890	1900	1910	1920	1930
Total farms	1,531,077	1,836,372	2,620,391	3,097,547	3,206,664	3,223,816
Farms operated by owners and managers	977,229	1,130,029	1,389,247	1,560,795	1,615,543	1,433,033
Tenant operated farms (incl. share-croppers)	553,848	706,343	1,231,144	1,536,752	1,591,121	1,790,783
Acreage harvested	15,921,000	20,937,000	24,886,000	31,508,000	34,408,000	42,444,000
Production (bales)	6,606,000	8,653,000	10,124,000	11,609,000	13,429,000	13,932,000
Average price (cents per lb.)	9.83	8.59	9.15	13.96	15.89	9.46

Source: U. S. Bureau of the Census, *Historical Statistics of the United States, Colonial Times to 1957* (Washington, D. C., 1960), 278, 301-302.

[43] Many Southerners, recognizing this dilemma, voiced their opposition to the views of the diversificationists. See Saloutos, *Farmer Movements in the South*, 99.

described a situation which differed from the 1890's only in that the problems had become more severe and pervasive.[44]

The leaders of the New South movement had envisioned a growing and prosperous South, a South freed from the shackles of King Cotton. On the land, cotton would be but one crop in a diversified agriculture; and in the cities, commerce and manufacturing, patterned after the North, would supply goods and services for the South and the rest of the nation. Not only would the South be prosperous, but it would achieve that economic independence which had eluded ante bellum reformers and had been denied on the battlefield. All that was required was energetic determination. In a manner reminiscent of similar ante bellum complaints, a Louisiana newspaper in 1868 warned of the consequences of a lack of enterprise: "The idea in Louisiana, that plantations cannot be run without the consent and assistance of New Orleans merchants, and that New Orleans can do nothing without the aid of Northern capitalists; that it is useless even to plan, contrive, and try to do anything till we get the written approbation of our financial masters, is unfortunate and ruinous to this State. While we sit down in despair over enterprises of vast importance, strangers snatch the work from our hands, and either snag the enterprise, or put it through, as their interests may require."[45] When the South failed to meet the sanguine goals of the New South enthusiasts, many again pointed to the section's lack of energy. This lament is implicit in the suggestions of the diversificationists that farmers grow their own food and buy only for cash. Since benefits would be so great, surely only those unwilling to practice the "earnest self-denial" required would not do so.

Admittedly, a diet of fatback and white bread was not one to endow a population with energy; but this abominable diet was the result more than a cause of Southern economic problems. The South's problems went deeper. The emphasis on cotton, the domination of the crop lien system, the general poverty of the section were all manifestations of more profound problems. Until these problems could be recognized and solved, the South could not escape the incubus of King Cotton. Nor could it achieve economic independence from the North.

[44] U. S. National Emergency Council, *Report on Economic Condition of the South* (Washington, D.C., 1938), *passim*.

[45] *Planters' Banner* (Franklin, La.), Dec. 5, 1868.

CHAPTER TWENTY-SEVEN

The South Remains Dependent: Conclusions

In 1894, Frederick W. Moore joined the widespread debate over the plight of the Southern farmer. After reviewing the workings of the credit system, he concluded that it was not "essentially bad." Like so many others, he traced the South's economic problems to individual inadequacy; the credit system created problems "because many who use it are morally too weak to use it successfully," and as a result, farmers go year after year under the yoke of debt.

Then, apparently forgetting his strictures concerning the moral inadequacy of the Southern farmer, Moore focused on more impersonal economic factors affecting the farmer, and, in so doing, asked a crucial question: "But why not sell the crop for cash, pay interest on the old debt and buy the new supplies for cash?"[1] This, of course, was a more meaningful way to approach the problem of the debt-ridden Southern farmer. What Moore suggested was a long-term loan similar to a bond issue enjoyed by the manufacturer or a land mortgage used by the Northern farmer. Obviously, it would not guarantee solvency, but it would allow the farmer to repay his loan piecemeal over several years and at the same time provide him with funds to make cash purchases—with the savings consequent to such purchases—over the year.

Moore answered his own question very simply. Neither the merchant nor anyone else in the South had the capital resources necessary to extend such long-term loans: "First of all, of course, because the merchant is not a capitalist-investor. He has done more than most retail merchants would consent to do when he arranges to have his capital turned over but once a year. At the end of that period he must have it to put into his business again. Secondly, there was no local capital at the close of the war to seek long investment; nor has the South yet become conspicuous for the amount of funded wealth accumulated."[2] Moore had recognized the South's chronic malady, a shortage of liquid capital. It was a problem familiar in prewar times, but one that was exacerbated by the Civil War and its aftermath. Its effect was to fasten and maintain the crop lien system on the South; and, as in prewar times, it served also to keep the South dependent upon the North.

Richard A. Easterlin's estimates of per capita income in the United States illustrate as well as help to explain the Southern farmers' economic plight. In 1900, per capita income in the states of Louisiana, Arkansas, Mississippi, and Georgia was below that of 1840, and the per capita income of South Carolina in 1900 about equaled that of 1840. Of the cotton states, only Tennessee and Alabama showed increases in per capita income; Tennessee increased about 30 percent and Alabama, about 17 percent between 1840 and 1900. For the nation as a whole, the increase over these years was about 75 percent, with the East North Central and West North Central states enjoying increases of 160 percent and 135 percent respectively.[3]

Low per capita income figures are, of course, a result of the South's continuing emphasis on agriculture, a generally low-income industry. But the section's poverty extended to nonagricultural pursuits as well. Low income meant meager savings and, as a result, a paucity of mortgage money. Indeed, the South lagged far behind the rest of the nation in its banking resources of all kinds, a problem familiar to ante bellum planters. When, in 1871, Louisianian Robert M. Davis complained about the "short-sighted policy of our banking system," his criticism was almost identical to that made by critics of the ante bellum banks. Banks were short-sighted, according to Davis, because they gave only short-term

[1] "The Condition of the Southern Farmer," *Yale Review*, III (May 1894), 62.

[2] *Ibid.*, 62-63. The first point was made again two years later by Pitt Dillingham, "Land Tenure Among the Negroes," *Yale Review*, V (Aug. 1896), 197.

[3] Calculations from figures given in Richard A. Easterlin, "Interregional Differences in Per Capita Income, Population, and Total Income, 1840-1950," *Trends in the American Economy in the Nineteenth Century* ("Studies in Income and Wealth by the Conference on Research in Income and Wealth," Vol. XXIV [Princeton, 1960]), 97-103.

loans on the security of commercial paper. But the borrowers —in this case, factors—needed longer-term credit and hence were forced to renew their bank loans "every sixty or ninety days, until the crops are made and sent to market. If the renewal of such loans is denied, the factor must have recourse to new discounts, generally upon a stringent money market, at increased rates of discount or interest."[4]

The problem Davis pointed out was a very real one, affecting not only factors but other merchants and planters as well. Long-term loans were usually very difficult to come by and always very expensive, as a customer of Savannah factors, Tison and Gordon, learned in early 1873. In early January, the customer had sent the factors three notes for a little over two thousand dollars each and had asked that they be discounted for cash. The first note was payable on August 23, 1873, the second on the same date in 1874, and the third in 1875. Gordon wrote that at the moment only the earliest note could be sold and that it might cost as much as 1.5 or 2 percent per month discount. He promised to seek a buyer for the longer notes, adding that "if I can get a chance to discount them at rate of 13% or even 15% per annum I will do so."[5] Not until mid-February could Gordon dispose of the shortest note and then it cost the owner 18 percent discount, or about 3 percent per month.[6] The other notes proved impossible to sell. In mid-April, Gordon wrote that money in Savannah cost as high as .5 percent per day![7]

Such exorbitant interest rates in early 1873 were not the result of a momentary aberration. Robert Somers in 1870 noted interest rates in various places ranging from 18 to 30 percent per annum.[8] In 1879, another visitor was told that loans even to "responsible men with much property" often cost as much as 2 percent per month, and 8 to 10 percent per annum was commonplace.[9] Legal

4 *The Southern Planter, the Factor and the Banker* (New Orleans, 1871), 9-10.

5 Wm. W. Gordon to Wm. H. Stiles, [Savannah], Jan. 24, 1873, Gordon Family Papers, Georgia Historical Society, Savannah, Ga.

6 Gordon to Stiles, [Savannah], Feb. 12, 1873, *ibid.*

7 Gordon to Stiles, [Savannah], April 15, 1873, *ibid.*

8 *The Southern States Since the War, 1870-1871* (New York, 1871), 45, 57, 63, 243.

9 Sir George Campbell, *White and Black* (London, 1879), 365. In 1875, Tison & Gordon were charging customers 15 percent per annum. See W. W. Gordon to Wm. H. Tison, Savannah, Oct. 12, 1875, Gordon Family Papers, Georgia Historical Society.

restraints would not solve the problem of high interest rates; indeed, such restraints threatened to dry up loans completely. Thus, when the Georgia legislature passed a usury law limiting interest rates to 8 percent per annum, it was reported that "the banks are refusing to discount or renew any outstanding paper." Bankers indicated that they were ready to discontinue business.[10]

The high interest rates charged by Southern banks were not the result of a conspiracy against the farmer and merchant; banks simply lacked the resources to give adequate loans at reasonable interest rates. Southern banking resources, never adequate to the section's needs during ante bellum times, had been virtually wiped out by the Civil War. Nor did the return of peace stimulate banking investment. Profit opportunities in cotton speculation and high interest rates did not induce banking investment under the national bank law. On the contrary, as Davis R. Dewey has put it, "the rates of interest in the South were so high that there was no profit in investing capital in government bonds at the high premiums which were current, in order to take out circulation limited to but 90 per cent. of the par value of the bonds."[11] By the 1870's, Southern banking facilities had increased, but they were still far below prewar levels.[12] Moreover, those bank funds which were available were seldom in the form of long-term mortgages. As before the war, bankers preferred to give short-term commercial loans to city merchants or at least to require a merchant's endorsement before discounting a planter's note.[13] Charles Nordhoff echoed the familiar lament of prewar days: "Some planters complained to me that they could never get advances from banks, which preferred to lend to factors."[14]

The banks' preference for short-term, commercial paper was based on sound economic principles. In an 1867 promotional tract urging Northern investment in the South, Theodore C. Peters reminded Northern capitalists of the advantages and safety of merchants' paper: "As a general rule, factors' bills are among the safest of negotiable securities that can be put upon the market. As a class they are exceedingly cautious, especially those who were

---

[10] *Bradstreet's*, I (Oct. 22, 1879), 1.

[11] "Banking in the South," *Economic History, 1865-1909*, Vol. VI of *The South in the Building of the Nation* (Richmond, 1909), 427.

[12] Somers, *The Southern States*, 45, 171, 184, 210-11, 243, 264-65.

[13] Davis, *The Southern Planter, the Factor and the Banker*, 5, 10.

[14] *The Cotton States in the Spring and Summer of 1875* (New York, 1876), 109.

in business before the war, and had built up a reputation for a high integrity, and great caution in their business relations with the planter. The answer invariably given by bankers was, that all things being equal, they considered a planter's bill with his factor's acceptance the safest paper that could be discounted."[15] Prewar banking experiences had taught bankers the advantages of short-term commercial paper and the dangers of making mortgage loans directly to the grower. As Southern banking was slowly rebuilt, loan policies tended to follow tested channels. Long-term mortgage loans required capital resources that the South did not have, as a New York business journal in a discussion of the needs of the New South made clear in 1881:

> Capital is . . . sorely needed for loan on security of land. The improvidence which mortgages the ungrown crop is a relic of slaveholding times, when the planter got into the hands of his factor, ground between enormous interest rates and wasteful methods; the enormous rates still exist, assisted by the temptation to rely on cotton alone, as being the crop of highest promise, and the southern farmer is consumed by the rates he pays, to-day going to help out yesterday. Capital for loan is as much wanted as capital for investment. Good management can make a mortgage business successful, and at the same time be building up the farmers who are now impoverished by a bad and grinding system.[16]

Such pleas for Northern investment in Southern mortgage banking went largely unheeded. In 1894, the president of the Alabama State Agricultural Society repeated the familiar complaint. A cotton grower was unable to borrow directly from the banks but had to turn instead "to his commission or advancing merchant" for the money he needed. The merchant, however, by adding his endorsement to the farmer's note or by using the farmer's crop lien as collateral, was able to borrow from the banks.[17]

Beginning with the 1890's, the number of Southern banks and the resources they could command began to increase, allowing some growers to deal directly with the banks in their neighborhoods.[18]

[15] *A Report Upon the Condition of the South* (Baltimore, 1867), 7.

[16] *Bradstreet's*, IV (Nov. 19, 1881), 322.

[17] U. S. Congress, Senate, Committee on Agriculture and Forestry, *Report . . . on Condition of Cotton Growers*, 53rd Cong., 3rd Sess., Report 986 (1895), I, 309.

[18] Dewey, "Banking in the South," 429; A. E. Nielsen, *Production Credit for Southern Cotton Growers* (New York, 1946), 46-47.

Direct dealings by farmers with local banks, however, did not become widespread until late in the second decade of the twentieth century. A government study, published in 1924, concluded that most cotton growers continued to deal with banks only indirectly: "The merchant is usually an intermediary between the farmer and the bank, or the factor in those occasional cases where the latter engages in financing. Similarly, the landowner is essentially an intermediary between the tenant and the bank or merchant, depending upon which of these two sources the landowner obtains his own credit from."[19] Where farmers owned their own land, tools, and other equipment, they could borrow from the banks on the security of their property but in the case of tenants, and especially sharecroppers, who owned little or no property, the banks required the endorsement of the landlord or merchant to secure their loans.[20]

Even when farmers did deal directly with the banks, the loan patterns remained the same. The banks, like the merchants, continued to lend money on short term; the farmer's promissory notes were secured by crop liens and chattel mortgages covering livestock, tools, machinery, and feed. Only rarely did they lend on the security of a land mortgage. Like merchant's loans, too, bank loans to cotton growers were timed to the crop season. Most were for periods of three to nine months and virtually none was given for more than a year. Interest rates were uniformly high, ranging, in 1921, from an average rate of 7.88 percent in Tennessee to 9.70 percent in Arkansas.[21]

Long-term real estate mortgages required a fund of capital which the South simply did not have. Although its banking resources increased sharply after 1890, the section lagged far behind the rest of the nation in per capita bank resources. In 1890, the cotton states had per capita bank resources of only $25, whereas the national figure was about $100.[22] Forty years later, on the eve of the Great Depression, the South's relative position had improved, but it still trailed the rest of the nation. (See Table 10.)

[19] Federal Trade Commission, *Report . . . on the Cotton Trade*, 68th Cong., 1st Sess., Senate Doc. 100, Pt. I, 30.

[20] Nielsen, *Production Credit*, 55-93.

[21] *Ibid.*, 53; Federal Trade Commission, *Report . . . on the Cotton Trade*, Pt. I, 3, 30-31.

[22] Calculated from figures given in Nielsen, *Production Credit*, 47; U. S. Bureau of the Census, *Historical Statistics of the United States, Colonial Times to 1957* (Washington, D. C., 1960), 7, 12, 624.

TABLE 10. NUMBER OF BANKS, TOTAL RESOURCES, AND PER CAPITA RESOURCES,
BY SELECTED SECTIONS, 1929

Section	Number of banks	Total resources (billions of dollars)	Per capita resources (dollars)
Total continental U. S.	25,260	71.8	588
New England	1,100	7.9	987
Middle Atlantic	3,297	30.6	1,176
East North Central	5,561	13.1	524
West North Central	6,477	5.0	384
South Atlantic	2,453	4.2	280
East South Central	1,746	1.9	211
West South Central	2,648	2.8	233

Sources: Number of banks and total resources from U. S. Department of Commerce, *Statistical Abstract of the United States, 1930* (Washington, D. C., 1930), 263.
Per capita resources calculated from 1930 Census figures as recorded in U. S. Bureau of the Census, *Historical Statistics of the United States, Colonial Times to 1957* (Washington, D. C., 1960), 7, 12.

The persistence of meager banking facilities in the South does not by itself explain the absence of mortgage lending to cotton growers. Had there been ample profit opportunities in mortgage banking, Northern investment in such enterprises would undoubtedly have found its way into the South. Yet, repeated pleas for such investments fell on deaf ears. In 1938, the National Emergency Council reported that Southern financial institutions accounted for only an insignificant proportion of the nation's investment and savings. Credit was considerably more expensive in the South and the section's banks were unable to make funds available unless given the security of easily negotiable securities.[23] The banks had insufficient funds to meet the credit needs of the farming population. "As a result, the majority of southern tenant farmers must depend for credit on their landlords or the 'furnish merchant' who supplies seed, food, and fertilizer."[24] In short, mercantile credit had persisted as the major means to finance cotton growing. Investors and bankers avoided lending money on the security of land simply because the South's farm real estate did not provide adequate security for loans. Chattel mortgages and crop liens seemed to provide far more security than did land.

Tenants and sharecroppers, of course, owned no land, and for

[23] U. S. National Emergency Council, *Report on Economic Condition of the South* (Washington, D. C., 1938), 50.
[24] *Ibid.* See also, Charles S. Johnson, Edwin R. Embree, and W. W. Alexander, *The Collapse of Cotton Tenancy* (Chapel Hill, 1935), 26-28.

them a real estate mortgage was impossible. The number of such tenants grew steadily after the Civil War, until by 1920 half the South's farms were run by tenants; this alone was a limiting factor in the development of mortgage banking in the South. Even when they owned their own land, however, Southern farmers could offer little real estate security. For one thing, Southern farms were, on the whole, much smaller than farms in the North. In 1900, for example, some 44 percent of the South's farms were under 50 acres in size; by 1925 this figure had risen to 50 percent. (See Table 11.) In part, of course, the prevalence of small farms in the South

TABLE 11. PERCENTAGE OF SMALL FARMS FOR SELECTED AREAS, 1900-1925

Area	Percentage of farms under 20 acres		Percentage of farms under 50 acres	
	1900	1925	1900	1925
East North Central	9	9	29	25
West North Central	4	5	15	13
South Atlantic	15	21	43	53
East South Central	17	22	48	57
West South Central	11	13	40	42
Total South	15	19	44	50

Source: Calculated from figures in U. S. Department of Commerce, *Statistical Abstract of the United States, 1930* (Washington, D. C., 1930), 628.

reflected the high rate of tenancy in the section. But it also reflected a labor-intensive industry, with farm size limited by the individual productivity of the owner or tenant. Small farms, *ceteris paribus*, meant small loans based on land as security.

But all other things were not equal. Not only were Southern farms small, Southern farm land was low in value per acre. In 1900 the average value of Southern farm land was far below the national average; although the relative standing of the South in terms of farm-land value improved during the first two decades of the twentieth century, in 1925 the Southern farm lands were still less valuable per acre than those for the nation as a whole. Moreover, even though the average value per acre of Southern farm lands was increasing at a rate that exceeded the national average, the South's standing in terms of the average value per farm was improving only very slightly. (See Table 12.) This, of course, was a reflection of the small size of Southern farms relative to the rest of the nation as well as of the lesser value of buildings and equipment on Southern farms.

That Northern funds did not enter the South as mortgage capital did not mean that Northern financial facilities were unavailable to Southern agriculture. On the contrary, Northern credit, backed by Northern capital resources, provided the main support for the merchants and bankers in the South, who financed the farmers.

When Sidney Andrews went South just after the Civil War, he met Southern merchants returning from the North where they had

TABLE 12. AVERAGE VALUE PER FARM AND PER ACRE, UNITED STATES AND SOUTH, 1900 AND 1925

Item	1900		1925	
	Average in dollars	Percentage of U.S. value	Average in dollars	Percentage of U.S. value
Value per farm				
United States	3,563	—	8,949	—
South Atlantic	1,511	42	4,205	47
East South Central	1,324	37	2,881	32
West South Central	2,146	60	5,600	63
Land value per acre				
United States	15.57	—	40.81	—
South Atlantic	8.63	55	33.65	82
East South Central	8.72	56	25.89	63
West South Central	5.40	35	25.31	62

Source: U. S. Department of Commerce, *Statistical Abstract of the United States, 1930* (Washington, D. C., 1930), 626.

gone to settle debts and make new purchases. He inquired as to their reception in the North and was told by most that they had been treated well and that some, at least, had received credit on their purchases of from 60 days to 4 months.[25] These were relatively short-term credits; longer-term credits that would allow a Southern merchant to withhold payment until the cotton came to market were slower in coming. After investigating the matter in the fall of 1865, a New York business journal concluded that "half the buyers pay in cash, and a large proportion of the remainder average less than three months in their credits, while but a very few obtain six or eight months." Merchants who had not been ruined by the war, and those who had been able to gain control of cotton during the period of high prices, were obviously able to pay cash for their purchases. The journal predicted that "so long as Northern jobbers

25 Sidney Andrews, *The South Since the War* (Boston, 1866), 5-6.

can sell all they want for cash or short time, it is evident that they will not care to sell to the South and wait upon the cotton crop for payment." But this condition would be temporary, the journal insisted, since only a relatively few were involved. Longer-term credit would soon become necessary if large-scale cotton planting was to resume and if the South was to recuperate.[26]

Indeed, short-term credits were only temporary. Within a few years cash payments decreased considerably. In April 1869, *Hunt's Merchants' Magazine* reported "improved confidence felt in Southern merchants" and indicated that the South was probably "buying upon credit to a much larger extent than during the late years."[27] Ten years later, *Bradstreet's* reported that long-term credit sales had reached prewar proportions. Significantly, the journal noted that credit was now going primarily to the storekeepers rather than to the factors, as it had before the war.[28] This change, as has been noted, reflected the growing importance of the furnishing merchant and also contributed to the decline of cotton factorage after the Civil War.

Like the merchants, Southern banks were also dependent upon Northern resources. In the early years after the Civil War, when the South's banking resources were virtually nonexistent, what meager bank capital it did have was supplemented by the influx of Northern funds. Robert Somers noted in 1870 that banking funds in the Southern markets were not adequate for the volume of trade; but, he added, the business in cotton and other merchandise was "transacted by credits established in New York, which are only banking in another form."[29]

New York, as the nation's monetary center, played a major role in moving all of the nation's agricultural products. In 1868, the *Commercial and Financial Chronicle* described the flow of funds from New York each year:

> In the Spring, currency is required for moving the balance of crops of the previous year and distributing the season's merchandise. In the Summer, the money sent out in the Spring, to accommodate the country banks and more produce, being

26 *Commercial and Financial Chronicle*, I (Sept. 9, 1865), 325-26.
27 LX (April 1869), 281.
28 II (April 7, 1880), 5.
29 *The Southern States*, 171.

no longer required for effecting retail exchanges, flows back into New York banks, and accumulates much in excess of their ability to find it employment. In the Fall, there is a very active demand for moving the crops of the West and the South and from the country banks generally to meet the wants of the retail trade. The banks then not only lose the deposits of the interior banks made during the Summer, but they are required to discount freely for their country correspondents, and to make advances to them; and this occurs simultaneously with an active demand from the City trade for discounts and loans. Toward the close of the year, the discounted paper begins to run off; money sent out for the purchase of produce returns in payment for merchandise; country banks deposit their surplus funds with their correspondents here; and again we have a plethora of money, which continues until the Spring demand sets in.[30]

For the Southern cotton grower, this meant simply that a good part of the credit he received came ultimately from the North. P. H. Lovejoy, a planter and furnishing merchant of Hawkinsville, Georgia, tersely described the process in his testimony before the Industrial Commission in 1899:

Q. How do they [Southern farmers] get supplies?
A. Through merchants.
Q. And the merchants?
A. Through the banks.
Q. And where do the local banks get their money?
A. New York.[31]

The flow of funds from the urban money markets to the country to move agricultural produce is, of course, a common feature of a modern market economy. The most important feature of financing cotton movements was not the usual movement of funds from city to countryside but the flow of funds primarily from Northern cities to the Southern countryside. While Western cities were developing money markets which aided significantly in the movement of Western crops, Southern banking facilities did not keep pace. A government survey over the three-year period ending in 1922 concluded that "New York is the most important source of cotton

[30] VII (Nov. 14, 1868), 615. See also, XI (Aug. 27, 1870), 261.
[31] U. S. Industrial Commission, *Report on Agriculture and Agricultural Labor* (Washington, D. C., 1901), 78; see also 120.

loans." Over 36 percent of the loans came from New York, or more than three times as much as was borrowed in New Orleans, the largest Southern money market in the cotton trade.[32]

The pattern of economic dependency that had characterized the ante bellum South was carried over into the postwar South. Many, recognizing and condemning this dependency, called for a change. Both their complaints and the solutions they offered were reminiscent of similar charges and proposals during the prewar period. Meager banking resources retarded the commercial development of the South, argued Isaac N. Maynard in 1875. Southern cities quickly used up their supply of capital and their business fell off. "The inability to make advances . . . diverts . . . trade into other channels, and the customary credits being denied to purchasers, country merchants lay in their supplies in other markets," he explained. His proposed solution was a Warehouse Bank that could lend money on stored merchandise.[33] All that was required, wrote the *New Orleans Price Current* in support of the proposal, was the required capital backing. If local funds were not forthcoming, the paper was sure that Northern or foreign capitalists, lured by the undoubted profits, would subscribe the necessary capital.[34]

But neither local nor outside funds were forthcoming and Maynard's plan remained a plan and nothing more, just as the plans of prewar reformers failed for lack of capital. In the early 1870's, Granges in Mississippi, Alabama, Georgia, and Louisiana set up cooperative marketing agencies, but these too failed for lack of adequate resources.[35] Complaints continued and always the refrain was the same. Growers were forced to give crop liens or chattel mortgages; merchants discounted the paper in local banks; local banks used it as collateral for loans from Northern banks. The end result was tragedy for the South. When the cotton was ready for shipment, each creditor pressed his debtor for payment, and all the cotton was forced on the market at the same time to meet financial obligations. This forced cotton prices down while interest

[32] Federal Trade Commission, *Report . . . on the Cotton Trade*, Pt. I, 54-55.

[33] *Notes on a Factors' Warehouse Bank (Loan and Pledge)* ([New Orleans], 1875), 1-6.

[34] Dec. 12, 1875, as reprinted, *ibid.*, 7-8.

[35] Federal Trade Commission, *Report . . . on the Cotton Trade*, Pt. I, 56.

payments drained funds from the South.[36] In 1910, Atlanta editor Henry S. Reed reviewed the problems involved in financing the cotton crop, raising the same problems which had been discussed for more than seventy-five years. Nor was his solution any different. He proposed "ample warehousing facilities" in the South and the establishment of "a great cotton bank and trust company, capitalized and managed in the sole interest of the cotton crop." "We must create a money center in the South," he declared. Apparently oblivious of the ancient vintage of his proposals, he envisioned a prosperous and independent South if his proposals, requiring "only . . . the co-operation of our southern bankers," were acted upon: "We must break away from the traditions of the past and become absolutely free and independent. The new gold which cotton brings from foreign lands is of such vast sums that it is absolutely unwise to permit it to be returned to New York instead of to New Orleans, for example."[37] Seventy-two years earlier George McDuffie and others had said much the same thing.

Like the ante bellum cotton factor, the furnishing merchant carried on his business in the context of a dependent South. If both, when successful, benefited from their favored position in cotton financing and marketing, both were in a very risky business. Indeed, the furnishing merchant, whose business practices had usually excited the greater obloquy, was, in fact, in a much more precarious position than the factor. Factors dealt with planters and merchants whose capital resources in slaves, land, and equipment often amounted to many thousands of dollars, whereas most of the furnishing merchants' customers were landless or, at best, owned only small plots of low-value land. "A mortgage given in January or February on a crop not to be planted until April, is not taken as a first-class commercial security, and consequently the charges on the advances are heavy," explained a perceptive South Carolinian in 1880.[38] Relying as he usually did on a single crop

[36] Senate Committee on Agriculture and Forestry, *Condition of Cotton Growers*, I, 309; U. S. Industrial Commission, *Report . . . on the Distribution of Farm Products* (Washington, D. C., 1901), 147.

[37] "Financing the Cotton Crop," *Annals of the American Academy of Political and Social Science*, XXXV (Jan. 1910), 16-24.

[38] Eugene Hilgard, "Report on Cotton Production in the United States," in U. S. Department of Interior, Census Office, *Tenth Census*, (1880) (Washington, D. C., 1884), VI, 518.

and dealing as he usually did with a farmer who could give virtually no security for his loans except his forthcoming crop, the merchant himself was a poor credit risk. Thus, his interest payments were extremely high and, as a consequence, he was "virtually forced to exploit the tenant if he is himself to survive."[39]

Yet, if the merchant can be relieved of the onus of the South's economic ills, it would be a mistake simply to see him as nothing more than a victim in a generally inefficient system.[40] Like the factor, he played a leading role in bringing capital into the South. His credit standing in the North enabled him to buy goods on credit; his endorsement on notes and liens made them more easily negotiable. In short, he was able to tap capital resources in the North that might not have been otherwise available. In the very process of performing this service, however, he helped to perpetuate the reign of King Cotton. He did this not by forcing Southern farmers to grow cotton but by enabling them to do so. A significant characteristic of agriculture is its ease of entry;[41] what is true of agriculture in general was even more true of postwar cotton production. Little in the way of tools and equipment was needed to begin cotton production. These minimal needs were easily met from the resources of the furnishing merchants. As a result, thousands could—and did—move into cash crop production even though they had virtually no capital resources to invest.

For well over one hundred years, cotton was king in the South, yet he had been unable to extend his hegemony beyond the South, as the Civil War had made abundantly clear. And even in his own domain his powers had been circumscribed, for he owed his perpetuation, indeed, his very existence, to more powerful rulers outside his realm. But, King Cotton's dependency exacted its toll, as Senator Benjamin Tillman noted in a flamboyant speech at the Atlanta Exposition (much to the chagrin of its New South organizers): "All the gold goes North and stays there. It does not return to beautify and adorn the South. They are enriching themselves at our expense and when you go there and see their palaces

[39] Johnson, Embree, and Alexander, *The Collapse of Cotton Tenancy*, 31. See also, Fred A. Shannon, *The Farmer's Last Frontier* (New York, 1945), 93-94.

[40] See Thomas D. Clark, *Pills, Petticoats and Plows: The Southern Country Store* (Indianapolis, 1944), 323.

[41] See Douglass C. North, *Growth and Welfare in the American Past* (Englewood Cliffs, N. J., 1966), 144.

and their wealth and their luxury, . . . reflect that it is not their country that has produced it, but that is the price which the South has paid for being conquered."[42]

Modern students, with a great deal less flourish and considerably more scholarship, have classified the economy of the South as "colonial."[43] In attempting to bring in Yankee enterprise and Yankee capital, the South, it is argued, lost control over her new industries. Southern businessmen, instead of becoming the local counterparts of the Northern industrial statesmen, became merely the agents of Northern interests. "The economy over which they presided was increasingly coming to be one of branch plants, branch banks, captive mines, and chain stores."[44] Recently, students have criticized this concept of a colonial South, arguing that it implies conspiracy against the South which simply did not exist.[45]

Students who regard the South as a colonial area emphasize the dependency of its manufacturing and industry. Critics of this interpretation focus on the same features in denying a Northern conspiracy to prevent economic development in the South. In a very real sense, however, both ignore the most essential aspects of the Southern economy. Agriculture, not industry, dominated the Southern economy until well into the twentieth century, and throughout the nineteenth century and beyond cotton dominated Southern agriculture. During this entire period the South was dependent upon the North for financing the growing and marketing of cotton. The peculiar evolution of the Southern economy and not a conspiracy sustained and perpetuated this dependent, colonial status. Cotton was king, but he was a puppet monarch.

[42] *The Cotton States and International Exposition and South, Illustrated* (Atlanta, 1896), 135.

[43] See, for example, B. B. Kendrick, "The Colonial Status of the South," *Journal of Southern History,* VIII (Feb. 1942), 3-22; C. Vann Woodward, *Origins of the New South, 1877-1913* (Baton Rouge, 1951), 291-320; William B. Hesseltine and David L. Smiley, *The South in American History* (2nd ed.; Englewood Cliffs, N. J., 1960), 393, 402; Walter Prescott Webb, *Divided We Stand* (New York, 1937).

[44] Woodward, *Origins of the New South,* 292.

[45] Clarence H. Danhof, "Four Decades of Thought on the South's Economic Problems," in Melvin L. Greenhut and W. Tate Whitman (eds.), *Essays in Southern Economic Development* (Chapel Hill, 1964), 7-68. See also George B. Tindall, "The 'Colonial Economy' and the Growth Psychology: The South in the 1930's," *South Atlantic Quarterly,* LXIV (Autumn 1965), 465-77.

Appendix

The following transcriptions of financial records from one cotton planter illustrate graphically the many services performed by the cotton factor for his client. The records selected show typical transactions: a domestic sale of 131 bales of cotton on the New Orleans market; a foreign sale made in Liverpool; and, finally, an annual account submitted by the factor. The originals are in the Hickman-Bryan Papers, Joint Collection, Western Historical Manuscripts Collection, State Historical Society of Missouri Manuscripts, Columbia, Missouri, and are used here with permission of the State Historical Society of Missouri, Columbia.

I. *Domestic sale*

The sale involves 131 bales that arrived in New Orleans via the steamboat "National" and were sold to Vunner & Mure on February 3, 1857. The weight of each bale is carefully noted, as is the sale price—12 cents per pound for the entire 58,383 pounds. The cotton was not of uniform quality, as is shown in the lower lefthand corner, where the valuation of the bales is given. The factor, instead of selling the cotton at prices varying from 11½ cents to 13⅛ cents per pound, decided to sell the entire lot at 12 cents. The list of "Charges" shows the payments made by the factor for his customer (drayage, storage, insurance) along with his 2½ percent commission on the gross proceeds. The final figure, $6,550.16, is the net proceeds going to the credit of the planter.

Sale of 131 Bales of Cotton Received pr Str "National"

Feby 3/57   To Vunner & Mure   acct. of Est. W. P. Hickman

Est W.P.H.
131

# 472	# 470	# 444	# 507	# 412	# 408	# 426
463	419	508	459	436	466	384
449	464	454	471	434	462	412
453	493	476	454	472	483	426
449	438	418	504	463	428	442
458	446	475	415	419	418	454
458	490	485	475	479	460	461
465	448	386	477	480	507	388
453	459	492	448	464	460	461
457	449	479	460	441	474	399
4577	4576	4617	4670	4500	4566	4253

# 400	# 418	# 378	# 398	# 428	# 402	# 432
405	424	409	461	445	443	
395	429	401	385	503	412	
466	438	417	390	484	468	
397	404	432	459	485	463	
444	404	454	449	423	508	
365	421	476	398	411	505	
468	439	475	463	468	380	
423	414	421	440	471	468	
480	452	461	476	454	442	
4243	4243	4324	4319	4572	4491	432

58.383 pounds @ 12 ¢ $ 7005.96

Charges

Frt as per B/L	131.00	
Drayage Storage &c	65.50	
River Insurance $6550 @ ¾ %	49.13	
Fire Insurance @ ½ %	35.02	
Commission @ 2½ %	175.15	455.80

Cr Estate W. P. Hickman $6,550.16

Valuation	New Orleans Feby 6/57
12 Bs @ 13⅛	R W Estlin & Co
35 " " 12⅜	pr Jas Rea
75 " @ 11½	

II. *Foreign sale*

The following two accounts are statements showing a sale of 13 bales of cotton in Liverpool. The planter, W. P. Hickman, sent the cotton to his factor in New Orleans, Dick & Hill, who then sent it to Astley & Williams in Liverpool, who sold it on August 12, 1847.

The account of the Liverpool factor shows the gross proceeds in pounds and shillings (£158 9). From this he deducted his costs (dock dues, freight, mending, insurance, etc.), interest on the sum advanced, and his selling commission. The net proceeds, still in pounds, are placed to the credit of Dick & Hill.

Dick & Hill then sent an account to the planter. This account reveals that Dick & Hill drew an advance on the Liverpool firm in May of £111 8 7 and paid interest on this advance. The advance, interest, and postage charges are subtracted from the net proceeds in Liverpool, leaving a sum of £23 6 5 due the planter. The factor thereupon drew on the Liverpool firm for this sum at 60 days, crediting the planter in addition with the 60 days of interest on his money. The bill drawn (in pounds) was discounted for local money, earning a 7 percent premium in the exchange. From this the factor deducted his commission and postage costs, and the net sum placed to the planter's credit came to $107.74. Thus, the factor had arranged a Liverpool sale for his customer and had negotiated an advance for him in Liverpool three months before the sale was made and six months before proceeds from the sale arrived in New Orleans. Moreover, he had arranged for all services on the cotton and had negotiated all the necessary exchange.

Account Sales of 13 Bales Cotton ex "Meteor" @ New Orleans Sold
for account of Est W P Hickman Esqr pr order of Messrs Dick & Hill

Aug 12	By E Hallam for 13 Bales payt 10 days & 3 mos		

```
                C  "  "
        WPH   51 1 9
        13           13
              ───────
              51 0 24
               1 3  9
                                              d
        49 1 15 ct. or 5531 lbs @ 6 ⅞ pr lb        158 9
              ═══════                              ═════
```

Charges

July 23	Dock dues 4/10 Town dues 2/2	7	
Oct 28	Freight on 5604 lbs @ ½d pr lb & 5%		
	Primage	12 5 2	
	Porters mending canvas & twine	17 6	
	Cartage & porterage 10/10 Whouse		
	Rent 4/8	15 6	
	Postage of remces 2d Bk Commr 9	11	
	Insurance from fire in Warehouse	4 10	
	Sea do on £141 @ 25/% £ 1.5.3		
	Policy 3/-	1 18 3	
	Interest on freight to 26 Novemr	1	
	Commission Brokerage & Guarantee		
	3¼%	5 3	21 13 2
	Nt. Pds at Cr of Messrs Dick & Hill		
	Cash 26 Nov		£136 15 10
E E			

Liverpool 2d September 1847
Astley & Williams

Statement of 13 Bales Cotton ex Meteor. Sold in Liverpool by
Astley & Williams for a/c of Estate Wm. P. Hickman

1847		
May 29	Received advance per Statement rend due in	
	Liverpool 27th Aug. $520. @ 5%	£111. 8. 7
	Interest in Liverpool to 26 Nov. 91 days. 5%	1.16. 2
	Postages in Liverpool	4. 8
		113. 9 5
	By proceeds Sales due 26 Nov 1847	136.15.10
		£ 23. 6. 5
Sep 29	„ Interest to maturity of a 60 d/s bill	
	drawn to day Say 28th Decr. 32 days 5%	2. 8
	gain over advance	£ 23. 9. 1

£23.9.1 @ 7% Ex.		$111.53
Commission on gain	2.79	
Postages	1.00	3.79
Cr Est of W P. Hickman in a/c		$107.74

with Hill McLean & Co.   Cash at Date

New Orleans Sep. 29, 1847
Dick & Hill in Liq
pr Robt Estlin

III. *Annual account*

After he had sold all the planter's cotton, the factor rendered his customer an account current. Here were listed all the items of expense and income handled by the factor for the entire year. The books were balanced and the records closed for the season. On the left side of the ledger were listed all the expenditures made by the factor for his customer, the date they were made, and the interest charges (calculated from the day the payment was made until the day the account was rendered). On the right side of the ledger were listed the income items—most commonly proceeds of cotton sales—along with interest earned (calculated from the day the income was received to the day the account was rendered). In the account here the planter ended the year on June 26, 1854, owing his factor a balance of $7,852.62. He paid this debt in two notes, one dated July 1, 1854, and the other dated January 19, 1855. Thus the factor carried his debt over until the next year.

Est W P Hickman   In a/c   Interest a/c @ 8%

Date	Description	Amount	Days	Interest
1853				
Sept 21	To Dft T J H fav E Parker 12 Sept 60 d/d due 14 Nov. 53	77 40	229	3 93
Dec. 2	„ Cash paid H R W Hill's Acceptance	1920 00	211	90 02
3	„ Cash paid Do „	259 27	210	12 08
1854				
Jany 4	„ Cash paid Note Mary A Hickman	241 56	178	9 53
14	„ Dft P. T. H. favor H Lynch & Co. 11 Jany due 4 March 54	1254 52	119	33 16
18	„ Cash paid H R W Hill's Acceptance	1320 00	164	48 10
25	„ Dft Mary Ann Hickman favor P T Hickman 16 Jany 12 m/d due 19 January 1855. 1468.60 bearing interest 8% from date 117.48	1586 08	down	
Feby 28	„ Invoice pork &c	149 14	123	4 45
	„ Cash paid order P T Hickman favor Henderson & Gaines	13 63		
	„ Dft P. T. H. favor Slack Day & Stauffer 27 Feby 60 d/d due 1 May 54	187 99	} 61	8 23
	„ Dft do favor Sickles & Co due 1 May	86 38		
	„ Dft do „ Dudley Nelson due 1 May	333 13		
	„ Dft do „ D H Holmes due 2 „	636 22	60	8 48
March 7	„ Dft do „ J. C. Wise 3 March 30 d/d due 5 April	230 21	87	4 44
April 8	„ Cash paid Dft. P. T. H. fav. Dr. Luckett	42 00	84	78
20	„ Dft P. T. H. fav. Dr. F W Marshall due 4 June '54	250 00	27	1 50
May 16	„ Invoice Lime &c	13 46	46	13
23	„ Invoice Pork &c	288 49	39	2 50
June 3	„ Cash paid Dft. P. T. H. fav. Dr. S A Smith	74 00	28	46
7	„ Cash pd. Hyde & Goodrich for repairing watch	13 50	24	07
10	„ Cash paid Dft fav. Toledano & Taylor	1000 00		
	„ Cash paid for check on N York $1000 @ 1⅝%	983 75	} 21	10 19
	„ Cash handed P T Hickman	200 00		
26	„ Amo. due Est. Hill 1 July '54 pr a/c	1431 33	x	x x
	„ Balance Interest a/c	161 30		
		$12753 36		238 05

To Balance due 1 July '54   6266 54
        19 January 55   1586 08
                    $ 7852 62

per Annum to 1 July '54   with   Estlin Leet Co.

1854					
March 28	By Proceeds 50 B/Cotton	1587 20	95	33 50
April 29	„ Proceeds 102 Do	2726 80	63	38 17
May 23	„ Proceeds 24 Do	586 74	39	5 08
	„ Balance Interest a/c			161 30
	Balance at Debit	7852 62		

                                           12753 36   238 05

E E

New Orleans June 26th 1854
Estlin Leet & Co.
pr H Thornhill

Bibliographical Note

Since bibliographical information on all the works and manuscript collections used and cited in the preparation of this book is available in the footnotes, my purpose here is to introduce the reader to some of the historiographical problems in Southern business and economic history in general and in cotton marketing in particular.

The most noteworthy fact about Southern economic history has been its relative neglect. Emory Q. Hawk's *Economic History of the South* (New York, 1934) is the only general economic history of the region and it is adequate only as a brief introduction to the subject. Although slavery has been given a great deal of attention, its economic aspects have not been emphasized, and in those works on the economics of slavery the emphasis has been on profits to the individual planter rather than on the effects of slavery on Southern economic development. [For an analysis of the literature on this subject, see my "The Profitability of Slavery: A Historical Perennial," *Journal of Southern History*, XXIX (Aug. 1963), 303-25.] Eugene D. Genovese's *The Political Economy of Slavery* (New York, 1965) is a recent outstanding effort to view slavery from a wider angle. Other work is also underway on this question. Douglass C. North's *The Economic Growth of the United States, 1790-1860* (New York, 1961) contains a splendid statement on "The Economic Structure of the South" (Chapter X) which should serve as the basis for a number of important specialized studies.

Nowhere has the neglect of Southern economic history been more obvious than in the field of commerce. When I first began this study I was warned that relevant manuscript material amounted to millions of pieces scattered from one end of the country to the other. I quickly learned that my informant did not exaggerate. Virtually every collection of planters' papers as well as the papers of storekeepers and other merchants contains invoices, accounts, and correspondence from cotton factors, buyers, and others involved in the marketing and financing of the Southern cotton crop. Yet, paradoxically, there are relatively few published analyses of the various agencies involved in the cotton trade.

This is especially true of the cotton factorage system, clearly the most important ante bellum agency in cotton marketing. Modern published descriptions of the factorage system almost universally rely upon the brief and perceptive article on the subject by Alfred Holt Stone: "The Cotton Factorage System of the Southern States," *American Historical Review*, XX (April 1915), 557-65. Valuable as it is, Stone's article unfortunately contains a number of serious errors which have regularly found their way into subsequent studies. The evidence does not support his insistence that commissions often exceeded 2½ percent, that interest was often charged for the entire year regardless of the length of time borrowed money was held, and that factors required planters to send a given amount of cotton to them, charging a penalty commission for failure to meet this stipulation. The most important weakness in Stone's article, however, is his contention that the factor was the power behind king cotton's throne, an argument that erroneously subordinates the country to the city in economic matters and implies political subordination as well.

Other useful general studies that deal with factorage are: John Spencer Bassett, "The Relation Between the Virginia Planter and the London Merchant," American Historical Association, *Annual Report for the Year 1901* (Washington, D.C., 1902), I, 551-75 (indispensable for the colonial background, but a subject which cries out for more extensive research); Thomas P. Govan, "Banking and the Credit System in Georgia, 1810-1860," *Journal of Southern History*, IV (May 1938), 164-84; Ralph W. Haskins, "Planter and Cotton Factor in the Old South: Some Areas of Friction," *Agricultural History*, XXIX (Jan. 1955). 1-14; Norman Sydney Buck,

The Development of the Organization of Anglo-American Trade, 1800-1850 (New Haven, 1925); Fred Mitchell Jones, *Middlemen in the Domestic Trade of the United States, 1800-1860* (Urbana, 1937). Local studies and studies of individual planters are often helpful. See Charles S. Davis, *The Cotton Kingdom in Alabama* (Montgomery, Ala., 1939); Edwin Adams Davis, ed., *Plantation Life in the Florida Parishes of Louisiana, 1836-1846 as Reflected in the Diary of Bennet H. Barrow* (New York, 1943); Louise Gladney, "History of Pleasant Hill Plantation, 1811-1867," unpublished master's thesis, Louisiana State University; Guion Griffis Johnson, *A Social History of the Sea Islands* (Chapel Hill, N.C., 1930); Weymouth T. Jordan, *Hugh Davis and His Alabama Plantation* (University, Ala., 1948); Weymouth T. Jordan, "The Elisha F. King Family: Planters of the Alabama Black Belt," *Agricultural History*, XIX (July 1945), 152-62; Wendell Holmes Stephenson, *Isaac Franklin, Slave Trader and Planter of the Old South* (Baton Rouge, La., 1938); Beatrice Marion Stokes, "John Bisland, Mississippi Planter, 1776-1821," unpublished master's thesis, Louisiana State University; Mack Swearingen, "Thirty Years of a Mississippi Plantation: Charles Whitmore of 'Montpelier,' " *Journal of Southern History*, I (May 1935), 198-211; Rosser H. Taylor, *Ante-Bellum South Carolina: A Social and Cultural History* (Chapel Hill, N.C., 1942); Alice Pemble White, "The Plantation Experience of Joseph and Lavinia Erwin, 1807-1836," *Louisiana Historical Quarterly*, XXVII (April 1944), 343-478. M[atthew] B[rown] Hammond, *The Cotton Industry* (New York, 1897) is mainly concerned with the post bellum period, but contains a number of good chapters on the ante bellum period also. Indispensable for any student of Southern agriculture are Paul W. Gates, *The Farmer's Age: Agriculture 1815-1860* (New York, 1960) and Lewis Cecil Gray, *History of Agriculture in the Southern United States to 1860*, 2 vols. (Washington, D. C., 1933). The works of Clement Eaton are perceptive and scholarly: *The Growth of Southern Civilization, 1790-1860* (New York, 1961); *A History of the Old South*, 2nd ed. (New York, 1966).

My own analysis of the factorage system has been based almost exclusively on contemporary documents. Travel accounts were sometimes helpful, but most have little to say about commercial procedures. They must, of course, be used with caution. Being outsiders, travelers often failed to understand or even to see routine business activities. Thomas D. Clark's splendid bibliography, *Travels in the Old South: A Bibliography,* 3 vols. (Norman, Okla., 1956-1959) will introduce the reader to this extensive literature. State court reports provide a mine of information on the factorage system as well as on other features of Southern economic life. Their enunciation of the law is only a part of their value. Testimony often reveals commercial practices which went far beyond the case at hand.

Manuscript collections remain the best sources. Planters' papers invariably contain correspondence and accounts from factors and other merchants. Footnote citations will lead the reader to those I have found most useful. The papers of cotton factors are more rare. Of those I have seen, I consider the following most valuable: Jackson, Riddle and Company Papers, Maunsel White Papers, Gordon Family Papers, Stephen D. Heard Papers, Southern Historical Collection, University of North Carolina Library, Chapel Hill; Gordon Family Papers, R. and J. Habersham Papers, Robert Habersham Papers, Georgia Historical Society, Savannah; Golsan Brothers Papers, Henry S. Leverich Correspondence, Charles P. Leverich Correspondence, Department of Archives and Manuscripts, Louisiana State University, Baton Rouge; Charles P. Leverich Papers, Mississippi Department of Archives and History, Jackson; Waring and Hayne Papers, South Carolina Historical Society, Charleston.

Neglect of the cotton factorage system is matched by neglect of Southern banking. There is no history of Southern banking in the nineteenth century although primary material is available in government (state and federal) documents and in Southern archives. There are a few state studies (see p. 100, note 4) but these are not adequate. The more general works of G. S. Callender, "Early Transportation and Banking Enterprises of the States in Relation to the Growth of Corporations," *Quarterly Journal of Economics,* XVII (Nov. 1902), 111-62, and Bray Hammond, *Banks and Politics in America from the Revolution to the Civil War* (Princeton, N. J., 1957), are fine studies that could serve as models for a history of Southern banking.

The economic history of the urban South is yet to be written. Weymouth T. Jordan's *Ante-Bellum Alabama: Town and Country*

(Tallahassee, Fla., 1957) is good, but it is only a first step. There are no studies of the ports of New Orleans, Mobile, Savannah, or Charleston to match Ralph Greenhalgh Albion's monumental *The Rise of New York Port [1815-1860]* (New York, 1939).

Fortunately, the ante bellum country store has been rescued from oblivion by Lewis Atherton in his splendid *The Southern Country Store, 1800-1860* (Baton Rouge, La., 1949). Thomas D. Clark's *Pills, Petticoats and Plows* (Indianapolis, 1944) is a spritely and scholarly study of the post-Civil War stores. This may be supplemented by the older, but still useful study by M. B. Hammond mentioned above.

The outstanding general work on the post-Civil War South is C. Vann Woodward, *Origins of the New South, 1877-1913* (Baton Rouge, La., 1951). Fred A. Shannon's *The Farmer's Last Frontier* (New York, 1945) is the best study of post-Civil War agricultural history.

A number of post bellum commercial developments have received scant attention from economic historians. None of the large cotton merchants such as Anderson, Clayton and Company have been studied; there is no history of the New York Cotton Exchange or the Memphis Cotton Exchange. James E. Boyle's *Cotton and the New Orleans Cotton Exchange* (Garden City, N.Y., 1934) is brief and anecdotal, but is the only study of this important exchange.

The Civil War has long been considered a turning point in American history and especially in American economic history. Recent scholarship, however, has tended to minimize its significance. Industrialism is said to have been well under way in the United States before the war; rapid economic growth—or the "take-off" to use W. W. Rostow's term—had already taken place. A convenient collection of essays on both sides of the controversy is Ralph Andreano, ed., *The Economic Impact of the American Civil War* (Cambridge, Mass., 1962). Broader in scope is David T. Gilchrist and W. David Lewis, eds., *Economic Change in the Civil War Era* (Greenville, Del., 1965) which is the proceedings of a "Conference on American Economic Institutional Change, 1850-1873, and the Impact of the Civil War" sponsored by the Eleutherian Mills-Hagley Foundation in 1964. Most participants in this conference found little institutional change arising as a direct result of the Civil War (banking was a notable exception). Changes were under way before the war and continued after the termination of conflict, a point of view that my own analysis tends to support.

For the economic history of the South, emphasis on the continuity of institutions is a necessary corrective in an area which has been traditionally divided at the Civil War. Further studies of such areas as banking, trade patterns, the internal market, and the like, which bridge the Civil War years, are clearly needed. Nevertheless, there is the danger of overcorrection. Unlike the North, the South did experience a major economic and social change as a result of Civil War—the end of slavery.

Index

Acceptances. *See* Endorsement

Accommodation paper: dangers of, 102-103, 117-19; defined, 116-17; transformed into long-term loans, 117; Edmond J. Forstall on, 117, 118; Louisiana Bank Law of 1842 on, 117, 118; contrasted to commercial paper, 117, 118*n*. *See also* Credit

Adams, Hopkins and Company, 17

Adams, John Quincy, 106

"Address to the People of the Southern and Southwestern States" (1838): quoted, 140-41

Adolphus C. Schaefer and Company, 248, 249, 276-77

Advances: defined, 34; advantages to planters of, 34, 134; availability of, 34-35, 35*n*, 82, 281, 286; law relating to, 62-63; by banks, 105, 106-113; criticism of, 132-33, 137-38; effect of on factors, 133, 281; by planters to tenants, 310. *See also* Credit

Agrarianism, viii, 144-45

Alabama: law concerning commission charges in, 55; internal improvements in, 88, 280; banking in, 98, 103, 105, 109, 122, 172; and Crisis of 1837, 181; interior cotton buying in, 275; population of, 190, 191; and New Orleans market, 280; Grangers in, 338; per capita income in, 346; cooperative marketing proposed in, 354, 356

Alabama and Florida Railroad, 88

Alabama River, 88

Alabama State Agricultural Society, 349

Albany, N.Y., 192

Alcorn, James Lusk, 219-20

Alexandria, La., 155

American Cotton Planters' Association, 252, 253

Americus, Ga.: ante bellum storekeeper's business in, 79; Civil War trade in, 227-34; cotton warehouse in during Civil War, 230; post bellum storekeeper's business in, 248, 249, 256-57, 302, 330; Grangers in, 334, 355

Anderson, Clayton and Company, 289

Anderson, Frank, 289

Anderson, Monroe, 289

Andrews, Israel, 133

Andrews, Sidney, 353

Andrews and Brother, 185

Annals of the American Academy of Political and Social Science, 336

Apalachicola River, 88

Arkansas: banking in, 98, 99, 102, 102*n*, 122, 172; population of, 189, 190, 191; and New Orleans market, 280; plantation stores in, 309; per capita income in, 346

Armour, James, 64, 185

Ashe, Thomas, 12

Athens, Ala., 93, 94

Atherton, Lewis E., 191

Atkinson, N. L., 95

Atlanta, Ga.: as an ante bellum cotton market, 15; railroad in, 88; wholesale grocery trade in during Civil War, 228; fall of, 232; post bellum businessmen in, 328-29

Atlanta and West Point Railroad, 88, 269

Gold (*continued*):
federacy, 217, 221; trade in Vicksburg during Civil War, 222; speculation, 330
Golsan, Eustace, 261-62, 263. *See also* E. F. Golsan and Company; Golsan and Sanders
Golsan, H. L., 262
Golsan, R. W. *See* Golsan, Eustace
Golsan and Sanders, 261-62, 283-84
Goodwyn, Philo, 16-17, 30
Gordon, A. and J. M., 79
Gordon, W. W., 247, 258-59, 291. *See also* Tison and Gordon
Gorrissen Brothers, 35
Govan, Thomas P., 110
Grace, Thomas A., 95
Grady, Henry, 296, 317, 323, 334, 341
Grain trade, 289
Grangers, 334, 335, 338, 356
Grant, Ulysses, 222
Grant and Nickels, 82
Green, Charles, 216
Green, General Duff, 204
Gribble, J. B., 137

H. R. Johnson and Company: ante bellum business of, 79, 157, 303; Civil War business of, 227-34, 235; post bellum business of, 248, 249, 250, 256-57, 285, 302, 303, 330; relations with New York after Civil War, 248, 250; cotton holdings at close of Civil War, 256-57; and Savannah factor, 285
Habersham, I. Rae, 18, 161. *See also* Robert Habersham and Sons
Habersham, Robert, 40-41. *See also* Robert Habersham and Sons
Habersham, William Neyle, 233-34. *See also* Robert Habersham and Sons
Hamburg, S. C., vii, 187
Hamilton, William S.: relations with factors, 40, 41-42, 45, 64-65, 67; credit purchases by, 41-42, 117, 155; interest paid, 52, 58; forced to sell to pay debt, 132
Hammond, Bray, 106*n*
Hammond, M. B., 336-37
Hampton, Wade, 47
Hardee, General William J., 237
Harrold, Thomas. *See* H. R. Johnson and Company
Harrold, U. B. *See* H. R. Johnson and Company
Harrold, Johnson and Company. *See* H. R. Johnson and Company
Hawkinsville, Ga., 355

Hayne, Robert Y., 136, 139, 149-51
Hayne and Waring, 5
Hazard, Isaac P., 156-57
Hazard, R. G., 79, 157
Hazlehurst, Miss., 301
Heard, B. W., 331
Heard, Stephen D.: ante bellum factorage business of, 19, 38, 39; and itinerant cotton buyers, 87-97; Civil War business of, 210-11, 238-39; post bellum business of, 249, 255, 276-77, 297-98, 331; relations with New York merchants, 276-77, 331; faces competition, 277; and crop liens, 297-98
Heard and Simpson. *See* Heard, Stephen D.
Hedging. *See* Futures system
Helper, Hinton Rowan, 145
Hester, Henry G., 280
Hickman, Peter T., 115, 123-24
Hickman, William P., 155
Hill, Harry R. W., 48, 124, 184
Hill, McLean and Company, 17, 40, 184
Holmes, Edmund G., 179
Holmes, George K., 336, 341
Homestead exemptions, 312
Hope and Company, 124
Hopkins, Dwight and Company, 276*n*
Hubbard, William Hustace, 287-88
Hudson, Thomas J., 205
Humphreys and Biddle, 106
Hundley, Daniel Robinson, 150*n*
Hunt's Merchants' Magazine: on furnishing merchant system, 303; on radical reconstruction, 319; on post bellum cotton trade, 320-21; on planter debts in 1868, 322; on credit from North, 354
Huntsville, Ala., 93, 105, 329
Hutchinson, Robert, 256

Ills of the South, The, 304
Impending Crisis of the South, The, 145
Income, per capita in post bellum South, 346
Industrialization: of post bellum South, 324-25; subordinate status of Southern industry, 359
Inflation in Confederacy, 218, 225, 226
Ingraham, Joseph Holt, 135, 193-94
Inman, Swann and Company, 331
Insurance costs, 177
Interest: ante bellum rates, 52-58, 124; how calculated, 56-57; paid to planter by factor, 57-58; charges by furnishing merchants, 303; post bellum rates, 347; rates in 1921, 350; rates in 1938,